BUSINESS VALUATION HANDBOOK

GLENN M. DESMOND and RICHARD E. KELLEY

VALUATION PRESS, INC.
Los Angeles, California 90292

Copyright 1988

VALUATION PRESS, INC.

All Rights Reserved

No part of this book may be reproduced or used in any form or by any means, graphic, electronic or mechanical, including photocopying, recording, taping or information storage or retrieval systems without the written permission of the publisher.

First Printing, April 1977
Revised Edition, June 1980
Twelfth Printing, March 1993

International Standard Book Number: 0-930458-03-6
Library of Congress Catalog Card Number: 80-51554

This publication is designed to provide accurate and authoritative information in regard to the subject matter covered. It is sold with the understanding that neither the authors nor the publisher is engaged in providing legal advice. If such advice is required, the services of an attorney should be sought.

Printed in the United States of America

ABOUT THE AUTHORS

Glenn M. Desmond is a professional appraiser. His designations include MAI (American Institute of Real Estate Appraisers—recipient of the Professional Recognition Award); and ASA (American Society of Appraisers).

He has gained special recognition as an expert in the appraisal of intangible assets and closely-held businesses. He is the developer and instructor for the business valuation seminar series sponsored by the American Institute of Real Estate Appraisers. He has conducted many courses and seminars on the subject throughout the United States. Besides the seminars, he lectures and writes on business valuation subjects regularly.

Mr. Desmond has an active business appraisal practice. He testifies regularly as an expert witness on business enterprise valuations for courts and commissions. He has represented governmental agencies, large and small businesses and private individuals. He holds a degree in economics from The Principia College.

Richard E. Kelley is an experienced financial executive, entrepreneur, and author. He has special expertise in the organization, financing, operation and appraisal of closely-held businesses. He was Deputy Administrator of the Small Business Administration in Washington, D.C. in charge of regulating and making loans to 700 privately-owned venture capital companies. These loans were based on valuation of several thousand closely-held businesses in which the venture capital firms had invested. He has formed, owned, or managed many closely-held businesses and presently manages several corporations and partnerships. Mr. Kelley has been vice president and department head of a large national bank, senior executive of an investment firm, president of a management consulting business, and president of a financial publishing company. He has testified before the Joint Committee on Taxation of the United States Congress, the House and Senate Banking Committees, and the House and Senate Small Business Committees. He has helped form tax policy with the U.S. Treasury Department and the Bureau of the Budget.

Mr. Kelley was the author of a highly successful book on venture capital which went into seven printings and was sold throughout the United States and in 20 foreign countries. In addition, he has written many articles on financial matters. He holds a degree with honors from Amherst College and a master's degree in business administration from Harvard Business School.

ACKNOWLEDGEMENTS

The authors are grateful for the constructive assistance of many persons who have made a contribution to this revised edition of the BUSINESS VALUATION HANDBOOK. We are particularly appreciative of the following persons. Alan Lannom, ASA, Business Valuation Services, Inc., Los Angeles; Joseph W. Marshall, ASA and Frank C. Swift, ASA, partners of Marshall & Swift Publication Company, Los Angeles; Clement H. Darby, Valuation Counselors, Inc., Princeton, New Jersey; John D. Huelster, CPA, partner in charge, Laventhol & Horwath, St. Louis, Missouri; Edgar Holton, CPA, Edgar Holton Accountancy Corporation, San Francisco; Richard Laskin, esquire; Thomas N. Dankert, attorney and partner with the law firm, Dankert & Kuetzing, Ventura, California.; and many other persons who have made suggestions.

PREFACE

This book deals with the valuation of closely-held businesses and the appraisal of goodwill and other intangible assets. It is not intended as an academic discourse nor as a theoretical approach to such appraisals. The stress is on the "how to do it" procedure rather than the "why?" Specific methods for valuation are taken up and examples given. Particular types of businesses and intangible assets are discussed. The very title "handbook" implies a volume intended for constant use and reference.

In their many years of work with closely-held businesses, the authors have been struck with the lack of a thorough, authoritative book on how such businesses should be appraised. Books and articles have been written on how to value publicly-owned companies. However, while some articles have appeared, no books could be found dealing with fundamental methods for the valuation of closely-held companies. Since literally thousands of such businesses change hands each year through decease, merger, or sale, and thousands more require appraisals for other purposes, the need for such a book seemed apparent.

The determination to write it now was sparked by a special circumstance. In July 1976, a new law went into effect in California which required compensation for goodwill lost when businesses were partially or fully taken in eminent domain proceedings. The California action appeared to be a harbinger for similar laws in many other states because the California goodwill loss provisions are essentially identical with those provided in the Uniform Eminent Domain Code proposed for adoption in all fifty states. Valuation of goodwill is frequently an integral element in the appraisal of closely-held firms. Since many goodwill valuations will be required in eminent domain proceedings, the timeliness of the book seemed apparent.

It is impossible to deal with appraisal of goodwill without covering valuation of other intangibles such as patents, copyrights, secret processes, and brand names. Too often some or all of these other intangible assets are erroneously commingled with goodwill, resulting in improper appraisals.

FOR WHOM THE BOOK IS PARTICULARLY USEFUL

It is difficult to specify all who may benefit from the information contained in this book because the range of uses is so widespread. However, the authors had in mind that the following would find it especially helpful:
1. Attorneys, accountants, and consultants specializing in gift, estate, and income taxes where the valuation of closely-held businesses and intangibles is important.
2. Appraisers who wish to sharpen their skills in the valuation of businesses, goodwill, and other intangible assets.

PREFACE

3. Attorneys and other eminent domain specialists concerned with the valuation of goodwill loss.
4. Judges concerned with deciding the value of closely-held businesses and intangibles.
5. Investment company executives who must value portfolio holdings of closely-held concerns.
6. Merger and acquisition specialists seeking to value potential acquisitions or sales of businesses.
7. Business owners and executives seeking guidance as to the value of their businesses for financing, sale, or tax purposes.
8. Owners of intangibles, such as patents, copyrights, employment contracts, and franchises who wish to know how these assets are valued.
9. Federal, state, and local governmental bodies concerned with the taxation or financing of closely-held businesses and intangible assets.
10. Banks, trust companies, and other financial institutions concerned with acting as executors of wills involving business assets or with financing closely-held businesses.

Some of the purposes for which business appraisals are made as cited at ¶ 1.05 of the text suggest many other possible uses.

FORMAT

It is recognized that all users may not be equally concerned with the details of each subject discussed. To accommodate the needs of the diverse group of readers, this format has been utilized:

1. At the beginning of the book there is a table of contents and at the end is a complete index by subject. Note that the index includes for each topic a reference to both the paragraph number and the page where it can be found.
2. At the start of each chapter on the reverse side of the flyleaf is a complete list of the topics discussed. Paragraph reference numbers are given. At the end of each chapter (except Chapter 12) there is a summary which covers the key points in non-technical language.
3. Each of the seven exhibits and each of the twenty-four major appraisal methods discussed in the book are indexed in black on the right margin of the applicable pages. These margin markers are staggered for quick finding.
4. At the end of the book following the appendix are a list of footnotes citing authorities or amplifying certain points.
5. Wherever practical to do so, examples have been used. A sample case entitled *BLM Electronics, Inc.* serves as a basis for most of the examples and helps to illustrate the coordination required in the use of different appraisal methods.

PREFACE

HOW TO USE IT

This book can be read in detail or skimmed. Normally, the best approach will be to first skim the book and then go back to those chapters which are of particular concern for a complete study. To skim the book, read Chapter 1 in detail. Next, glance through the topics listed on the flyleaf for each chapter and read the summary at the end of the chapter. Chapter 12 can be quickly reviewed by reading the questions together with only those answers which are of immediate interest. Having thus covered the whole book in perhaps thirty to forty-five minutes, the reader can return to each chapter for thorough study.

Topics can be found quickly by referring to the Table of Contents, the Topics Discussed page at the head of each chapter, or by reference to the Index. Examples and major appraisal methods can be located easily by use of the right margin markers.

CONTENTS IN BRIEF

The first chapter clarifies the meaning of business value, defines closely-held businesses both as to management and legal form, covers reasons for appraising them, and outlines a ten-step valuation process. Chapter 2 deals with the compilation and analysis of financial statements for appraisal purposes. Chapter 3 sets forth a format for conducting interviews and for compiling information for a business appraisal using the case study, *BLM Electronics*, to illustrate the procedure. Chapter 4 illustrates the reconstruction of financial statements usually needed to convert accounting data into a form useful for appraisal purposes.

Chapter 5 describes eight appraisal methods which are useful in valuing professionally-managed, closely-held businesses. Chapter 6 covers the process whereby the differing results obtained from application of the eight methods previously described can be coordinated into a single value. It also sets forth a method for valuing promissory notes.

Chapter 7 deals with valuation of smaller, personally-managed businesses and sets forth some methods for doing so. Certain businesses of this type are specifically discussed.

Chapter 8 is the first of three chapters dealing with the appraisal of goodwill and other intangible assets. Chapter 8 specifically discusses the nature of goodwill, how it can be distinguished from other intangible assets, and how its existence can be ascertained. Chapter 9 deals with other intangibles and sets forth several methods for their valuation together with specific suggestions for the appraisal of certain assets. Chapter 10 is focused on valuation of goodwill loss under the Uniform Eminent Domain Code.

Chapter 11 concerns methods for valuing fractional interests in closely-held businesses, whether minority or majority holdings. Chapter 12 poses a series of

PREFACE

questions and answers intended to clarify points not fully explained in other parts of the text.

We enjoyed writing this book and felt we were assembling some useful disciplines in convenient form. We hope you will agree.

Glenn M. Desmond
Richard E. Kelley

Los Angeles, California

TABLE OF CONTENTS

CHAPTER 1

FUNDAMENTALS OF BUSINESS APPRAISAL

	Page
Removing the Aura of Mystery	3
Business Value: the Future, Not the Past	3
What is a Professional Business Appraisal?	5
What is a Closely-Held Business?	5
The Personal Business	5
The Professionally-Managed Business	6
Businesses Difficult to Classify	7
Common Legal Entities Used	7
Class of Trade	11
Why Businesses are Appraised	11
Sale or Purchase of a Business	12
Allocation of Purchase Price	12
Divorce	12
Sale of a Business Asset	12
Estate and Inheritance Tax	13
Gift Tax	13
Spinoff of Part of a Business	13
Determine True Return on Investment	13
Dissident Owner	14
Liquidation of a Business	14
Condemnation by a Governmental Body	14
Employee Benefit Plans	14
Buy and Sell Agreements Between Owners	14
Financing Purposes	15
Certain Property Taxes	15
Other Purposes for Business Appraisals	15
Who Should Make the Business Appraisal	15
The Ten Step Valuation Process	16
Summary	19

Chapter 2

FINANCIAL STATEMENTS: A PROLOGUE TO VALUATION

Financial Statements are Historical	23
Statements Conform to GAAP	23
The Deficiencies in GAAP	24
How the Appraiser Views Financial Statements	27
The Case of BLM Electronics, Inc.	28
Steps in Statement Analysis	28

TABLE OF CONTENTS

    Step 1 - Arrange statements in comparative form 28
    Step 2 - Compute analytical ratios 29
    Step 3 - Look for unusual, misvalued or omitted items 36
Multiple Entities and Consolidated Statements 39
Summary 41
Exhibits ....
    BLM Electronics, Inc. Balance Sheet, Last Five Years 43
    BLM Electronics, Inc. Income Statements, Last Five Years 45
    BLM Electronics, Inc. Income Statement Detail, Last Five Years 47

CHAPTER 3

INTERVIEWS: ADDING LIFE TO THE VALUATION

Who Should be Contacted? 51
Format for Conducting Interviews and Assembling Data 51
    Date of Appraisal 52
    Purpose and Scope 52
    History of the Business 53
    Legal Entities 53
    Detail on Subsidiaries or Affiliates 53
    Locations at Which the Business Operates 54
    Present Ownership of the Business 54
    Products and Services Sold 54
    Industry Classification 55
    Creditor Names 55
    Major Customers 55
    Employee Plans 55
    Property Occupancy Information 56
    Physical Condition of the Plant 56
    Appraisals and Plans 57
    Ownership Transfers and Offers 57
    Information Sources 58
    Owner Profiles 58
    Key Personnel Information 59
    Special Queries Regarding Statements 59
    Contingencies 60
    Industry Study 61
    Independent Financial Study 61
    Key Personnel Interviews 61
    Appraise Tangible Assets 61
    Appraise Goodwill and Intangibles 62
Summary 62

TABLE OF CONTENTS

CHAPTER 4

HOW TO RECONSTRUCT FINANCIAL DATA

Statements Required for Valuation Purposes	65
Adjusted Historical Balance Sheet	65
Economic Balance Sheet	65
Adjusted Historical Income Statements	65
Pro Forma Income Statements	66
Balance Sheet Adjustments	66
Preparing the Adjusted Historical Balance Sheet (BLM Case)	66
Key Percentages	68
Preparation of the Economic Balance Sheet (BLM Case)	68
Income Statement Adjustments (BLM Case)	70
Preparation of Pro Forma Income Statements	74
Industry Comparisons	75
Adjustment Principles	77
Summary	78
Exhibits	
BLM Electronics, Inc. Adjusted Historical Balance Sheet And Economic Balance Sheet	81
BLM Electronics, Inc. Adjusted Historical Income Statements	83
BLM Electronics, Inc. Pro Forma Income Statement For The Period April 1, 1976 to March 31, 1977	85
BLM Electronics, Inc. Comparison With Industry Data	87

CHAPTER 5

VALUING THE PROFESSIONALLY-MANAGED BUSINESS

Subjective Nature of Business Valuation	91
A Framework for Judgment	91
Check for Market Formulas	92
Balance Sheet Methods	93
Method 1 - Net Worth Per Books	93
Method 2 - Tangible Net Worth at Market	95
Earnings and Cash Flow Methods	96
Method 3 - Excess Earnings (or Excess Profit) Method	97
The Meaning of Capitalization Rates and Multipliers	102
Method 4 - Capitalization of Net Profit	103
Method 5 - Discounted Cash Flow	107
Market Data Comparison Methods	111
Method 6 - Price Earnings Ratio	111

TABLE OF CONTENTS

    Method 7 - Dividend Capitalization 119
    Method 8 - Ration of Market Price to Book Equity 123
Market Price Premiums 126
Summary 126

CHAPTER 6

DECISIONS! DECISIONS!

The Need for Correlation 131
All Assets Have Not Been Valued 131
Valuation of Other Tangible Assets 131
    Method 9 - Note Valuation 132
The Correlation Process 133
Summary 136

CHAPTER 7

VALUING THE PERSONALLY-MANAGED BUSINESS

Special Problems 139
The Basic Limits of Value 140
The Search for Formulas 142
The Typical Formula Approach 144
    Method 10 - Asset-Based Formula 144
    Method 11 - Sales-Based Formula 146
    Correlation of Formula Methods 148
    Flexibility of Formulas 148
    Formula Guidelines 148
    What To Do When No Formulas Emerge 149
Examples of Businesses Sold by Formula 151
    Auto Repair Garages 151
    Liquor Stores 151
    Insurance Agencies 152
    Accounting Practices 152
    Legal Practices 153
    Advertising Agencies 153
    Convenience Groceries 154
    Bars and Cocktail Lounges 154
    Newspapers and Periodicals 154
    Auto Wrecking Yards 155

TABLE OF CONTENTS

Funeral Homes	155
Real Estate-Related Businesses	155
Hotels and Motels	155
Nursing Homes	156
Mobile Home Parks	156
Summary	156

CHAPTER 8

WHAT IS GOODWILL?

The "Big Pot" Theory of Goodwill	161
Elements of Goodwill and Other Intangible Assets	163
Intangible assets non-severable from the business	164
Intangible assets non-severable from the person	164
Intangible assets generally severable from the business	164
How to Distinguish Goodwill from Other Intangibles	165
General definition of goodwill	166
Definition of other intangible assets	166
Can goodwill and other intangibles be commingled?	167
Going Concern Value	167
Court definitions of goodwill	168
The Internal Revenue Service view of intangibles	170
How to Determine the Existence of Goodwill	174
Earnings test	174
Market test	175
Question and answer test	175
Summary	176

CHAPTER 9

HOW TO VALUE GOODWILL AND OTHER INTANGIBLES

Goodwill Valuation and the IRS	181
Method 12 - IRS Goodwill Formula	181
Intangible Valuation Methods	184
Method 13 - Profit Advantage	184
Method 14 - Relief from Royalty	185
Variations on Profit Contribution Methods	187
Method 15 - Cost Savings	188
Method 16 - Cost to Create	189
Method 17 - Cost to Purchase	191
Method 18 - Accountants' Method	191
How to Value Specific Intangible Assets	192

TABLE OF CONTENTS

    Brand Names and Registered Trademarks................................ 192
    Copyrights 193
    Contracts 194
    Employment Contracts 194
    Covenants Not to Compete.. 195
    Affiliation Agreements... 196
    Patents 196
    Franchises 197
    Licenses 198
    Secret Processes, Methods, and Formulas 198
    Lists 199
        Specialized Mailing Lists 199
        Customer Lists... 199
        Subscription Lists.. 200
    Leasehold Interests 201
    Technical Libraries and Newspaper Morgues.......................... 202
    Drawings 202
    Water Rights... 203
    Film Rights 204
    Tax Credits for Past Losses 205
Summary 206

CHAPTER 10

VALUING GOODWILL IN EMINENT DOMAIN CASES

California Innovation in Goodwill Loss Compensation 209
Legal History of Goodwill in Eminent Domain Actions..................... 209
Uniform Eminent Domain Code Proposed 211
Goodwill Under the Eminent Domain Code 212
    Loss of Patronage... 212
    Expanded Concept of Goodwill 212
    Goodwill Must Be Lost 214
    Compensation for Goodwill Loss Must Not be Duplicative............. 215
    No Betterments May Be Created 216
Special Considerations 216
    Businesses with Improving Trends 217
    Owner Preferences and Physical Condition 217
    Personal Goodwill Versus Business Goodwill 217
    Tenancy Versus Ownership 218
    History and Longevity of the Business 218
    Multiple Businesses 219
    Total Versus Partial Loss... 219
Appraisers' Definition of Goodwill Loss..................................... 220

TABLE OF CONTENTS

Goodwill Loss Valuation Methods 221
    Goodwill as a Special Purpose Property 221
    Method 19 - Capitalization of Excess Earnings Lost 222
    Method 20 - Goodwill Loss Based on Market Formulas 225
    Method 21 - Cost to Restore Goodwill Loss 227
Summary 228

CHAPTER 11

VALUING FRACTIONAL INTERESTS IN CLOSELY-HELD BUSINESSES

The History of Minority-Interest Discounts 233
Minority-Interest Valuation Methods 234
    Method 22 - Cost to Market 235
    Method 23 - Comparable Letter Stock 235
    Method 24 - Dividend Yield 236
Valuing Majority Interests 237
Blockage 238
Stocks Held in Trust 239
Restrictive Agreements 239
    Buy-Sell Agreements 239
    Option Agreements 239
    Right of First Refusal 239
Valuing Different Classes of Stock 240
Summary 241

CHAPTER 12

QUESTIONS AND ANSWERS

Estate Tax - Decease of Key Owner 245
Divorce - Valuation of Professional Business 245
Intangible Valuation ....
    Choice of Method 246
    Multiple Assets 247
    Choice of Remaining Life 247
    Loss in Value of Assets 248
Definitions ....
    IRS "Fair Market Value" 248
    IRS "Closely-Held Corporation" 249
    Market Value 249
    Value in Exchange 250
    Value in Use 250
    Value in Place 251

TABLE OF CONTENTS

  User-in-Possession 251
  Going Concern 252
  Working Capital for Appraisal Purposes 252
Special Purpose Properties - Choice of Appraisal Method 253
Stock Valuation ....
  Employee Stock Ownership Trusts (ESOTS) 253
  Majority Interest in Trust 254
  Minority Interest Transfers Within Family 254
  Appraisal of Tangible Assets 255
  Preferred Stock 255
Appraisal Methods - Capitalization Rate Versus Multiplier 256
Comparability ....
  Use of Similar Businesses 256
  Importance of Location 257
Excess Earnings Method - Handling Interest Expense 257
Goodwill in Tax Cases - Inclusion of Other Intangibles 258
Goodwill in Eminent Domain - Inclusion of Tangible Assets 259
Real Estate - Separation of Business Values 260
Debt Consideration - Real Estate Versus Business Operations 260
Business Sales - Large Versus Small Businesses 261
Market Data - Reliability 262
Multiple Entities - Approach to Segregation 262
Appraisers ....
  Used as Consultants 263
  Procedure in Hiring 263
  Trial Preparation 264
  As Witnesses 264
  Tips for Trial Attorneys 265

APPENDIXES

1. Ratio Analysis for Small Business - Excerpts 269
2. Court Decisions Regarding Depreciation of Intangibles 297
3. Revenue Rulings Respecting Valuation 301

FOOTNOTE REFERENCES   311

INDEX   317

CHAPTER 1

FUNDAMENTALS OF BUSINESS APPRAISAL

Everything is worth what its purchaser will pay for it.

PUBLIUS - 1st Century B.C.

TOPICS DISCUSSED IN THIS CHAPTER

[¶1.01]	—	**Removing the Aura of Mystery**
[¶1.02]	—	**Business Value: the Future, Not the Past**
[¶1.03]	—	**What is a Professional Business Appraisal?**
[¶1.04]	—	**What is a Closely-Held Business?**
[¶1.04-1]	—	**The Personal Business**
[¶1.04-2]	—	**The Professionally-Managed Business**
[¶1.04-3]	—	**Businesses Difficult to Classify**
[¶1.04-4]	—	**Common Legal Entities Used** Proprietorship—Partnership—Ordinary Corporation—Pseudo Corporation—Trusts—Multiple Entities
[¶1.04-5]	—	**Class of Trade**
[¶1.05]	—	**Why Businesses are Appraised**
[¶1.05-1]	—	**Sale or Purchase of a Business**
[¶1.05-2]	—	**Allocation of Purchase Price**
[¶1.05-3]	—	**Divorce**
[¶1.05-4]	—	**Sale of a Business Asset**
[¶1.05-5]	—	**Estate and Inheritance Taxes**
[¶1.05-6]	—	**Gift Tax**
[¶1.05-7]	—	**Spinoff of Part of a Business**
[¶1.05-8]	—	**Determine True Return on Investment**
[¶1.05-9]	—	**Dissident Owner**
[¶1.05-10]	—	**Liquidation of a Business**
[¶1.05-11]	—	**Condemnation by a Governmental Body**
[¶1.05-12]	—	**Employee Benefit Plans**
[¶1.05-13]	—	**Buy-and-Sell Agreements Between Owners**
[¶1.05-14]	—	**Financing Purposes**
[¶1.05-15]	—	**Certain Property Taxes**
[¶1.05-16]	—	**Other Purposes for Business Appraisals**
[¶1.06]	—	**Who Should Make the Business Appraisal?**
[¶1.07]	—	**The Ten-Step Valuation Process** 1. Determine the date of valuation. 2. Define what is to be valued. 3. Obtain and analyze the financial statements. 4. Interview the owners, managers and others. 5. Prepare adjusted and projected financial statements. 6. Develop comparative data. 7. Value individual tangible assets. 8. Value goodwill and other intangibles. 9. Apply established valuation methods to the business. 10. Correlate data and develop value opinion.
[¶1.08]	—	**Summary**

CHAPTER 1

FUNDAMENTALS OF BUSINESS APPRAISAL

[¶ 1.01] REMOVING THE AURA OF MYSTERY

The valuation of a going business has always been an enigma, even for the financially sophisticated. The technical jargons of the professional appraiser, the accountant, the courts, the securities markets, and the tax collector, further obscure the subject. A portion of an appraiser's opinion with respect to the valuation of a company might read as follows:

> In valuing the business, I considered the approach set forth by ARM 34 and 68 [Internal Revenue Service rulings], its book value [an accounting term], and comparable price-earnings ratios [securities market terminology]. I also capitalized the income stream, considering known risk factors [appraisers' terminology]. A non-competition agreement [commercial jargon] was valued using principles described in the Houston Chronicle case [a court decision].

If the reader was not confused, baffled, or apprehensive about the subject of business valuation before, he doubtless would be after reading this statement.

This book is intended to cut through such technical verbiage and describe business valuation in terms both the layman and the professional can understand. Since the vast majority of businesses are privately owned and closely held, the emphasis here is on appraising these concerns. A critical matter in the valuation of all businesses is the proper appraisal of goodwill and other intangibles, such as patents, copyrights, mailing lists, employment contracts, and sales contracts. Therefore, considerable space is devoted to the subject of intangible valuation.

While business and intangible valuation have been simplified, they cannot be made easy. The techniques used by the professional business appraiser are explained in straightforward terms, but a great deal of research, judgment, and common sense are still necessary in their application. The results of the various methods described here must be correlated and weighed to arrive at proper opinions of value, whether for a whole enterprise, a fractional interest, or for individual assets of a business, such as goodwill, patents, or copyrights.

[¶1.02] BUSINESS VALUE: THE FUTURE, NOT THE PAST

Oliver Wendell Holmes said, "All values are anticipations of the future." Put in the context of business, it means that people buy businesses, not to enjoy their past performance, but rather to realize a present and future benefit. The benefit may not be predominantly monetary. A man might purchase a business because it was founded in 1872, has an excellent reputation, and he wishes the prestige of being chairman of the board of directors. While the prestige represents a present and future benefit of owning a business, it is seldom the primary reason for purchase.

FUNDAMENTALS OF BUSINESS APPRAISAL

Usually the buyer is seeking a monetary return on the investment of his savings, and perhaps on his time. The proposed acquisition represents but one of many alternative places in which his money could be invested. If he plans to be an owner-manager, the purchase may also represent but one of several employment opportunities open to him.

A seller is faced with similar choices. He could continue to own the business and derive future monetary benefits from it. Or he could sell it and invest his money, and perhaps his talents, in some other place for present and future benefit. Both buyer and seller will necessarily value the business based on its future benefits.

As will be noted later, there are many reasons other than sale or purchase which cause a business to be appraised. To name but a few: the owner may have died and estate taxes must be computed on its value; husband and wife owners may be contemplating divorce and split up of their equity in the business; or the owners may plan to liquidate the business and wish to know what it would bring in bits and pieces.

The values may differ according to the purpose of the appraisal. Taxable value of a business for estate tax purposes, while theoretically representing fair market value, may in fact be considerably different from the price it would command upon sale in the open market. While there are a number of reasons for this, one which is readily apparent is the fact that the estate is usually appraised as of an arbitrary date in the past, namely, the date of death. Market conditions could have changed considerably by the date of sale. Liquidation value is generally different from the fair market value of an ongoing operation.

One theme is pervasive. Almost without exception, the purposes for which business valuations are made entail an opinion of the future benefits the business can provide expressed in monetary terms. That is, the appraiser must give his opinion that a business is worth $200,000 or $500,000 or $1,000,000 for purposes of sale, for estate tax purposes, for liquidation, or for whatever purpose appraisal is contemplated. The fair market value of a going business could be $1,000,000, whereas its liquidation value might be only $500,000. Regardless of the purpose, the value must be expressed in terms of money.

Most business valuations are made by laymen whose knowledge of appraisal techniques is limited. The research involved in such lay approaches may also be limited. In many cases this restricted knowledge is satisfactory, or all that can be afforded. An example might be the sale of a franchised service station, which typically sells for inventory valued at cost, plus equipment at economically depreciated cost. In such an instance, the buyer and seller arrive at a value, usually with the assistance of a representative of the supplying oil company. More knowledge could be unnecessary and too expensive.

FUNDAMENTALS OF BUSINESS APPRAISAL

On the other hand, for many businesses a similar approach is not feasible because there is no convenient, generally accepted, widely-known, single method of valuation. In addition, the stakes may be too high to accept any formula approach as a true measure of value.

[¶1.03] WHAT IS A PROFESSIONAL BUSINESS APPRAISAL?

A professional business appraisal requires the determination of the present and future rewards of owning all or part of a business, expressed in monetary terms. In arriving at these rewards, one or more methods or disciplines will be used which have been found useful in similar situations. Once these methods have been applied, the results are correlated and weighed by the appraiser, who then expresses an opinion as to the value of the business for a specified purpose.

To arrive at his opinion, the professional appraiser must analyze pertinent facts relative to the past of the business, its present status, and the outlook for its future, including the outlook for the industry of which it is a part. He must know how similar businesses are valued by knowledgeable buyers and sellers.

This book describes for various types of businesses the methods and techniques used by the professional appraiser to make his value judgments. These methods may be applied by anyone facing a business valuation problem, not simply by the professional.

[¶1.04] WHAT IS A CLOSELY-HELD BUSINESS?

A closely-held business is usually privately owned by individuals, as opposed to having its shares or ownership interests held by the general public. Most often, effective control is lodged in a small group ranging from one to six people, although ownership could extend to forty or fifty. A subsidiary of another business would not generally be considered closely held unless the parent firm was closely held. A publicly-owned company could have many of the characteristics of a closely-held business if effective control were lodged in a small group of individuals, if there were few public shareholders, and if the stock had been traded infrequently. While such a business might be valued using many of the techniques described here for closely-held businesses, it would not generally be considered closely held.

There are two basic types of closely-held businesses described in the following paragraphs.

[¶1.04-1] THE PERSONAL BUSINESS

The most common type of closely-held venture can be characterized as a very personal business operated primarily by and for the benefit of a single individual,

FUNDAMENTALS OF BUSINESS APPRAISAL

or a partnership of relatively few individuals. It is tied closely to the personality of the owners who are directly involved in all aspects of the enterprise. Most single retail or wholesale outlets are in this category. Also included are most smaller professional firms, such as real estate brokerages, insurance agencies, medical and legal practices. Usually the personal business is small, although size is a difficult criterion to apply since what is large in one industry may be small in another. For years, the Small Business Administration has tried, with dubious success, to define small business in terms of sales, assets, net worth, and employees.

For purposes of appraisal, the degree of personal control is more important than a determination of whether it is truly large or small. The personally-controlled business tends to be valued in the marketplace on the basis of its tangible assets plus an arbitrary amount for goodwill, or on the basis of a formula acceptable within the industry. The formula is usually related directly to gross income and net profits, including provision for the owners' salaries. While earnings are important and should be considered, this factor is usually given secondary consideration.

Earnings are deemphasized because the owner-manager of such a business can directly influence the amount earned. Often, too, the owner does not distinguish between business profit and his salary. The buyer of such a business usually recognizes these facts and values the operation by putting greatest weight upon its assets (less any liabilities he will assume) or upon its gross income. He generally believes that no matter how well the previous owner-manager has operated the business, he, the buyer, can make improvements. The appraisal problems and techniques applicable to such personal, closely-held business are described in detail in a later chapter.

[¶1.04-2] THE PROFESSIONALLY-MANAGED BUSINESS

A second category of closely-held concerns may be regarded as the professionally-managed business. Although closely held, it has typically grown to the point where the individual owner is unable to personally control a significant number of its activities. It has become necessary to employ management personnel, who have little if any ownership interest in the company. The emphasis of the firm has shifted primarily to maximization of earnings over and above owner salaries. Greater attention is paid to the basic financial strength of the operation.

Valuation of the professionally-managed business becomes a much more sophisticated problem than appraisal of the personal business. Greater attention must be paid to earnings potential. While formula approaches to valuation may be used, often more than one formula must be applied, and a number of other tests of value must be used as well. The judgment and experience of the appraiser become much more important in the interpretation of the valuation methods.

FUNDAMENTALS OF BUSINESS APPRAISAL

[¶1.04-3] BUSINESSES DIFFICULT TO CLASSIFY

Unfortunately, in the world of business, all closely-held firms do not fit neatly into the two categories cited above. There is no handy quantitative measure for distinguishing one from the other. Some enterprises appear to have the characteristics of both the personal and the professionally-managed business.

One of the authors of this book was employed for several years as the treasurer of a firm which was fully staffed in all departments with professional executives. It was of large size in its industry and employed several hundred people. However, ninety percent of the stock was owned by one individual, who was also the chief executive. He strongly influenced the earnings and investments of the firm to suit his personal desires and to minimize his personal income taxes.

The appraisal of such a business may involve a mixture of some of the methods usually reserved for personal businesses together with techniques generally applicable only to the professionally-managed concern.

[¶1.04-4] COMMON LEGAL ENTITIES USED

Closely-held firms can operate in one of several forms, or in a combination of forms or entities. It is helpful to understand the various legal ways in which such businesses are organized, because the financial data collected by the appraiser from the company will reflect the form of operation, and the form may raise significant appraisal problems. Also, any comparative data on other companies in the industry must be viewed with the legal form in mind.

For instance, if the business being appraised is a proprietorship, its financial statements usually will not reflect salary to the proprietor nor income taxes payable on the business profit. Furthermore, if most of its competitors are corporations, comparisons of operating results cannot be made unless the company's figures are adjusted to what would be reflected if it were a corporation. A good way to obtain a quick check on the legal organization of the company to be appraised is to look at its income tax filings. Each different type of business entity must file a different income tax form.

PROPRIETORSHIP

By far the most common business entity is the proprietorship. Under this form of operation, legal requirements of organization are at a minimum. The business can be owned only by a single individual or by a man and wife as joint owners. Filings with governmental bodies charged with controlling the existence of business entitles are minimal. No permission is needed to operate in this form. Sometimes there will be a recording of the business name in the county or counties in which it maintains offices, if the business operates under a name other than that of the proprietor.

FUNDAMENTALS OF BUSINESS APPRAISAL

Proprietorships file Schedule C to Federal Income Tax Form 1040 and can be thus recognized. If the individual operates more than one proprietorship, he files a separate Schedule C for each business.

PARTNERSHIP

The second most common entity used by closely-held businesses is the partnership. In most cases this means that there is a partnership agreement and that two or more individuals are owners who are not husband and wife. It is possible for a husband and wife to have a partnership, rather than operating as a proprietorship under the husband's name, but this is unusual.

The formalities of a partnership are not extensive. Like the proprietorship, it usually need not file with any government body controlling legal entities unless it operates under an assumed name, or if it is a limited partnership.

The simplest situation is a general partnership where the owners have an equal vote in the affairs of the company and they are jointly responsible for its debts. There may or may not be a partnership agreement covering such items as division of property, buy-out in the event of decease or disagreement, etc. When more than two individuals are involved in a partnership, an agreement is usual.

A more complex form is known as a *limited* partnership. In this case there will always be a partnership agreement. There will always be at least one general partner and one or more limited partners. The general partner or partners are responsible for most management decisions and assume legal responsibility for the debts of the partnership. One reason limited partners are so termed is because their liability for partnership debts is either zero or limited to certain items specified in the partnership agreement. The term *limited* is also applicable because limited partners may have no vote in the conduct of the business, or their vote may be restricted to certain major decisions, such as sale of all or nearly all of the assets of the partnership. The partnership agreement often specifies that if a partner wishes to sell his partnership interest, he must first offer it to the remaining partners.

All partnerships file Federal Income Tax Form 1065. Limited partners will almost never be paid a salary. Usually there will be no provision for income taxes on partnership books because taxes on partnership earnings are the responsibility of the individual partners.

It is important for the business appraiser to obtain and read any partnership agreements. The agreements may restrict the salability of a partnership interest, specify the share of profits payable to various classes of partnership owner interest, limit voting rights, and limit or extend liability. Any or all of these factors can have considerable bearing on the value of the partners' individual and collective equity.

FUNDAMENTALS OF BUSINESS APPRAISAL

ORDINARY CORPORATION

A closely-held business may be operated as an ordinary corporation chartered by one of the states. In unusual instances, such as a national bank, it may be chartered by the Federal Government. The corporate form entails shareholders electing a board of directors and the directors in turn making most major policy decisions and appointing the corporate officers. The corporate officers make the day-to-day operating decisions. Minutes should be kept in more or less complete form, recording actions taken at shareholders' and directors' meetings.

In practice, most closely-held corporations dispense with all but the absolute minimum of formality with respect to shareholders' and directors' meetings, since the controlling group, by definition, is small. Meetings and minutes take on the appearance of sitting down to write oneself a letter. However, usually goaded by the company public accountant or attorney, most closely-held corporations do write up minutes on major policy matters. These writings are often self-serving for tax or regulatory purposes, but, nevertheless, important facts about the business can be learned by examining the minutes. For instance, there may be a buy-sell agreement between various shareholders which affects the value of their stock, or there may be comments as to why dividends have not been consistently paid. Wherever possible, the appraiser should obtain and read the minutes of shareholders' and directors' meetings.

The corporate charter, bylaws, and stock record book should also be examined to understand the rights and privileges of various classes of stock. Usually there is only one class of stock in a closely-held corporation, namely, voting common. The owners of such common stock vote and receive dividends in proportion to the number of shares owned. Nevertheless, it is not a rarity to find a preferred stock or a non-voting common designed to accommodate shareholders who have made an investment in the business, but who do not have a voice in operating it. Stock with restricted dividends or voting rights has a different value than voting common. There may also be a trust set up to hold and vote part or all of the shares of the corporation. Such a trust also affects stock values.

The existence of the corporate form may be revealed by the name, since the word *corporation, inc.,* or *incorporated* can not be used in the company name unless it is a corporation. As noted before, another quick check can be made by referring to the income tax forms filed by the business. Ordinary corporations file Federal Income Tax Form 1120. This form will also reveal other characteristics of the corporation, such as its date of formation and the predominant class of trade of which it is a part.

PSEUDO-CORPORATION

Many closely-held businesses operate as so-called *Pseudo* or *Subchapter S* corporations. These are ordinary corporations afforded certain tax privileges by the

FUNDAMENTALS OF BUSINESS APPRAISAL

Federal Government and by some, but not all, states. By law, there can not be more than 15 individual shareholders (formerly 10 shareholders until amended by the Tax Reform Act of 1976, P.L.94-455). Sub-chapter S corporations are always closely held because of the legal limitations on the number of shareholders.

Subchapter S corporations in most respects are taxed like a partnership. Therefore, salaries to managing owners may be minimal or non-existent, and most Federal income taxes on the business earnings are not reflected on the company books. Certain classifications of Federal capital gains taxes may be imposed at the corporate level and state corporate taxes may be recorded if state law does not provide a tax privilege similar to the Federal. Subchapter S corporations file Federal Income Tax Form 1120-S.

TRUSTS

A closely-held business may be operated as a trust, with control vested in an individual trustee or trustees, or in a corporate trustee. Usually, the trustee operates the business for the benefit of a rather small group of individuals, such as the relatives of a business founder. However, there may be a broader group of trust beneficiaries.

For instance, the sole trustee of a water company in California protects beneficial interests in the trust owned by as many as 200 individuals. This operation has all of the characteristics of a closely-held business, although there are many diverse, unrelated owners.

At times a trust is set up by will to operate a business until the son of the founder becomes 21 years of age, at which time it will be terminated and the son will take over direct control of the business or become trustee. A so-called *living trust* may also be set up, wherein the founder within his lifetime transfers the business to a trust for the benefit of his family or others. Trusts file Federal Income Tax Form 1041.

When a business is operated as a trust, there is always a written trust agreement. The appraiser will wish to study this document carefully, as it can have a profound effect on the profitability, marketability, and fair market value of the business. In the water trust referred to earlier, the trustee is prohibited from raising the rates for water service above a stated level without obtaining the written permission of the owners of over 50% of the beneficial interests in the trust. The trustee may be restricted in selling the business. Following the same illustration, the trustee of the water company can sell only to specified types of water companies or to a governmental body.

MULTIPLE ENTITIES

Sometimes a closely-held business will operate in several forms, all essentially in one class of business, or there may be a different entity for each class. For ex-

FUNDAMENTALS OF BUSINESS APPRAISAL

ample, a professionally managed, closely-held corporation engaged in the manufacture and sale of rubber parts had one subsidiary corporation located in another state which also manufactured and sold similar parts. It had another subsidiary corporation which purchased already manufactured parts from the parent corporation and sold them exclusively in one state. It had a majority interest in a partnership with an individual who was conducting experiments to develop a new type of processing equipment to be sold to the parent and its subsidiaries and to be offered on a royalty basis to other rubber manufacturers. Another subsidiary corporation was engaged in leasing industrial equipment. Substantial annual contributions were made by the parent corporation to a charitable foundation which held non-voting stock in the corporation and which was part of the controlling shareholder's estate planning. Another subsidiary corporation was engaged in converting single engine aircraft to twin engine, partly because a large market was expected for the converted aircraft, and partly because flying was a hobby of the controlling shareholder. Later, when the major shareholder died, the parent corporation was controlled by three unrelated, individual co-executors of his estate, who later relinquished control to a trust administered by a single trustee. A professional business appraiser was employed to determine the market value of this business for estate and inheritance tax purposes.

[¶1.04-5] CLASS OR TRADE

A closely-held company can operate any type of business. It can be a service business, a retailer, a wholesaler, a manufacturer, a utility, or any of several thousand subcategories. The appraiser will wish to determine the class or classes of trade in which the business is engaged in order to obtain information on competing business, including any special valuation methods or problems incident to that trade. The U.S. Government and many research organizations collect comparative statistics according to so-called *SIC*, or Standard Industrial Classification codes which are specified in the standard industrial code manual published by the U.S. Government.[1] A clue to the class of trade into which a company fits may be gained from its income tax form, wherein it must select an SIC code which presumably represents its major business activity. This selection may be arbitrary and inaccurate, however, and the appraiser must select for himself the proper classifications based on his own analysis of the firm to be sure his comparable company statistics and other information are truly comparable.

[¶1.05] WHY BUSINESSES ARE APPRAISED

A list of all of the reasons for which closely-held businesses are appraised could be quite voluminous. Nevertheless, it is helpful to understand some of the more common purposes of appraisal. In all of the instances cited below, a professional appraiser may not be employed, or even desired. In all cases, however, the methods and techniques of the professional appraiser can be helpful, and virtually essential, in developing realistic values which can be defended.

FUNDAMENTALS OF BUSINESS APPRAISAL

[¶1.05-1] SALE OR PURCHASE OF A BUSINESS

Sale of larger closely-held businesses often calls for the application of the appraisal techniques described in this book as well as the use of a professional appraiser. The seller may wish help in substantiating his price based on an appraiser's review of future outlook and comparable sales. Intangible assets with significent values, such as mailing lists, copyrights, secret processes, and leasehold interests may add unexpected value to the balance sheet. The buyer may learn of overvalued assets, such as outmoded tooling or equipment, or he may have reason to believe some assets still appearing on the books have been sold or lost. Or he may discover that earnings prepared according to generally accepted accounting principles, when adjusted by appraisal techniques, indicate the business is really making far more or far less than he thought.

[¶1.05-2] ALLOCATION OF PURCHASE PRICE

Often the assets of a going business will be purchased for a set price without determining the dollar value of its various components; or a premium over book value will be paid for the stock of a corporation, and the corporation is liquidated in a reorganization. It becomes necessary to assign values to the components of the purchase for purposes of depreciation, amortization, tax planning, and proper accounting. A professional appraisal is most often made in such situations to protect the buyer against the tax collector's allocation of excessive amounts to non-amortizable goodwill. A full discussion of the problems and appraisal techniques applicable to goodwill appears later in this book.

[¶1.05-3] DIVORCE

In property settlement, both husband and wife wish to be convinced that each is receiving his proper, agreed share of the commonly-owned assets, which many times includes a closely-held business. It may be obvious to either or both parties that the balance sheets and income statements prepared by the usual accounting methods do not reflect the true value of the business. The wife, for instance, may be aware that all assets have been depreciated as rapidly as possible to save taxes and that earnings have been deflated by heavy entertainment expenses. Her only method of obtaining an objective valuation may be a professional appraiser.

[¶1.05-4] SALE OF A BUSINESS ASSET

Business management may wish to sell a process, a mailing list, a subsidiary, or a leasehold interest and may have no idea how to price the item to be sold. Or, it may have a price in mind but no basis for supporting the price. Business appraisal techniques can assist in arriving at sustainable asking prices.

FUNDAMENTALS OF BUSINESS APPRAISAL

[¶1.05-5] ESTATE AND INHERITANCE TAXES

Frequently, a closely-held business will be part of a decedent's estate. The estate beneficiaries are essentially in an adversary position with the Internal Revenue Service and the state inheritance tax appraisers. The tax collector may seek to prove an excessively high fair market value for the business, often based on its past performance rather than its future outlook. Inadequate consideration may be given to the lack of marketability of stock in a closely-held business. A professional appraisal should uncover fallacies in the tax collector's reasoning. If the appraisal is made by a professional, he can also serve as a witness for the taxpayer before taxing bodies or the courts.

[¶1.05-6] GIFT TAX

As an aid to estate or income tax planning, substantial ownership interests in a closely-held business may be given by one family member to another. It is then essential to file a gift tax return and equally essential to measure the value of the gift in a defensible way. Application of the techniques described in this book to the valuation problem provide the basis for defending the value reported when the return is audited.

[¶1.05-7] SPINOFF OF PART OF A BUSINESS

Although it happens most frequently to publicly-owned companies due to their larger size, closely-held businesses may be forced to divest themselves of a subsidiary or a division to meet requirements of the Federal Trade Commission, the Securities and Exchange Commission, the Internal Revenue Service, the Department of Justice, or some other governmental agency. In other cases, the owners of a company may decide to sell a subsidiary or division to raise cash or to simplify management. In many instances, an appraisal is needed to identify and arrive at values in order to set a selling price, to substantiate tax filings, and to properly account for the transaction.

[¶1.05-8] DETERMINE TRUE RETURN ON INVESTMENT

For reasons explained in the next chapter, return on investment as determined from a company's books of account generally does not coincide with the return on market value of the owner's investment. For instance, the market value of assets will often exceed their book value. It sometimes becomes pertinent to evaluate management performance in light of the true value of assets and to consider use of invested funds in some other manner. Sale of high-value, low-return assets and investment of cash received in a high-return part of the business could greatly increase owner rewards.

FUNDAMENTALS OF BUSINESS APPRAISAL

[¶1.05-9] DISSIDENT OWNER

It is not infrequent for a closely-held corporation or partnership to have an owner who is in radical disagreement with the other owners. It becomes necessary to set a value on his interest as a step toward buying him out. The seller will often be antagonistic, causing values set by established appraisal principles to be most acceptable.

[¶1.05-10] LIQUIDATION OF A BUSINESS

Sometimes there are no logical successors to the owner-manager of a closely-held firm; the owner wishes to retire and no buyer can readily be found for the business. It becomes essential to know what the assets of the business would bring upon liquidation, both to determine the funds the owner will have to invest elsewhere and to decide whether liquidation is indeed the best course of action. A professional business appraisal for liquidation can be invaluable in such a decision.

[¶1.05-11] CONDEMNATION BY A GOVERNMENTAL BODY

There is a trend in many states toward compensating businesses for the loss of goodwill when they are forced to move or curtail their activities as a result of eminent domain proceedings. For example, in California the law on eminent domain was amended effective July 1, 1976 to provide: "The owner of a business conducted on the property taken, or on the remainder, if such property is part of a larger parcel, shall be compensated for loss of goodwill..."[2] The subject of goodwill is discussed more fully later. Suffice it to say here that it is frequently necessary to appraise an entire closely-held business to determine the value to be assigned to goodwill. In such eminent domain cases, both the governmental bodies involved and the owners have a direct interest in establishing the value, if any, of goodwill, hence, either or both may require professional business appraisals.

[¶1.05-12] EMPLOYEE BENEFIT PLANS

Where employees are to be partially compensated in stock of a closely-held firm, as in the case of Employee Stock Ownership Trusts (ESOT), the stock must be valued to meet requirements of both the U.S. Department of Labor and the Internal Revenue Service. These values are subject to audit and must be defensible. The application of professional appraisal techniques in setting these values provides a basis for defense.

[¶1.05-13] BUY-AND-SELL AGREEMENTS BETWEEN OWNERS

Business appraisals may be made to set up formulas and techniques whereby owners agree in advance how their shares will be valued for buy-out in the event of disagreement or in the event of their decease. Such appraisals and agreements can

FUNDAMENTALS OF BUSINESS APPRAISAL

provide important methods of saving estate and inheritance taxes and can resolve many potential disagreements between owners by expedited, inexpensive means.

[¶1.05-14] FINANCING PURPOSES

While it is traditional to present financial statements to lenders and potential investors essentially on the basis of cost, such a presentation may overlook substantial additional values which would support larger loans or investments in the business. Machinery and equipment depreciated for accounting and tax purposes well below their economic value might support a loan or sale and lease-back well in excess of book value, if discovered and valued in an appraisal. Value might be developed on a favorable patent or franchise which was not even shown on the balance sheets. The fact that these values were set by recognized business appraisal techniques also adds to their credibility for financing purposes.

[¶1.05-15] CERTAIN PROPERTY TAXES

Ad valorem (property) taxes are sometimes levied on the basis of business operations. For instance, some hotels are valued for property tax purposes, not on the basis of their tangible assets, but on their income statements, including goodwill. Water rights may be valued on the basis of the actual or theoretical selling price of the water received under the rights. Completed movies (known as "film in the can") are valued for property tax purposes based on their potential earnings. Professional business appraisals which cover these operations could result in values widely divergent from those used by the tax assessor.

[¶1.05-16] OTHER PURPOSES FOR BUSINESS APPRAISALS

Business appraisals can be useful in reorganizations, consolidations, and conversions of one class of stock to another. Tax planning in advance of estate and gift tax filings and tax planning to minimize income taxes can often benefit from an analysis of the market value of closely-held business interests. A business appraisal may be required in rate-setting cases for public utilities. Related to but distinct from the subject of eminent domain discussed at ¶ 1.05-11 are so-called inverse condemnation cases, where the actions of public bodies are viewed as reducing business values without actual condemnation. In such instances, the operating business may need to be valued before and after the governmental action.

[¶1.06] WHO SHOULD MAKE THE BUSINESS APPRAISAL?

As noted earlier in this chapter, a professional appraiser is often not needed or justified when a small, personal business changes hands. Likewise, the professional appraiser may not be needed if the primary purpose of the appraisal is for the internal management of the business. The firm's public accountant or a financial executive may be well equipped to apply the methods and techniques described in this book.

FUNDAMENTALS OF BUSINESS APPRAISAL

On the other hand, when a third party opinion on value is needed, the professional business appraiser should be selected. In a tax dispute, for instance, he can testify before the taxing authority and before the courts as an independent expert on business valuation, thereby giving added weight to the values determined. The public accountant could use the same appraisal techniques and arrive at a similar opinion of value. However, the values reported may be very different from those reflected on the financial statement he has prepared from the company's books, thereby putting him in the difficult position of having to defend disparate values for the same business. The firm's attorney is also in an awkward position to defend a business valuation which he has prepared. As the taxpayer's advocate, he is expected to develop facts which are favorable to his client and not detrimental. This casts doubt on the objectivity of his appraisal.

Aside from instances which involve disputes, the independent business appraiser may also be sought where the amount of money involved is substantial. In such cases, his experience and judgment developed in numerous business valuations may uncover assets, liabilities, or profit opportunities which might be missed by others.

[¶1.07] THE TEN-STEP VALUATION PROCESS

An essential element in making realistic business valuations is the development of a thorough, orderly approach to the task. Such an approach will help prevent the overlooking of important considerations and facts. The procedure found most helpful by the authors is described briefly below. It will be expanded upon in later chapters.

STEP 1   DETERMINE THE DATE OF VALUATION

It is important to determine whether the business is to be valued retroactively, as of a past date, such as the date of an eminent domain taking or date of death of a major owner, or if it is to be valued as of the present date.

STEP 2   DEFINE WHAT IS TO BE VALUED

The next step is to determine and actually write down what is to be appraised and for what purpose. It is important to clearly define whether a company's stock is to be valued in whole or in part; or whether its assets alone are to be valued in whole or in part. If the stock or other ownership equity is to be valued, the appraisal must be in much greater depth than if assets alone are involved. Valuation of equity interests requires consideration, not only of the assets of the subject business, but also of its liabilities, profitability, competitive position, and stock marketability, to mention but a few of the added requirements.

If a minority holding is to be valued, there may be a considerable discount over the relative value assigned a majority holding. If only certain assets out of

FUNDAMENTALS OF BUSINESS APPRAISAL

the total business holding are to be valued, it may or may not be necessary to value all assets.

If the objective of the appraisal is to determine fair market value, it is quite a different task than were the objective to arrive at liquidation value. The resulting values and the procedures followed in arriving at them will usually be quite different.

STEP 3 OBTAIN AND ANALYZE THE FINANCIAL STATEMENTS

The appraiser should obtain the firm's latest five years of income statements and balance sheets—audited, if possible. It is helpful to get the income tax returns of the business for the same period. The statements will then be put in comparative form and analyzed for unusual fluctuations and changes. A series of questions will be developed to be resolved by interviews and other research.

STEP 4 INTERVIEW THE OWNERS, MANAGERS, AND OTHERS

It almost goes without saying that a vast amount of written material and general information pertinent to the valuation can be obtained only from the owners and managers of the closely-held business. They alone can produce minute books, confidential payroll records, important contracts, and patent or copyright data. They alone can explain the company's history, policies, and performance in the detail necessary to a good approach.

It often is desirable to go beyond the owners and interview the company's banker, trade association executives, selected creditors and competitors, and key company personnel. The interview procedure is described in Chapter 3.

STEP 5 PREPARE ADJUSTED AND PROJECTED FINANCIAL STATEMENTS

After analysis of the historical financial statements, interviews with owners and managers and parties outside the firm, and after market appraisal of the assets as required, the appraiser will change the most recent balance sheet to reflect economic values. All tangible and intangible assets will be so valued, except for goodwill, the valuation of which is described later in this book. Liabilities will also be analyzed to eliminate such items as amounts due owners, which would not be pertinent to outsiders, and to add in unstated liabilities, such as so-called financial leases. The result may be termed the "economic balance sheet."

Next, an adjusted historical income statement will be prepared. The past accounting reports will be altered to remove unusual or improper income and expense items and to adjust as required to reflect reasonable salaries to the owner-managers. Depreciation and other capital charges will be added back so that the statements represent profits before tax and before capital charges.

Finally, the appraiser will prepare projected, or pro forma, income statements

FUNDAMENTALS OF BUSINESS APPRAISAL

for a relatively short period ahead—usually one year. The resulting profit will be before taxes, depreciation, and other capital charges, but after owner-manager salaries.

The complete procedure in making up the foregoing statements is described in Chapter 4

STEP 6 DEVELOP COMPARATIVE DATA

With the adjusted historical and projected statements in hand, the appraiser obtains statistical data, including operating ratios on comparable companies, if available. This data is put in a form which allows comparison with the company being appraised, or the data developed for the subject company can be cast in a form comparable with published data on other concerns in its industry. Compilations of this data can be expedited through the series of interviews mentioned in Step 4. The development and use of comparative data is fully described in Chapter 4.

STEP 7 VALUE INDIVIDUAL TANGIBLE ASSETS

The valuation of tangible assets, such as machines and equipment, land and buildings, is not the subject of this book, but these assets may have to be valued using established appraisal techniques. This will be necessary if there is reason to believe some of the tangible assets are carried at values significantly below market value; if earnings on such assets are insufficient; or if certain appraisal techniques are used, such as the Excess Earnings Method described in Chapter 5.

STEP 8 VALUE GOODWILL AND OTHER INTANGIBLES

Appraisal techniques applicable to goodwill and other intangibles are fully discussed in the latter part of this book.

STEP 9 APPLY ESTABLISHED VALUATION METHODS TO THE BUSINESS

Commencing at Chapter 5, the business valuation methods used by professional appraisers are described. It should be noted that it will often be necessary to apply several methods to the same business. The referenced discussion also covers the limitations and advantages of each method.

STEP 10 CORRELATE DATA AND DEVELOP VALUE OPINION

When all of the data has been collected and analyzed and several appraisal techniques have been used, a range of values is developed. The appraiser must correlate and evaluate all of the results and arrive at his opinion of the proper value. This will usually involve a combination of experience, judgment, and factual data.

FUNDAMENTALS OF BUSINESS APPRAISAL

[¶1.08] **SUMMARY**

This book simplifies business and intangible valuation by describing in non-technical language the processes and techniques professional appraisers use to appraise these assets. Whether he is a professional appraiser or a layman in these matters, the reader should gain a clear understanding of the entire appraisal process and be in a position to apply the methods. Sustainable values require careful, painstaking research, common sense, and judgment applied to the facts at hand.

Business values are based on the present and future monetary rewards to be gained from owning all or a portion of a business. The values to be established by the appraiser, therefore, may be quite different from those shown on the company's books, because book figures are typically based on cost, not market value or even liquidation value.

Closely-held businesses are those firms which are usually privately owned by a few individuals, as opposed to companies owned by the general public. Usually, effective control is in the hands of one to six individuals.

Single businesses frequently fall into one of two categories. The first and most common type is the personal business operated primarily by and for the benefit of a single individual or a partnership of a relatively few individuals. A second category is the professionally managed business, wherein the owners have delegated a significant share of the management to professional executives. The valuation of the professionally managed business generally requires different and more complex methods than do personal businesses. Some closely-held firms have characteristics of both types and may involve appraisal methods applicable to both.

Closely-held businesses operate in many legal forms, and these forms can have significant effects on the appraisal. Proprietorships and partnerships are most common, followed by ordinary corporations and pseudo-corporations. Sometimes the business will be operated as a trust. It is not unusual for several legal entities to be used within a single business. The legal forms involved can be readily determined by reference to the Federal Income Tax filings.

It is desirable to reach a conclusion as to the class of trade into which the business falls so that comparisons can be made with other firms in the industry. Usually the process requires selection for the firm of an applicable Standard Industrial Classification Code (SIC).

Businesses are appraised for many different reasons. Some of the more frequent purposes are enumerated at ¶ 1.05.

A professional appraiser is seldom sought when the business involved is small and personal unless there is need for a third party in a legal action. Larger, closely-held businesses, being more complex, require the special knowledge and judgment of the professional with greater frequency.

FUNDAMENTALS OF BUSINESS APPRAISAL

There are ten basic steps in the appraisal process recommended by the authors. These steps, explained fully in the balance of the book, are summarized in this chapter.

CHAPTER 2

FINANCIAL STATEMENTS: A PROLOGUE TO VALUATION

The absence of romance in my history will, I fear, detract somewhat from its interest; but I will be content if it is judged useful by those inquirers who desire an exact knowledge of the past as an aid to the interpretation of the future, which in the course of human things must resemble if it does not reflect it.

THUCYDIDES - 413 B.C.

TOPICS DISCUSSED IN THIS CHAPTER

[¶2.01] — **Financial Statements are Historical**

[¶2.02] — **Statements Conform to GAAP**

[¶2.03] — **The Deficiencies in GAAP**
        Most Assets are Reported at Cost
        Valuation Accounts Do Not Really Value
        Some Assets and Liabilities are Omitted Entirely
        Estimates are Required
        Different Accounting Methods are Permitted
        1. Cash versus accrual accounting. 2. Inventory costing methods differ. 3. Depreciation methods vary. 4. Research and development accounting varies.

[¶2.04] — **How the Appraiser Views Financial Statements**

[¶2.05] — **The Case of BLM Electronics, Inc.**

[¶2.06] — **Steps in Statement Analysis**

[¶2.06-1] — **Step 1 - Arrange Statements in Comparative Form**

[¶2.06-2] — **Step 2 - Compute Analytical Ratios**
        Current Ratio - Quick Ratio - Collection Period - Inventory Turnover - Debt-to-Worth Ratio - Net Profit on New Worth - Net Worth Turnover - Net Profit on Sales - Other Ratios - Purchases to Trade Payables - Fixed Assets to Worth

[¶2.06-3] — **Step 3 - Look for Unusual, Misvalued or Omitted Items**

[¶2.07] — **Multiple Entities and Consolidated Statements**

[¶2.08] — **Summary**

Exhibit 1 — **BLM Electronics, Inc.**
        Balance Sheet - Last Five Years

Exhibit 2 — **BLM Electronics, Inc.**
        Income Statements - Last Five Years

Exhibit 3 — **BLM Electronics, Inc.**
        Income Statement Detail - Last Five Years

CHAPTER 2

FINANCIAL STATEMENTS: A PROLOGUE TO VALUATION

[¶2.01]   FINANCIAL STATEMENTS ARE HISTORICAL

"What's past is prologue" wrote Shakespeare, and that well explains the relationship of financial statements to the appraisal of a business. As indicated in Chapter 1, the appraiser is concerned with the present and future monetary returns to be derived from a business. The accountant is concerned principally with the past. The balance sheet prepared by the public accountant represents a company's financial position as of a date in the past. The income statement records the results of its operations for the accounting period preceding the date of the balance sheet.

Despite the historical aspects of the financial statements, no intelligent projection of the future can be made without a careful look at the past. The most complete and accurate record available is the financial data prepared from the books of account. The best summaries of that data are the periodically-prepared balance sheet and income statements. If these are audited by a CPA, their reliability is further increased.

[¶2.02]   STATEMENTS CONFORM TO GAAP

In spite of the foregoing, it is important to recognize that financial statements are seldom really accurate representations, even of the past. How can this be true when the standard auditor's opinion reads: "In our opinion, the aforementioned financial statements present fairly the financial position of X Company at December 31, 19____ and the results of its operations and the changes in its financial position for the year then ended"?

The key to the inaccuracy of the statements lies in the next phrase of the accountant's opinion, which reads, "in conformity with generally accepted accounting principles applied on a basis consistent with that of the preceding year." Properly interpreted, this statement means that the financial statements fairly present the financial position and past operations of the business, if one is willing to agree with the premises set forth by Generally Accepted Accounting Principles, or GAAP, in accounting parlance; and to understand that GAAP condones many different methods which could produce vastly different results were one method chosen over another; and to understand that the accountant is usually most concerned with the consistency with which the selected accounting methods are applied from year to year, not with the economic reality of the results.

To understand all of the artificial results which GAAP produces requires in-depth training in accounting and years of experience in the analysis of financial statements. Thus, a full presentation of the subject goes beyond the scope of this book. A basic knowledge of accounting, its terminology and its deficiencies must be assumed. Nevertheless, an understanding of the deficiencies of financial state-

FINANCIAL STATEMENTS: A PROLOGUE TO VALUATION

ments is essential so that the appraiser can make necessary corrections to reflect true values. Furthermore, many who are knowledgeable in using these statements do not take the time, or have not had the occasion, to make the in-depth, methodical analysis required of the appraiser. Therefore, this chapter will highlight the more common deficiencies of financial statements prepared according to GAAP, as well as the appraisal techniques used to analyze them. Later chapters show how the statements can be reconstructed to reflect the values and operating results needed by the appraiser.

[¶2.03] THE DEFICIENCIES IN GAAP

No one will deny that generally accepted accounting principles developed over the years serve a useful purpose. They bring a measure of order out of what would otherwise be a chaotic diversity of reporting methods. Still, the business appraiser must be concerned with economically real values, and the statements have glaring deficiencies from his standpoint. A few of the more important deficiencies, in addition to the historical nature of the data discussed earlier, are cited below:

MOST ASSETS ARE REPORTED AT COST

In inflationary periods, such as the present, this often means values are understated.

VALUATION ACCOUNTS DO NOT REALLY VALUE

Reserves for depreciation or amortization and other similar captions are called *valuation accounts* by accountants, but they are misnomers to the appraiser. They merely represent reductions in the cost of the assets to which they apply, which reductions may have been arrived at by a variety of methods.

SOME ASSETS AND LIABILITIES ARE OMITTED ENTIRELY

It is common practice to omit certain assets entirely, such as the value of patents, licenses, trademarks, copyrights, technical libraries, sales contracts, advertising materials, and goodwill. It is acceptable to omit certain liabilities, such as lease contracts, executive compensation contracts, and pending litigation claims, although these items may be noted in the accountant's footnotes to the financial statements if, in his judgment, they are important to a fair presentation.

ESTIMATES ARE REQUIRED

Estimates must be applied to many assets and liabilities, which in turn affect net income and balance sheet items. For instance, uncollectable accounts receivable, the life of depreciable and amortizable assets, and income taxes all must be estimated. The appraiser often does not agree with the estimates applied by the accountant.

FINANCIAL STATEMENTS: A PROLOGUE TO VALUATION

DIFFERENT ACCOUNTING METHODS ARE PERMITTED

A wide variety of accounting methods is permitted by GAAP. While the same methods will usually be applied by the same company, the methods used can have a tremendous effect on the results, even when applied consistently. Also, different companies in the identical type of business may use different methods of accounting, making comparisons difficult and tricky. It is important that the appraiser understand the different permissible methods. Some of the more important are as follows:

1. **Cash Versus Accrual Accounting**

    While nearly all large businesses employ accrual accounting, many closely-held businesses use the so-called cash basis. This is true because the closely-held firm is often more interested in saving income taxes than in accurately reporting income. The cash basis is acceptable to the Internal Revenue Service in many cases, and it can save, or at least defer, income taxes. Some businessmen believe it can save on bookkeeping as well.

    On the cash basis, income is realized when invoices are collected, not when they are rendered. Expenses are recorded when they are paid, not when they are incurred. The opportunities for income or expenses to be accelerated or deferred with tremendous effect on earnings are quite obvious. Often deferral or acceleration will not be deliberate, but will be dictated by the availability of cash and the pressures for payment exerted on customers or by suppliers.

    It is not quite correct to say that cash basis accounting is acceptable under GAAP, because most public accountants will convert cash books to accrual statements when they believe the distortion is too great. Yet, use of cash basis accounting is not actually prohibited by GAAP. *Montgomery's Auditing*, written by authorities in the field, merely says: "The accrual basis rather than the cash basis is preferred."[3]

    For appraisal purposes, it is not really important to determine the acceptability of cash basis accounting under GAAP. Rather, the appraiser must realize that whether or not the accountants like it, the cash basis is widely used among closely-held firms. When used, significant adjustments of the accounting records and statements are usually required to arrive at realistic figures.

2. **Inventory Costing Methods Differ**

    Inventories can be costed by a number of different methods, all acceptable under GAAP, but with a broad variation in the result. Inventories may be costed on the basis of actual cost, or standard cost, or by the retail method, to name three of the more common. The movement of inventories may be determined on the basis of First In, First Out (FIFO); Last In, First Out (LIFO); and the Average Method—again to name but a few. Different methods may and often do apply to inventories of raw

FINANCIAL STATEMENTS: A PROLOGUE TO VALUATION

materials, work-in-process, and finished goods. The methods by which overhead is applied to work-in-process and finished goods may vary. Inventories are customarily carried at cost unless the market price is lower, in which case market value is used.

For a full discussion of inventory accounting methods, the authors suggest reading an authoritative text, such as *Montgomery's Auditing*. A single illustration may indicate the broad difference in possible accounting results.

EXAMPLE:

In a period of rising prices, a company wholesaled a single, unchanging product, granulated sugar. At the close of its accounting period, just before the rapid price escalation in sugar, it had 10,000,000 pounds in inventory at a cost of 10c per pound, which was 5c per pound under the market value of 15c per pound. During the next year, the cost rose steadily, and the company purchased and sold 5,000,000 pounds, again closing with 10,000,000 pounds on hand. The 5,000,000 pounds purchased cost 40c per pound. The market price at the end of the second accounting period was 45c per pound.

Under the FIFO method, it would be assumed that the sugar sold was from the initial inventory, which cost 10c a pound. Therefore, the cost of the 5,000,000 pounds sold would be $500,000. On the other hand, were the LIFO method used, it would be assumed the 5,000,000 pounds sold were from the current purchases at 40c per pound. In this case, the cost of the 5,000,000 pounds sold would be $2,000,000, or a difference in profitability reported on the same transaction of $1,500,000.

Notice that neither the FIFO nor the LIFO method reflected the true market value of the sugar in inventory. In the FIFO case, the inventory would be carried on the statements as worth $2,500,000 (5,000,000 lbs. at 10c and 5,000,000 lbs. at 40c). Under LIFO, the inventory would be worth $1,000,000 (10,000,000 at 10c). Its economic value at the end of the period was actually $4,500,000 (less the cost of selling it). This type of distortion did occur during the sugar price rise, the Arab oil boycott, and more recently, in the coffee market.

3. Depreciation Methods Vary

The CPAs define depreciation accounting as follows: "Depreciation accounting is a system of accounting which aims to distribute the cost or other basic value of tangible capital assets, less salvage (if any), over the estimated useful life of the unit (which may be a group of assets) in a systematic and rational manner. *It is a process of allocation, not of valuation.*"[4] [Italics added]

Acceptable depreciation methods are heavily influenced by those acceptable for income tax purposes. Among the more common are the straight-line, sum-of-the-digits, and declining-balance methods. All three are acceptable under GAAP as well as income tax accounting.

FINANCIAL STATEMENTS: A PROLOGUE TO VALUATION

EXAMPLE:

A new automobile costing $6,000 is purchased on January 1, 1976 for business use. It is expected to have a useful life of five years, at the end of which time it can be sold for $500 salvage value. Depreciation for the year 1976 would be as follows: $1,100 under the straight-line method; $2,000 under the sum-of-the-digits method; and $2,400 under the double-declining-balance method.[5] The remaining undepreciated cost at the end of 1976 under the three methods would be: $4,900, $4,000, and $3,600 respectively.

Note that the market value of the automobile in the foregoing example is probably different from any of the three resultant figures.

It is also pertinent to observe that regardless of the depreciation method selected, there can be different acceptable ways in which it can be applied. Thus, assets may be individually depreciated, or they may be grouped into classes. The grouping approach may give the appraiser a particular problem in determining the age of specific items. If the assets in question are significant enough, a physical tabulation and economic valuation may be required.

4. Research and Development Accounting Varies

It is permissible under GAAP to either write off research and development costs in the year the expenses are incurred, or to set them up as an asset to be amortized over future years. If $1 million was incurred in such expenditures in a given year, the profit or loss reported by the business in that year would be $1 million more or $1 million less, depending on which choice was made.

The foregoing examples highlight but a few of the many choices open to businesses under generally accepted accounting procedures. For a more comprehensive discussion, the reader should refer to any of the standard texts on accounting or to authoritative compendiums, such as *The Handbook of Modern Accounting, Montgomery's Auditing,* or the *Accountants' Handbook*.[6] For an overly critical but nevertheless readable and revealing commentary on the deficiencies of GAAP, two books written by CPA Abraham J. Briloff can be instructive. One is entitled *Unaccountable Accounting* and the other *More Debts Than Credits*.[7]

[¶2.04] HOW THE APPRAISER VIEWS FINANCIAL STATEMENTS

Since the business appraiser must be concerned with economically real values, it is apparent he can *never* afford to accept financial statements prepared according to generally accepted accounting principles as being true economic representations of a company's financial position or of its real profitability. This is not to say that accounting statements never reflect economic values, but it would be unusual for them to do so, and the appraiser must research and test the values so represented before accepting them. This is even more true when the statements are prepared by the company itself and have not been subjected to a certified audit. In practice, the

FINANCIAL STATEMENTS: A PROLOGUE TO VALUATION

statements presented to the appraiser by a closely-held business are very often of the latter type, or they are prepared by a public accountant without audit.

The unaudited statements may include all sorts of unusual transactions which a public accountant would not condone. Capital items of some consequence may be expensed. Personal expenses may be charged to accounts such as travel and entertainment. Personal dwellings may be carried as assets. The owners' wives may drive company automobiles. Such actions are more characteristic of the personal business described in Chapter 1, but may occur in all closely-held firms. The appraiser cannot be expected to be an auditor, but he must do his best to isolate true business expense and assets from those not necessary to its operation. The steps described below can be helpful in this regard, together with the interviews suggested in Chapter 1 and the industry data described in Chapter 4.

[¶2.05] THE CASE OF BLM ELECTRONICS, INC.

Since statement analysis and many of the valuation techniques described hereafter can be quite esoteric and difficult to grasp in the abstract, the authors will weave a single case study through much of this book. The company is named BLM Electronics, Inc. It is not an actual company but represents data drawn from several businesses known to the authors, which facts are combined to illustrate valuation methods. More data on the company will be drawn out in subsequent chapters. For purposes of this chapter on Financial Statements, it will be assumed the appraiser has been presented with five years of financial statements prepared by company accountants. These statements have been excerpted from year-end figures prepared by a CPA.

[¶2.06] STEPS IN STATEMENT ANALYSIS

The following procedure will be found helpful in analyzing the financial statements of most companies:

[¶2.06-1] STEP 1 ARRANGE STATEMENTS IN COMPARATIVE FORM

Wherever possible, obtain at least five years of balance sheets and income statements, including those nearest the date of valuation. If prepared by an outside accountant, be sure to obtain all related notes. If prepared internally, obtain copies of workpapers and journal entries wherever possible. Obtain copies of income tax returns covering the statement periods.

Arrange the balance sheets and income statements in comparative form on columnar pads, leaving a blank column between each year's figures for detail references. These blank columns can be used for cross-reference to subsidiary schedules or for comments as needed.

Balance sheets and income statements for BLM Electronics, Inc. arranged in comparative form are shown at Exhibits 1 through 3.

FINANCIAL STATEMENTS: A PROLOGUE TO VALUATION

[¶2.06-2] STEP 2 COMPUTE ANALYTICAL RATIOS

There are many ratios which can be used to help analyze financial statements. Those described below have been particularly helpful in a wide variety of business appraisals. The listing is by no means all-inclusive. The need to compute other ratios may be suggested by the peculiarities of the company being analyzed, or by ratios which are widely used in the compilation of comparative statistical data for the industry of which the company is a part. More detail on ratios can be obtained by reading portions of books such as *Business Finance Handbook*, published by Prentice-Hall, and *Understanding Corporate Reports* by Bernstein.[8] The Small Business Administration has compiled a useful booklet entitled *Ratio Analysis for Small Business*.[9]

Each of the ratios below has been computed for BLM Electronics, Inc. using the material compiled in Exhibits 1 and 2. The dates heading the columns below refer to fiscal years ending on March 31 of the respective years.

RATIOS FOR BLM ELECTRONICS, INC.

Usual Ratios	**1972**	**1973**	**1974**	**1975**	**1976**
Current Ratio	3.8	3.4	3.4	3.3	2.8
Quick Ratio	2.0	1.8	1.6	1.6	1.2
Collection Period	87	86	80	75	74
Inventory Turnover	2.8	2.7	2.5	2.5	2.4
Debt/Worth	.2	.2	.2	.3	.3
Profit/Worth	21.2%	17.1%	19.5%	20.6%	17.1%
Worth Turnover	1.5	1.5	1.5	1.5	1.7
Profit/Sales	14.4%	11.5%	13.1%	13.5%	10.1%
Special Ratios for BLM					
Purchases/Payable	59	57	55	116	129
Fixed Assets/Worth	.2	.2	.1	.1	.2

The computation and meaning of the above ratios follows:

CURRENT RATIO

Computation

The total of current assets is divided by the total of current liabilities.

Purpose

To test the ability of the company to meet its current obligations.

FINANCIAL STATEMENTS: A PROLOGUE TO VALUATION

Example

For BLM, the current ratio at March 31, 1976 was 2.8. This was computed by taking from Exhibit 1 total current assets of $699,091 and dividing by total current liabilities of $251,895.

Results

BLM has 2.8 times more current assets than it has current liabilities. While this result is a generally good indicator, it cannot be accepted as final evidence that the firm can easily pay its bills. See other ratio comments below. Note, also, that the current ratio has declined from 3.8 to 2.8 over the past five years.

QUICK RATIO

Computation

Subtract from current assets all except cash, short-term marketable securities, and accounts receivable net of bad debt reserves. Divide the result by total current liabilities.

Purpose

To further test the company's ability to pay short-term obligations by considering only those assets which can be quickly converted into cash (hence called the Quick Ratio) against obligations due within twelve months.

Example

For BLM, the Quick Ratio at March 31, 1976 was 1.2. This was computed by taking from Exhibit 1 total current assets of $699,091 less prepaid expenses of $16,271 less inventories of $380,373, resulting in a figure of $302,447. Divide $302,447 by total current liabilities of $251,895.

Results

Considering only cash and accounts receivable (BLM had no marketable securities), it appears that BLM can meet its current liabilities with .2, or 20% to spare. Note, however, that the Quick Ratio has declined even more rapidly than the Current Ratio. It was 2.0 at March 31, 1972 and is only 1.2 at March 31, 1976. By referring to Exhibit 1, the reason is apparent: inventories have increased from $247,850 to $380,373 over five years. The appraiser will wish to discuss the reasons for this inventory increase with key personnel and will add this point to his standard owner-manager checklist discussed in Chapter 3.

FINANCIAL STATEMENTS: A PROLOGUE TO VALUATION

COLLECTION PERIOD

Computation

Divide net sales by 360 days to get average daily sales. Divide total net trade accounts and notes receivable by average daily sales. [Memo: 360 days are recommended because bankers and many comparative statistical sources use this instead of 365 days.]

Purpose

To determine how many days' sales are tied up in accounts receivable. If the company sells on 30-day terms, and 90 days sales are represented by accounts receivable, a problem is indicated. This computation refines the Quick Ratio and gives a further indication of the company's ability to pay its debt.

Example

For BLM, there were 74 days' sales in accounts receivable at March 31, 1976. This was computed by taking from Exhibit 2 total sales of $1,274,893 and dividing by 360 days. The result is average daily sales of $3,541 during this fiscal period. Next, take from Exhibit 1 accounts receivable-trade (net of the reserve for bad debts) in the amount of $263,512. Divide $263,512 by $3,541, the average daily sales.

Results

If BLM's usual terms of sale are net 30 days, a significant problem is indicated. The reader will notice, however, that there has been a steady improvement from year to year. At March 31, 1972, 87 days' sales were tied up in accounts receivable, whereas by March 31, 1976, only 74 days were involved. Even so, the appraiser will certainly wish to add a question to his client interview checklist regarding the slow collection period.

INVENTORY TURNOVER

Computation

Divide cost of goods sold by the inventory at the end of the fiscal period.

Purpose

To see how rapidly inventory is turned over. A slow rate of turnover may indicate excessive inventories, possible outdated stock, or an unusual buildup of some type. A very fast turnover may reflect good inventory management, or it might indicate hand-to-mouth buying, with sales missed due to inadequate stocks. The inventory turnover is a further test of the firm's ability to liquidate assets to pay its bills.

FINANCIAL STATEMENTS: A PROLOGUE TO VALUATION

Example

For BLM, the inventory turned over 2.4 times in the fiscal year ended March 31, 1976. This was computed by obtaining from Exhibit 2 the cost of goods sold of $904,879 and dividing by the ending inventory of $380,373.

Results

The inventory turnover for BLM seems slow, and it has declined over the past five years. This is at least partly the result of the inventory buildup highlighted in connection with the Quick Ratio computation above. However, it raises a further question of how much inventory is really needed to run the operation. The appraiser may wish to expand his client interview checklist still further, since a turnover ratio of 2.4 means the inventory is turning only five times per year.

DEBT-TO-WORTH RATIO

Computation

Divide total liabilities by tangible net worth. Tangible net worth is the worth of a business minus intangible items, such as goodwill, trademarks, patents, capitalized research and development, etc. This ratio is sometimes computed using book net worth, but many industrial statistical compilations include tangible net worth, because intangibles are seldom properly reported or valued on accounting statements. Therefore, use of tangible net worth is recommended.

Purpose

To provide a quick measure of the ratio of owner's capital to borrowed funds, frequently referred to as "leverage." When borrowed funds exceed the owner's capital, the pressure of debt on the operation tends to increase. Expressed as a ratio, the lower the ratio, the lower the debt pressure.

Example

For BLM, the debt to tangible net worth ratio is .3 for the fiscal year ended March 31, 1976. This was computed by obtaining from Exhibit 1 total liabilities of $261,895 (Ignore deferred income as a liability for this purpose) and dividing by $755,973, tangible net worth. Tangible net worth is derived by deducting from the book net worth of $915,184 shown on Exhibit 1 new product investment of $134,210 and other assets of $25,001. Note that other assets consists of goodwill and patents.

Results

Although the ratio of debt to worth has increased since 1972, the ratio looks highly favorable for BLM. Outside creditors have only 30% as much invested in the business as do the owners. This indicates that the company probably has some available borrowing capacity if needed.

FINANCIAL STATEMENTS: A PROLOGUE TO VALUATION

NET PROFIT ON NET WORTH

Computation

Divide net profit before tax by tangible net worth.

Purpose

To evaluate the profitability of the operation to the owners and to form a partial basis for weighing the profitability of the business against alternative investments.

Example

For the fiscal year ending March 31, 1976, BLM realized a net profit before tax of 17.1% on tangible net worth. This was computed by dividing net profit before tax from Exhibit 2 of $129,054 by $755,973 tangible net worth. The tangible net worth was derived as described under the above example for the Debt-to-Worth Ratio.

Results

Whether the net profit on investment for BLM is satisfactory depends on several factors which cannot be fully determined at this point, such as (1) What comparable returns are other industry members realizing? (2) What are other investments of like risk yielding? (3) Is salary to the owners high or low? (4) How much of this profit can be realized after tax? If desired, the ratio can be developed on an after-tax basis, but this result is not as readily found in comparable industry figures.

NET WORTH TURNOVER

Computation

Divide net sales by tangible net worth.

Purpose

This ratio indicates how thoroughly invested capital is being used. If the ratio increases from year to year, it implies that owner's capital is being used more and more. If the ratio climbs very high on the basis of comparison with other companies in the industry, the company being valued may be undercapitalized, or it may indicate the management is not sufficiently conservative. On the other hand, it can indicate careful management of assets.

FINANCIAL STATEMENTS: A PROLOGUE TO VALUATION

Example

In the fiscal year ended March 31, 1976, BLM turned over its net worth 1.7 times. This result was obtained by taking from Exhibit 2 total sales of $1,274,893 and dividing this by tangible net worth of $755,973. Tangible net worth was derived as described under the above example for the Debt-to-Worth Ratio.

Results

The turnover ratio of 1.7 appears low. Note that the ratio has been consistent over the past five years, improving somewhat in the latest fiscal year.

NET PROFIT ON SALES

Computation

Divide net profit before tax by net sales.

Purpose

To determine the profitability of the operation based on sales and to form a basis for comparing this result with industry figures. A high rate of return may or may not be favorable. An above-industry rate may indicate the firm is exceptionally profitable, or it may suggest that many sales are lost due to overly high prices. Were prices lower, the greater volume of sales might lead to a greater total profit for the firm.

Example

In the latest fiscal year, BLM realized a net profit before tax of 10.1%. This was computed by obtaining from Exhibit 2 net profit before tax of $129,054 and dividing by total sales of $1,274,893. (As noted earlier, for purposes of illustration, total sales are here assumed to be net sales.)

Results

Until a comparison is made with industry figures, it is difficult to judge whether the 10.1% return is favorable. The appraiser will note that the ratio has declined in the fiscal year ended March 31, 1976 over the level of the previous two years. He may wish to add a question on this point in his client interview.

OTHER RATIOS

Among the many other ratios that could be computed, the following two seem particularly desirable in the BLM case.

FINANCIAL STATEMENTS: A PROLOGUE TO VALUATION

PURCHASES TO TRADE PAYABLES

Computation

Divide purchases for the year by 360 days to obtain average daily purchases. Divide trade accounts payable by average daily purchases.

Purpose

To see whether inventory purchases are putting a strain on accounts payable.

Example

For BLM there are 129 days' purchases included in accounts payable. This results from taking purchases for the fiscal year ending March 31, 1976 of $402,792 from Exhibit 2 and dividing by 360 days to obtain average daily purchases of $1,119. Trade accounts payable from Exhibit 1 of $144,138 is then divided by $1,119.

Results

When compared with the same calculation for preceding periods, it is apparent that not only is there an indication of a present problem with excessive accounts payable, but also there is a definite unfavorable trend. In the fiscal years ending in 1972, 1973, and 1974, less than 60 days of purchases were involved in accounts payable. Then in the fiscal year ending in 1975, this figure more than doubled. In fiscal 1976, it increased further. The appraiser may wish to obtain an aging of accounts payable as a further check on accounts payable, and he will certainly want to question BLM owners on this topic.

FIXED ASSETS TO WORTH

Computation

Divide total fixed assets after depreciation and amortization by tangible net worth.

Purpose

To determine whether a high or low ratio of net worth is tied up in fixed assets.

Example

In the BLM case for the fiscal year ending March 31, 1976, take Equipment & Improvements - Net of $120,774 from Exhibit 1 and divide this by tangible net worth of $755,973. As in other preceding examples, tangible net worth is derived as explained under the Debt-to-Worth Ratio.

FINANCIAL STATEMENTS: A PROLOGUE TO VALUATION

Results

The ratio of .2 seems low. Noting this fact and the substantial charges for equipment rental in Exhibit 3, the appraiser should add a query regarding leased equipment to his client check list. He may also wish to check the level of fixed asset investment in the industry of which BLM is a part.

[¶2.06-3] STEP 3 LOOK FOR UNUSUAL, MISVALUED OR OMITTED ITEMS

Having completed the ratio analysis, the business appraiser will next turn to the detail of the comparative financial statements. He will look for captions which might indicate unusual expenditures or income, undervalued or overvalued assets, or clues to assets and liabilities which have been omitted entirely. Such an analysis will raise a multitude of questions to be posed in the client interview and will help to define the required scope of the appraisal. So diverse are the possible results that a full explanation of what to look for would be far too lengthy, complex and confusing. Therefore, reference will be made to the BLM case as an example.

FROM RATIO ANALYSIS

The ratio analyses just explained brought out certain questions, such as increasing inventories and low fixed-asset investment, which questions are also raised by the statements alone. Further comment on these items will not be included here.

FROM THE BALANCE SHEET - EXHIBIT 1

1. **Possible Soft Receivables**

The item "Other Accounts and Notes Receivable" of $20,000 looks suspicious. The even dollar amount seems to indicate it is not simply a trade receivable converted to a note. Could it be an officer loan or an advance to an affiliated company? If so, is it really collectable within 12 months (hence current) or is it collectable at all?

2. **An Unusual Receivable**

The item "Notes Receivable - Long Term" for $297,648 bears checking because it suddenly appeared as $312,000 at March 31, 1975. This is clearly unusual. Is it worth the book figure?

3. **Investment in Affiliate**

What is the nature of the partnership interest carried at $53,580 at March 31, 1976? Why did it increase $30,000 between March 31, 1973 and March 31, 1974? For a further discussion of appraisal problems raised by affiliates and by wholly and partially-owned subsidiaries, see ¶ 2.07.

FINANCIAL STATEMENTS: A PROLOGUE TO VALUATION

4. **Equipment and Improvements**

Why did machinery and equipment, furniture and fixtures, and tools and dies increase markedly between March 31, 1975 and March 31, 1976? Is there any old, outdated equipment? Are any tools and dies now obsolete? What is the nature and economic value of the leasehold improvements? Is the total cost of equipment and improvements reduced by the reserve for depreciation close to their fair market value? (Liquidation value is not an issue in the case.)

5. **Research and Development Policies**

What comprises New Product Investment of $134,210? Is this simply capitalized research and development, or does it have some relationship to the value of new products? Why did it increase so markedly in the fiscal year ending March 31, 1976? See also Exhibit 3, Research and Development.

6. **Disappearance of an Asset**

What happened to $168,295 of other assets between March 31, 1974 and March 31, 1975? Is it somehow related to the unusual receivables cited at item 2 above and the new item of deferred income discussed at 9 below?

7. **Goodwill and Other Intangibles**

Determine the origin of the $25,000 goodwill and the $1.00 set up for patents. Does the goodwill figure have any relation to economic value? Obviously, the patent valuation is for record purposes only.

8. **Possible Soft Payables**

What is the nature of the $8,320 "Accounts Payable-Other", which has been carried at a like amount for the past five years? Is it really payable, and, if so, should it not be considered long term?

9. **Handling of Deferred Income**

What comprises the deferred income item, and is the income properly deferred from an economic standpoint? Is this possibly related to items 2 and 6 above?

FROM THE INCOME STATEMENTS - EXHIBIT 2

1. **Shift In Sales Mix**

What is the significance of the increase in commercial sales and the fall-off of U.S. Government instrument sales over the past five years? What effect does this apparent trend have upon the company's future profitability?

FINANCIAL STATEMENTS: A PROLOGUE TO VALUATION

2. Increase in Direct Labor

In FYE 1972 Direct Labor-Factory was 9.8% of total sales, whereas in FYE 1976 it reached 12.7%. Is this a trend involving a further projected increase in the percentage, or has it stabilized?

3. Increase in Miscellaneous Income

Over the five years, miscellaneous income has increased from $7,520 to $48,419. What is included in this amount?

4. Low Income Taxes

Why does the corporation pay only about 9% of its net profit in income taxes? Is there a loss carry-forward, or is this a Subchapter S corporation paying only state income taxes? The latter seems more plausible, since the loss carry-forward would tend to wipe out all income taxes.

5. Dividends and Surplus Charges

Why were dividends of $100,000 per year paid, when this level of payment left the company with only $18,935 in cash at March 31, 1976? If dividends are assumed to be $100,000 for the latest fiscal year, what is the nature of the additional $2,250 appearing in the Dividends and Other Surplus Charges account?

FROM INCOME STATEMENT DETAIL - EXHIBIT 3

1. Depreciation Policy

Why did depreciation expense under factory overhead jump suddenly in FYE 1973 and FYE 1976? Is this a tip-off to the use of accelerated depreciation on new equipment?

2. Increase In Equipment Rental

Why did equipment rental increase by $6,800 between FYE 1972 and FYE 1973? Is there a lease that has economic value, such as one which permits renewal at the end of the lease for a nominal rental?

3. Possible Building Write-off

Why did maintenance and repair and outside services increase by almost $25,000 between FYE 1974 and FYE 1975? Why did insurance and property taxes escalate in FYE 1976? Could this be a tip-off as to a hidden asset, such as a building addition expensed for tax purposes but economically valuable?

FINANCIAL STATEMENTS: A PROLOGUE TO VALUATION

4. **Possible Machinery Write-off**

Why did expendable tools increase by $10,500 in FYE 1973? Could this indicate valuable tools written off for tax purposes? The subsequent increase in utility charges from $3,503 in FYE 1973 to $4,187 in FYE 1974 might also indicate added equipment in use.

5. **Possible Hidden Promotional Asset**

Why did advertising suddenly jump by over $14,000 in FYE 1976? Could there be catalogs and other advertising material which have been expensed but which are valuable for the future and represent an asset?

6. **Increase In Commissions**

Why have commissions increased dramatically over the past five years?

7. **Possible Hidden Liability**

Why did legal and audit fees jump perceptibly in FYE 1976 after having been relatively steady for several years? Could this indicate some costly litigation under way, or possibly a pending income tax assessment?

8. **Possible Personal Expenses**

Why did travel and entertainment jump by almost $7,000 between FYE 1975 and FYE 1976? Did some of the owners take an expensive personal trip which was charged to business? Or is the increase related in whole or part to the increase in commercial business?

In the foregoing manner, the business appraiser must develop his own list of further items to explore with client personnel. Every set of financial statements will present different questions and different facts, so that no set rules can be developed for where to look for problems and questions. Once the data is spread, however, as the BLM case demonstrates, the queries will almost suggest themselves.

[¶2.07] MULTIPLE ENTITIES AND CONSOLIDATED STATEMENTS

The authors find that approximately 60% of their work in valuing closely-held firms involves multiple entities. The controlling owners may be engaged in a single business but use different corporations, partnerships or trusts to operate certain functions, such as manufacturing or sales. In the alternative, the owners may be engaged in many different types or classes of business, each with a separate entity but still inter-related. Sometimes the related businesses are wholly-owned subsidiaries. Sometimes the owners have only a controlling interest, with others owning the minority. Sometimes only a minority is owned. At times, commonly-controlled companies are not formally inter-related on the company's records, but there are

FINANCIAL STATEMENTS: A PROLOGUE TO VALUATION

substantial inter-company dealings involving accounts and notes receivable and payable.

The client company's use of multiple entities for whatever reason raises a number of special problems for the business appraiser in analyzing the financial statements and in putting this data in a form he can use for appraisal. In addition to the normal problems presented by GAAP, as described in the preceding sections of this chapter, he must be concerned with the following:

1. Were the subsidiary entities acquired by purchase, start-up, or consolidation? If acquired by purchase, assets may have been revalued to a considerable extent to reflect market values at the date of acquisition. Otherwise, subsidiary assets will usually be carried at cost.

2. Have subsidiary operations been consolidated with the parent in consolidated financial statements? If so, financial ratios may be distorted and the income of different constituent subsidiaries may be distorted. Statements may have to be constructed and analyzed on each subsidiary entity to arrive at real values.

3. If statements have not been consolidated, are there unrealistic allocations of income or costs between the subsidiary or affiliated entities? Are inter-company receivables and payables realistic? Will they be paid?

4. Are different accounting methods and procedures followed by various entities? For instance, does one entity value its inventories on a LIFO basis where the others use FIFO? Is one entity on the cash basis while others are on the accrual method? Are there different fiscal years?

Example

On March 31, 1976, BLM Electronics, Inc. had a $53,580 interest in a partnership. As will be developed in the next chapter, the partnership is 53% owned and is engaged in the restaurant business. The restaurant was started by an individual partner who was a former employee of BLM. What effect does this operation have on BLM reported results?

As will be seen in the next chapter, the foregoing example is a simple form of multiple entity operation. Even so, it means business appraisals of essentially two separate and distinct businesses. It requires analysis of any possible inter-company accounts to remove the effect, if any, of one business on the other. However, the unscrambling required is minimal in contrast with the situations where there are more massive inter-company relations, or consolidated statements have been prepared.

In the BLM case, the appraiser himself may be able to make the necessary adjustments for inter-company transactions, although his work could be expedited considerably by discovering from the firm's CPA or internal accountant which account or accounts carry inter-company dealings. When the situation becomes more complex, and especially where consolidated statements are involved, the authors

FINANCIAL STATEMENTS: A PROLOGUE TO VALUATION

recommend an early conference with the CPA (or internal accountant, if no CPA is involved) to obtain full information on adjustments already made plus those which might still be required. Trying to ferret out the adjustments and trying to deduce what was involved can be costly to the client and frustrating to the appraiser.

Caveat: If multiple entities are involved, be prepared to spend considerably more time on the appraisal than were there a single entity. Be particularly alert to inter-company distortions, and call upon the company accountant for help.

[¶2.08] SUMMARY

Financial statements prepared according to generally accepted accounting principles (GAAP) are historical. As such, their usefulness to the business appraiser is limited, since he must determine the present and future worth of the business. He must realize that generally accepted accounting principles (GAAP) do not result in statements which reflect value. Assets are generally carried at cost. Valuation accounts do not really value. Some assets and liabilities are completely omitted. Many estimates are required. Different accounting methods, all permissible under GAAP, can result in widely different results.

The statements, with all of their deficiencies, represent the best record of the past, and they form a prologue to the present and future figures needed by the appraiser. However, it is important that he *never* merely accept financial statements as being true economic representations of a company's financial position, nor of its real profitability. In unusual instances, they might represent economic value and real earnings, but he cannot assume this to be the case.

To simplify the development of facts the reader needs to know about financial statements and appraisal techniques, the case of BLM Electronics, Inc., is used in this chapter and subsequently in the book. It is not a real company, but it is a composite of real company problems faced by the authors.

There are three steps represented in analyzing financial statements for appraisal purposes. First, arrange the statements in comparative form. Second, compute eight key analytical ratios plus such others as may seem logical. Analyze the meaning of the ratios developed and make up specific questions for the client interview. Third, look for unusual, misvalued or omitted items by reviewing the comparative financial statements. Add these to the list of questions for the client interview.

If the business operates through several entities which are subsidiaries or affiliates, be particularly careful to look for figures which are distorted by inter-company transactions. Also, realize that each business may not have its assets listed at cost, and different accounting methods may be used by the different entities. In short, be prepared to spend extra time on the appraisal, and be particularly alert to unrealistic figures.

EXHIBIT 1

BLM ELECTRONICS, INC.

BALANCE SHEETS - LAST FIVE YEARS

	3-31-72	3-31-73	3-31-74	3-31-75	3-31-76
Cash	49,096	47,852	22,766	89,764	18,935
Accounts Receivable - Trade	267,085	261,800	250,018	259,840	266,986
Less: Reserve for Bad Debts	(8,038)	(3,782)	(2,552)	(12,333)	(3,474)
Accounts Receivable - Net	259,047	258,018	247,466	247,507	263,512
Other Accounts & Notes Receivable	-	-	10,000	10,000	20,000
Inventories	247,850	275,122	300,434	330,085	380,373
Prepaid Expenses	14,253	14,780	15,175	15,353	16,271
TOTAL CURRENT ASSETS	570,246	595,772	595,841	692,709	699,091
Notes Receivable - Long Term	-	-	-	312,000	297,648
Partnership Interest	23,580	23,580	53,580	53,580	53,580
Equipment & Improvements:					
Machinery & Equipment	40,188	52,105	52,105	53,288	74,101
Furniture & Fixtures	39,018	40,988	40,988	42,100	45,191
Leasehold Improvements	45,384	45,384	45,384	49,210	49,210
Tools, Dies & Molds	36,013	38,222	41,003	46,022	66,436
Total Cost-Equip't & Improvements	160,603	176,699	179,480	190,620	234,938
Less: Reserve for Depreciation	(42,011)	(60,160)	(75,678)	(90,444)	(114,164)
Equipment & Improvements - Net	118,592	116,539	103,802	100,176	120,774
New Product Investment	50,024	65,330	80,422	97,722	134,210
Other Assets	193,296*	193,296*	193,296*	25,001*	25,001*
TOTAL ASSETS	955,738	994,517	1,026,941	1,281,188	1,330,304
Notes Payable - Short Term	69,993	87,301	83,580	70,000	60,000
Accounts Payable - Trade	46,651	48,421	47,733	102,080	144,138
Income Taxes Payable	11,758	9,478	13,162	14,424	11,615
Accounts Payable - Other	8,320	8,320	8,320	8,320	8,320
Other Taxes Payable	6,618	9,500	7,299	4,993	8,649
Other Current Liabilities	6,554	10,421	12,692	10,759	19,173
TOTAL CURRENT LIABILITIES	149,894	173,441	172,786	210,576	251,895
Notes Payable - Long Term	-	-	-	10,000	10,000
Deferred Income	-	-	-	160,617	153,225
TOTAL LIABILITIES	149,894	173,441	172,786	381,193	415,120
Common Stock	10,000	10,000	10,000	10,000	10,000
Paid-In Surplus	200,000	200,000	200,000	200,000	200,000
Earned Surplus	595,844	611,076	644,155	689,995	705,184
TOTAL CAPITAL	805,844	821,076	854,155	899,995	915,184
TOTAL LIABILITIES & CAPITAL	955,738	994,517	1,026,941	1,281,188	1,330,304

*Includes Goodwill at $25,000 plus Patents at $1.
 Land at $168,295 also included through 3-31-74.

EXHIBIT 2

BLM ELECTRONICS, INC.

INCOME STATEMENTS - LAST FIVE FISCAL YEARS

	3-31-72	3-31-73	3-31-74	3-31-75	3-31-76
Instrument Sales - Commercial	287,611	330,240	371,864	415,404	467,116
Instrument Sales - U.S. Government	510,242	432,702	360,590	302,992	258,327
Medical-Dental Sales-Professional	175,259	220,011	275,064	348,830	437,288
Medical-Dental Sales - U.S. Government	98,342	102,814	105,330	118,225	112,162
TOTAL SALES	1,071,454	1,085,767	1,112,848	1,185,451	1,274,893
Beginning Inventories	238,743	247,850	275,122	320,434	330,085
Material Purchases	286,286	307,930	313,792	316,717	402,792
Direct Labor - Factory	105,005	110,741	120,189	133,962	162,315
Factory Overhead*	215,644	240,634	230,440	258,167	248,282
Direct Labor - Engineering	34,386	35,563	36,230	39,155	44,919
Engineering Overhead*	67,436	69,645	69,256	76,050	96,859
Subtotal	947,500	1,012,363	1,045,029	1,144,485	1,285,252
Less: Ending Inventories	(247,850)	(275,122)	(300,434)	(330,085)	(380,373)
TOTAL COST OF GOODS SOLD	699,650	737,241	744,595	814,400	904,879
GROSS PROFIT	371,804	348,526	368,253	371,051	370,014
Administrative Expense*	217,847	229,359	234,202	237,201	286,154
PROFIT FROM OPERATIONS	153,957	119,167	134,051	133,850	83,860
Miscellaneous Income	7,520	12,618	20,113	35,432	48,419
Miscellaneous Expense	6,770	7,075	7,923	9,018	3,225
NET PROFIT BEFORE TAX	154,707	124,710	146,241	160,264	129,054
Income Taxes	11,758	9,478	13,162	14,424	11,615
NET PROFIT AFTER TAX	142,949	115,232	133,079	145,840	117,439
Dividends & Other Surplus Charges	100,000	100,000	100,000	100,000	102,250
NET PROFIT TO SURPLUS	42,949	15,232	33,079	45,840	15,189

*See Exhibit 3

EXHIBIT 3

BLM ELECTRONICS, INC.

INCOME STATEMENT DETAIL - LAST FIVE FISCAL YEARS

	3-31-72	3-31-73	3-31-74	3-31-75	3-31-76
Salaries and Wages	130,183	131,523	132,004	134,218	136,009
Payroll Taxes and Insurance	16,501	16,918	17,160	17,213	17,734
Depreciation	10,510	15,197	12,308	11,540	21,026
Equipment Rental	2,215	9,053	9,004	9,108	9,299
Insurance	2,305	2,318	2,331	2,450	2,951
Maintenance and Repair	2,614	2,782	2,542	18,118	2,761
Outside Services	3,814	4,022	3,978	13,344	4,185
Property Taxes	9,237	9,523	9,598	9,987	11,298
Rent	15,780	15,780	17,358	17,358	17,358
Tools - Expendable	3,941	14,522	4,083	4,123	4,239
Utilities	3,484	3,503	4,187	4,342	4,824
All Other	15,060	15,493	15,887	16,366	16,598
TOTAL FACTORY OVERHEAD	215,644	240,634	230,440	258,167	248,282
Salaries	33,758	34,923	35,084	38,102	39,682
Payroll Taxes and Insurance	4,505	4,684	4,800	5,205	5,450
Depreciation	1,338	1,434	1,508	1,410	1,238
Outside Services	555	602	481	523	516
Research and Development	35,321	37,420	34,425	40,347	66,510
Rent	3,218	3,354	3,689	3,689	3,689
All Other	8,919	9,342	8,602	9,821	9,796
Less: Capitalized New Product Invest't.	(20,178)	(22,114)	(19,333)	(23,047)	(30,022)
TOTAL ENGINEERING OVERHEAD	67,436	69,645	69,256	76,050	96,859
Salaries	94,818	97,221	97,422	100,112	112,345
Payroll Taxes and Insurance	3,854	4,055	4,078	4,222	4,705
Advertising	12,888	15,144	13,005	12,132	26,350
Bad Debts	5,357	5,429	5,564	5,927	6,374
Commissions	23,621	28,002	32,993	38,975	46,574
Conventions	3,575	3,515	5,132	5,284	7,314
Depreciation	1,558	1,518	1,702	1,816	1,456
Interest	4,242	5,011	6,303	7,605	6,789
Legal and Audit	12,233	11,847	12,134	12,063	18,278
Proposal Expense	12,118	10,025	8,333	5,100	3,366
Rent	4,736	4,736	5,210	5,210	5,210
Royalties	6,888	6,933	6,705	6,888	6,941
Telephone	7,023	7,440	7,718	7,513	8,032
Travel and Entertainment	12,713	14,854	13,008	12,144	19,022
All Other	12,223	13,629	14,895	12,210	13,398
TOTAL ADMINISTRATIVE EXPENSE	217,847	229,359	234,202	237,201	286,154

CHAPTER 3

INTERVIEWS: ADDING LIFE TO THE VALUATION

Ask, and it shall be given you; seek, and ye shall find; knock, and it shall be opened unto you:

                THE BIBLE - MATTHEW 7:7

TOPICS DISCUSSED IN THIS CHAPTER

[¶3.01] — Who Should be Contacted?

[¶3.02] — Format for Conducting Interviews and Assembling Data

[¶3.02-1] — Date of Appraisal

[¶3.02-2] — Purpose and Scope

[¶3.02-3] — History of the Business

[¶3.02-4] — Legal Entities

[¶3.02-5] — Detail on Subsidiaries or Affiliates

[¶3.02-6] — Locations at Which the Business Operates

[¶3.02-7] — Present Ownership of the Business

[¶3.02-8] — Products and Services Sold

[¶3.02-9] — Industry Classification

[¶3.02-10] — Creditor Names

[¶3.02-11] — Major Customers

[¶3.02-12] — Employee Plans

[¶3.02-13] — Property Occupancy Information

[¶3.02-14] — Physical Condition of the Plant

[¶3.02-15] — Appraisals and Plans

[¶3.02-16] — Ownership Transfers and Offers

[¶3.02-17] — Information Sources

[¶3.02-18] — Owner Profiles

[¶3.02-19] — Key Personnel Information

[¶3.02-20] — Special Queries Regarding Statements

[¶3.02-21] — Contingencies

[¶3.02-22] — Industry Study

[¶3.02-23] — Independent Financial Study

[¶3.02-24] — Key Personnel Interviews

[¶3.02-25] — Appraise Tangible Assets

[¶3.02-26] — Appraise Goodwill and Intangibles

[¶3.03] — Summary

CHAPTER 3

INTERVIEWS: ADDING LIFE TO THE VALUATION

[¶3.01] WHO SHOULD BE CONTACTED?

In any closely-held firm, it is essential to conduct comprehensive interviews with the owners. These will uncover many pertinent facts regarding the business and will give an insight into the owners' operating philosophy. Often, considerable information can be learned about the industry of which the company is a part, the competition, its bank and supplier relations, as well as the competency and experience of key personnel.

Interviews should not stop with the owners, however, unless it is a personal business as described at ¶ 1.04-1 where management and ownership are synonomous. Even so, key personnel may need to be consulted, such as the inventory control clerk, if inventories are substantial, to see if there are outmoded or slow-moving items in stock. In the professionally-managed business, interviews should be held with key management personnel. This is true even where there may be some repetition of topics discussed with the owners. The sales manager, for instance, may reveal some important contracts the owners forgot to mention, or he may point up a competitive situation which would affect the appraisal. The production manager may indicate that a new machine just acquired is cutting production costs significantly. Each of these revelations may have a significant effect on the forecasts the appraiser will develop to arrive at the future level of profitability.

Nor should the interviews stop with company personnel. It is desirable to talk to the firm's banker, who may provide further data on the company's history and may give his opinion of its future. The public accountant, if any, who prepares the statements and makes up the tax returns, must be contacted. Judicious contacts with key competitors can often be fruitful in gleaning information about the industry and even about the client company. Trade association executives can be an excellent source of data on the industry and its outlook, and they can frequently supply helpful statistical data as well.

[¶3.02] FORMAT FOR CONDUCTING INTERVIEWS AND ASSEMBLING DATA

From experience in making many appraisals of closely-held firms, the authors have developed a format, or checklist, which they follow in compiling information from interviews with client company personnel and with others contacted on behalf of the client. This checklist is equally useful in assembling data for goodwill valuation. The use of this or a similar checklist is recommended.

INTERVIEWS: ADDING LIFE TO THE VALUATION

To assist the reader in use of the checklist, pertinent facts on the BLM case are provided in this format. These facts, in turn, will be used to help illustrate suggested methods for further processing financial data and for actually appraising businesses. To avoid irrelevant detail, however, only the facts pertinent to this appraisal are included. In the actual valuation process, much more information would be assembled, including a considerable amount that would prove to be irrelevant. The process of determining what information is pertinent is an integral part of the appraisal process, but being a matter of judgment, it is not possible to adequately explain this step. Furthermore, such a discussion could tend to obscure, rather than clarify, the principal points the authors wish to make.

A summary of the key facts learned through personal interviews and other research on the BLM case are as follows:

[¶3.02-1] DATE OF APPRAISAL

The appraisal is to be made as of March 31, 1976, which is 10 days after the appraiser was engaged.

Comment

In practice, appraisals seldom are conveniently made as of the date an accounting year closes. Hence, it is usually necessary to obtain interim financial statements as well as those regularly prepared at the end of the fiscal period. This added data will not be required in the BLM case.

[¶3.02-2] PURPOSE AND SCOPE

The owners wish to know the fair market value of the company if sold. They also want to know the fair market value of a 33⅓% interest if sold separately for cash.

The purpose is to provide a basis for pricing the company in negotiations to sell out completely to another company for cash. If this sale is not completed, the company proposes to sell for cash its majority interest in a short order food operation, referred to after this as the "Fast Burger operation." One of the owners would also sell his 33⅓% holding of BLM to an unrelated outsider for cash.

Comment

The fact that all transactions would be for cash eliminates the necessity of setting a value on the stock or other consideration to be received in trade. Three distinct valuations are involved, however. 1. A value of 100% of the stock. 2. The value of 33⅓% of the stock. 3. The value of a majority holding in the Fast Burger operation. The fact that 33⅓% of the same stock is involved, with respect to which 100% must be valued, does not mean the one-third interest is worth the proportion it bears to the whole.

INTERVIEWS: ADDING LIFE TO THE VALUATION

[¶3.02-3] HISTORY OF THE BUSINESS

The business was formed in 1952 as a general partnership, with Messrs. Gregory M. Bellini, George P. Love, and Walter R. Murphy as partners. It was successful from the start because all three men were experienced in the field and they had developed a good line of products and knew many agents and distributors of similar lines. In 1961, the firm was incorporated. In 1970, Walter R. Murphy retired as the chief marketing executive but retained his directorship. In 1975, George P. Love retired as Treasurer and sold his stock to Edward F. Mondale. (See ¶ 3.02-16) From 1961 to April 1, 1971, the firm cumulated an earned surplus of $538,645, but no dividends were paid. With the retirement of Murphy and upon advice of tax counsel, dividends of $100,000 per year were instituted in 1971.

[¶3.02-4] LEGAL ENTITIES

BLM Electronics, Inc. is a California corporation incorporated October 31, 1961. There is one class of voting, common, $1 par stock. Ten thousand shares have been issued. A Subchapter S election has been in effect since incorporation. The State of California does not recognize Subchapter S corporations for tax purposes and taxes them at the regular corporation rate of 9%. (This rate was lower through March 31, 1973.)

The Fast Burger operation is a general partnership formed April 1, 1971. It has a common fiscal year with BLM.

Comment

The case is simplified by there being one class of stock and by the Fast Burger operation having a common accounting year with BLM. Often, this is not the case in practice, where different classes of stock must be valued and different accounting periods between related companies must be reconciled. On the other hand, BLM requires special adjustments because of the Subchapter S election and the different tax treatment between Federal and state law—not an uncommon situation.

[¶3.02-5] DETAIL ON SUBSIDIARIES OR AFFILIATES

There are no subsidiaries or affiliates other than the Fast Burger operation. This operation is 47% owned by a former employee of BLM who operated an in-house cafeteria for the company. He is unrelated to the owners of BLM, but he operates the business with little or no management guidance from BLM.

Comment

Pertinent financial data is included in the discussion of Valuation Methods 10 and 11 in a later chapter. Further discussion of the operation is also found at that point. It can be assumed that income statements, balance sheets, and tax returns were obtained for the latest five years and that these were analyzed as required and the appropriate adjustments were made in deriving the figures used for appraisal purposes.

INTERVIEWS: ADDING LIFE TO THE VALUATION

[¶3.02-6] LOCATIONS AT WHICH THE BUSINESS OPERATES

BLM operates at a single location in leased premises in an industrial park located in Santa Monica, California. The Fast Burger operation is located nearby, also in leased premises.

[¶3.02-7] PRESENT OWNERSHIP OF THE BUSINESS

BLM Electronics, Inc. is owned as follows: Gregory M. Bellini, Chairman—334 shares; Walter R. Murphy, Director—333 shares; Edward F. Mondale, Director—333 shares.

The Fast Burger operation is owned 53% by BLM Electronics, Inc. and 47% by Wilson F. Blaine, General Manager of Fast Burger.

[¶3.02-8] PRODUCTS AND SERVICES SOLD

The company has two major lines of products. Both are sold through manufacturers' representatives on a consignment basis with the representatives billing BLM for commissions when sales are consummated. One line consists of medical, dental, and laboratory diagnostic lights which are sold principally to doctors and dentists. The other line consists of instruments sold to industrial firms for medical research. Both lines are also sold to the U.S. Government, but such sales are made directly by company personnel, who receive no commissions.

Capitalized new product development in the amount of $134,210 (Exhibit 1) has been largely devoted to revising and perfecting the "Belmur process." This secret (but unpatented) process allows the company to manufacture and sell an average of 10,000 units per year of one of its most popular diagnostic lamps for $1.50 more per unit than the price its competitors can command. Company and industry personnel estimate this price advantage will be sustained for seven to ten years. The consensus was about eight years.

Some research and development also went into developing a patent (just received) on a new explosion-proof lamp. This patent has been licensed to another firm at a royalty to BLM of 7% of annual sales up to and including $60,000; 6% on annual sales of $60,000 to $90,000; and 5% on annual sales of over $90,000. The appraiser estimates from company and industry sources that these sales will run $50,000 during the fiscal year ending March 31, 1977, $75,000 in the next fiscal year, and $100,000 in the year ending March 31, 1979. Thereafter, he estimates sales will be $50,000 per year for the following seven years, after which time the patent will be rendered of no value by improved technology.

Comment

See ¶3.02-20 for data on the financial effects of this method of selling. Also see Valuation Methods 13 and 14 for an approach to valuing the Belmur process and the lamp patent.

INTERVIEWS: ADDING LIFE TO THE VALUATION

[¶3.02-9] INDUSTRY CLASSIFICATION

By reference to the *Standard Industrial Classification Manual*[10] and after discussion with the company owners and personnel, the appraiser concludes that the company's activities place it about equally in SIC 3841, Manufacturers of Surgical and Medical Instruments and Apparatus, and in SIC 3843, Manufacturers of Dental Equipment and Supplies.

Comment

It is not unusual for a firm to fall into two or more SIC categories. Usually, the appraiser must decide which category is dominant in order to find suitable industry statistics. In this case, however, the best comparative statistics are concluded to be those published by Robert Morris Associates, and this publication conveniently combines SIC Codes 3841 and 3843.[11]

[¶3.02-10] CREDITOR NAMES

It can be assumed that the appraiser has obtained the names of several principal creditors of BLM and that some have been interviewed. The results of this check indicate that the company is chronically slow in paying its bills, with many accounts as much as 90 to 120 days past due. Cash discounts are not taken, and in the past year some sellers have refused credit, forcing the company to buy from higher cost suppliers.

[¶3.02-11] MAJOR CUSTOMERS

The appraiser can be assumed to have obtained from BLM a list of major customers, including the name, address, and telephone number of a knowledgeable party at each firm which could be contacted. He would determine typical products purchased by these accounts and past volumes of purchases.

Comment

While no significant findings are assumed from the BLM customer review, as an appraisal proceding, such a review can be helpful in revealing product deficiencies, inadequate service, late delivery, or other matters which would affect the appraiser's projected income, expense, and cash requirement figures for the company.

[¶3.02-12] EMPLOYEE PLANS

In the BLM case, company-paid medical insurance is provided at competitive rates. There is no company pension or profit-sharing plan. The company is not unionized.

Comment

The foregoing assumptions have been made to simplify the case, but the appraiser will always wish to check out employee benefit plans and union contracts.

INTERVIEWS: ADDING LIFE TO THE VALUATION

The benefit plans may contain significant unfunded liabilities which are not reflected on the company's financial statements. There may be an Employee Stock Option Plan (ESOP) which has an effect on stock prices. Union contracts may reveal added expenses to be borne in future years affecting pro forma profits developed by the appraiser.

[¶3.02-13] PROPERTY OCCUPANCY INFORMATION

BLM leases a modern factory building which houses 200 employees and has parking for 150 cars. The building is 100% occupied by BLM. The rent is competitive for the space provided at $26,000 per year on a net lease. The lease expires in six years on March 31, 1982.

For accounting purposes, the company splits the rent approximately two-thirds to factory overhead and the balance is split between engineering overhead and administrative expense. (See Exhibit 3.)

The Fast Burger operation lease has several years to run and is at a competitive rental for such facilities.

Comment

The significant fact for the BLM case is that the rent is competitive and that the lease for the parent operation (i.e., excluding Fast Burger) has six years to run. However, this step in the usual appraisal process could reveal a lease that had an escalation clause affecting projected income, or one that was especially favorable or unfavorable. A particularly favorable lease could well add a value to the business which was not reflected on the balance sheet. An unfavorable lease could add a liability which should be considered. If the lease had only a short time to run, it could also signal an impending rent increase or a costly move.

[¶3.02-14] PHYSICAL CONDITION OF THE PLANT

Discussion with the owners and company personnel as well as physical inspection of the plant by the appraiser indicates the following:

1. A new wing was added in the fiscal year ended March 31, 1975. The material was charged to maintenance and repair and the labor was charged to outside services. The approximate cost was $24,000. This accounts for the unusual increase in the captions in FYE 3/31/75 revealed by the review of accounting statements at ¶ 2.06-3, Step 3.

2. Several major pieces of equipment were expensed in the fiscal year ended March 31, 1973. The total amount involved was estimated at $10,500. This fact explains the increase in expendable tools in that year, first noted in the accounting statement review.

INTERVIEWS: ADDING LIFE TO THE VALUATION

The owners, indicated, and physical inspection confirmed, that the condition of the plant, equipment, fixtures, and furnishings was generally good. A physical examination of some of the tools and dies indicated some possible obsolete material in this category, however. See confirmation at ¶ 3.02-24.

[¶3.02-15] APPRAISALS AND PLANS

At the request of the business appraiser, the company had a qualified machinery and equipment appraiser value all categories of equipment and improvements at fair market value as of March 31, 1976. The results of this appraisal are as follows:

Machinery and equipment	$ 80,000
Furniture and Fixtures	50,000
Leasehold improvements (includes wing discussed at ¶ 3.02-14)	70,000
Tools, dies and molds	50,000
Total Fair Market Value	$250,000

The company has made a detailed marketing and financial study which indicates sales of $1,400,000 to be a reasonable expectancy for the fiscal year ending March 31, 1977. The company believes this can be done at a Gross Profit of 33⅓%. This was the approximate gross profit percentage prior to the fiscal years ending in 1975, when the new wing was written off, and in 1976, when research and development expense was exceptionally high. Administrative costs are expected to be about the same for fiscal 1977. Heavy space advertising incurred in fiscal 1976 to introduce a new line is expected to decrease markedly in 1977. Travel and entertainment expenses and proposal expense were both extra high in the 1976 fiscal year. These expenses are expected to decrease for the next year or two and offset other increases in administrative expense which might be associated with the extra volume.

Comment

In practice, the appraiser will seldom find this material as neatly and appropriately packaged for his use. However, a review of appraisals, studies, and forecasts already made by the company, or at its direction, can reveal facts which may save a great deal of time and research.

[¶3.02-16] OWNERSHIP TRANSFERS AND OFFERS

The appraiser learned from his interview with the company owners that George P. Love, one of the company founders, sold his 333 shares to Edward F. Mondale for $290,000. The price was based on the book net worth at March 31, 1975 of approximately $900,000, plus estimated profits after tax of $20,000 for April and May 1975, less an adjustment of $50,000 for additional bad debt reserves, outdated inventory, and obsolete tools and dies.

INTERVIEWS: ADDING LIFE TO THE VALUATION

An interview with Mr. Mondale revealed that he was a financially sophisticated former stockbroker and that this book formula had been used because it was the easiest approach to Mr. Love. However, he had actually computed the purchase using a different valuation approach which yielded similar results. His approach had been basically the price earnings ratio method.

It also developed that the company owners had been offered $1,500,000 for all of their stock in October 1975, but this offer involved only $300,000 down and a note for $1,200,000, the payment of which was contingent on future earnings.

[¶3.02-17] INFORMATION SOURCES

The appraiser would normally compile from his interview with company owners a list of sources of good information on the company and its industry. This list might include the company's bankers, trade association officials and trade journals, as well as the creditor and customer names already elicited. Trade sources might also be uncovered at the public library.

[¶3.02-18] OWNER PROFILES

The pertinent facts on the company owners of BLM are as follows: Only Gregory Bellini is active in the business, and this is on a half-time basis doing research and development on product improvement. He was responsible for developing the Belmur process several years ago and worked to constantly improve it. He holds an M.E. degree from MIT and has had many years of experience in the company and in the industry. He draws $20,000 per year for his half-time work. However, in the fiscal year ended March 31, 1976, he was paid a bonus of $21,000 which was written off to research and development but actually had no relation to his work. It was simply in the nature of largess agreed to by his co-owners to help him pay a large medical bill. Bellini is 69 and in poor health. Nevertheless, he apparently gives the company good value for his basic salary. He has no plans to retire, but would do so and would sell his interest if the other two owners decide to sell as well.

Murphy has not been active in the business for several years and is age 66. He would like to sell his stock regardless of whether or not the other two owners sell.

Mondale, the recent buyer, is age 56. He is an investor only and is not active in the business. He is agreeable to selling if the other owners wish to do so.

Comment

Were the owners active in the business, an in-depth review of their abilities and intentions would be most desirable. Specifically, it is recommended that the appraiser determine for each active owner the following: 1. Approximate age. 2. Physical condition. 3. Specialized knowledge of the company and the industry of which it is a part. 4. Education. 5. Time in the business. 6. Future intentions.

INTERVIEWS: ADDING LIFE TO THE VALUATION

[¶3.02-19] KEY PERSONNEL INFORMATION

As a result of the owner interviews, background on key personnel can be assumed to have been obtained. Pertinent to the case are the following facts:

1. All sales, production, engineering and financial personnel are professionals who are reasonably competent in their jobs. There is a competent back-up research man should Bellini resign.

2. The President and Executive Vice President are experienced in the industry but are rather poor in financial control. As a result, the company does not do as well in cash management as its competitors. However, it produces better than average profits.

Comment

In practice, the appraiser should list the names, ages, tenure, and special skills of all key personnel. This would include personnel in the fields of management and administration, finance and accounting, production, engineering and research, sales and marketing.

[¶3.02-20] SPECIAL QUERIES REGARDING STATEMENTS

A long list of questions regarding BLM financial statements was compiled from the analysis made in the previous chapter. The owners would be queried on many of these items, and those which still remained unanswered would be covered with the company's accounting personnel and independent public accountant, together with any other knowledgeable parties. Except for those points specifically discussed in this chapter, it is assumed for purposes of the BLM case that all questions raised have been answered to the appraiser's satisfaction. Conclusions not covered elsewhere in this outline are as follows:

1. Inventories have increased because more consignment agents have been added. This has placed a strain on working capital and caused the company to delay payments to trade creditors.

2. Accounts receivable are typically slow in the industry because of dealing through consignment agents who have less incentive to follow up on their sales than do company personnel. Government sales are also slow pay, and 30% of the company's sales are in this category. Collections have improved over the years as the government sales percentage has decreased.

3. The item in Exhibit 1 "Other Accounts and Notes Receivable" is a loan to Director Murphy in the amount of $20,000 made to offset the $21,000 bonus given Chairman Bellini. Repayment is not expected.

4. The item in Exhibit 1 "Notes Receivable—Long Term" for $297,648 represents the sale of land which the company bought for speculation in 1971. It cost

INTERVIEWS: ADDING LIFE TO THE VALUATION

$168,295 and was sold in early 1975 for $347,000, with $35,000 down payment and the balance of $312,000 secured by a first mortgage on the land payable at the rate of $31,200 per year including interest at 8% per annum until paid. The balance due on the note at March 31, 1976 and the item "Deferred Income" represents the remaining profit on the transaction which is being reported as payments are received. In the fiscal year ended March 31, 1975, $18,025 was recorded in Miscellaneous Income on this note. The comparable figure for March 31, 1976 was $30,480. Prior to the date of sale, property taxes on the land were as follows: FYE 1972 - $4,000; FYE 1973 - $4,200; FYE 1974 - $5,000; and FYE 1975 - $6,000.

5. Partnership income reported by fiscal year was as follows: 1972 - $5,000; 1973 - $10,000; 1974 - $15,000; 1975 - $15,000, and 1976 - $15,000. This represents 53% of the total partnership income for these years.

6. Goodwill of $25,000 included in "Other Assets" on Exhibit 1 was the difference between the cash, accounts receivable, and tangible assets, which were valued at $185,000, and the capital stock of $10,000 plus paid-in surplus of $200,000 received by the corporation from the Bellini, Love and Murphy Company when the partnership was incorporated. The item $1.00 for patents was a nominal value given to a now-expired patent.

7. The item, "Accounts Payable—Other," represents an advance made by former owner George Love which inadvertently has not been written off the books.

8. High dividends have been paid to eliminate undistributed earned surplus for tax reasons incident to the Subchapter S election. All owners agree this has aggrevated the company's cash problem.

9. The surplus charge of $2,250 represents a dispute with company accountants over the proper handling for Internal Revenue Service purposes of some customer gifts.

10. Commissions have increased considerably over the past five years as civilian sales have increased. However, civilian sales are more profitable than U.S. Government sales, even after considering added commissions.

[¶3.02-21] CONTINGENCIES

The owners should be asked whether they are aware of any contingencies not reflected as liabilities on the balance sheet, such as lease contracts, pending law suits, IRS audits in process, patent expirations, etc.

In the BLM case, the appraiser is advised of the existence of an equipment lease contract signed in 1972. The reply resulted from the appraiser's query as to why equipment rental had increased in that year. (See Exhibit 3.) Upon further investigation, the lease is discovered to be, in effect, a purchase agreement in which the company built up an equity as follows: FYE 1973 - $2,000; FYE 1974 - $2,500; FYE 1975 - $2,800; and FYE 1976 - $3,000.

INTERVIEWS: ADDING LIFE TO THE VALUATION

There are no other contingencies or unreported liabilities.

[¶3.02-22] INDUSTRY STUDY

A study of the industry reveals a trade association headquartered in Washington, D.C., the members of which are manufacturers and distributors of scientific apparatus and equipment similar to that made by BLM. From this association, information is gained which tends to substantiate the company's forecast sales gains for 1977 as being consistent with industry trends.

No business brokers were active in the sale of firms such as BLM, nor are there any formulas by which such businesses are valued including their goodwill. However, the appraiser does discover that businesses such as the Fast Burger operation are often valued by formula. One formula is a multiple of 25% times annual net sales weighed against a second formula of 4 times net profit before tax but after provision for salary to the owner. Another typical approach would add one year's net profit before tax to the value of the tangible assets plus the market value of the franchise.

No recent sales of businesses similar to BLM were discovered, nor were people in the trade aware of any significant technological changes.

[¶3.02-23] INDEPENDENT FINANCIAL STUDY

Normal procedure would be to obtain and review the latest five years of balance sheets, income statements, and income tax returns as described earlier. The company's independent public accountant and chief accounting officer would then be questioned for detail on all income, expense, and balance sheet items of consequence. Interim statements and any prepared pro forma, or projected, statements would be obtained and reviewed. Creditors would be interviewed as noted at ¶ 3.02-10. The company bankers would be interviewed.

For purposes of the BLM case, all pertinent facts have already been brought out as a result of statement studies and owner, industry, creditor and customer interviews.

[¶3.02-24] KEY PERSONNEL INTERVIEWS

As a result of interviews with key personnel, the appraiser confirms the existence of obsolete tools, dies, and molds. (See ¶ 3.02-14.) It also appears that there is $10,000 more of probable bad debts in accounts receivable than has been covered in the reserve for bad debts. (Exhibit 1) Also, the inventory control clerk identified about $20,000 in obsolete stock.

[¶3.02-25] APPRAISE TANGIBLE ASSETS

The checklist would contain a notation to appraise tangible assets as required. Since a machinery and equipment appraiser has already been engaged to do this

INTERVIEWS: ADDING LIFE TO THE VALUATION

for BLM, the business appraiser will not make this valuation. (See ¶ 3.02-15.) He may review the appraisal, however, to see that no elements of goodwill have been inadvertently included in the fixed asset values. If such elements have been included, he would have to consider this in his valuation of goodwill.

[¶3.02-26] APPRAISE GOODWILL AND INTANGIBLES

The checklist would include this reminder. Since the appraisal of such assets is described in detail later, further comments will not be made here.

[¶3.03] SUMMARY

In a closely-held firm, it is very important to interview the owners in depth, because many facts can only be discovered in this way. The interviews should go much further, however, and cover key personnel, customers, creditors, bankers, suppliers, and trade association people as required to learn all possible about the company and the industry. A format for conducting these interviews and assembling data for the appraisal is suggested in this chapter. Pertinent facts on the BLM case which will be used to illustrate various business appraisal techniques are placed in this format and discussed in this chapter. The results as described are much less complete than those found in an actual appraisal, but they serve to illustrate the types of data needed.

CHAPTER 4

HOW TO RECONSTRUCT FINANCIAL DATA

To grasp this sorry scheme of things entire, would not we shatter it to bits—and then remold it nearer to the Heart's Desire!

EDWARD FITZGERALD - 1809-1883

TOPICS DISCUSSED IN THIS CHAPTER

[¶4.01] — **Statements Required for Valuation Purposes**
　　Adjusted Historical Balance Sheet
　　Economic Balance Sheet
　　Adjusted Historical Income Statements
　　Pro Forma Income Statements

[¶4.02] — **Balance Sheet Adjustments**

[¶4.02-1] — **Preparing the Adjusted Historical Balance Sheet (BLM Case)**
　　A. Notes Receivable-Long Term and Deferred Income are Eliminated
　　B. Partnership Interest is Eliminated
　　C. New Product Investment is Removed
　　D. Other Assets Caption is Deleted (Goodwill and Patents)
　　E. Reduction in Income Taxes Payable

[¶4.02-2] — **Key Percentages**

[¶4.02-3] — **Preparation of the Economic Balance Sheet (BLM Case)**
　　A. Accounts Receivable-Net are Decreased
　　B. Other Accounts and Notes Receivable are Eliminated
　　C. Inventories are Reduced
　　D. Fixed Assets are Increased in Value
　　E. Accounts Payable-Other are Eliminated
　　F. Notes Payable-Long Term are Eliminated

[¶4.03] — **Income Statement Adjustments (BLM Case)**
　　A. Add the Value Build-up in Leased Equipment
　　B. Add Write-off of New Wing
　　C. Add Equipment Written Off
　　D. Add Unusual Research and Development Expense
　　E. Add Depreciation on the Wing and Equipment
　　F. Deduct Unrelated Partnership Income
　　G. Deduct Land Sales Income
　　H. Restore Taxes on Unrelated Land
　　I. Owners' Salary Adjustment
　　J. Add Interest Expense
　　K. Add Regular Depreciation Expense
　　L. Add Depreciation Deducted at "E" Above

[¶4.04] — **Preparation of Pro Forma Income Statements**

[¶4.05] — **Industry Comparisons**

[¶4.06] — **Adjustment Principles**

[¶4.07] — **Summary**

CHAPTER 4

HOW TO RECONSTRUCT FINANCIAL DATA

[¶4.01] STATEMENTS REQUIRED FOR VALUATION PURPOSES

All that has preceded this chapter leads to a single objective. That objective is to provide figures on the business being appraised which are acceptable for valuation purposes—not simply for accounting and tax purposes. Once these figures have been assembled, it becomes possible to apply established appraisal methods and arrive at a defensible opinion as to the company's value.

To arrive at figures acceptable for valuation purposes requires reconstruction and extension of the accounting data. The results of this reworking are as follows:

ADJUSTED HISTORICAL BALANCE SHEET

This will be the latest balance sheet, prepared according to generally accepted accounting principles and reconstructed to eliminate all intangible assets, such as capitalized research and development, patents and goodwill. Also eliminated will be assets which are extraneous to the company's basic business activities, and assets which would distort comparison with other firms in the same industry as the company being appraised. The end result is to arrive at a restatement of the owners' equity which includes only the tangible assets of the business at their book values. This will be referred to as "Historic Tangible Net Worth."

ECONOMIC BALANCE SHEET

The "Economic Balance Sheet" is the adjusted historical balance sheet described above with substitution of economic values for book values. Fixed assets are included at their fair market value. Accounts and notes receivable and accounts and notes payable are analyzed to be certain all are truly receivable or payable. Necessary adjustments are made for those which are not. The end result of this reconstruction of the balance sheet is to restate owners' equity in terms of tangible assets *at economic or market value*. This will be referred to as "Economic Tangible Net Worth."

ADJUSTED HISTORICAL INCOME STATEMENTS

The "Adjusted Historical Income Statements" consist of the latest five years' of income statements (plus interim statements, if required) adjusted to eliminate certain items. These items are those which would distort the true profits, items which are unrelated to the company's main activity, and items which would distort comparisons with other firms in the same industry. Another adjustment is to make any required addition or reduction in salaries paid the business owners so that their compensation is included at competitive levels. Finally, the historic figures are adjusted to restore interest paid, depreciation, and amortization to arrive at figures which represent "Adjusted Profit Before Tax and Before Capital Charges."

HOW TO RECONSTRUCT FINANCIAL DATA

PRO FORMA INCOME STATEMENTS

The "Pro Forma Income Statements" represent the business appraiser's best judgment as to the future profits of the company. Such statements will usually be prepared for only a year or two into the future and will generally be on a before tax and before capital charge basis. A further projection into the future may be required if the appraiser chooses to use the "Discounted Cash Flow Method" of appraisal.

* * * * *

The figures and accounting captions necessary to arrive at the adjusted statements described above will vary with each company being appraised. The authors can only describe the principles involved in the changes, then the appraiser will have to adapt these principles to the requirements of the valuation with which he is involved.

To keep the discussion from becoming too esoteric and to demonstrate the application of the adjustment principles, the BLM case has again been used. Each revised statement is described in terms of the case. Data for the adjustments, is drawn from Chapters 2 and 3. The basic principles are summarized at the end of this chapter.

[¶4.02] BALANCE SHEET ADJUSTMENTS

The latest five years of balance sheets for BLM as prepared by its public accountants are shown at Exhibit 1. No interim statement is needed, since the appraisal is to be made as of March 31, 1976, a regular fiscal year statement date. For worksheet purposes in making the required balance sheet adjustments, the last column of Exhibit 1 (i.e., the book figures for 3-31-76) has been copied into the first column of Exhibit 4. Exhibit 4 is the basic worksheet, to which reference will be made in describing below the balance sheet adjustments.

[¶4.02-1] PREPARING THE ADJUSTED HISTORICAL BALANCE SHEET

In the second column of Exhibit 4, five adjustments have been made which result in the "Adjusted Historical Balance Sheet" for BLM Electronics as of March 31, 1976. The letter before each explanation refers to the same letter opposite the item affected in Column 2 of Exhibit 4. The adjustments are as follows:

A. **Notes Receivable-Long Term and Deferred Income are Eliminated**

This adjustment has been made because the appraiser learned that these two items resulted from the sale of land held for speculation. (See ¶ 3.02-20, item 4.) Removal is necessary for two reasons: (1) the note must be valued separately from the BLM manufacturing operation, and (2) if not removed, it would distort comparison with other firms in BLM's industry. Such firms do not generally engage in land

HOW TO RECONSTRUCT FINANCIAL DATA

speculation, and the $297,648 note and $153,225 of deferred income are significant amounts in the BLM balance sheet.

B. **Partnership Interest is Eliminated**

The appraiser learned that this caption represented an interest in the Fast Burger operation. (See ¶ 3.02-4 and 5.) Removal is required because (1) the partnership must be separately valued, and (2) such an operation is not typical of firms in the medical-dental instrument field. Were the partnership engaged in the same or a similar line of activity as BLM, a different approach would be taken; namely, the assets would be consolidated with those of BLM for industry comparisons.

C. **New Product Investment is Removed**

The purpose in so doing is to delete an intangible which has been recorded on the books.

Comment

Such intangibles as may appear on the books usually are recorded at values considerably different from their market values. Therefore, all are eliminated as part of the statement reconstruction process. After they have been separately appraised, they will be restored in arriving at the total value of the company.

D. **"Other Assets" Caption is Deleted**

This adjustment includes goodwill of $25,000 and $1 for an expired patent. (See ¶ 3.02-20, item 6.) These are intangibles which must be eliminated under the same theory applied to New Product Investment above.

Comment

It is not customary to eliminate "Other Assets" automatically. This would be done only when an analysis of the caption reveals an intangible or other item which must be deleted.

E. **Reduction in Income Taxes Payable**

This reduction, which amounts to $2,383, represents the difference between California income taxes actually payable and those which would be payable were the income on the $297,648 note and on the Fast Burger operation deleted. Since the note and the restaurant operation have been removed from assets, it is logical to also remove the taxes payable on the income for industry comparison purposes.

Comment

It could be argued that the historic tax figures before and after this adjustment are still not comparable to the industry figures, since BLM is a Subchapter S corporation. (See ¶ 3.02-4.) Most statistical compilations include only ordinary corporations, and these pay Federal income taxes, as well as state.

HOW TO RECONSTRUCT FINANCIAL DATA

With the completion of the foregoing adjustments, column 2 of Exhibit 4 represents the "Adjusted Historical Balance Sheet" for BLM Electronics as required for appraisal purposes. The "Total Capital" shown on the next to the last line in this column is the "Historic Tangible Net Worth" figure required for some industry comparisons.

[¶4.02-2] KEY PERCENTAGES

To further assist in making comparisons with statistical data on other firms in the industry, percentages have been computed for certain key captions. These percentages, which appear in column 3 of Exhibit 4, have been calculated using the figures developed in column 2 of Exhibit 4.

[¶4.02-3] PREPARATION OF THE ECONOMIC BALANCE SHEET

Column 4 of Exhibit 4 shows the Economic Balance Sheet developed for BLM Electronics. By cross-reference to columns 1 and 2 of the same exhibit, the reader can observe the transition from one set of figures to the next. Letter references below relate to the letter opposite the item being adjusted in column 4 of Exhibit 4. The adjustments which are needed to convert the Adjusted Historic Balance Sheet to the Economic Balance Sheet are as follows:

A. **Accounts Receivable - Net Are Decreased**

This adjustment has been made by increasing the reserve for bad debts shown in columns 1 and 2 of Exhibit 4 from $3,474 to $13,474. The added $10,000 is the appraiser's estimate of additional accounts receivable which should be considered doubtful.

Comment

While the existence of such accounts was indicated by key personnel, (See ¶ 3.02-24) the appraiser must draw his own conclusions. He probably would supplement the interview with an aging of accounts receivable and specific review of major accounts.

B. **Other Accounts and Notes Receivable Are Eliminated**

The interviews with BLM owners indicated this account in the amount of $20,000 was a note due from owner-director Murphy which the company did not expect to collect. (See ¶ 3.02-20, item 3.)

Comment

It is not at all unusual in closely-held businesses to find amounts due from and to owners which are not valid. Sometimes such items remain on the books due to an oversight. More often, there would have been an adverse income tax effect on the owners were they eliminated.

HOW TO RECONSTRUCT FINANCIAL DATA

C. Inventories Are Reduced

The reduction of $20,000 between the book value of $380,373 and the market value of $360,373 was instigated because of an interview with the inventory control clerk. (See ¶ 3.02-24.)

Comment

In view of the significance of inventories among the company's assets, it can be assumed the appraiser also made a market value study. Such a study would often be calculated as follows:

Current Market Selling Price of the Inventory	$621,333
Less:	
Normal Cost of Selling the Inventory at 10%	(62,133)
Normal Profit Margin at 32%	(198,827)
Current Market Value of the Inventory	$360,373

In this case the book value less $20,000 is identical with the market value. In practice, one would not expect such a precise coordination of the figures. The result would more likely be a few thousand dollars different than that obtained by merely deleting obsolete stock.

D. Fixed Assets Are Increased In Value

This increase is based upon the market value appraisal of these items discussed at ¶ 3.02-15. The four balance sheet items appraised, entitled "Equipment and Improvements," totaled $120,774 on the books after depreciation, whereas the appraiser valued them at $250,000. This wide differential of $129,226, resulted from the following:

1. Due to inflation, the equipment actually depreciated very little in recent years.

2. Repairs and maintenance which actually increased value were expensed rather than being capitalized. From the owner and key personnel interviews, the appraiser knows of the following items which were expensed: a wing of the building which cost $24,000; equipment which cost $10,500 (See ¶ 3.02-14); and equipment which actually was owned but had been written off as being under lease. In addition to these specific items, there probably were many smaller improvements expensed.

3. Accelerated depreciation which exceeded economic depreciation was taken for tax purposes.

4. Offsetting these positive factors was the acknowledged existence of obsolete tools, dies, and molds.

HOW TO RECONSTRUCT FINANCIAL DATA

Comment

Such wide variation between appraisal and book values of fixed assets is not unusual in practice—especially in closely-held firms. The combination of wishing to maximize income tax write-offs plus the effects of inflation can produce some major differences between book figures and actual values.

E. **Accounts Payable - Other Are Eliminated**

This adjustment of $8,320 resulted from the owner interviews. (See ¶ 3.02-20, item 7.) It represented an overlooked item which should have been written off.

Comment

It may seem strange to one accustomed to rather sophisticated accounting to find an item such as this which inadvertently was not written off. Such is not unusual in smaller businesses of all kinds—even those which one might class as medium-to-large. It has been put in this case to demonstrate a common situation to which the business appraiser must be alert.

F. **Notes Payable - Long Term Are Eliminated**

Subsequent to the interviews described in Chapter 3, the appraiser discovered that $10,000 appearing as due owner-director Mondale would probably never be paid, despite earlier indications that payment was anticipated shortly.

Comment

It is not unusual in practice to believe one has all of the facts, only to discover additional significant matters shortly before the valuation is completed. The important thing is to make the discovery before the appraisal is delivered.

Further Comment

As an end result of the preparation of the Economic Balance Sheet there has also been derived a value which can be expressed as "Tangible Net Worth at Market." This value will be useful in applying appraisal techniques in the next and subsequent chapters. Note, however, that while it contained a realistic appraisal of the basic assets of the firm, it has given no consideration to the value of the Belmur process, the lamp patent, goodwill, the Fast Burger operation, or the land sale note.

[¶4.03] INCOME STATEMENT ADJUSTMENTS

The latest five years of income statements for BLM as prepared by its public accountants are shown at Exhibits 2 and 3. As in the case of the balance sheet adjustments, no interim statement is needed, because the appraisal is to be made as of March 31, 1976. A worksheet has been prepared at Exhibit 5 which indicates the changes needed in the historic income statements to arrive at the Adjusted Historical Income Statements for BLM. Notice that some adjustments are required in all

HOW TO RECONSTRUCT FINANCIAL DATA

five fiscal years. These changes are as follows: (Letter references below relate to the letter opposite the item being adjusted in Exhibit 5.)

A. **Add the Value Build-up in Leased Equipment**

In reviewing Factory Overhead, shown in Exhibit 3, the appraiser noticed a significant increase in Equipment Rental commencing with the fiscal year ended March 31, 1973. As a result of owner and key personnel interviews, it was discovered that the equipment rental expense account actually reported payments on a lease which essentially transfered ownership to the lessee. An equity build-up in the lease resulted which must be restored to profits. As discussed at ¶ 3.02-21, the adjustments required on Exhibit 5 are as follows commencing with the fiscal year ended in 1973: $2,000; $2,500, $2,800, and $3,000.

B. **Add Write-off of New Wing**

A plant inspection and personnel interviews revealed a new wing constructed in the fiscal year ended in 1975 which was written off to expense. (See ¶ 3.02-14.) This $24,000 cost must be restored to the profits of that year.

C. **Add Equipment Written Off**

In the fiscal year ended in 1973, equipment totaling $10,500 in cost was written off to Expendable Tool Expense. (See ¶ 3.02-14.) This asset must be restored to profits.

Comment

It is common practice in many businesses to expense some capital improvements to save income taxes. Usually this is done under the pretext that the improvement was in the nature of a repair. For instance, a new tile roof might replace an old composition roof. Part of such an expenditure could well be a repair and part added value. When there is any doubt, many closely-held firms expense it all. Generally, the addition of a whole wing would not be expensed, but the authors have seen it done.

D. **Add Unusual Research and Development Expense**

The interview with BLM owners indicated that one reason Research and Development expense had been so high in the fiscal year ended March 31, 1976 was because one of the owners, Chairman Bellini, had been given a cash gift which was written off in this account. The amount was $21,000, and since the gift had no relationship to proper business expense, it must be restored to the profits for that year.

E. **Add Depreciation on the Wing and Equipment**

Since the cost of the new wing and the cost of equipment written off on the company records were added back at "B" and "C" above, it is also necessary to add back as an economic expense depreciation and amortization applicable to these

HOW TO RECONSTRUCT FINANCIAL DATA

assets. The lease-purchase equipment has been handled differently. There has been added to profit at "A" above the net economic buildup in the lease. Presumably, this takes depreciation into account.

Comment

The two methods of handling equipment written off have been used to call attention to both appraoches to restoring profits. Under the first approach, the full cost of the equipment is added back to profits, then this amount is reduced by depreciation that would have been taken had the items been properly capitalized at the time. If the equipment had been financed, any interest would already have been recorded as interest expense.

The second appraoch is more applicable to equipment acquired under a socalled financial lease where the lesee is building up a substantial equity in the lease by virtue of his right to renew at the end of the prime term for less than the economic rent then payable. He may never actually purchase the equipment, but he has all of the benefits of ownership.

Most experts would agree with the handling of the items restored to profits. However, some might not agree with the manner in which the authors have added the equity buildup in the equipment lease. It could be argued that the full amount of the rental payments should be restored to profits and then separate entries made to deduct interest and depreciation on the cost of the equipment. The authors have in effect combined these items into one adjustment reflecting the equity buildup in the lease. Were three entries made instead, the adjusted profit before tax and before capital charges might be slightly higher, because interest and depreciation are added back. In this case, the effect is of minor significance, however.

F. **Deduct Unrelated Partnership Income**

Since the Fast Burger operation was removed from the balance sheet, (See ¶ 4.02-1, item B.) the same reasoning requires removal of income on this asset in arriving at the Adjusted Historical Income Statements. The amounts involved for each fiscal year were determined in the owner interviews as noted at ¶ 3.02-20, item 5.

G. **Deduct Land Sales Income**

Since the note receivable which resulted from the unrelated land sale was removed from the balance sheet (See ¶ 4.02-1, item A), the income incident to the note must also be removed. The amount of miscellaneous income involved is discussed at ¶ 3.02-20, item 4.

H. **Restore Taxes on Unrelated Land**

Before the land held for speculation was sold in 1975, there were property taxes deducted as miscellaneous expense. Therefore, it is necessary to restore

HOW TO RECONSTRUCT FINANCIAL DATA

these taxes to income for the affected years by making appropriate reductions in miscellaneous expense. The amounts to be adjusted are noted at ¶ 3.02-20, item 4.

I. Owners' Salary Adjustment

None is required for BLM. The only owner working for the firm is Chairman Bellini, whose salary for half-time work at $20,000 per year is judged about right from an economic standpoint. (See ¶ 3.02-18.)

Comment

This item was placed on Exhibit 5 to highlight the necessity of reviewing owners' salaries. The BLM situation is unusual in not requiring such an adjustment. Typically, owner salaries in Subchapter S corporations tend to be lower than industry levels, and sometimes they are non-existent, because there is no real tax incentive to take a salary. The salary becomes more of an economic adjustment between various owners to even out their relative contribution of time to the business. On the other hand, closely-held firms operating as ordinary corporations will often pay excessive salaries because the tax advantage lies in doing so.

Note, too, that compensation may come in many forms. In the BLM case it was a gift to Bellini which probably would be challenged upon IRS audit as compensatory, even though the case assumes it is intended as a gift. Compensation may include many diverse perquisites whose relevance to the business will challenge the appraiser's analytical ability. When is a hunting lodge a necessary business expense and when is it not? If there are many vehicles, are all really business related? Are significant charitable contributions to a family foundation formed to aid in estate planning proper business expenses and, if so, is some adjustment still needed to make valid industry comparisons? The list of such items is long in closely-held businesses, and the appraiser must be very inquisitive if he is to arrive at cogent figures.

J. Add Interest Expense

To arrive at adjusted profit before taxes and before capital charges, it is necessary to add to net profit before tax any interest paid by the company. The amount to be added back in the BLM case is the interest expense reported in Exhibit 3 as part of Total Administrative Expense.

K. Add Regular Depreciation Expense

Depreciation must also be added back to arrive at profit before taxes and capital charges. In the BLM case, the total amount of depreciation taken is reported in three places, and the figure shown at item K of Exhibit 5 is the total of all three. See specifically Exhibit 3, Income Statement Detail, where depreciation is reported under Factory Overhead, again under Engineering Overhead, and again under Administrative Expense. Depreciation for BLM also includes amortization of leasehold improvements.

HOW TO RECONSTRUCT FINANCIAL DATA

Comment

Depreciation frequently is reported under several captions in many businesses. The appraiser should use the company's tax return and books of account to see that he has isolated all of the depreciation. It is important to see that amortization as well as depreciation is restored—such as amortization of leasehold improvements, of patents, and of organization expense.

L. **Add Depreciation Deducted at "E" Above**

Since reported profits were reduced by a depreciation and amortization deduction on equipment and on the new wing, it is necessary to add these charges back to arrive at adjusted profit before tax and before capital charges. In other words, this deduction was appropriate in deriving adjusted net profit before tax, but it should be excluded in arriving at profits before capital charges.

Comment

Note that the Adjusted Profit Before Tax and Before Capital Charges differs from the historic profits, in that income and expense items which are not economically proper have been adjusted, as well as income items extraneous to the main thrust of the firm's business. The latter will be separately valued. *What has not been removed, however, is any income resulting from the Belmur process, the lamp patent, goodwill, and any other intangibles which might exist.* The reasons for this will become apparent as appraisal methods are discussed in subsequent chapters.

[¶4.04] PREPARATION OF PRO FORMA INCOME STATEMENTS

The business appraiser needs Pro Forma (projected) profits because business value involves the future, not the past. Past income statements are merely an indicator of what the business is likely to do in the future. Unless he is buying assets for liquidation, the purchaser of a business looks to what the firm will produce in the way of future profits. Although projections well into the future could be helpful, the appraiser is an economic realist and is aware of the difficulty of making such estimates with any degree of assurance. Therefore, it is recommended that a pro forma income statement be prepared for only one year in the future.

For some appraisal methods, the Pro Forma Profit Before Tax and Before Capital Charges is needed. For others, Pro Forma Profit After Tax is required. The Discounted Cash Flow Method of appraisal requires a projection beyond one year. The authors have included at Exhibit 6 for BLM Electronics only the Pro Forma Profit Before Tax and Before Capital Charges for one year. When other forms of the pro forma earnings statements are required to demonstrate appraisal techniques, the necessary transition from Exhibit 6 will be discussed.

The projection of total sales of $1,400,000 is based on the marketing and financial study made by BLM and discussed at ¶ 3.02-15. It can be assumed the appraiser

HOW TO RECONSTRUCT FINANCIAL DATA

has made his own evaluation of this forecast and agrees with it. He should not blindly accept the company's figures, which often are unduly optomistic.

It can be further assumed that the appraiser does not quite agree with the company's projection of a gross profit of 33⅓%. (See ¶ 3.02-15.) A calculation of Adjusted Gross Profit on Exhibit 5 indicates gross profits by fiscal years as follows: 1972 - 34.7%; 1973 - 33.2%; 1974 - 33.2%; 1975 - 33.1%; and 1976 - 30.5%. The appraiser believes some of the manufacturing costs which contributed to the decrease in gross profit for the year ended March 31, 1976, will persist into the near future. Therefore, he bases his projection on a gross profit of 32%. He believes, for some of the reasons cited at ¶ 3.02-15 that Total Administrative Expenses will be only slightly higher in the near future than they were in the fiscal year ended in 1976. Without including income from the Fast Burger operation and from the land sale note, he believes other income and other expense will remain at close to their historic levels as shown at Exhibit 5.

Since it is necessary to obtain net profit before capital charges, projected interest expense of $4,000 and projected depreciation of $28,000 must be added back. The result is projected profit before capital charges of $190,000 for the fiscal year ending March 31, 1977.

Comment

Preparation of the pro forma income statements and the accounting and financial analysis which goes behind them have been given little space here because a lengthy discussion of all of the considerations involved in arriving at accurate projections goes beyond the scope of this book. Good projections are important, nevertheless, and should be carefully made.

[¶4.05]   INDUSTRY COMPARISONS

One part of the process of arriving at accurate projections does require amplification. The business appraiser will generally make a careful study of the industry of which the company being appraised is a part. He will interview trade association executives where possible and appropriate. He will discuss the outlook for the industry and, where judiciously possible to do so, the outlook for the company being appraised. Similar discreet discussions will be conducted with customers and competitors. It will be part of the analysis the appraiser makes when he assesses the future earnings prospects for the company.

An integral part of this industry study is to make a comparison of the company's financial results with those of other firms in the same industry. As discussed at ¶ 3.02-9, it was concluded that BLM operations fell closest to Standard Industrial Classification Codes 3841 and 3843. The most meaningful statistics on firms in these code classifications were assumed to be those prepared by Robert Morris Associates. Accordingly, the appraiser in the BLM case prepared the comparison shown at Exhibit 7.

HOW TO RECONSTRUCT FINANCIAL DATA

The figures for the industry were excerpted from the Robert Morris study referenced at Exhibit 7. The BLM asset, liability, and net worth figures were taken from column 3 of Exhibit 4. The income data are computed using the adjusted historical income statement for the period ending March 31, 1976 shown in column 5 of Exhibit 5.

The ratios used for the industry comparison are different in some respects from those computed in Chapter 2 and summarized at ¶ 2.06-2. This is because the ratios computed in Chapter 2 were based on the historic balance sheet and income statements, whereas the ratios computed for industry comparison were based on the *adjusted* historic balance sheet shown in column 2 of Exhibit 4 and on the *adjusted* historic income statement for April 1, 1975 to March 31, 1976 shown in column 5 of Exhibit 5. The historic figures were adequate for spotting problems within the company, but the adjusted figures were needed for industry comparison.

Comment

Normally, one would not compare adjusted figures for a company to unadjusted figures for an industry, because the industry figures are presumably the composite of unadjusted financial statements as reported. Such a comparison would usually be distorted. In the BLM case, however, some eliminations were necessary for a good comparison—i.e., the fast food operation and the speculative land sale. Companies which manufacture surgical, medical and dental instruments and supplies seldom include in their statements such diverse activities. Also, the industry figures are weighted by the accounting policies generally found in publicly-held concerns, whereas BLM is closely held. Therefore, items such as gifts to owners and substantial asset write-offs were removed as not being typical of the industry operating results. One adjustment to the historic income statements which could provide a minor distortion for industry comparison is the economic build-up in the equipment lease. However, as noted earlier, the effect is minor.

The industry comparisons shown at Exhibit 7 indicate the following:

BLM has less cash than most firms in its industry; however, it has more current assets. This is because it has more in accounts receivable and inventories than do its competitors. The excessive accounts receivable, excessive inventories, and excessive accounts payable all tend to confirm the weak financial management of BLM mentioned at ¶ 3.02-19. However, BLM has less debt than its competitors and therefore should have the ability to raise more cash.

BLM's fixed assets are lower than its competitors, probably due to the leased equipment and faster-than-average depreciation.

While its net worth is greater than the average as a percentage of total assets, this is not necessarily good. It appears to mean more capital is invested than is actually required. Were excessive accounts receivable and inventories reduced, or were more borrowed capital used, net worth could be reduced.

HOW TO RECONSTRUCT FINANCIAL DATA

On the plus side, BLM stacks up well on its profits—primarily because it seems to have kept its overhead expenses below the industry average. While Cost of Goods Sold is well above the industry level as a percentage of sales, this is offset by all other expenses (basically overhead items) which are well below the industry level. One could question the long-run outlook for profits under these circumstances. Perhaps extra profits are being made at the expense of low salaries, a condition which could lead to loss of key people. Lower manufacturing costs would give more cause for comfort.

Based on the comparisons of key company figures with others in its industry, BLM does not come off too well. The management does *not* seem to be doing a particularly good job. For purposes of this case, it will be assumed that other industry checks and interviews tend to confirm the figures.

Comment

The fact that BLM does not appear to be well managed, will be an important factor in deciding what capitalization rates to use in some of the appraisal methods described in subsequent chapters. In other words, having money invested in this company is fairly risky. The present profits may not be sustained.

[¶4.06]   ADJUSTMENT PRINCIPLES

The adjustments for BLM Electronics just reviewed are intended to demonstrate certain principles usable in converting accounting data to figures useful for valuation purposes. These principles are summarized below.

To prepare the Adjusted Historical Balance Sheet, first eliminate all intangibles which appear on the books. These items will be valued by techniques which are not applicable to the business as a whole. Next remove assets which are extraneous to the company's major business activity, so that industry comparisons will not be distorted. Examples are the Fast Burger operation and the land sale note in the BLM case. Finally, adjust liability accounts, such as income taxes payable, to reflect the removal of the assets just discussed. The result is a balance sheet, at book value, which contains no intangibles or assets which would not usually be found in balance sheets of companies in the same industry. Another result is a restatement of owner's equity in terms of tangible assets pertinent to the company's basic line of business. The balance sheet as so constituted is useful for comparison with other firms in the same industry. It also is a valuation yardstick, albeit somewhat limited in scope.

In preparing the Economic Balance Sheet, first review all semi-tangible assets, such as accounts and notes receivable, and make such adjustments as may be required to reflect true collectability. Next, carefully review inventories and revalue them at their market selling price less the normal cost to sell them and less the normal profit margin.[12] Then eliminate any notes and accounts receivable due from owners, unless there is strong evidence that they are actually collectable or payable. Be sure all liabilities are truly owed. Finally, revalue fixed assets, such as machinery and equipment and leasehold improvements at market value. This may entail a separate appraisal of these items. The result is a restatement of the adjusted historic balance sheet in terms of market values and a restatement of owners' equity in terms of tangible assets pertinent to the company's basic line of business *at market values*. This so-called Economic Balance Sheet is useful in the application of several appraisal techniques discussed later.

In preparing the Adjusted Historic Income Statement, first determine any significant assets of the business which may have been written off to expense. Restore these to profits as appropriate for each of the five years being reviewed. If there have been any improper expenses taken, add these back to profit. If expensed assets have been added back, be sure that depreciation on these assets is considered in arriving at the adjusted profits. In some cases, such as a financial lease with valuable reversion rights or nominal rental on renewal, the adjustment to profits may take the form of the net economic value added each year by way of rental payments. Remove the income on assets which are extraneous to the company's main line of activity, such as, in the BLM case, income on the Fast Burger operation and on the land note. Be sure any expenses incident to unrelated assets are also considered. In this way, adjusted net profit before tax can be derived, and this is useful for some industry comparisons.

A further step is desirable with respect to the Adjusted Historic Income Statement to produce adjusted net profit before tax and before capital charges. The appraiser must consider whether the business owners are paid at competitive rates. If not, the profit must be adjusted for this. Interest expense and depreciation plus all other capital charges, if any, are then added back. The result is adjusted net profit before tax and before capital charges, a figure useful for industry comparisons and useful for the application of appraisal techniques described later.

Finally, based on all of the information gleaned from interviews, industry study, and analysis of the company's statements, the appraiser must prepare Pro Forma Income Statements. Usually, these are prepared for just one year ahead, due to the difficulty of making accurate predictions beyond that point. This statement, too, is most useful if prepared on a before tax and before capital charges basis. The pro forma statements will be benefited considerably in their accuracy if a thorough industry study is made, together with a careful analysis of comparative statistics.

[¶4.07] SUMMARY

The objective of all of the analysis which preceded this chapter was to provide figures acceptable for valuation purposes, not simply for accounting and taxes. Essentially, this means preparation of the following: (1) an adjusted historical balance sheet as of the date of appraisal; (2) an economic balance sheet which represents the fair market value of tangible assets, including cash, accounts receivable,

HOW TO RECONSTRUCT FINANCIAL DATA

and inventories as part of the tangibles; (3) an adjusted historical income statement; and (4) a pro forma income statement.

To arrive at these adjusted statements, a number of changes are needed in the historic data. Activities or assets which are not usually found in the industry of which the firm is a part should be removed. Such items can be separately valued, and removal will improve comparison with the industry statistics. Adjustments should also be made to remove the effect of the unusual accounting often found in closely-held firms. The adjustments made in this chapter result from the analysis described in Chapter 2 and from the interviews covered in Chapter 3. All adjustments are described in terms of the BLM case so that the reader can easily determine where the figures originated and so he can see the basic principles involved in more concrete terms.

Part of the process of reconstructing the figures is to make a comparison between the company being valued and its competitors. This will accomplish two important things: (1) it will help in developing meaningful projections for the company, including not only profit projections, but also capital requirements, and (2) it will help weigh the effectiveness of management. The industry comparison is not simply statistical; it also includes interviews with knowledgeable people in the industry. The evaluation of management will be an important factor in determining capitalization rates applied to future earnings. Good management often means a relatively safe investment—especially if industry trends are strongly upward. Weak management increases the risks of having funds in the business.

Just prior to this summary is a section called "Adjustment Principles" which summarizes the principles involved in adjusting financial statements. In effect, the section says, "We have reviewed all of these adjustments for the BLM Electronics case. Now what do they mean in terms of appraisal principles?"

EXHIBIT 4

BLM ELECTRONICS, INC.
ADJUSTED HISTORICAL BALANCE SHEET AND ECONOMIC BALANCE SHEET

	1. Historical 3-31-76 from Exhibit 1	2. Adjusted Historical 3-31-76	3. Adjusted Historical Percentages 3-31-76	4. Economic Values 3-31-76
ASSETS				
Cash	18,935	18,935	2.3	18,935
Accounts Receivable - Trade	266,986	266,986		266,986
Less: Reserve for Bad Debts	(3,474)	(3,474)		(13,474)
Accounts Receivable - Net	263,512	263,512		253,512 A.
Other Accounts & Notes Receivable	20,000	20,000	34.6	- B.
Inventories	380,373	380,373	46.4	360,373 C.
Prepaid Expenses	16,271	16,271	2.0	16,271
TOTAL CURRENT ASSETS	699,091	699,091	85.3	649,091
Notes Receivable - Long Term	297,648	A.		
Partnership Interest	53,580	B.		
Equipment and Improvements:				
Machinery & Equipment	74,101	74,101		80,000 D.
Furniture & Fixtures	45,191	45,191		50,000 D.
Leasehold Improvements	49,210	49,210		70,000 D.
Tools, Dies, and Molds	66,436	66,436		50,000 D.
Total Cost - Equipment & Improvements	234,938	234,938		250,000
Less: Reserve for Depreciation	(114,164)	(114,164)		-
Equipment & Improvements - Net	120,774	120,774	14.7	250,000
New Product Investment	134,210	C.		
Other Assets	25,001	D.		
TOTAL ASSETS	1,330,304	819,865	100.0	899,091
Notes Payable - Short Term	60,000	60,000	7.3	60,000
Accounts Payable - Trade	144,138	144,138	17.6	144,138
Income Taxes Payable	11,615	9,232 E	1.1	9,232
Accounts Payable - Other	8,320	8,320		E.
Other Taxes Payable	8,649	8,649	4.4	8,649
Other Current Liabilities	19,173	19,173		19,173
TOTAL CURRENT LIABILITIES	251,895	249,512	30.4	241,192
Notes Payable - Long Term	10,000	10,000	1.2	- F.
Deferred Income	153,225	A.		
TOTAL LIABILITIES	415,120	259,512	31.6	241,192
Common Stock	10,000	10,000		10,000
Paid-in Surplus	200,000	200,000		200,000
Earned Surplus	705,184	350,353		447,899
TOTAL CAPITAL	915,184*	560,353*	68.4	657,899*
TOTAL LIABILITIES & CAPITAL	1,330,304	819,865	100.0	899,091

Footnotes:
*Column 1 Net Worth is exactly per the company's books of account. Net Worth in Columns 2 & 4 consists of tangible items only.
A to E of Column 2 and A to F of Column 4 are explained in Chapter 4.

EXHIBIT 5

BLM ELECTRONICS, INC.
ADJUSTED HISTORICAL INCOME STATEMENTS

	3-31-72	3-31-73	3-31-74	3-31-75	3-31-76
TOTAL SALES*	1,071,454	1,085,767	1,112,848	1,185,451	1,274,893
TOTAL COST OF GOODS SOLD*	699,650	737,241	744,595	814,400	904,879
ADD:					
A. Value Buildup-Leased Equipment	-	(2,000)	(2,500)	(2,800)	(3,000)
B. Write-off of New Wing	-	-	-	(24,000)	-
C. Equipment Write-off	-	(10,500)	-	-	-
D. Unusual Research & Development	-	-	-	-	(21,000)
E. Depreciation on Wing & Equipment:					
Wing	-	-	-	4,000	4,000
Equipment	-	1,000	1,000	1,000	1,000
ADJUSTED COST OF GOODS SOLD	699,650	725,741	743,095	792,600	885,879
ADJUSTED GROSS PROFIT	371,804	360,026	369,753	392,851	389,014
Administrative Expense	217,847	229,359	234,202	237,201	286,154
ADJUSTED PROFIT - OPERATIONS	153,957	130,667	135,551	155,650	102,860
Miscellaneous Income	7,520	12,618	20,113	35,432	48,419
F. Deduct Unrelated Partnership Income	(5,000)	(10,000)	(15,000)	(15,000)	(15,000)
G. Deduct Land Sales Income	-	-	-	(18,025)	(30,480)
ADJUSTED MISCELLANEOUS INCOME	2,520	2,618	5,113	2,407	2,939
Miscellaneous Expense	6,770	7,075	7,923	9,018	3,225
H. Deduct Taxes on Unrelated Land	(4,000)	(4,200)	(5,000)	(6,000)	-
ADJUSTED MISCELLANEOUS EXPENSE	2,770	2,875	2,923	3,018	3,225
ADJUSTED NET PROFIT BEFORE TAX	153,707	130,410	137,741	155,039	102,574
. Owners' Salary Adjustment	None Required	-	-	-	-
. Add: Interest Expense	4,242	5,011	6,303	7,605	6,789
. Add: Regular Depreciation	13,406	18,149	15,518	14,766	23,720
. Add: Depreciation taken at "E" above	-	1,000	1,000	5,000	5,000
ADJUSTED PROFIT BEFORE TAX AND BEFORE CAPITAL CHARGES	171,355	154,570	160,562	182,410	138,083

EXHIBIT 6

BLM ELECTRONICS, INC.
PRO FORMA INCOME STATEMENT FOR THE PERIOD
APRIL 1, 1976 TO MARCH 31, 1977

Total Sales	$1,400,000
Cost of Goods Sold (68% of Sales)	952,000
Gross Profit (32% of Sales)	448,000
Operating Expenses	258,000*
Profit from Operations (Before Depreciation, Interest and Income Taxes)	190,000

* Note that the interest expense and depreciation are already excluded from operating expenses.

EXHIBIT 7
BLM ELECTRONICS, INC.
COMPARISON WITH INDUSTRY DATA

	RMA* Industry Figures	BLM 3-31-76 Adjusted Historical	Difference
Cash	7.1%	2.3%	(4.8)
Accounts Receivable - Net	30.7	34.6	3.9
Inventories - Net	33.1	46.4	13.3
All Other Current Assets	.9	2.0	1.1
TOTAL CURRENT ASSETS	71.8	85.3	13.5
Fixed Assets - Net	21.2	14.7	(6.5)
All Other Assets	7.0	-	(7.0)
TOTAL ASSETS	100.0%	100.0%	
Notes Payable - Short Term	14.4%	7.3%	(7.1)
Accounts Payable - Trade	13.7	17.6	3.9
Income Taxes Payable	2.4	1.1	(1.3)
All Other Current Liabilities	9.9	4.4	(5.5)
TOTAL CURRENT LIABILITIES	40.4	30.4	(10.0)
Long Term Debt	15.2	1.2	(14.0)
TOTAL LIABILITIES	55.6	31.6	(24.0)
Tangible Net Worth	44.4	68.4	24.0
TOTAL LIABILITIES & CAPITAL	100.0%	100.0%	
INCOME DATA			
Net Sales	100.0%	100.0%	
Cost of Goods Sold	61.9	69.5	7.6
Gross Profit	38.1	30.5	(7.6)
All Other Expense - Net	31.6	22.5	(9.1)
Profit Before Taxes	6.5	8.0	1.5
RATIOS			
Current	1.9	2.8	.9
Quick	.8	1.2	.4
Collection Period	50 days	74 days	24 days
Inventory Turnover	4.1	2.3	(1.8)
Debt to Worth	1.2	.5	(.7)
Profit on Investment	17.7%	18.3%	.6
Net Worth Turnover	4.3	2.3	(2.0)
Purchases to Trade Payables	N/A	129 days	-
Fixed Assets to Worth	.5	.2	(.3)

Footnote

*This column was excerpted from *Annual Statement Studies (Revised)*, 1975 edition, by Robert Morris Associates, Credit Division, Philadelphia National Bank Building, Philadelphia, Pa. 19107. The data is shown on page 82 of that publication under the caption, "Manufacturers of Surgical, Medical & Dental Instruments & Supplies. The sub-caption for firms with $250,000 to $1,000,000 of assets was chosen, rather than that for firms with over $1,000,000 and less than $10,000,000 in assets, because BLM was judged closer to the smaller firms, based on its adjusted historic balance sheet figures shown in column 2 of Exhibit 4.

CHAPTER 5

VALUING THE PROFESSIONALLY-MANAGED BUSINESS

It is common sense to take a method and try it. If it fails, admit it frankly and try another. But above all, try something.

FRANKLIN DELANO ROOSEVELT - May 22, 1932

TOPICS DISCUSSED IN THIS CHAPTER

[¶5.01] — **Subjective Nature of Business Valuation**

[¶5.02] — **A Framework for Judgment**

[¶5.03] — **Check for Market Formulas**

[¶5.04] — **Balance Sheet Methods**

[¶5.04-1] — **Method 1 - Net Worth Per Books**
Basic Concept - Limitations - Advantages
Procedure - Example

[¶5.04-2] — **Method 2 - Tangible Net Worth at Market**
Basic Concept - Limitations - Advantages
Procedure - Example

[¶5.05] — **Earnings and Cash Flow Methods**

[¶5.05-1] — **Method 3 - Excess Earnings (or Excess Profit) Method**
Basic Concept - Limitations - Advantages
Procedure - Example

[¶5.05-2] — **The Meaning of Capitalization Rates and Multipliers**

[¶5.05-3] — **Method 4 - Capitalization of Net Profit**
Basic Concept - Limitations - Advantages
Procedure - Example

[¶5.05-4] — **Method 5 - Discounted Cash Flow**
Basic Concept - Limitations - Advantages
Procedure - Example

[¶5.06] — **Market Data Comparison Methods**

[¶5.06-1] — **Method 6 - Price Earnings Ratio**
Basic Concept - Limitations - Advantages
Procedure - Example

[¶5.06-2] — **Method 7 - Dividend Capitalization**
Basic Concept - Limitations - Advantages
Procedure - Example

[¶5.06-3] — **Method 8 - Ratio of Market Price to Book Equity**
Basic Concept - Limitations - Advantages
Procedure - Example

[¶5.06-4] — **Market Price Premiums**

[¶5.06-5] — **Summary**

CHAPTER 5

VALUING THE PROFESSIONALLY-MANAGED BUSINESS

[¶5.01] SUBJECTIVE NATURE OF BUSINESS VALUATION

In valuing real property or machinery and equipment, a substantial degree of objectivity is possible. There are three highly developed, well recognized methods for estimating value; namely, cost summation, income capitalization, and market comparisons. Sales of comparable properties are usually available. In valuing a parcel of business-zoned land, for example, there is a high probability that a number of similarly zoned parcels will be discovered in the area which can be compared on a per acre, per square foot, or per front foot basis. The property being valued is entirely tangible.

On the other hand, valuing any operating enterprise is at best somewhat subjective. When the business is closely-held with no substantial public market for its stock, the problem is compounded. While there are well-developed methods for valuing such businesses, they are not as widely known and hence not as broadly accepted as are those used for real property and equipment. The methods must be applied to operating businesses with more judgment and subjectivity than comparable methods applied to real estate.

Likewise, although there may be many sales of businesses of similar types within a given geographic area, the factors influencing the selling prices are much more difficult to measure. The success of a business is closely related to management skills, personalities, and other intangible elements. In addition, there are special influences, such as income tax considerations, union contracts, and foreign competition, which are usually much more complex than the factors which affect the value of real or personal property.

The relative financial strength of a company, its management ability, the transferability of the skills, intangibles such as patents and licenses, and an endless list of other concerns require a substantial degree of individual analysis. Then there must be an analysis of the interrelationship of all of these factors. The end result is that there is no set formula to be applied to comparative data which automatically assures objectivity. The appraisal must be subjective, and the final opinion of value must be based upon a series of judgments by the appraiser.

[¶5.02] A FRAMEWORK FOR JUDGMENT

Despite the subjective nature of the business valuation process, there are basic techniques which have gained acceptance. These methods provide a framework within which the appraiser can operate in an orderly manner, and they form a basis for explaining his value conclusions. Also, they demonstrate principles which can be followed in developing hybrid approaches to meet special needs.

It is the objective of this chapter to bring together and explain the basic ap-

VALUING THE PROFESSIONALLY-MANAGED BUSINESS

praisal methods which have gained widest acceptance in valuing entire business enterprises of the professionally-managed type. (See ¶ 1.04-2.) A presentation of all of the methods which might be used is not possible, since so many could be listed. However, a reasonably complete listing of basic techniques is discussed. The number of possible yardsticks applicable to value are limited. Value must be related to tangible assets, or to intangibles, or to a combination of tangibles and intangibles, or to total sales (or revenues), or to profits. The methods discussed here show how to measure all of these ingredients of an operating enterprise—often in more than one way.

Methods for valuing businesses have evolved from many sources. Government regulatory bodies have spawned some which have gradually gained acceptance. Court decisions based upon evidence presented by expert witnesses have led to others. The accounting profession, appraisal theorists, and regulations of the Internal Revenue Service are responsible for some. In addition, a wide array of methods have been evolved in the marketplace as a result of negotiations between buyers, sellers, and underwriters.

[¶5.03] CHECK FOR MARKET FORMULAS

As noted earlier, this chapter deals with valuation of the professionally-managed business. Such businesses present much more complex appraisal problems than do personal businesses. (See ¶ 1.04-1 and 2.) Personal businesses tend to be sold more on the basis of a formula determined in the marketplace. This is because personal businesses are usually less complex, often being small retailers or professional offices, and because they are more numerous and hence more often sold.

Larger, professionally-managed firms are much less likely to sell by formula. However, the possible existence of marketplace formulas should not be overlooked simply because a business is relatively large and is professionally managed. One might think, for instance, that businesses as complex and professionally managed as commercial banks would not be sold by formula. However, many commercial banks are sold with heavy emphasis on a formula related to net worth at book value - i.e., one to two times book net worth. This doesn't mean that an appraiser should blindly follow such a formula in valuing a bank, but he should know of its existence and test its applicability to the bank being appraised.

A starting point in the valuation of any closely-held business is a check of the market to see if any valuation formulas are being widely used. A further check for formulas should be made with the trade association which serves the industry of which the firm being appraised is a member. Court cases involving the sale of similar companies should be reviewed. Internal Revenue rulings may provide helpful guidelines.

Since marketplace formulas are not widely applicable to professionally-managed, larger businesses, they will not be discussed in this chapter. Such formulas

VALUING THE PROFESSIONALLY-MANAGED BUSINESS

are covered in detail in the later review of methods for appraising personal type businesses.

[¶5.04]   BALANCE SHEET METHODS

The methods described in this section can be broadly categorized into three classes: namely, balance sheet, earnings and cash flow, and comparable sales. In logical progression, the balance sheet methods are first discussed.

[¶5.04-1]   METHOD 1 - NET WORTH PER BOOKS

Basic Concept

The net worth of an enterprise as expressed on its balance sheet is the difference between all of the assets of the firm and all of its liabilities as recorded on its books of account. Net worth so defined represents the book value of the owners' equity.

Limitations

The net worth per books seldom represents economic value, for reasons explained in detail in Chapter 2 at ¶2.01 through ¶2.04. In essence, this is because traditional accounting methods and statements do not generally reflect market values. Consequently, this measure of value must be viewed as merely a starting point in the appraisal process.

Advantages

Net worth per books is readily available. Because of a long tradition of usage, it is understood by most businessmen, by all public accountants, most lawyers, and even by many laymen who may be serving on juries where value is an issue. Furthermore, a careful test of the unadjusted balance sheet may indicate that there are offsetting factors on both the asset and liability sides which taken together result in a book value which by coincidence may be economic. However, one would be ill-advised to adopt the book net worth as the final value conclusion without checking each item on the balance sheet carefully and without comparing the book values shown on the balance sheet with those resulting from other valuation methods.

After doing the necessary checking and after applying other valuation techniques, the conclusion may be reached that book net worth is the best indication of value. If so, the appraiser should adopt it as the principal basis for his final value conclusion, because it is so much more readily explained than are other valuation methods.

Book net worth is most apt to approach economic net worth when businesses are relatively new; or where there have been management or other problems in the past; or where a key person is no longer involved in the operation (such as the

VALUING THE PROFESSIONALLY-MANAGED BUSINESS

void caused by the death of a sole owner-manager); or where the future outlook of the business is less than bright for a wide variety of reasons.

Procedure

Net worth per books means accepting the net worth shown on the financial statements and books of account without adjustment. However, the appraiser will seldom use this figure without at least some adjustment. Generally, he will remove any intangible assets recorded on the books. While it is not common, intangibles such as goodwill, patents, secret processes, and new product development do sometimes appear in the financial records of the business. Seldom are the values assigned to them realistic, and seldom can they be defended unless tested by other valuation methods. Consequently, adjustments are usually made to reduce book net worth by any such intangibles, resulting in a restatement of net worth that can be designated *Tangible Net Worth Per Books*.

Tangible net worth per books may be further adjusted to remove assets which are extraneous to the main business of the firm being appraised. This is done because such extraneous assets normally must be separately valued and because they tend to distort comparisons which the appraiser will wish to make with other companies in the same basic industry.

Example

In the BLM case, net worth per books at March 31, 1976 was $915,184. This figure appears in the last column of Exhibit 1 and in the first column of Exhibit 4. The transition from this figure to the tangible net worth figure which is useful for industry comparisons is described in Chapter 4 at ¶ 4.02-1 and illustrated in Column 2 of Exhibit 4. In summary, this is what was done:

Net Worth Per Books			$915,184
Less Intangible Assets:			
New Product Investment		134,210	
Other Assets (Goodwill & Patent)		25,001	159,211
Tangible Net Worth Per Books			755,973
Less Unrelated Business Items:			
Notes Receivable - Long Term	297,648		
Net of Deferred Income	(153,225)	144,423	
Partnership Interest		53,580	
Plus: Income Tax on Unrelated Income		(2,383)	195,620
Tangible Net Worth for Industry Comparisons			$560,353

VALUING THE PROFESSIONALLY-MANAGED BUSINESS

[¶5.04-2] METHOD 2 - TANGIBLE NET WORTH AT MARKET

Basic Concept

The existing unadjusted balance sheet is used as a tool for developing an adjusted balance sheet which reflects the tangible assets of the business and its liabilities at their economic worth. In this regard, tangible assets include all assets except those defined as intangibles later in the book. That is, one could regard accounts receivable or prepaid expenses as intangibles in a sense, but such items are not excluded under this method of valuation. Only such intangibles as goodwill, patents, and new product development are deleted, and this is because they are to be revalued using a specific appraisal method described later. At the completion of the valuation process, the intangibles will be added to the tangible net worth at market. (See Chapter 6.)

Limitations

The balance sheet adjusted to reflect market values is far superior to the balance sheet at book values discussed under Method 1. However, it does not reflect intangibles and therefore is not conclusive as to value. Tangible net worth at market must be compared with the results of the earnings valuation methods described as Methods 3 through 7 in this chapter.

Advantages

The principal advantage of the Tangible Net Worth at Market method is that this approach is more apt to reflect the economic worth of a business than is the unadjusted balance sheet, or net worth per books. In the case of certain types of businesses which are primarily fixed asset related, determination of tangible net worth at market may provide the best method for developing the market value of the enterprise. Indeed, it could be the only acceptable approach. The value of the underlying assets of most holding companies, or of such real estate related operations as motels or hotels, is usually the value of these businesses. The assumption that this may be true does not relieve the appraiser of the necessity of comparing tangible net worth with the results of earnings valuation methods and with commonly-used market tests of value.

Procedure

The principles involved in developing the Economic Balance Sheet are discussed in Chapter 4 at ¶4.06. They need not be restated at this point. However, to these principles should be added the need to eliminate for industry comparison purposes those assets and liabilities which would not be found on the balance sheets of most of the companies in the industry. If there are no such unrelated assets or liabilities, none need be eliminated.

VALUING THE PROFESSIONALLY-MANAGED BUSINESS

Example

The adjustments required to convert the BLM balance sheet prepared for accounting purposes at March 31, 1976 to an economic balance sheet are described in detail in Chapter 4 at ¶ 4.02-3. The results are shown in Exhibit 4 at column 4 under "Economic Values at 3-31-76." In summary, the transition from the tangible net worth per books, which was developed for industry comparison under Method 1 above, is as follows:

Tangible Net Worth Per Books for Industry Comparison		$560,353
Less Decreases in Book Values to Economic Values:		
Greater Reserve for Bad Debts	10,000	
Note Due from Owner Eliminated	20,000	
Reduction in Inventories by Appraisal	20,000	50,000
Subtotal		510,353
Plus Increases in Book Values to Economic Values:		
Increase in Fixed Assets by Appraisal	129,226	
Accounts Payable Officer Eliminated	8,320	
Note Payable Owner Eliminated	10,000	147,546
Tangible Net Worth at Market		$657,899

[¶5.05]   EARNINGS AND CASH FLOW METHODS

It is evident that the two most important factors which affect the value of an operating enterprise are the market value of its assets and the value of its earnings. Both factors are extremely important, but, in the final analysis, earnings carry the greatest weight. This axiom is based on the premise that an operating enterprise is worth only what it will earn. Indeed, a business is an investment where a return is expected. Therefore, the amount of investment is logically dictated by the anticipated return compared to alternative investments.

The balance sheet items, including net worth, are essentially passive in nature. The balance sheet as adjusted to market is presumably a summation of what the revalued assets could be sold for independently or as part of an operating enterprise. But this would not really be representative of the investment value of the business. If an investor wished to purchase accounts receivable, for example, he would not pay the book value, or even an adjusted book value. For investment purposes, he would pay some discounted price which would allow him a competitive return on the investment. The same would be true of most of the other assets. Thus, the mere accumulation of assets is really not what it's all about—to use the current idiom. The true concern is the income which the assets are capable of generating when they are assembled together in a harmonious and productive manner.

VALUING THE PROFESSIONALLY-MANAGED BUSINESS

The earnings of the going concern take on prime importance in the valuation of a business. They are of greatest concern to the investor, and this means they are also of greatest concern in the valuation process.

Several representative types of earnings valuation methods have evolved over the years. There are imperfections in all of them, but at least they provide organized methods for processing earnings into estimates of value. These estimates may be compared with one another; or with values derived from the balance sheets; or with values arising from specialized formulas derived from market transactions; or with value indications resulting from previous sales of interests in the company being appraised.

[¶5.05-1]   METHOD 3 - EXCESS EARNINGS METHOD

Basic Concept

This technique may begin with either pro forma operating profit or after-tax earnings. For illustration here, operating profit is utilized. The basic objective of this method is to provide a format for the provision of economic depreciation, amortization and return on all components of the business investment. These component requirements for return of and return on capital are deducted from the profit. If there are residual profits, this residual may indicate the presence of intangibles and goodwill.

Limitations

Many going businesses do not have sufficient profit to make this method operable as a test for intangible values. Yet these values may be known to exist.

Advantages

The method causes the appraiser to think through carefully the return of and return on investment requirements for all components of the business.

Procedure

1. Develop a pro forma income statement for the company to be appraised following the recommended approaches discussed in Chapter 4 at [¶4.04]. Regardless of the legal form in which the business operates, it is usually helpful to think of it operating as an ordinary corporation. The primary effect of this assumption is to require an appropriate level of salaries for the owners as an expense item. If the method is to be utilized with after-tax earnings, then provision must be made for normal state and federal income taxes. If the method is to be applied on an operating profit basis, then no other adjustment needs to be made in the pro forma income statement at this point. However, it is critical for the appraiser to be aware that if

VALUING THE PROFESSIONALLY-MANAGED BUSINESS

operating profit is to be used as a starting base, the capitalization rate applied to the excess profit should be higher than the rate applied to the excess after-tax earnings. The rates are different to account for income taxes in one instance whereas they have already been accounted for in the other.

2. Draw Up an Economic Balance Sheet

Preparation of an Economic Balance Sheet which reflects the market value of tangible assets and liabilities was described in Chapter 4 at ¶ 4.02-3. It also forms the basis of the Tangible Net Worth at Market technique described in this chapter as Method 2 at ¶ 5.04-2. The balance sheet so restated is needed for this method as well.

3. Develop Pro Forma Operating Profit

If the projected operating profit has not already been converted to a "before capital charges" basis, this should be done. The process involves adding depreciation and interest to income.

Depreciation so added includes any amortization of assets such as leasehold improvements and organization expense. It conforms to depreciation and amortization allowable for income tax purposes. As such it will usually be depreciation and amortization shown on the historical statements adjusted for pro forma purposes to compensate for additions and deletions of assets. It is not depreciation based on the market value of assets. The same depreciation and amortization which was used as an expense in arriving at pro forma net profit before tax is added back at this point.

The result of these adjustments is pro forma operating profit before capital charges.[13]

4. Provide for Economic Depreciation of Tangible Assets

List each tangible asset and provide economic depreciation or amortization based on its remaining useful life. Basic categories would include buildings, if owned, or leasehold improvements, if buildings are leased; furniture and fixtures; machinery and equipment; special tools; vehicles; and other depreciable assets of a tangible nature.

Land is not included, because it is not depreciable. Also, accounts receivable and inventories are not depreciated, even though they were considered to be tangible assets for purposes of developing the economic balance sheet.

VALUING THE PROFESSIONALLY-MANAGED BUSINESS

5. **Provide for Amortization of Intangible Assets**

At this point, provision should be made for amortization of intangible assets which have ascertainable lives and for which separate values can be established. This may entail a dual approach, depending upon the purpose of the appraisal. If it is for tax purposes, consideration must be given to court rulings and to Internal Revenue regulations as to whether an intangible is depreciable or amortizable for income tax purposes. If the asset can be depreciated or amortized, then it should be included at this point. If the asset cannot be depreciated or amortized because the Internal Revenue Service does not consider it to have a determinable life, then the IRS will consider it to be part of goodwill. If part of goodwill, it should be included in the final step under this Method 3, namely, capitalization of excess net profit.

On the other hand, if the appraisal is not for tax purposes, it would be appropriate to include all identifiable intangibles which can be amortized or depreciated, whether or not acceptable to the taxing authorities. The depreciation and amortization provided here is the actual economic decline in value which is anticipated, based on the remaining useful lives of the assets involved.

6. **Provide for an Economic Return on Investment**

A realistic return on the investment in major categories of assets should be provided, including land, equipment, leasehold improvements, and other tangible assets. A return should also be computed on intangibles other than goodwill.[14] Also, a return should be provided on working capital, but this may not be synonymous with working capital as it appears on the historic balance sheet. The working capital shown on the Economic Balance Sheet (See ¶ 4.02-3.) is a better starting point. However, the cash included in the economic balance sheet is the actual cash on hand, and this may not be adequate for the firm's needs. If this is so, for purposes of this calculation working capital should be increased by the added cash requirements.[15]

7. **Deduct Depreciation and Investment Return from Profits**

The total requirement for economic depreciation and amortization and for return on investment is deducted from pro forma operating profit and before capital charges. In other words, the results of items 4, 5 and 6 above are deducted from the profit described at item 3.

8. **Develop Goodwill from Excess Earnings**

The result of the step taken above was to develop what may be termed "Excess Earnings." The resulting figure from that calculation represents earnings which are

VALUING THE PROFESSIONALLY-MANAGED BUSINESS

in excess of those needed to provide for depreciation and amortization on a realistic basis; in excess of those needed to provide a reasonable return on identifiable assets of the business; and in excess of those needed to pay interest on working capital permanently invested (cash, accounts receivable, inventory less trade accounts payable). Such excess earnings must be attributable to the goodwill and other unidentifiable or unmeasurable intangibles which the business has created.

To convert such excess earnings into a value for goodwill and other intangibles, the excess earnings are capitalized at a rate which is commensurate to the risks of the investment. The risks to be considered are those inherent in the business, with particular emphasis on the relative certainty or uncertainty that the excess earnings will continue at their projected level into the future.

9. **Summarize for Total Value**

The final step under this method entails a summation of the value of the goodwill, the tangible net worth developed from the Economic Balance Sheet, and the separate value of the intangibles which were separately valued. The total of all equals the value of the entire basic business. If extraneous assets or affiliates were excluded and valued separately, their value would still have to be added in to arrive at the value of the entire business. This latter step would not actually be a part of the Excess Earnings Method.

VALUING THE PROFESSIONALLY-MANAGED BUSINESS

Example

Computation of the value of BLM Electronics, Inc. by Method 3 - Excess Earnings - is recapitulated as follows:

Pro Forma Operating Profit (Exhibit 6, Chapter 4) $190,000

1. Deduct Economic Depreciation on Tangible Assets

	Economic Value	Economic Deprec. Rates		
Machinery & Equipment	80,000	.167 (6 yr. life)	13,360	
Furniture & Fixtures	50,000	.125 (8 yr. life)	6,250	
Leasehold Improvements	70,000	.167 (6 yr. life)	11,690	
Tools, Dies & Molds	50,000	.250 (4 yr. life)	12,500	(43,800)

2. Deduct Economic Amortization of Intangibles

	Economic Value	Amortization Rates		
Belmur Process	75,000	.125 (8 yrs.)	9,375	
Lamp Patent	15,000	.100 (10 yrs.)	1,500	(10,875)

3. Deduct Economic Return on Investment

	Amount	Rate of Return		
Working Capital	407,899	10%	40,790	
Equipment & Improvements	250,000	14%	35,000	
Belmur Process	75,000	20%	15,000	
Lamp Patent	15,000	15%	2,250	(93,040)

4. Excess Earnings 42,285

5. Value of Goodwill (Excess Earnings at 20% Capitalization Rate) $211,425

6. Summary of Value

Adjusted Tangible Net Worth (Exhibit 4, Column 4)	657,899
Economic Value of Belmur Process	75,000
Economic Value of Lamp Patent	15,000
Value of Goodwill	$211,425
VALUE OF BLM (excludes Land Note and Fast Burger)	$959,324

The foregoing example of the Excess Earnings Method applied to the figures for BLM requires some amplification. The economic values for the tangible assets were obtained from the appraisal mentioned in Chapter 3 at [¶3.02-15]. The value of the Belmur Process has been determined by separate appraisal, using Method 13, which is described later. The value of the Lamp Patent has also been derived by separate appraisal using Method 14.

VALUING THE PROFESSIONALLY-MANAGED BUSINESS

[¶5.05-2] THE MEANING OF CAPITALIZATION RATES AND MULTIPLIERS

From time to time throughout the discussion of valuation methods, reference will be made to capitalization rates. The use of such a rate is an integral part of the Excess Earnings Method. It is also used in the method called "Capitalization of Income Stream" which will be discussed next.

A capitalization rate as used herein means the divisor that is used to divide into an amount of income so that the quotient will be a principal or capital amount which would yield the rate of return envisioned by the capitalization rate. If this sounds like double-talk, it is not surprising. It really takes an example to clarify the meaning.

In the foregoing BLM example, excess income of $42,285 was capitalized at a rate of 20%, yielding a value of $211,425 for goodwill. Now what was really being said? Simply, that with the known risks in this business as compared to other forms of investment, a prudent businessman would not want to make a basically unsecured investment in a very intangible asset of the company unless it would yield at least 20% per annum on the investment. Starting with that conclusion and with the knowledge that such an intangible produced earnings of $42,285, it should be possible to determine the principal amount which one would be required to invest in such an asset to produce the annual yield of $42,285. At this point it can really be reduced to a formula taught in high school mathematics; namely, if $.20X = \$42,285$ what does X equal? The answer is $211,425. In this case, that must be the value of the goodwill.

Now re-read the definition in the earlier paragraph and it should make some sense with these substitutions: A capitalization rate (20%) as used herein means the divisor (.20) that is used to divide into an amount of income ($42,285) so that the quotient ($211,425) will be a principal or capital amount which would yield the rate of return (20% per annum) envisioned by the capitalization rate.

Sometimes, however, one may use a multiplier instead of a capitalization rate. In speaking of a price earnings ratio, it will often be said that a stock is priced at so many times earnings. Thus, if a stock is earning $2.00 per share per year and it sells for $20 a share, its price earnings ratio is 10; or put another way, the earnings are multiplied by 10.

In reality, a multiplier is merely the reciprocal of a capitalization rate. In the BLM case just cited, the same result would have been obtained had the excess earnings of $42,285 been multiplied by 5.0. Where did 5.0 come from? It results from the simple logic that if $20 return is desired on each $100 invested, how many times would $20 go into $100? The answer is 5.0. Therefore, if the earnings of $42,285 are known and these

VALUING THE PROFESSIONALLY-MANAGED BUSINESS

earnings are to represent a return of $20 per $100 invested, one could find the investment needed to provide this yield by multiplying $42,285 by 5.0. This does indeed also result in $211,425.[17]

The multiplier concept occasionally is used in capitalizing excess earnings. The multiplier would correspond to the number of years of excess profits an informed buyer would be willing to pay for goodwill. The decision as to whether to use a capitalization rate or its reciprocal, the multiplier, will often be determined by the custom in the market for particular businesses, or the appraiser may decide to use it because a multiplier is easier to explain to a jury of laymen. Regardless of which method is used, the value conclusion would be the same. Indeed, as noted, a multiplier of 5.0 would result in the same value as its reciprocal 20%.

[¶5.05-3] METHOD 4 - CAPITALIZATION OF NET PROFIT

Basic Concept

The net profit from a business has a value to its recipients which can be appraised in various ways. There are several variations of net profit capitalization (or multipliers) commonly used. Examples include price earnings ratio multiplier, dividend capitalization and discounted cash flow, all of which are described in this text.

The distinctive feature of the method described here as "Capitalization of Net Profit" is that it entails a comparison of the available income flow from the business appraised with other business investment opportunities where the appraiser can perceive similar risk characteristics.

The net profit before taxes is capitalized at a rate taken from market data. The source of market data might be publicly-traded companies. Very often this is the only available source for a reasonable amount of information useful for developing capitalization rates. Ideally, the information would be obtained from the sale of closely-held companies where a total sale price and net profit before tax income history relationship can be developed. However, such information is often difficult to obtain.

Development of an overall capitalization rate from publicly-traded stocks requires the following essential information; aggregate selling price of stock (the total number of shares outstanding times the average price), and all long-term debt, including the current portion. These two items, aggregate price and long-term debt, are totaled. Net profit before taxes plus depreciation and interest expenses are totaled. The total net profit before taxes and interest is divided by the aggregate stock price and long-term debt. The result is an overall capitalization rate. If data on a sufficient sampling of companies can be found, a realistic composite rate for the industry should develop. The appraiser may have to adjust when comparing publicly-traded companies with an established market to a closely-held company with no established market for its stock or factors.

Additionally, the appraiser should compare the results of the overall rates from the public market with other industry data if available. Trade associations specializing in a particular industry may be a source for such data.

Another method for developing an overall rate is a summation technique. The method begins with a safe rate such as that represented by yields on savings accounts, U.S. Government Notes and Bonds. To this is added factors for lack of liquidity, risks of a company which may have a relatively narrow product line, investment management requirements and other factors the appraiser considers appropriate in a particular instance.

Once a capitalization rate has been computed, it is applied to the stream of net profit the business can be expected to generate. The net profit is thus capitalized; that is, a determination is made of the amount of capital which must be invested to produce the net profit generated by the business, assuming a given rate of return.

Limitations

One of the difficulties with this method is obtaining comparable data. A great deal of common sense and good judgment must be applied.

Advantages

Despite its limitations, net profit capitalization provides a technique which reflects the attitude of the market and adjustments can be made for each situation.

Procedure

The first problem is to develop a source of comparative information. Data may be derived from publicly-traded companies, related industry sources such as trade organizations, brokers, accountants or other business consultants specializing in a particular industry or with unique knowledge about the details of the transfers of interests in closely-held companies.

Sufficient information is needed in order to develop an overall capitalization rate for each comparative company. Naturally, the more companies used in the comparison the better. It is recognized that ideal comparatives are rarely available. Therefore, the appraiser must use companies which generally reflect the investment community attitude about the industry of which the appraised business is a part.

VALUING THE PROFESSIONALLY-MANAGED BUSINESS

Overall Capitalization Rates

What is meant by an overall capitalization rate? The process of capitalization been explained previously in this text. However, the meaning of an overall rate may require some additional explanation. The term, overall rate, is defined as the direct ratio between Annual Net Operating Income (NOI) and Value or Sales Price. That overall rate includes provision for both return of and return on capital invested. The rate derived by this procedure is a debt-free rate. That is, it is assumed the business has no long-term debt. It will be noted that the long-term debt has been added to the aggregate market price as though that total represented a 100% equity in the business. Then, the net profit before income taxes is added to depreciation and interest. That is, the long-term debt has been added to equity on the asset side of the balance sheet and by the same token, interest on that debt is added back to profit. Furthermore, depreciation and amortization deducted for income tax purposes have been added back to net profit. These items, as allowable deductions for tax purposes, do not necessarily represent provision for economic return of capital. The result is that an overall capitalization rate is derived which provides all return of (depreciation and amortization) and return on (interest) capital on everyone's equity, including the owners and the long-term debt creditors.

For the purposes of this text, the example used assumes data from publicly-traded companies to be reasonably comparative to BLM. A step-by-step procedure for development of an overall capitalization rate follows:

Step 1. An average aggregate price (average for a particular day, several months, a year or even two or three years may be utilized depending upon what is considered a most representative period uninfluenced by very unusual conditions such as the death of a President or war, and so forth) is developed. The aggregate price per share is multiplied by the average number of shares of common stock outstanding for the same period. Adjustments might have to be made for preferred shares and other classes of stock. The result of this multiplication is the aggregate market price of all of the stock (column 1 of the example).

Step 2. The total long-term debt for the same average period is added to the aggregate market price of all of the outstanding common stock (column 3).

Step 3. The net profit before income taxes is added to the total depreciation and amortization expenses deducted for income tax purposes and the total interest expenses deducted for income tax purposes (column 6).

Step 4. The total of the net profit before income taxes, depreciation and amortization and interest is divided by the total of the aggregate market price of the outstanding stock and the long-term debt. The result of these computations is an overall capitalization rate (column 7).

VALUING THE PROFESSIONALLY-MANAGED BUSINESS

Step 5. The appraised company net profit before income taxes, depreciation, amortization and interest is computed.

Step 6. The appraised company's net profit before income taxes, depreciation, amortization and interest is divided by the market-derived overall capitalization rate.

If sufficient and meaningful market rate data is not available, an alternate rate development can be utilized or even used to supplement the market data. One such method is the rate summation technique.

Step 7. Dividing the appraised business net profit before income taxes, depreciation, amortization and interest expense by the market-derived overall capitalization rate develops an indicated value of the total equity and debt of the appraised company. Remember that in the development of the overall rate from comparative companies, long-term debt has been treated as though it were equity. Therefore, in developing an indicated owner equity value, the appraised company's long-term debt must be deducted.

EXAMPLE: COMPUTING OVERALL CAPITALIZATION RATES FROM PUBLICLY TRADED STOCKS

(Add 000 to columns 1 - 6)

Comparative Company	Col. 1 Aggregate Price	Col. 2 Long Term Debt	Col. 3 Total (1) + (2)	Col. 4 Net Profit Before Taxes	Col. 5 Depreciation And Interest	Col. 6 Total (4) + (5)	Col. 7 Indicated Overall Capitalization Rate (6) ÷ (3)
1	$ 15,268	$ 8,486	$ 23,754	$ 9,420	$ 2,358	$11,778	50.0
2	200,413	68,614	269,027	31,390	19,779	51,169	19.0
3	68,026	19,536	87,562	12,050	4,322	16,372	19.0
4	93,263	2,300	95,563	11,060	4,500	15,560	16.0
5	56,334	1,040	57,374	13,361	3,390	16,751	29.0
Composite rate (Totals of Col. 6 ÷ Col. 3)							21.0
Average rate							27.0
Rate Range							16.0 - 50.0

VALUING THE PROFESSIONALLY-MANAGED BUSINESS

In applying this method to BLM, the starting point is the operating profit before income taxes, depreciation and interest expenses. The figure is $190,000. This is derived from Exhibit 6, page 85.

The market-derived composite overall capitalization rate is 21%. See the example which follows. It will be noted that 21% was the composite rate from the 5 comparative companies. A composite rate may be used, or an average or a rate selected from the individual comparatives depending upon appraisal judgment and the circumstances of each case.

BLM's $190,000 is divided by 21% ($190,000 ÷ .21) which results in a total value of equity and debt of $904,762. From this sum is deducted the $60,000 long-term debt. This can be seen on Exhibit 4, page 81. The resulting indicated value is $844,762.

COMPUTATION OF THE VALUE OF BLM ELECTRONICS, INC. BY METHOD 4—CAPITALIZATION OF OPERATING PROFIT IS SHOWN BELOW:

Pro Forma Operating Profit Before Interest, Depreciation and Taxes (See Exhibit 6)	$190,000
Overall Capitalization Rate (Using Composite Rate)	21.0%
VALUE OF BLM EQUITY AND DEBT (Excludes Land Note and Fast Burger)	904,762
Less Long-Term Debt	60,000
VALUE OF BLM EQUITY	$844,762

[¶5.05-4] METHOD 5 - DISCOUNTED CASH FLOW

Basic Concept

This method requires a forecast of cash flow for a given number of years into the future. The present value of this cash flow is then computed using a discount rate. Any value of the assets of the business which is expected to remain at the end of the cash flow period is next valued on a discounted basis. The value of the company is the present worth of the cash flow plus the present worth of the residual assets less any liabilities expected to remain if it is assumed that the business will cease at the end of the projected term. If the business is expected to continue beyond the projection period (the terminal year) then the terminal year cash flow can be capitalized (using an after tax cash flow price/earnings multiple) discounted to the present. The sums of the discounted year by year cash flows are added to the terminal year capitalized value for a total business value indication.

VALUING THE PROFESSIONALLY-MANAGED BUSINESS

Limitations

For many going businesses, the limited period of time for which a cash flow is assumed to continue may set an arbitrary and unrealistic restriction.

Advantages

This method is very useful for a business whose existence is dependent on a single contract, at the end of which there is a high probability the business will be discontinued. It is also useful in valuing a new company where there is a relatively high risk. The length of the cash flow projection may be based upon the period for which the appraiser believes a prudent investor would be willing to risk his capital to achieve its full recovery. If, for example, he believes an investor, considering the inherent risks of the business, would wish to see his capital returned in no less than five years, he may estimate the cash flow for a five year period, then add to its present worth the worth of the assets which could be expected to remain at the end of that period.

Procedure

The pro forma net profit after tax is estimated for the desired period, such as five years into the future. To these profits is then added depreciation and amortization, which are non-cash expenses. The result is pro forma cash flow before debt service and other capital requirements. From this result, for each year of the projection is then deducted loan amortization requirements and cash needed for other purposes, such as working capital. The final result of these steps is to derive pro forma cash flow available for capital recovery or general reinvestment.

The crux of the method is the determination of the present worth of this flow of cash as well as the present worth of any assets which may remain at the end of the projected period. The computation of the present worth of such future benefits involves a widely-used technique, namely, the use of "Present Worth Tables." Such tables are in effect merely a variation on compound interest tables.[18]

To understand the theory of the present worth tables, it is helpful to first review the concept of compound interest. This theory hypothesizes that if $1,000 were invested today at a known rate of interest and where the compounding periods are known, it is possible to look up in a table and determine what that $1,000 will be worth at any given date in the future. Thus, $1,000 invested at 8% interest and allowed to compound monthly for five years will be worth $1,489.85 at the end of the fifth year.

The present worth tables start by reversing this theory. The rhetorical question is asked, how much would one have to invest today at 8% interest compounded monthly to have $1,000 at the end of five years? The answer, drawn from a present worth table, is $671.21. A corollary to this answer is the proposition that if one were to acquire the right to receive at the end of five years $1,000 in cash, or an

VALUING THE PROFESSIONALLY-MANAGED BUSINESS

asset worth $1,000, and if, considering the risks of the investment, he were satisfied that 8% was an adequate return on his money, he would be willing to pay $671.21 *today* for such a right.

Carried a step further, the value of $1,000 received at the end of this year is worth more than if it were received five years from the present. This is true because the money received at the end of this year can be invested to gain compound interest for the next four years, so it would be worth more than $1,000 at the end of five years. This forms the basis for determining the present value of $1,000 received once a year for five years. Thus, using the same table cited (an 8% compound interest table with interest compounded monthly) in computing the present worth of $1,000 at the end of five years one finds the following: The present worth of $1,000 is $923.36 if received at the end of one year; $852.60 if received at the end of two years; $787.26 if received at the end of three years; $726.92 if received at the end of four years; and $671.21 if received at the end of five years. If one were faced with valuing the present worth of $1,000 per year to be received at the end of each year for five years, he would merely add $923.36 + $852.60 + $787.26 + $726.92 + $671.21, and the present value of such a stream of cash would be $3,961.35. All of this assumes that one were satisfied with 8% per annum compounded monthly. If one analyzed the risks and found 7% to be a satisfactory return, then the income stream cited would be worth more. On the other hand, if 9% is required, the present value would be less than $3,961.35. Similarly, the compounding period will affect the value conclusion.

Under the Discounted Cash Flow Method, a present worth table is selected which is based on interest (the discount rate) at the desired rate compounded at suitable intervals. The projected cash flow available for capital recovery and/or general reinvestment is then valued on a present worth basis for each year of the projection. The total of these year-to-year values is then obtained, and this represents the value of the cash flow for the selected period.

To the present value of the cash flow is then added the present value of the assets of the business which are expected to remain at the end of the projected period. Usually, goodwill is assumed to be non-existent at the end of the period. Often the residual values to which the present worth factors are applied are liquidation values rather than fair market values, since this method assumes the termination of the business at the end of the projected period.

As a final step, add the present worth of the cash flow and the present worth of the residual assets and deduct any liabilities which are expected to remain at the end of the projected period. The final result so obtained is the value of the company.

Example

The discounted cash flow method may not be particularly applicable to the BLM case, since there is no assumption in the case that the firm will be liquidated at the end of a given period. However, it might be useful to apply the method to see what

VALUING THE PROFESSIONALLY-MANAGED BUSINESS

would happen if the owners could not sell the business on a basis satisfactory to them and decided to operate if for five years and then liquidate. What would a prudent investor be willing to pay as of the appraisal date for the cash flow the company would generate during this period and for the assets that would remain at the end of the five years? In other words, what is the company really worth to the owners if they follow such a program?

Computation of the value of BLM Electronics, Inc. by Method 5 - Discounted Cash Flow - is recapitulated as follows:

Fiscal Year Ending:

	3-31-77	3-31-78	3-31-79	3-31-80	3-31-81
Pro Forma After-Tax Earnings	81,000	100,000	125,000	135,000	140,000
Add: Depreciation (after-tax basis)	21,741	21,741	21,741	21,741	21,741
Cash Flow Before Debt Service	102,741	121,741	146,741	156,741	161,741
Less:					
Loan Amortization Needs	10,000	10,000	10,000	20,000	—
Additional Working Capital Needs	15,000	15,000	20,000	20,000	20,000
Pro Forma Cash Flow	77,741	96,741	116,741	116,741	141,741
Present Worth Factor (18% Rate)	.847	.718	.609	.516	.437
Present Worth of Pro Forma Cash Flow	65,847	69,460	71,095	60,238	61,941

Total Present Worth of Cash Flow	328,581
Pro Forma Liquidation Value of Assets at 3-31-81:	
Accounts Receivable	300,000
Inventories	325,000
Prepaid Expenses	5,000
Machinery & Equipment	14,000
Furniture & Fixtures	19,000
Leasehold Improvements	12,000
Tools, Dies & Molds	5,000
Belmur Process	5,000
Lamp Patent	8,000
Goodwill	-0-
Present Worth of Non-Cash Assets	693,000
Present Worth Factor Five Years Hence (12% Rate)	.567
Present Worth of Liquidation Value of Assets	392,931
Subtotal	721,512
Less: Liabilities Remaining at 3-31-81	10,000
VALUE OF BLM (Excluding Land Note and Fast Burger)	$711,512

In making the foregoing valuation, pro forma after-tax earnings for the fiscal year ending March 31, 1977, was computed as follows assuming a 49.0% effective tax rate (both state and federal):

$158,000 x 1.00 − .49 = $80,580, rounded to $81,000

VALUING THE PROFESSIONALLY-MANAGED BUSINESS

Note that an overall rate of 21% was used with Method 4 and 18% with Method 5. A lower rate is appropriate as Method 5 is on an after-tax basis. If a single year was being used for Method 5 and not a projection of five years, an even lower rate might be considered. However, the projected figures increase the possibility of error, thus a higher risk and the need for a higher rate.

It is assumed that $50,000 was borrowed at the beginning of the fiscal year ending March 31, 1977 which had to be repaid in annual installments of $10,000 through fiscal year ending March 31, 1979 with the residual of $20,000 due by March 31, 1980. As with the previously discussed methods, the values of the land note and the Fast Burger operation are not included.

[¶5.06] MARKET DATA COMPARISON METHODS

[¶5.06-1] METHOD 6 - PRICE EARNINGS RATIO

Basic Concept

The price earnings ratio is a multiplier applied to the after-tax earnings of the company being appraised. It is usually derived from an analysis of the price earnings ratios applicable to publicly-traded companies considered to be reasonably comparable to the firm being valued. While such a ratio may be developed for any class of stock, it is most commonly used to reflect the value of common stocks or preferred stocks with common stock characteristics.

The price earnings ratio for a company having only common shares outstanding is derived by first dividing its total net profit after tax for the most recent fiscal year by the number of shares outstanding at the end of that year. This results in earnings per share.[19] These per-share earnings are then divided into the selling price of each share at any desired date following the fiscal year end. The result is the price earnings ratio.

For example, if a firm earned $1,000,000 and had 100,000 shares outstanding, the earnings per share would be $10. If the firm's stock sold for $150 per share, the price earnings ratio would be 15. ($150 ÷ $10 = 15.) Using this ratio of 15 as a multiplier applied to the earnings of $10 per share, one can work back to the selling price of the stock, or $150 per share.

Limitations

There are many problems involved in developing a price earnings ratio from the public stock market which is then applied to the earnings of a closely-held company. Some of the more significant of these problems are as follows:

1. Stock of the closely-held firm is not publicly traded.

This means the appraiser must hypothesize as to what would occur if the firm's stock were publicly traded—even though it may be highly improbable, and perhaps impractical as well, for it to be so traded. How many shares would likely be issued? Could a broadly-based public market be developed? What degree of public

VALUING THE PROFESSIONALLY-MANAGED BUSINESS

acceptance would the stock enjoy? How long would it take to achieve an active market? These and many other questions have to be answered on a theoretical basis.

2. It is difficult to find truly comparable companies.

Many closely-held firms are highly specialized or involve activities which cross over into several industries. If specialized in one activity, this activity may represent such a small market that there are no public companies which are competitors. If, on the other hand, the company performs activities which are part of several industries, the public may value the stock of these industries on a widely divergent basis. For example, the price earnings ratio of a firm owning retail drug stores may be 5, whereas a hospital supply firm might enjoy a ratio of 21. If the company being appraised is in both activities, what public company price earnings ratio is comparable to its situation?

3. Public shares usually trade as fractional interests.

Virtually all publicly-traded stock quotations involve a fraction of the total shares of each firm's outstanding stock. Seldom do the quotes involve sale of a controlling interest. On the other hand, most appraisals of closely-held businesses involve 100% of the stock, even though it may be necessary at some point in the appraisal to develop the value of specific fractional interests. The question arises as to whether the value of an entire closely-held company is more or less than the selected price earnings ratio would indicate when that ratio resulted from the public market valuation of fractional interests.

4. Earnings of the closely-held firm may be distorted.

As has been discussed in some detail in Chapter 2, the earnings of closely-held firms may not reflect the real earning capacity of these firms. The controlling parties may write off questionable expenses, or accelerate expenses for tax reasons, or salaries may be unrealistically high or low. Public companies, on the other hand, are usually under some pressure to maximize earnings, since stock prices and shareholder satisfaction tend to improve with higher earnings. Hence, an opposite bias tends to affect the reported earnings of privately-owned companies as opposed to their public counterparts.

Faced with this problem, the appraiser has three basic choices: (a) He may elect not to use the price earnings ratio method at all. (b) He may apply a price earnings ratio to the unadjusted earnings of the closely-held firm, compensating for the inherent bias by using a substantially higher price earnings ratio than could be justified in the market (resulting in a lower value for the company) or (c) He may apply the market-derived price earnings ratio to adjusted earnings of the firm being appraised.

VALUING THE PROFESSIONALLY-MANAGED BUSINESS

With larger closely-held companies, it usually is not prudent to completely disregard the price earnings ratio method. This is true because it is so generally used in the marketplace, and the appraiser must be in a position to show that he has tested the method. He may then go on to show why it is not suitable for the situation at hand.

To apply the price earnings ratio to unadjusted earnings has the advantage of being easy to explain, and in the marketplace such ratios are applied to unadjusted earnings. That is, the *reported* earnings of the publicly-owned companies form the basis of their price earnings ratios. Whatever biases or distortions these earnings contain are built into the result. Therefore, it could be argued that a price earnings ratio taken from the market "as is" should be applied to the closely-held firm's earnings "as is." At first glance, this seems logical, but for the reasons cited earlier, the appraiser may find it very difficult to accept this approach. It is interesting to note that the courts have accepted both actual and adjusted earnings as a base for the application of price earnings ratios derived from the market.

In many instances, the appraiser will conclude that the most reasonable approach using this method is to apply a market-derived price earnings ratio to adjusted historical earnings. It is important not to use pro forma or projected earnings, because this would tend to make this method a mere restatement of some of the other methods which do use pro forma earnings.[20] It is important in the valuation process to keep each appraisal method independent from all others so that each technique will provide a separate and distinct measure of value. Probably one of the greatest problems with the price earnings ratio method is the difficulty of being certain that it does indeed constitute a method distinct from the others described in this book.

Advantages

This method is relatively easy to understand compared to the other valuation methods described here. It has gained broad acceptance in the courts and can be explained with relative ease to a jury. It is a method commonly used in the marketplace to value both fractional interests and total business enterprises.

Procedure

1. Make up adjusted historical income statements and balance sheets.

Following the procedure suggested in Chapter 4 (¶ 4.02 and 4.03), prepare adjusted historical income statements and balance sheets for the company to be appraised. Instead of merely adjusting the balance sheet for the latest year, however, it is desirable to do so for the latest five years, putting the results in comparative form. Also, instead of computing adjusted net profit before tax and before capital charges as was done for BLM in Exhibit 5, develop adjusted net profit after allowance for a proper salary to the owner-managers and *after corporate income taxes*. This should be done for the latest five years and put in comparative form. The

VALUING THE PROFESSIONALLY-MANAGED BUSINESS

statements so prepared contain adjustments necessary to remove unusual or improper figures not apt to be found in the statements for most public companies.

2. Make a careful industry or sub-industry classification of the company.

This procedure has already been described in some detail in Chapter 4 at ¶ 4.05. However, for purposes of the price earnings ratio method, an industry classification may be needed which is more comprehensive than that suggested earlier. It is crucial to the success of this method that companies be selected which are as truly comparable as possible. As was noted earlier, closely-held companies often do not neatly fit into a single industry classification, and even when they do, there may be no publicly-held counterparts.

3. Select publicly-held companies for comparison.

Selection of appropriate publicly-held companies for comparison with the company being appraised is next required. The list should be as extensive as possible, because further analysis may necessitate dropping a number of the concerns initially selected as not being adequately comparable.

There is an abundance of financial information on all publicly-traded companies. The most commonly used sources are services such as *Moody's* and *Standard and Poor's*. These can be found in most public libraries, in college or university libraries, and at stock brokerage offices. Daily issues of *The Wall Street Journal* and many general newspapers show price earnings ratios for stocks listed on the New York and American stock exchanges. *The Wall Street Journal* also lists many over-the-counter stocks, whose price earnings ratios can be developed with further research. Some stocks of a regional nature may be active primarily in regional exchanges, such as those located in Boston, Detroit, or Los Angeles. In addition, many less active over-the-counter stocks are not listed in the newspapers, but quotations and earnings data can be obtained from brokers who subscribe to the appropriate quotation services.

The publicly-traded companies selected for comparison may be taken from any of the stock markets. There is some benefit in selecting stocks which have a broad market and are actively traded. The broader the market, the more likely the stocks will reflect a typical investor opinion of the stock and of the industry. Thinly traded securities (i.e., those which are traded infrequently and in relatively small amounts) normally do not provide meaningful samples for developing market value comparisons.

It is desirable to avoid the selection of low-priced stocks. Such stocks often attract speculators, and other unusual circumstances may influence their price earnings ratios. The authors suggest choosing comparative stocks which sell for at least $5.00 per share.

VALUING THE PROFESSIONALLY-MANAGED BUSINESS

The product or service furnished by the comparative public companies should be as closely related as possible to the company being appraised. If there are no publicly-traded companies with comparable products or services, it will be necessary to select public companies which are subject to the same general economic influences and whose products or services could be expected to follow trends similar to the company being appraised. For instance, assume the company being valued manufactures a single line of plastic seals sold predominantly to automobile manufacturers. There are only two competitors, neither one of which is publicly traded. It probably would not be appropriate to merely compare this company with others in Standard Industrial Classification 3079 "Manufacturers of Miscellaneous Plastic Products," because this classification includes everything from manufacturers of aquarium accessories to manufacturers of plastic overshoes and window screens. More reliable results might be obtained by choosing public companies that manufacture other relatively small parts also sold predominantly to automobile manufacturers. Such companies would be subject to the same economic cycles as the company being appraised, at least in so far as their market is concerned.

Selling costs should be similar. There could be other factors affecting the manufacture of the product itself, such as price boosts in the cost of the material used by the publicly-owned firms, which boosts do not affect the plastic parts made by the subject company; or there may be pending technological changes which are dissimilar. If these latter factors are important, it may be necessary to look further for comparable public companies, perhaps ending up with publicly-traded manufacturers of parts sold to automobile manufacturers which use different materials from those just selected. If the company is diversified in its products and customers and if there are no public companies for direct comparison, a similar process may have to be followed for each line of products. That is, it may be necessary to select similar but not identical manufacturers from more than one industry.

The foregoing is by no means a comprehensive description of all of the considerations necessary in choosing comparable companies, but the appropriate line of reasoning is suggested.

In some cases, geographic location may influence a particular industry, making it preferable to find comparative companies operating in the same or a similar geographic area. One instance might be a home builder. Publicly-owned companies are admittedly not plentiful in this industry, but if the company being appraised is a home builder in Maine, it is obvious that a much better comparison could be made with publicly-owned home builders operating in New England than with those operating in California. Likewise, a public company whose profits are strongly influenced by its foreign markets might not be a suitable comparable for a closely-held firm which operates almost exclusively in the domestic market, even if the products of the two firms are similar.

Extreme differences in sales volume between public companies in the same line as the company being valued will be a reason to reject them as comparables.

VALUING THE PROFESSIONALLY-MANAGED BUSINESS

On the other hand, differences in the number of employees alone would not be decisive.

The number of shareholders a public company has could be an influence in its selection. A closely-held company which markets its shares publicly, normally will not start out with millions of shareholders. It is more likely to count them in the thousands. On the other hand, as noted earlier, care should be exercised not to select public companies with markets which are too thin. The companies selected for comparison should not be giants, nor should their shares be infrequently traded.

Public companies with a history of extreme financial difficulties usually are not appropriate for comparison, unless the company being appraised has a similar history.

4. Collect necessary data on publicly-held companies.

Once the publicly-owned companies have been chosen, it is desirable to collect fairly comprehensive information on those finally selected. The latter phrase is important. Initially, one would select companies for potential comparison, compiling as long a list as possible. This list should then be screened. Companies that might at first glance look like good comparables may be discarded for some of the reasons cited under "3" above. The appraiser should at first collect only as much information as is necessary to weed non-comparable firms from his list.

Assuming the list has thus been reduced to those firms which will be used, it is suggested that wherever possible the following data be compiled on each company:

a. The most recent five years of income and balance sheet data should be put in comparative form, as will have been done for the company being appraised.
b. All available balance sheet data should be included.
c. Income statement data put into the comparative form should be summarized into the following categories:
 Gross Sales
 Net Sales
 Cost of Goods Sold
 Gross Profit
 Expense Items
 Operating Profit
 Other Income
 Other Expenses
 Net Profit Before Taxes
 Income Taxes
 Net Profit After Taxes
 Dividend Payments

VALUING THE PROFESSIONALLY-MANAGED BUSINESS

In connection with the foregoing, it is desirable to obtain expenses broken down into manufacturing expense, selling expense, and general and administrative expense. Within these categories, also obtain interest and depreciation expense. Any unusual income or expense items should be noted. If there are any special matters affecting income taxes, such as loss carry-forwards, these should be noted. The form of dividends should be described; that is, whether dividends are paid in stock or in cash.

d. Equity capital should be classified, showing the number of shares of each class of preferred and common outstanding for each of the five years. Any subordinated debentures should be noted.

e. The high, low, and average price at which each class of stock traded should be compiled for each year.

f. Any other information deemed pertinent for comparative purposes should be noted.

g. The same ratios developed for the company being appraised should be obtained or computed for the public companies. It may be desirable to compile these figures for *each* of the five years, both for the public companies and for the company being valued. In all cases, the price earnings ratios should be compiled for each year for the public companies. The use of five years of ratios is desirable to see how closely the various public companies correlate with one another. If similar ratios are evident, and especially if the price earnings ratios are reasonably close to one another, the validity of the block of companies selected for comparison is established. If there are some dissimilarities in the price earnings ratios for some of the five years, the detailed comparative data and other ratios may help to explain it.

5. Select an appropriate price earnings ratio.

After consideration of the data described above and after comparison of this information with similar data on the company being appraised, a price earnings ratio can be selected. The ratio to be used for the subject company would be chosen because, in the appraiser's judgment, it represents a consolidation of the external and internal factors that would probably affect the company were its stock publicly traded. In the selection process, the appraiser would weigh the fact that a 100% interest is being valued in the subject company, whereas the market data was based on fractional interests. He would also consider all of the positive and negative characteristics of the company being valued, including but not limited to its financial situation, management strengths and weaknesses, market mix, its prospects for increasing, declining, or level profits, and its reputation.

As was noted earlier, the price earnings ratio selected may be applied to either unadjusted or adjusted earnings. If unadjusted earnings are to be used, the price earnings ratio selected will be different from that applied to the adjusted earnings.

VALUING THE PROFESSIONALLY-MANAGED BUSINESS

(See item 4 under "Limitations" under this method.) This is another way of saying one will either adjust the price earnings ratio derived from the market to compensate for the differences between the company being appraised and its publicly-owned counterparts, or he will use a market ratio and adjust the company data to more closely resemble the public companies. Since the authors recommend the latter approach, it is assumed the price earnings ratio selected under this method is one which reflects the market.

6. Apply the selected price earnings ratio.

The price earnings ratio method may be applied in different ways. Which approach is used depends upon the appraiser's judgment as to which will result in the most representative measure of market value at the date of valuation. One approach is to use a price earnings ratio developed on the basis of the most current year's data for the selected comparable companies. Another approach is to develop a separate price earnings ratio for each of the five years being analyzed, then pick one which is typical. A third approach is to compute these same five ratios and then consolidate them into a single ratio by simple averaging or by a weighted average.

There is considerable risk in using mathematical averages. A mathematical average may be a correct computation, but it may not be a good appraisal conclusion. *In the valuation of any property, including an operating enterprise, a unique asset is being considered for which there is no such thing as a 100% pure comparable, or an average which can be confidently applied.* If careful study indicates the price earnings ratio applicable to the company being appraised is equal to the highest ratio developed for any comparable company, then that ratio should be used. On the other hand, if the lowest ratio seems appropriate, that should be applied. An average ratio may fortuitously turn out to be proper, but the chances are it is just that - fortuitous.

Once the proper price earnings ratio has been selected, the authors suggest it be applied to the latest year's net profit after tax and after adjustments which make that year's profits reasonably comparable with those reported by public companies. In the terms used in this book, the price earnings ratio is applied to the "Adjusted Historical Net Profit After Tax" for the most current year.

Example

In the BLM case, Method 6 - Price Earnings Ratio - may be applied as follows:

Adjusted Historical Net Profit Before Tax (Exhibit 5, column 5)			$102,574
1. Deduct Applicable Corporate Taxes:			
State Corporate Income Tax		9,200	
Federal Corporate Income Tax		38,300	47,500
2. Adjusted Historical Net Profit After Tax			55,074
(Same as adjusted historical earnings)			

VALUING THE PROFESSIONALLY-MANAGED BUSINESS

    3.   Applicable Price Earnings Ratio   15

    4.   VALUE OF BLM (excludes land note & Fast Burger) $826,110

In the foregoing example, it can be assumed the applicable price earnings ratio of 15 resulted from an intensive industry study of the type suggested in the foregoing discussion. It is also pertinent to note that the case assumes owner-manager salaries are at competitive levels so that no adjustment is needed. Were this not true, a further adjustment should be made to the historical net profit before tax to provide proper salaries. Also, as was done under the previous methods discussed in this chapter, the resulting value for BLM, using the figures cited above, does not include the value of the land note and the Fast Burger operation.

[¶5.06-2] METHOD 7 - DIVIDEND CAPITALIZATION

Basic Concept

The first step is to select publicly-owned companies that are comparable to the firm being appraised. The same public companies used in connection with the Price Earnings Ratio Method (¶ 5.05-5) should be suitable for this method. A typical dividend yield rate is then selected for the comparable companies. That is, one rate should be chosen which would be reasonably representative for all of the comparable companies.[21]

The next step is to develop the "dividend paying capacity" of the company being appraised. This capacity to pay dividends may be more or less than the actual dividends paid, for the reasons cited below under "Limitations." The dividend paying capacity represents a judgment made by the appraiser as to how much of the company's earnings can appropriately be devoted to paying dividends.[22]

The final step is to divide the dividend paying capacity by the typical "dividend yield rate." In effect, the dividend yield rate is used as a capitalization rate (¶ 5.05-2.), the result being another measure of the value of the company's stock.

Limitations

In using this method to value closely-held companies, it becomes necessary to substitute the artificial measure called "dividend paying capacity" for the actual dividends used when this same method is applied to publicly-owned companies. How realistic the resulting value may be depends a great deal upon the judgment of the appraiser.

Comment

Actual dividends paid by closely-held firms tend to be meaningless in the valuation procedure, since they are almost never based on the capacity to pay. Closely-held companies operating as ordinary corporations usually disburse as little in divi-

VALUING THE PROFESSIONALLY-MANAGED BUSINESS

dends as possible for two reasons. First and foremost, there can be significant income tax savings through retaining the earnings in the corporation. Secondly, financing is not easy or inexpensive for privately-owned firms, so there is a strong incentive to retain as much self-generated capital as possible. On the other hand, if the firm operates as a pseudo corporation (¶ 1.04-4), income tax considerations often dictate paying the largest possible dividend, whether or not the company can really afford it. In view of these built-in biases, it becomes necessary to make changes in the general method by introducing dividend paying capacity.

In addition to the artificiality of dividend paying capacity, a number of adjustments to historic profits are required to remove distortions.[23] To this adjusted historical data is applied an unadjusted market rate, i.e., a dividend yield rate derived from the market. The applicability of unadjusted market data to adjusted company figures may cast some doubt on the validity of this technique.

Despite the limitations cited, the Dividend Capitalization Method has gained sufficient acceptance so that the appraiser is well advised to always test its applicability, even if this test only permits him to comment effectively on why it is not pertinent.

Advantages

The Internal Revenue Service maintains that dividend paying capacity is one of the important factors to be considered in valuing closely-held firms.[24] There are a number of court cases which support the concept of dividend capitalization.[25] Earnings and dividends are major factors considered by investors, and this method relates to both of these factors. The mathematical procedure is relatively simple and easy to explain. There is a great deal of information publicly available regarding the dividend yields of publicly-traded companies.

Procedure

Start with the adjusted historical net profit after tax as developed for the Price Earnings Ratio Method [¶5.06-1].[26] Determine how much of the earnings can logically be devoted to dividend payout.

The process of determining dividend paying capacity usually involves a number of considerations. It is necessary to analyze the firm's near term capital needs, not only for working capital but also for any probable expansion. There must be sufficient capital to provide for new technology, special advertising, new sales programs, additional personnel, acquisition of new plants, and expansion of existing facilities, to the extent these expenditures seem appropriate. In-depth interviews will be required with the owners and key managers, including but not limited to those handling accounting and finance. In no other way can the appraiser hope to arrive at a realistic judgment as to capital requirements.

VALUING THE PROFESSIONALLY-MANAGED BUSINESS

Part of the study should include an evaluation of past dividends paid by the company. These dividends generally should be analyzed in the light of past cash flow. This will probably require the development of adjusted historical cash flow, not only for the current year, but also for the previous four years. If no dividends have been paid, or dividends have been very modest, or if dividends appear excessive, the reasons for such non-typical payments should be noted and carefully considered.

The dividend payment history of the public companies chosen for comparison should be studied next. Such payouts are usually expressed as a percentage of earnings or cash flow. In some cases it may be helpful to develop a weighted average payout rate for the five year period for each comparative company. From this, a weighted average could be developed for all of the companies. Another approach would be to develop a weighted average payout rate for all comparable companies for each of the five years and then draw up a composite figure. If weighted averages appear to result in distorted figures, then simple averages or typical payment rates can be used. The objective is to arrive at a typical payout rate which can be defended as realistic and typical of the comparative companies so that this rate can be applied to the subject company's cash flow or earnings to arrive at a defensible dividend paying capacity for that company. Notice that the dividend payout rate is *not* the same as the dividend yield rate. The payout rate is the percentage of earnings or cash flow which the comparative companies typically disburse as dividends. Dividend yield rates are the ratio dividends paid bear to the market price of the stock of each comparative company.

A comparison should then be made between the dividend paying capacity of the firm being appraised, as determined from the industry study, and its actual dividend payments. If there appears to be a wide difference, satisfactory explanations should be garnered. For example, if comparable companies typically pay out 30% of their net profits after tax as dividends, and the company being valued has historically paid out only 10%, the appraiser should satisfy himself as to why this has occurred.

Once the dividend paying capacity has been settled upon, it is relatively simple to arrive at a theoretically proper dividend for the subject company. Carrying the above example further, if the subject company had after-tax earnings of $50,000 and its dividend paying capacity is accepted to be 30% of these earnings, the proper dividend would be $15,000 - i.e., $50,000 times 30%.

The final step is to divide the proper dividend for the subject company (in this case $15,000) by the industry dividend yield rate. If this yield rate were 4%, the company would have a value of $375,000, using this method.

Industry dividend yield rates are usually low, ranging from less than 1% to highs of 5% or 6%. This is a dangerous generalization, as yields will vary, depending upon market conditions, the economics of the particular industry, the avail-

VALUING THE PROFESSIONALLY-MANAGED BUSINESS

ability and cost of borrowed funds, and a multitude of other factors. However, it is reasonable to say that such rates appeared typical when this book was written.

When the industry dividend yield rate is computed, it is important to be certain that it is calculated on a basis consistent with the industry dividend payout rate. That is, if the payout rate was based on a weighted average of some type, then the yield rate should also be based on a similar weighted average.

Similarly, if a weighted average has been used in arriving at the industry payout rate and the industry yield rate, weighted averages should be used with the company earnings. That is, if a weighted average of five years has been used to develop the industry dividend payout and yield rates, a five year weighted average should be used for the company being appraised.

Example

Computation of the value of BLM Electronics, Inc., by Method 7 - Dividend Capitalization - is recapitulated as follows:

	Fiscal Year Ending				
	3-31-72	3-31-73	3-31-74	3-31-75	3-31-76
1. Net Profit Before Tax (Exhibit 5)	153,707	130,410	137,741	155,039	102,574
2. Deduct Corporate Taxes:					
State Corporate Income Tax	(11,682)	(9,911)	(12,397)	(13,954)	(9,200)
Federal Corporate Income Tax	(61,672)	(51,340)	(53,665)	(61,221)	(38,300)
3. Net Profit After Tax Earnings	80,353	69,159	71,679	79,864	55,074
4. Average Earnings					71,226
5. Dividend Paying Capacity Based on Comparable Firms:					
50% of Average Net Profit After Tax ($71,226 X 50%)					35,613
Dividend Paying Capacity, Rounded					36,000
6. Dividend Yield Rate Based on Comparable Firms					4%
7. VALUE OF BLM (Excludes land note & Fast Burger)					$900,000

The net profit before tax figures used above are adjusted historical profits as recorded in Exhibit 5 in Chapter 4. It can be assumed that a study of comparable companies indicated that a simple five-year average of net profits after tax provided the best basis for computing dividend payment rates and dividend yields.

VALUING THE PROFESSIONALLY-MANAGED BUSINESS

Since simple averages based on a five year period were used for the comparative companies, the same type of average was used for BLM. Thus, the total of the net profits after tax shown on line 3 above was $356,129. Dividing this figure by 5 years results in average net profits after tax of $71,226. The comparable companies typically paid out 50% of their average after-tax profits as dividends. Using this measure, BLM had a dividend paying capacity of $35,613. Using the alternative test, the total cash flow for five years as shown on Line 5 above was $453,688. Dividing this figure by 5 years results in average annual cash flow of $90,738. The comparable companies paid out 40% of their average cash flow in dividends. Using this approach, BLM had a dividend paying capacity of $36,295. Since the results of the two methods were quite close, each result was rounded to the nearest $1,000, resulting in a consolidated dividend paying capacity of $36,000.

The final step was to use the dividend yield rate derived from the study of comparative firms to capitalize the dividend paying capacity. In other words, $36,000 was divided by .04, resulting in a value for BLM of $900,000, using this method. Once again, this value does not include the land note and the Fast Burger operation, which are separately valued.

It is pertinent to note that the actual dividends paid by BLM were far in excess of its computed dividend paying capacity; namely, $100,000 per year in actual dividends versus a capacity to pay of $36,000. Dividends were abnormally high because BLM is a Pseudo or Subchapter S corporation. If most of the earnings had not been withdrawn, there would be a danger that undistributed earnings could be locked in and subjected to double taxation at a later date. Also, since the corporation itself pays no taxes, dividends must be sufficient to allow the owners to pay their individual taxes on the earnings. There are indications that this heavy withdrawal has steadily impaired BLM's liquidity, and it probably will have to borrow funds and reduce dividends in the future. The difference between the average cash flow of $83,794 and the $36,000 dividend paying capacity is about $48,000 per year, which the appraiser feels is realistic retention requirement for debt service and future capital needs.

[¶5.06-3] METHOD 8 - RATIO OF MARKET PRICE TO BOOK EQUITY

The final approach suggested is one of several types of market data comparisons which may be utilized in developing an indicated value of an operating business. The method is a ratio of market price to book equity of publicly-traded stocks.

VALUING THE PROFESSIONALLY-MANAGED BUSINESS

Basic Concept

The procedure involves gathering data on the book equity and average market price of publicly-traded companies in comparable industries. The data utilized would usually be from the same sources as suggested for Method 6 - Price Earnings Ratio [¶5.06-1] and Method 7 - Dividend Capitalization [¶5.06-2]. If a sufficient sampling of publicly-traded stock information can be obtained, the relationship of the book equity on a per share basis to the average market price per share of the stock is computed as a composite ratio. The ratio of the individually selected companies, or the companies as a composite, is applied to the book value of the appraised company to develop an indicated value of the equity in the appraised business.

Limitations

Often suitable public companies cannot be found for the purpose of developing comparative data. Publicly-traded stocks often represent companies which are considerably larger than the appraised business and usually have a wider product mix. In addition, many involve divergent business operations, such as a large conglomerate, and have no parallel with the appraised business. Also, the public company has an established market. These are basically the same disadvantages discussed previously with the price earnings ratio and dividend capitalization methods. There are, however, some additional limitations. One of the major ones is using book values for comparative purposes. As has been discussed in a previous chapter, depreciated book costs are usually not the same as market values. Furthermore, companies have different policies regarding how fixed assets are handled. The fixed asset category can have a major impact on book tangible net worth. For example, one company may operate primarily with leased equipment and another owns all or most of its equipment. Another operates with assets that have been greatly depreciated for income tax purposes. Depreciation methods vary widely, too. One company uses straight line depreciation and another takes advantage of maximum accelerated methods.

Another important consideration is at any time, the market price of a publicly-traded stock is not necessarily the same as the true investment (market) value.

Advantages

This or any similar market comparison method has some validity if a large sampling of data can be obtained. Very often there will be compensating differences that tend to even out on a weighted-average basis. The resulting ratio can be applied with careful judgment and common sense. The result is another expression of the attitude of the investing public in a particular industry.

VALUING THE PROFESSIONALLY-MANAGED BUSINESS

Procedure

Utilizing an appropriate source of market data, the ratio of market price to net book equity is computed. As broad a sampling as possible should be utilized. For BLM, the same publicly-traded comparative companies used for price earnings ratio, dividend yield and overall capitalization rates have been used for developing the ratio of market price to book equity.

The aggregate price has been used in this instance. If there are preferred or other classes of stock, some adjustments might be required.

The aggregate price, or the price per share, is divided by the total book equity or the book equity per share. Intangibles of the comparative companies should be eliminated before the ratio is computed.

For BLM, a composite ratio computed from the market data has been used for the purpose of estimating an indicated market value of the equity in this business by use of the ratio of market price to book equity method.

The composite ratio from this data of 1.73 is used for BLM.[27] This ratio is multiplied by the adjusted historical tangible net worth (See Column 2, page 81) of $560,353. When 1.73 is multiplied by this historical tangible net worth, the resulting indicated market value of BLM is $969,411.

Example

Comparative Company	Aggregate Market Price (000)	Book Equity (000)	Ratio
1	$ 15,268	$ 10,550	1.45
2	200,413	100,710	1.99
3	68,026	38,220	1.78
4	93,263	70,650	1.32
5	56,334	30,290	1.86
Composite			1.73
Average			1.68
Range			1.32-1.99

VALUING THE PROFESSIONALLY-MANAGED BUSINESS

[¶5.06-4] MARKET PRICE PREMIUMS

The prices paid for factional interests in publicly-traded stocks do not always represent the true investment (market) value of those shares assuming the entire company, or at least a majority interest, is being acquired. Very often a premium wil be paid for a controlling interest. This is vividly illustrated with most tender offers for publicly-traded stocks when a company is offering to buy back its own shares (going private) or when another company or an individual is offering to acquire a substantial interest in a publicly-traded company. Tender offers are usually higher than the going price per share in the market for the same stock.

In appraising a closely-held company for the purpose of estimating the market value of a 100% stockholder equity, consideration should be given to such premiums if any are shown. This is not to suggest premiums are always appropriate and indeed in the BLM case example, no premium has been applied for a 100% interest when developing value indications by the price earnings ratio method and the dividend capitalization method. However, an appraisal cannot be complete unless consideration is given to all market influences.

[¶5.06-5] SUMMARY

The valuation of an operating enterprise is much more subjective than the valuation of tangibles, such as real property and machinery. This is particularly true when the business is closely-held with no substantial market for its shares. Despite this, a number of appraisal techniques have gained recognition and acceptance as being suitable for such valuation. They provide a framework within which the appraiser can accumulate facts in an orderly manner and form a basis for his value conclusions. This chapter describes eight such techniques that can be applied to professionally-managed businesses. Two are based principally on the company's balance sheet, five are based on earnings and cash flow and one involves an analysis of market prices and their relationship to book values. Another method, not discussed in the text, involves the analysis of sales of interests in the company being appraised. Unfortunately, adequate details on the transfer of closely-held companies is difficult to obtain unless that company has been acquired by a public company where information must be disclosed to the Securities and Exchange Commission. However, when closely-held companies are purchased by private individuals or other closely-held businesses, the data is not usually public.

While not normally applicable to the larger, professionally-managed businesses, a check should also be made for any market formulas that may be commonly used in selling companies within the industry.

The first method discussed relates value to net worth per books. This is seldom useful without adjustment. Therefore, the second method shows how book figures can be adjusted to arrive at tangible net worth at market. Both of these methods, however, fail to consider earnings and intangibles such as goodwill. The third

VALUING THE PROFESSIONALLY-MANAGED BUSINESS

method, called the excess earnings method, interrelates net worth, earnings and goodwill. The fourth method involves a projection of the net profit the company can expect in the near future. Alternate business opportunity investments such as publicly-traded stocks in the industry may be used as a basis for developing a capitalization rate to be applied to the net profit. Alternately, a summation rate may be used beginning with a safe yield rate represented by quality stocks, government bonds, certificates of deposit and so forth. Added to this rate are factors for the additional risks of a closely-held company such as narrow product mix and lack of liquidity.

The fifth method, called discounted cash flow, requires a projection of cash flow for the company in the future. However, it is one of the least reliable methods and should not be utilized alone, but supported with other techniques. The sixth method is an adaptation of one widely used for publicly-owned companies, the price earnings ratio. Under this method, a price earnings ratio is selected that is typical for those companies. This ratio is used as a multiplier applied to the historical after-tax earnings of the company. These historical earnings often must be adjusted to remove biases introduced by the closely-held nature of the company. If not corrected, such biases would make the price earnings ratios derived from publicly-owned companies difficult to apply to closely-held counterparts. A comment is also made by the authors on premiums often paid for companies when a tender offer is made for a public company. Such attempts to acquire a signigicant interest in a publicly-traded company often result in premiums and this market data must not be overlooked. However, in the examples in this text, no premium has been added. A method called dividend capitalization requires an analysis of publicly-owned companies that are reasonably comparable to the firm being appraised to determine the usual percentage of earnings these companies pay out in dividends and to determine their typical dividend yield rate. With this information, dividend paying capacity of the subject company is determined by applying the public dividend payment percentages to the company's most recent after-tax earnings or several years' average. However, the appraiser must make appropriate adjustments for consideration of the true cash needs of the business. The dividend capitalization method should be considered if practical, but it is not always a suitable technique. Many closely-held businesses cannot truly afford to pay dividends. Very often these companies depend on all their earnings for future capital requirements. Public companies, on the other hand, are more under the scrutiny of the public investor who may demand dividends. Finally, one other market data comparison technique is described, ratio of market price to book equity, Method 8. This is one of several market data comparative techniques that could be considered. In addition, consideration should be given to possible formulas used by the industry (usually more applicable to smaller companies), offers to purchase or actual purchases of interest in the company being appraised and comparisons with other comparable closely-held companies that have sold.

CHAPTER 6

DECISIONS! DECISIONS!

*The prologues are over. It is question, now,
Of final belief . . . It is time to choose.*

WALLACE STEVENS - 1879-1955

TOPICS DISCUSSED IN THIS CHAPTER

[¶6.01] — **The Need for Correlation**

[¶6.02] — **All Assets Have Not Been Valued**

[¶6.03] — **Valuation of Other Tangible Assets**

[¶6.03-1] — **Method 9 - Note Valuation**
Basic Concept - Limitations - Advantages
Procedure - Example

[¶6.04] — **The Correlation Process**

[¶6.05] — **Summary**

CHAPTER 6

DECISIONS! DECISIONS!

[¶6.01] THE NEED FOR CORRELATION

In the previous chapters, eight valuation methods were discussed that can be applied to professionally-managed businesses. Each method used a different approach to value and predictably resulted in a different value for BLM Electronics, Inc. The values ranged from $560,000 to $969,411. If each approach has some validity for BLM, it becomes essential to reconcile the differences and arrive at an expression of value that correlates the methods. Such a divergence of results is not unusual, nor need it be disturbing when put in the proper perspective.

[¶6.02] ALL ASSETS HAVE NOT BEEN VALUED

One reason for the wide divergence in values is the two balance sheet techniques (Methods 1 and 2) omit consideration of the Belmur Process and of the explosion-proof Lamp Patent (¶3.02-8). For purposes of these methods, the process and the patent are to be separately valued. It is natural, therefore, such omissions would cause variations in indicated values between the methods discussed.

Each of the other seven methods omitted the value of the land sale note (See ¶3.02-20, item 4) and the value of the Fast Burger operation (See ¶3.02-5) because these assets were to be valued separately from the seven methods.

[¶6.03] VALUATION OF OTHER TANGIBLE ASSETS

In many business appraisals it is necessary to set a market value on certain tangible assets. In the BLM case, a market value appraisal was made of machinery and equipment, furniture and fixtures, leasehold improvements, tools and dies. The methods used were not described because they are outside the scope of this book. Approaches to the valuation of accounts receivable and inventories were discussed at ¶4.02-3. These methods were not described in detail because such a discussion would tend to divert the reader from the main thrust of the book, and the suitable methods are widely known to most accountants and appraisers.

Essential to the appraisal of the entire BLM enterprise, however, is the valuation of the land sale note discussed at item 4 of ¶3.02-20. This asset is of importance to the whole BLM appraisal. The valuation of similar notes may arise often enough to warrant a brief discussion of one acceptable method for appraising them.

DECISIONS! DECISIONS!

[¶6.03-1] METHOD 9 - NOTE VALUATION

Basic Concept

Notes frequently arise from the sale of a business asset. The rate of interest applicable to such notes tends to be below the market rate for so-called hard money loans. This is especially true of land sales where the seller takes an installment note. Where one might have to pay 10% - 12% to borrow money from a bank to buy real estate, the seller is in a less advantageous position and may be forced to charge only 7% - 8%. The buyer assumes the seller is making a profit on the real estate, and hence he is unwilling to pay the going market rate for what amounts to a loan from the seller. Regional patterns often develop as well, where all sellers of land in a given area customarily apply a given interest rate on notes resulting from their sales of land.

Given this situation, it is reasonable to assume that a note arising from the sale of a business asset—especially land— probably carries a below-market interest rate. Were the note to be sold to an investor, it would have to be discounted to provide a satisfactory yield. It is often possible to determine at what yields similar notes are selling. Then by reference to financial tables, it is possible to determine how much discount should be applied to the note being valued.

Limitations

Each business asset or parcel of land has some distinct qualities which impair its comparability to other like assets. Of even greater importance, each debtor has different payment habits and different amounts of net worth and financial stability. If the note resulting from the sale is collateralized by a lien on the asset sold, this asset may be worth more or less than other similar assets. Whether the note is secured or not, the debtor is of prime importance, and he may not be comparable to debtors in other similar asset purchases.

Advantages

The method is relatively simple and well recognized. If the note is seasoned—i.e., the debtor has been paying regularly for some time—he becomes reasonably comparable with other debtors who have demonstrated their payment capability and intentions. Yield rates on similar seasoned notes are therefore reasonably good measures of the yield which must be provided on the subject note.

Procedure

If there is an active market for comparable notes, as would be the case with land notes secured by first or second mortgages, the yield rates should first be determined on the sale of such notes to investors. In many states, there are brokers in such notes listed in the telephone book.

As much information as possible should be collected on the other sales to be

DECISIONS! DECISIONS!

certain they are truly comparable. Was land sold in comparable sales also unimproved? Were the notes seasoned for about the same time? Were all payments current?

Having determined the desired yield rate, it is possible to determine the market value of the note from financial tables. See the example below.

Example

The BLM land sale note had a balance due at March 31, 1976 of $297,648, payable at the rate of $31,200 per annum including interest at 8%. After a careful check of other sales of land, it is found that the BLM note is competitive in interest rate with other such sales. Notes seasoned for a similar period also secured by unimproved urban land were being actively traded at discounts sufficient to yield the buyer of the note 12% per annum.

The first step is to determine the Annual Constant percentage. In the BLM case, the Annual Constant is 10.48%. ($31,200 per year payments divided by $297,648 principal balance due) This rate includes 8% interest and means the loan will pay off in 19 years.

Next, by reference to published financial tables, find the Annual Constant percentage necessary to amortize a 12% loan in 19 years. This percentage is 13.58%.

To determine the market price of the note discounted to yield 12%, divide 10.48 by 13.58, which equals 77.2%. Therefore, the BLM note of $297,648 has a market value of $229,784 ($297,648 times 77.2%). The rounded value is $230,000.

[¶6.04] THE CORRELATION PROCESS

A correlation of the eight methods used to value BLM can best be summarized in tabular form. To these values developed in Chapter 5 are added, where appropriate, the value of the land note as computed above at ¶6.03-1 together with the value of other omitted assets. It is pertinent to note that the Fast Burger operation was valued using Methods 10 and 11. The Belmur process was appraised by Method 13, and the explosion-proof lamp patent by Method 14. All of these methods are described in later chapters, and only the final value determinations are reflected in this chapter to illustrate the correlation process necessary between the results of the basic business appraisal methods.

DECISIONS! DECISIONS!

BLM - CORRELATION OF VALUATION METHODS

Method	Value	Fast Burger	Land Note	Belmur Process	Patent	Total Value
1	560,353	58,000	230,000	75,000	15,000	938,353
2	657,899	58,000	230,000	75,000	15,000	1,035,899
3	959,324	58,000	230,000	75,000	15,000	1,337,324
4	844,762	58,000	230,000	—	—	1,132,762
5	711,512	58,000	230,000	—	—	999,512
6	826,110	58,000	230,000	—	—	1,114,110
7	900,000	58,000	230,000	—	—	1,188,000
8	969,411	—	—	—	—	969,411

The methods referred to by number above, together with the paragraph references in the text where they are described, are as follows: Method 1 - Net Worth Per Books [¶5.04-1], Method 2 - Tangible Net Worth at Market [¶5.04-2], Method 3 - Excess Earnings [¶5.05-1], Method 4 - Capitalization of Net Profit [¶5.05-3], Method 5 - Discounted Cash Flow [¶5.05-4], Method 6 - Price Earnings Ratio [¶5.06-1], Method 7 - Dividend Capitalization [¶5.06-2] and Method 8 - Ratio of Market Price to Book Equity [¶5.06-3].

The value of BLM as computed by Method 1 gives no consideration to goodwill, and yet the firm obviously has goodwill, as proven by the Excess Earnings Method. It also is based strictly on book values that differ from market value. Therefore, the value so developed, even when adjusted for the omitted assets (Fast Burger, the land note, the Belmur Process and the Lamp Patent) is too low at approximately $938,000. This approach is therefore discarded.

The tangible net worth at market is much more realistic when the omitted items are added back, but the value of about $1,036,000 does not include goodwill. Therefore, this value seems low.

The excess earnings method, Method 3, has considered all elements of value when expanded to include the four separately valued assets, the Fast Burger operation, land note, Belmur Process, Lamp Patent and goodwill. It is tangible net worth at market plus goodwill.

The value of approximately $1,132,762 developed by Method 4 - Capitalization of Net Profit, provides a fairly realistic measure of the value of the business when compared to alternative stock investment opportunities. It should be noted the total income stream has been valued except for income from the Fast Burger operation and the land note. This means the Belmur Process, Lamp Patent and goodwill have all been rolled into the final value. The result is a value for BLM that should be given serious consideration.

DECISIONS! DECISIONS!

Method 5, Discounted Cash Flow, also provides a value for everything except Fast Burger and the land note. When adjusted for these assets, the result of $999,512 is very close to the tangible net worth at market, Method 2. This suggests that it probably does not give adequate consideration to the value of goodwill. This is understandable, since Method 5 assumes an arbitrary five-year life for BLM, whereas it most probably will continue more of less indefinitely beyond that period. Therefore, this method appears to result in an unrealistically low value. As such, it should be set aside.

Method 6, Price Earnings Ratio, also considers indirectly all elements of the business except the separately-valued Fast Burger operation and the land note. When adjusted for these omissions, the value of $1,114,110 for BLM provides for some goodwill value. The method includes many judgments and assumptions but it also reflects investor attitudes.

Method 7, Dividend Capitalization, when adjusted to add in the value of the Fast Burger operation results in a value slightly higher than developed by Method 4 and lower than Method 3. The many assumptions that are necessary cause the method to be somewhat questionable, yet the value developed falls between those developed by two plausible methods. As a value indicator, this approach has proven useful.

Method 8 results in an overall company value of $969,411 that appears to be somewhat low. The disadvantages of developing a market value based upon a book value ratio have been discussed. It may be the sampling of five comparative companies used for the development of the ratio is too small for a proper value indication. Only secondary weight is given to the result of Method 8.

In conclusion, the methods given most weight indicate BLM is worth somewhere between $1,100,000 and $1,300,000. Of the remaining four methods, the tangible net worth at market method would probably result in a similar range were some reasonable measure of goodwill added to the tangible worth. Two of the remaining three methods have defects when applied to this company; Net Worth Per Books omits economic values and goodwill and the Discounted Cash Flow method assumes an arbitrary liquidation.

On balance, therefore, the appraiser concludes BLM is worth $1,133,000. Each of the methods that resulted in this range of values is reviewed and Method 4, Capitalization of Net Profit, is relied on. The result of this method appears to express a realistic value for BLM supported by the value indications of Methods 2, 3, 6 and 7.

DECISIONS! DECISIONS!

[¶6.05] **SUMMARY**

The values developed in Chapter 5 made it obvious the results needed close analysis. However, analysis reveals the values that were developed are much closer together than would be indicated if book value based methods are put in proper perspective.

A method for valuing notes receivable, Method 9, is discussed because it is pertinent to the BLM case and there is often a need to value notes in business appraisals.

The process of correlating the value results obtained by the eight business valuation methods discussed in Chapter 5 entails analysis of the logic behind each approach as applied to the company being valued. If several methods all support a single value, which seldom happens, the appraiser has several ways to support his value opinion. On the other hand, if one method stands out as the best for the company involved, this single method should be used. The appraiser should not be tempted into arbitrarily applying mathematical averages.

CHAPTER 7

VALUING THE PERSONALLY-MANAGED BUSINESS

It's a fine thing to have a finger pointed at one, and to hear people say "That's the man."

PERSIUS 34 - 62 A.D.

TOPICS DISCUSSED IN THIS CHAPTER

[¶7.01]	—	Special Problems
[¶7.02]	—	The Basic Limits of Value
[¶7.03]	—	The Search for Formulas
[¶7.04]	—	The Typical Formula Approach
[¶7.04-1	—	Method 10 - Asset-Based Formula Basic Concept - Limitations - Advantages Procedure - Example
[¶7.04-2]	—	Method 11 - Sales-Based Formula Basic Concept - Limitations - Advantages Procedure - Example
[¶7.04-3]	—	Correlation of Formula Methods
[¶7.04-4]	—	Flexibility of Formulas
[¶7.04-5]	—	Formula Guidelines
[¶7.04-6]	—	What To Do When No Formulas Emerge
[¶7.05]	—	Examples of Businesses Sold By Formula
[¶7.05-1]	—	Auto Repair Garages
[¶7.05-2]	—	Liquor Stores
[¶7.05-3]	—	Insurance Agencies
[¶7.05-4]	—	Accounting Practices
[¶7.05-5]	—	Legal Practices
[¶7.05-6]	—	Advertising Agencies
[¶7.05-7]	—	Convenience Groceries
[¶7.05-8]	—	Bars and Cocktail Lounges
[¶7.05-9]	—	Newspapers and Periodicals
[¶7.05-10]	—	Auto Wrecking Yards
[¶7.05-11]	—	Funeral Homes
[¶7.06]	—	Real Estate-Related Businesses
[¶7.06-1]	—	Hotels and Motels
[¶7.06-2]	—	Nursing Homes
[¶7.06-3]	—	Mobile Home Parks
[¶7.07]	—	Summary

CHAPTER 7

VALUING THE PERSONALLY-MANAGED BUSINESS

[¶ 7.01]   **SPECIAL PROBLEMS**

The vast majority of personally-managed businesses are single service, cash and carry, general retail or wholesale enterprises. A significant minority also includes various types of professional operations, such as legal, medical, or accounting practices. As business activities, nearly all are relatively simple. However, such firms can be difficult and time-consuming to appraise.

A significant problem can be ferreting out the facts as to exactly what the business really owns, what it owes, and what profit it is really producing. Audited financial statements are seldom available, and the quality of record-keeping is often, to put it charitably, an aberration. Cash basis accounting is commonplace. So the appraiser frequently is faced with a considerable task in seeking to arrive at adjusted historical balance sheets, income statements, and pro forma profits which are truly representative of the business.

The foregoing may be countered by those who would contend that a careful analysis of the business is unnecessary. It is common knowledge that most firms of this type tend to sell on the basis of a market-derived formula. Frequently, this formula will be a multiplier applied to sales or billings. Thus, if one can reasonably ascertain the sales and can discover the commonly accepted multiplier, why spend all the time and effort to go deeper into the operation?

The answer has several facets. First, only an unsophisticated buyer or seller would rely strictly on such a formula. It is merely a starting point for negotiation with numerous deviations being both typical and plausible. Secondly, most such formulas are two step. The first step may involve a multiple of sales, but somewhere along the line a second step is used which also weighs profitability in some manner. Third, there may be no discernable formulas in existence. It may be rumored that firms in a certain industry sell strictly by formula, but a closer analysis may show this to be untrue. Or there may not even be the hint of a formula. Finally, if ever a business is likely to be individualistic and not conform to pattern, it would be the personally-managed firm. Such businesses tend to be an extension of the lifestyle of the owner. Its goodwill is integrally bound up in his personality.

This is not to say that the appraiser should ignore the existence of market formulas or fail to search for them. In fact, where none appears to exist, he may even try to evolve one of his own from a study of comparable sales. He will always want to check for the existence of market formulas. The point is that such formulas, whether existing or derived, are merely indicators of value. Just as in the case of professionally managed firms, no one appraisal method can be taken to be a final conclusion as to value, so no formula can be considered the final measure of value for the personally-managed business.

VALUING THE PERSONALLY-MANAGED BUSINESS

[¶7.02] **THE BASIC LIMITS OF VALUE**

There is no universal formula which can be applied to all personally-managed businesses, or even to all those within a given industry classification. However, there is a universal logic that can be applied. The first element of this logic tends to set a floor on the value of the business. The second element establishes a basic ceiling.

The floor value usually is the tangible net worth of the business, with its assets and liabilities revalued to their economic worth. Put another way, the floor tends to be the tangible net worth developed according to the concepts discussed at ¶ 5.04-2. If the assets do not contribute to a viable going concern, the value of assets may be best represented by a liquidation value.

Nevertheless, this floor may be breached in some cases, with the liquidation value of assets substituted for their market values. While the business may evidence a reasonable living for the owner, it may produce no more. In such an instance, a prudent buyer would pay no more than liquidation value, because it seems evident the business will steadily decline and even the owner's living will be in jeopardy. For a business to continue its existence, it must generate earnings over and above the owner's living requirements. Stores and offices need modernization from time to time. Depreciating machinery and equipment must be replaced. In most retail and wholesale establishments, money is needed for advertising in order to hold the clientele. Usually, too, a business can not simply float. It must grow and expand and keep in step with the times. It is not unusual to find owners who ignore the prospective decline and rationalize the low profitability by stressing their independent status. Most buyers, however, do not wish to be independent today and on welfare tomorrow.

At the other extreme, there is a logical ceiling to the value of the business. That ceiling is usually a price which is no more than the number of years investors are willing to await the full return of invested capital. The pro forma earnings would be developed according to the techniques discussed at ¶ 4.04. The reasoning behind the ceiling is as logical as that behind the floor value. Given the uncertainties of the future with respect to any business, including ever-changing economic conditions and constantly revised tax laws, few well-informed buyers are willing to pay for more than a few years of future profits. For example, if it would take five years to recover the investment only then would it start to return on the investment. In fact, it probably would be considerably longer before the return materialized, because the five years of earnings will be taxable to the buyer.

VALUING THE PERSONALLY-MANAGED BUSINESS

Where between the floor and the ceiling a business is actually valued is a matter of negotiation which is influenced by a number of factors. A business which produces only a living to its owner and provides the minimal excess earnings necessary to continue its existence may still command some premium over tangible net worth. This generally happens when the firm has some special value to a buyer—perhaps a non-economic value. Thus, some people will pay a premium to buy a business college, because there is a measure of prestige involved in being a college president. A considerably different consideration might cause one restaurant to command a slight premium over tangible net worth, whereas others with identical profits could not. There are those who would give such a bonus for a restaurant which served only breakfast and lunch rather than one of identical profitability which served three meals a day. The reason? The owner can work shorter hours. Such non-economic premiums tend to price the marginal business only a little above the tangible net worth floor.

The primary factors which govern the level of value of a business are economic. How long has the business been established? What has been its earnings history? How transferable is its goodwill? How easy is it for new competitors to enter the field and lure away valued customers? All of these and similar questions must be considered.

When the business being valued has a poor earnings history, the appraiser should analyze it carefully to ascertain the cause of the trouble. The problem may be poor management, or other factors which could be corrected. If so, and if it would be reasonable to presume that prospective buyers would have the ability to make the business reach reasonable levels of earnings, pro forma earnings should be adjusted to reflect this fact. Thus, although past earnings do not justify it, the outlook for the firm may be such that a buyer would be willing to pay a premium over tangible net worth, because the business is pre-assembled, start up costs are behind, and there is a going concern value.

On the other hand, if a business is new and not well established, there may be no premium, even though it has made profits well in excess of the minimum necessary to provide the owner with a living. The newness of the business means its continued profitability and existence have not been proven, so the buyer may be justified in paying only for its tangible net worth. At the other extreme, there are many instances where a business is well established and very profitable, but it still commands no premium because it is too closely tied to a single owner. When the owner departs, the business goes with him. This often happens in the sale of a medical practice. One way around the problem is to enter into a contract with the seller to remain for a given period. In such an instance, however, the business may still be worth only its tangible net worth, and any premium is really paid for the employment contract.

Within certain limits, the length of time a personally-managed firm has been established may be of lesser importance than other factors. If it is very new, it is

VALUING THE PERSONALLY-MANAGED BUSINESS

adversely affected. If it is very old, such as 50 years in the same location, there may be added value. Between such extremes, however, the age of the business may have little effect. For instance, it is not unusual to find two similar restaurants with similar volume selling for the same price, even though one is two years old and the other has existed for ten years. The former might command a slight premium if its equipment were newer, but that may be all.

On the other hand, the transferability of the goodwill of a business can be extremely important, not only with respect to the individuals involved, as cited for a medical practice, but also with respect to the nature of the business itself. Thus, an insurance agency will generally sell for a much higher premium over tangible net worth than would an advertising agency. The insurance agency receives premiums on past business more or less automatically, without personal involvement. Many of its customers tend to renew their policies because it is the easiest thing to do and the service is needed. Advertising agencies, however, tend to handle a few ads or an ad campaign for a client, and then they must look for new clients because the campaign served its purpose, or it was not successful, or the extremes of competition force an old agency to be replaced by a new one.

In summary, the basic limits of value for personally-managed businesses are:
1. A floor of tangible net worth at market value, if the business produces enough profits to assure its owner a living and to perpetuate its existence.
2. A ceiling of five times pro forma profits before tax but after a salary allowance to the owner.

Where in between these extremes the price falls depends on any special non-economic values the business involves, how well established it is, how profitable it is, and, particularly, how transferable its goodwill may be.

[¶7.03] THE SEARCH FOR FORMULAS

If no goodwill were involved, the pricing of personally-managed businesses would be relatively simple. The appraiser would determine the tangible net worth at market for the business, and that would be the selling price. For many small, personally-managed businesses this approach is satisfactory, because there is no goodwill. This is true because the firm is too new, earns too little in profits, or the goodwill it has is not transferable. However, for a significant number of such firms there is transferable goodwill, and a market established formula may enter into pricing it. Or the business may change hands at the equivalent of its tangible net worth, but the market arrives at this result by a different approach. If formulas exist which are widely used in selling firms within the industry of which the subject business is a part, the appraiser must discover these formulas and use them in his valuation, if only to prove they do not fully apply. Or he may find that no such formulas exist, but that he can better explain and justify his values by deriving formulas of his own from market data.

VALUING THE PERSONALLY-MANAGED BUSINESS

A good beginning point in the search is to talk to people who have been involved in the transfer of similar businesses. These contacts would often include business brokers, buyers, sellers, and trade organizations. Such parties may be located by referring to classified advertisements in local newspapers, trade journals, the yellow pages of telephone directories, and by discussions with bankers. Some bankers may themselves be knowledgeable as to the prices and conditions applicable to the sale of many businesses, or they may be able to suggest knowledgeable business brokers. As broad a survey as possible should be made of such sources by telephone and by personal interviews.

Only in a limited number of cases will the appraiser find an existing formula neatly applicable to the business being valued. More often than not he will have to create his own formula from the market information he has assembled. If sufficient research is undertaken, it will generally provide enough data so that he can develop such a formula if he chooses. Even if a rule of thumb method for valuing a particular business is uncovered, the appraiser should view it with suspicion and test it with enough factual data from actual sales to satisfy himself as to its validity. Also, as stated earlier, he will usually use such a formula as only one test of value.

In turning to the market for data, one should realize that despite some indications to the contrary (i.e., the lists of business opportunities in most daily papers), the marketplace is not highly organized as to valuation methods. The price of any closely-held business is subjective and as such may vary from logical norms. The final price is determined by negotiation between buyers and sellers who arrive at the price by compromising ideal objectives. A rule of thumb, or formula, may be a starting point for negotiation, but often the final result is far removed from it.

In these negotiations, buyers and sellers often have opposite objectives, and this may tend to pull the negotiation away from a set pattern. For instance, the seller will usually wish as much of the selling price as possible allocated to goodwill because he can clearly obtain a capital gain on that portion of the sale. Were more of the price allocated to depreciable assets, he might realize some income which would be taxable as a capital gain, but a portion may well be taxable at ordinary income rates because of depreciation recapture provisions of the Internal Revenue Code.[28] The buyer, on the other hand, wants as much of the price as possible allocated to depreciable assets because he can deduct depreciation each year. Goodwill is not depreciable to him and offers no tax advantage. If the buyer prevails, it may appear that a given business sold for tangible net worth at market with no goodwill, whereas in fact it sold at a multiple of earnings which included goodwill. The market value of the assets was inflated to disguise this fact. If, in the alternative, the seller prevailed, the price may appear to have been derived by taking a multiple of earnings which resulted in substantial goodwill over book values. If the appraiser accepted tangible net worth at market as the formula in the first instance, he would err, because he would conclude no goodwill was involved. If he accepted the earnings multiple in the second instance, he would also err, because goodwill was overstated.

VALUING THE PERSONALLY-MANAGED BUSINESS

Another factor which complicates the data collection process is the fact that buyers and sellers do not neatly package the results of their negotiations. Thus, a buyer may purchase the business for *some* of its tangible assets and *some* of its liabilities plus a bonus. The seller might retain certain accounts receivable whose collection was partially uncertain and he might assume all past income tax liabilities for the corporate business. In such a case, what is the real selling price and the real formula? Or the seller may retain certain perquisites after the sale as part of the selling price but not stated as such. He may keep a company leased car until the lease runs out, or enjoy a club membership paid by the company for a year or so on the income tax pretext that it will help him to carry over customers to the buyer. In fact, neither the car nor the club membership may have any continuing business purpose. Again, what is the true selling price?

Formulas, even when discovered, can be fraught with fallacies. The appraiser must look behind them with great care.

[¶7.04] THE TYPICAL FORMULA APPROACH

Whether the formula is taken directly from the market or is developed by the appraiser, it is usually a two step procedure. There are a number of possible combinations of such two-step methods. Occasionally, there are also three and four-step approaches.

[¶7.04-1] METHOD 10 - ASSET-BASED FORMULA

Basic Concept

The business is valued on the basis of tangible net worth at market plus a bonus for goodwill. The goodwill bonus is based on a multiplier times a typical monthly pre-tax profit after provision for a suitable owner's salary.

Limitations

The formula could result in an excessive or inadequate provision for goodwill when viewed on the basis of return on investment. The typical profit multiplier used in the industry may tend to weigh goodwill on an average investment, but few prices are average. Thus, a firm with average monthly profits of $2,000 having assets worth $20,000 probably should have a different value than a similar firm with average monthly profits of $2,000 and assets worth $40,000.

Advantages

The approach is simple. There is provision for the differing values of assets themselves as between firms through the tangible net worth at market calculation. (See Method 2, ¶5.04-2.) Variations in reasonable returns on investment as between firms in the same industry may be partially compensated for by varying the sales

VALUING THE PERSONALLY-MANAGED BUSINESS

multiplier used within the range which has gained acceptance. To the degree the method has been widely used, the reasonableness of an appraisal is easier to justify to the interested parties.

Procedure

Develop tangible net worth at market using the techniques described at ¶ 5.04-2. Prepare adjusted historical income statements for the most recent five years as explained at ¶ 4.03, deriving adjusted net profit before tax but after owner's salary. Depending on the usual procedure dictated by the market, either select a typical level of monthly profits based on past performance, or develop pro forma monthly profits using the process described at ¶ 4.04.

Determine the range of multipliers applicable to profits within the industry and select the high, low, or median multiplier (if a range exists) depending upon the risks of the particular firm being appraised. Apply the selected multiplier to the typical monthly historical profits or to the monthly pro forma profits as the situation dictates. Total the tangible net worth at market value plus the goodwill value determined by the multiplier. The result is the value of the business.

Example

In the BLM case correlation at ¶ 6.04 it was noted that a value of $58,000 had been developed for the Fast Burger operation. In arriving at this value, two formula approaches were used—each in itself a two-step method. The first of these is Method 10, described in general above.

It will be recalled that Fast Burger is a general partnership. It is operated by a single individual manager with little or no guidance from BLM management. (See ¶ 3.02-4, ¶ 3.02-5, and ¶ 3.02-7.) As such, it is essentially a personally-managed business. BLM has invested $53,580 in Fast Burger, for which it received a 53% interest in the business. This can be assumed to be effective control should BLM decide to exercise its rights. BLM's 53% interest entitled it to a similar share of the restaurant operation's earnings. The BLM share of earnings was as follows by fiscal years: 1972 - $5,000; 1973 - $10,000; 1974 - $15,000; 1975 - $15,000; and 1976 - $15,000. (See ¶ 3.02-20, item 5.) It can be assumed that Wilson Blaine, the General Manager of Fast Burger, has drawn a competitive level salary before the earnings were computed. It is a franchised fast food operation, and franchises for this size and type of operation are valued at $20,000.

Other pertinent facts are as follows: Total net profits before tax but after a reasonable salary to Blaine were by fiscal years: 1972 - $9,400; 1973 - $18,900; 1974 - $28,300; 1975 - $28,300; and 1976 - $28,300.[29] The industry formula is based on typical historical profits. Since the last three years' earnings are stable, the level of $28,300 per annum, or $2,360 per month, is considered typical. The goodwill multiplier obtained from industry checks ranges from 10 to 14 times average monthly profit. A multiplier of 12 is selected as proper for firms of the same relative

VALUING THE PERSONALLY-MANAGED BUSINESS

size and profitability as BLM. Tangible assets at market value are as follows: Accounts Receivable - $15,000; Inventories - $30,000; Fixtures and Equipment - $30,000. There is $15,000 owed to suppliers and for payroll taxes withheld.

The computation of value using Method 10 is as follows:

Step 1 - Compute Tangible Net Worth at Market

Accounts Receivable	$15,000
Inventories	30,000
Fixtures and Equipment	30,000
Total Tangible Assets	75,000
Less: Liabilities	(15,000)
Plus: Value of Franchise	20,000
Tangible Net Worth at Market	$80,000

Step 2 - Compute Addition for Goodwill

Typical Average Monthly Profit	$ 2,360
Market Multiplier	12
Value of Goodwill	$28,300

Following Method 10, the Value of Goodwill of $28,000 is added to the Tangible Net Worth at Market of $80,000, yielding a value of $108,000 for the whole business. Since BLM's holding is a controlling block of 53%, the appraiser concludes that it is appropriate to use 53% of $108,000, or $57,000, as its value. It could be argued that BLM's interest is worth more than its proportionate share of the total because it is a controlling block and that Blaine's interest is worth less than his share because it is a minority. However, for purposes of this example it will be assumed BLM and Blaine propose to sell as a unit and split the return according to their interests.

[¶7.04-2] METHOD 11 - SALES-BASED FORMULA

Basic Concept

The average annual sales of a business (pro forma or typical historical) are valued using a market-derived multiplier such as .25, .50, 1.5, etc. However, the value so computed should be no more than the typical annual net profit (after owner's salary adjustment) times a second market-indicated multiplier such as 1, 2, or 3.

Limitations

Sales-based formulas tend to overlook return on investment as far as the *seller* is concerned. The fact that a certain level of sales produces certain minimal profits is not in turn related to tangible net worth.

VALUING THE PERSONALLY-MANAGED BUSINESS

Advantages

As in the case of asset-based formulas, the approach is simple and understandable. If the buyer in effect purchases the business on the basis of its ability to create sales and he can be assured that these sales are reasonably profitable, there is a relationship between the price he paid and the return on *his* investment.

Procedure

Develop annual pro forma or typical historical sales. Which measure of sales is used will be dictated by the market review. Then develop annual net profit before tax but after owner salary adjustment, again on either a pro forma or typical historical basis as called for by the market. Use the techniques discussed at ¶ 4.03 and ¶ 4.04. Determine the market multiplier to be applied to sales and the market multiplier to be applied to profits and apply them. If the value determined by the sales method does not exceed the value determined by the profit multiplier, the sales multiplier approach prevails. Otherwise, the profit multiplier approach constitutes the value. This points out the effect of the logical limit on value discussed at ¶ 7.02.

Example

See the previous example for basic facts regarding the Fast Burger operation. Assume the industry check indicated typical historical sales and profits were the basis of most calculations. Typical historical sales for Fast Burger were $500,000 per year, and as noted in the previous example, the typical annual profit was $28,300. A market analysis indicated that similar franchised operations sold for .25 times annual sales, with a ceiling of not more than four times typical annual profits.

Step 1 - Compute Value Based on Sales

Typical Annual Historical Sales	$500,000
Market Multiplier	.25
Indicated Value of the Business	$125,000

Step 2 - Compute Top Value Based on Profits

Typical Annual Historical Profit	$28,300
Market Multiplier	4
Indicated Value of the Total Business	$113,200

Since the profit multiplier sets the effective ceiling, it governs, resulting in a value by Method 11 of $113,000. Had the sales multiplier produced a lower value, such as $100,000 instead of $125,000, that figure would have prevailed. The value of BLM's share of the total is $60,000 based on its 53% interest. As in the previous example, it is assumed that no premium will be paid for the BLM interest simply because it constitutes effective control.

VALUING THE PERSONALLY-MANAGED BUSINESS

[¶7.04-3] CORRELATION OF FORMULA METHODS

Methods 10 and 11 have certain limitations. There can be merit in applying both methods to an operation such as BLM, as was done at ¶7.04-1 and ¶7.04-2. There still remains the need to reach a conclusion as to which value is correct. By Method 10, the whole company was valued at $108,000, and 53% represented $57,000. Using Method 11, the company was worth $113,000, and 53% represented $60,000.

The range of value on the 53% holding is actually narrow at $57,000 - $60,000. The appraiser concludes that Method 10 better sustains the values and hence elects to use this approach. He decides, however, that inventories could be properly valued upwards by about $2,000 so that the final value conclusion as to the 53% interest is $58,000.

In effect, by using both Methods 10 and 11, the appraiser has used a four-step approach. Method 10 has two steps—one based on assets and the other on profits. Method 11 also has two steps—one tied to sales and the other to profits.

[¶7.04-4] FLEXIBILITY OF FORMULAS

Even when the market indicates that an average net sales multiplier is three months, for example, it does not necessarily follow that this average should be applied to the business being appraised. The formulas should be used with flexibility to fit the circumstances. Thus, a sales multiplier can be adjusted up or down, giving consideration not only to the relative strengths or weaknesses of the subject company as compared to others in the market, but also based upon what assets are to be included and their condition. A firm with more modern equipment than its competitors might justify a greater sales multiplier. The same logic applies to net profit multipliers.

[¶7.04-5] FORMULA GUIDELINES

Multipliers applied to the sales of smaller service, cash-and-carry, retail and wholesale businesses are usually expressed in terms of one, two, or three months of typical monthly sales. These businesses usually have relatively narrow margins of profit. Therefore, the multipliers in use are intended to include primarily the tangible assets, sometimes including inventories and sometimes not, plus a modest amount for goodwill. In some cases there is no allowance for goodwill. The larger and stronger service-type firms with stable back-up managements which would continue with the business may command higher multipliers. These may run six months of typical monthly sales, or in some instances, twelve or more months. Usually, service-oriented businesses have relatively low fixed asset values, with most of their value represented by goodwill or other intangibles.

Net profit multipliers used in valuing the entire enterprise typically range from

VALUING THE PERSONALLY-MANAGED BUSINESS

one to five times the annual net profit before tax but after provision for salary to the owner. Relatively few businesses sell for a multiple of five, for reasons cited at ¶ 7.02. To do so, they must be exceptionally good, and there must be a strong probability of continued growth.

Multipliers applied to net profit for the purpose of estimating a bonus for goodwill usually range from one to two months of typical net profits before tax but after a salary allowance to the owner. Better established, stronger, or unique businesses which are difficult to start may command multipliers of six to twelve months net profit for their goodwill.

It is always preferable to have the tangible assets appraised. Such assets would include furniture, fixtures, machinery, equipment, inventories, and any other tangible assets necessary to operate the business at a given level of sales and profitability. Book values are just as meaningless for valuation purposes in the personally-managed business as they are for the larger professionally-managed firms. If anything, they are even less representative of value because of the generally poorer level of accounting in small versus larger businesses.

Particular care must be exercised in handling the owner's salary. Since most smaller, personally-managed businesses are not regular corporations, income tax returns or statements prepared by the owner's accountant usually do not show a salary to the owner. As part of his investigation of market data, the appraiser should *always* determine whether or not the owner's salary was specifically provided for before net profit multipliers were applied. It will be found that multipliers are sometimes applied to the total profit before tax, including an owner's salary, whereas in other cases they are used only with net profit after an owner's salary provision has been deducted.

In making a study of the market for any kind of business, an appraiser can usually find some instances where goodwill was purchased. This does not mean that goodwill exists for all similar businesses. Each situation must be considered individually. It is important not to create a bonus for goodwill when none is warranted, regardless of the outcome of a market-derived formula.

[¶7.04-6] WHAT TO DO WHEN NO FORMULAS EMERGE

While an analysis of actual sales of many personally-owned smaller firms will often reveal the use of a formula, this will not always be true. There are many instances where it is impossible to conclude that a definite formula has been used. If this is the case, the appraiser must come up with a practical solution. A consideration of the basic limits of value discussed at ¶ 7.02 will be helpful in this regard. From these basic value limits, together with data on comparable businesses sold, the appraiser may develop a formula of his own to which he can relate his conclusions. He might consider some form of the Excess Earnings Method. (See Method 3 at ¶ 5.05-1.) This approach is useful when the firm has a history of reasonable profits.

VALUING THE PERSONALLY-MANAGED BUSINESS

Frequently, however, smaller businesses do not show a sufficient record of earnings to provide a full return on tangible assets, let alone any excess earnings. Yet, even without excess earnings, it may appear that most businesses comparable to the one being appraised do sell for a value which includes goodwill. This value may be due to the fact that the business is already pre-assembled, has a favorable reputation, has a lease at a good location, and has regular patronage. In other words, a bonus is paid because it is not a start-up situation. It may appear that this premium has been arrived at on an arbitrary basis by negotiation between buyer and seller. Yet, the appraiser must arrive at a sustainable value for such goodwill if it exists in the business he is valuing. Most of the methods applicable to larger professionally-managed businesses discussed in Chapter 5 are useless, due to the low level of earnings.

One method of determining a reasonable level of bonus for goodwill would be to make a study of other types of businesses with characteristics similar to the one being appraised. If a formula or method of valuing goodwill can be developed for these similar firms, it could be concluded that such a formula or method could logically be applied to the firm being valued. Certain cautions are necessary to be certain that there is a proper level of comparability between the other firms and the subject business. The other firms should be similar in the following respects to the business being appraised:
1. Dollar volume and profit margins should be similar.
2. The type and degree of skill required to operate the businesses should be comparable.
3. The relative amount of tangible asset investment should be similar.
4. The difficulty and expense of start-up should be comparable.
5. Businesses which require special and difficult-to-obtain licenses should not normally be compared with those which do not require licensing.[30]

Another method for developing goodwill value involves the comparison of a non-franchised business with similar businesses which are franchised. Thus, a non-franchised restaurant could be compared with a similar franchised restaurant. The applicable franchise fee may be a reasonable measure of the going concern value of the non-franchised business. This involves certain assumptions, namely: (1) that the business being appraised is a successful, going concern which warrants a goodwill bonus, and (2) that payment of the franchise fee with its attendant assistance in advertising, uniformity of products, management aid, merchandising, and special training will bring the franchised firm to a level of profitability relatively close to that of the non-franchised business. If these assumptions are valid, the franchise fee would become a useful consideration in goodwill valuation. An investor who has many opportunities open to him could very feasibly compare franchised and non-franchised business opportunities. The franchised operation has certain advantages over its non-franchised comparable firm, and these might cause the investor to discount the goodwill bonus somewhat from the franchise fee he might

VALUING THE PERSONALLY-MANAGED BUSINESS

otherwise pay. On the other hand, the fact that the non-franchised business is already a going concern might more than offset this consideration.

It is useful to view the business being appraised as just one of many investment opportunities open to a prospective purchaser. This frees the appraiser from being forced to use formulas or approaches which may have only marginal applicability to the firm in question. He may apply any formula or approach which appears to be a reasonable test for measuring the relative risk of an investment in the business being appraised compared with alternative investments. He might, for example, use a variation of Method 4 - Capitalization of Income Stream (¶ 5.05-3) which compares the flow of income anticipated from a business with that which can be expected from other investments with similar risks. The problem would be to find investments with comparable risks and to clearly segregate the profits of the business being appraised from earnings which are actually in lieu of salary to the owner.

[¶7.05] EXAMPLES OF BUSINESSES SOLD BY FORMULA

A review of business opportunity advertisements and contacts with business brokers will reveal formulas which are used in the negotiations for sale or purchase of many small, personally-managed businesses. A listing of all businesses which might be considered by a formula approach could be quite extensive. Some are larger, professionally-managed firms, such as commercial banks and life insurance companies. At the other extreme are the more numerous small restaurants, retail stores, and professional practices. The listing below is not intended to be all-inclusive, but rather to give an indication of the type of formulas an appraiser is likely to find with respect to the sale and purchase of predominantly small, personally-managed businesses.

[¶7.05-1] AUTO REPAIR GARAGES

Usually, there must be a minimum income for the owner-mechanic before a formula is applied. The level of income required depends upon the earnings of mechanics in the part of the U.S. where the business is located. If this income is available, then a multiplier of two times the typical historical monthly receipts is generally used. To this amount is added the market value of all tangible assets, including machinery and equipment, less any liabilities assumed. The result is the price of the business.

[¶7.05-2] LIQUOR STORES

One of the most important assets owned by a liquor store is its license to operate. The licenses are handled differently in different states. Where they are freely transferable, this value will range from about $6,000 to $40,000. (See further comments on liquor licenses at ¶ 7.05-8.)

VALUING THE PERSONALLY-MANAGED BUSINESS

Liquor stores often sell by formula, frequently with a two-step approach. Step No. 1 involves the application of a multiplier of 3 - 5 to typical monthly historical sales. To this is added the value of the inventory. The result is the price of the total business.

Step No. 2, which may be used as a check on the first step, requires a multiplier of 1½ - 2½ times typical monthly historical sales, to which is added the value of the liquor license and the inventory. Note that the liquor license was included in Step No. 1 and was not considered as a separate item under that approach.

[¶7.05-3] INSURANCE AGENCIES

Often, negotiations for an insurance agency begin with a formula based upon 125% - 150% of the annual fees or commissions received. Receipts are based upon typical levels derived from the most recent two or three years. To the formula result there is usually added separate values for the client list, working capital, and fixed assets.

The basic value in a going insurance agency is the annuity type income it receives from the sale of renewal policies on casualty insurance and from the continuing premiums received on life insurance policies. Renewals on casualty policies and payment records on life policies can be established by a study of the books. Customer dropouts and failures to pay on life policies can be converted into a customer turnover or departure rate. This rate will have a significant bearing upon the multiple applied to annual receipts. Although not stated as part of the formula approach, an analysis of the profitability of the agency would be made, and this would enter into the selection of the annual receipts multiplier.

As was discussed earlier, the transferability of customers is extremely important, as is the continuance of key employees. For this reason, the formula approach is generally used only where the agency is owned by more than one individual and where it has some staff which will remain. Individual proprietorships may also start negotiations with the formula approach, but the final value arrived at is more apt to be a significant departure from this method.

[¶7.05-4] ACCOUNTING PRACTICES

Accounting practices usuallly are priced with a three-step formula as the basis. The first step involves a determination of the price to be paid for goodwill. This usually ranges from 75%–150% of typical annual historical billings. The second step is to apply a multiplier of 2 - 5 to the typical historical profits before tax but after provision for a salary to the owner. Within this range, a multiplier of 3 or 4 times is typical. The second step is not in addition to the first but is used as a test which sets a maximum on the premium for goodwill.

The third and final step involves the addition of the assets of the business to the value determined for goodwill. Included at market values would be fixed assets,

VALUING THE PERSONALLY-MANAGED BUSINESS

accounts receivable, work-in-progress, and any other essential assets. Liabilities assumed would normally be deducted.

As in the case of insurance agencies and other professional practices, the price of sole proprietorships tends to depart from the formulas due to problems of client transferability. The goodwill premium would tend to be smaller or, in some cases, non-existent.

[¶7.05-5] LEGAL PRACTICES

A formula approach similar to that used in pricing accounting practices is often used for legal practices. However, there is a question with respect to legal practices as to whether the legal code of ethics will allow the sale of clients and, hence, goodwill. This same ethical question arises with respect to medical practices, and it could be raised with accountants as well. If the ethical problem becomes important to the buyer, the seller may be able to receive only the economic value of his tangible assets, such as furniture, fixtures, and law library. This would generally be the case anyway where the practice being sold is that of a sole practitioner, because the goodwill attached to such an individual is difficult to transfer. A solution to this ethical problem may involve the selling attorneys entering into an employment contract with the buyers. If this contract is sufficiently profitable to the sellers, it may compensate for the lack of consideration for goodwill, and the procedure can assist in the transfer of clients.

[¶7.05-6] ADVERTISING AGENCIES

Advertising agencies are higher risk businesses than insurance agencies, legal or accounting practices. The latter three professions tend to retain clients even when there is a change of ownership, because insurance, legal and tax aspects of a business are sufficiently complex to require the retention of an experienced professional who becomes intimately acquainted with the business. It is easier and often more satisfactory to stay with the firms which have been handling these matters, rather than to shop for another broker, lawyer, or accountant. Although advertising agencies may be well acquainted with client businesses, there is not the same strong tie. Therefore, goodwill premiums tend to be lower than those applicable to insurance agencies, and if ethical considerations are not involved, also lower than the premium for goodwill in the sale of accounting and legal practices.

The sale of advertising agencies often involves the use of one of two possible formulas. The first formula entails the computation of a premium for goodwill based on 30% - 50% of typical recent annual billings. To this is added the market value of the tangible assets of the business less any liabilities assumed. Where between 30% and 50% the actual multiplier should be depends on the risks involved in retaining the clientele and in continuing prior levels of profit.

The second formula is based on profits. A multiplier of 8 - 12 is applied to typical historical monthly profits before tax but after provision for salaries to the

VALUING THE PERSONALLY-MANAGED BUSINESS

owners. The result of this calculation is the value placed on goodwill. To the goodwill is again added the market value of the tangible assets less any liabilities assumed.

It is apparent that the appraiser may wish to use both approaches. Each involves a different method of computing goodwill, hence one can serve as a useful check on the other.

[¶7.05-7] CONVENIENCE GROCERIES

Such groceries often sell for a price equal to 3 to 4 months typical monthly sales. The resulting amount represents the value of the entire business, excluding real estate. Fixtures, equipment, inventory, supplies, and goodwill, if any, are all included. A minimum annual sales volume of $200,000 - $300,000 is usually required before any goodwill bonus is paid. Put another way, unless there is at least this much volume, these stores typically sell for their tangible net worth at market value.

[¶7.05-8] BARS AND COCKTAIL LOUNGES

Such businesses are usually valued at 4 to 6 times monthly net sales plus the value of the liquor license. As in the case of liquor stores, the license can range in value from $6,000 - $40,000.

In determining the value of the liquor license, there are a number of factors to be considered. Often governmental agencies control the transferability of the license and may even control the maximum price for which it can be sold. Also, different types of transfers are viewed differently. Thus, the values and transferability of the license may be different, depending upon whether the transfer involved is from person to person, from one premise to another, or from one county to another within a state. Beer and wine licenses generally have a lower value than do those which authorize the sale of all types of alcoholic beverages. When valuing any licensed operation, the appraiser must become thoroughly familiar with the governmental regulations which affect the value of the licenses.

[¶7.05-9] NEWSPAPERS AND PERIODICALS

Publications of this type are often valued using a two-step approach. The first step is based upon paid circulation. A check in the market where the publication circulates should result in the determination of a price per unit of circulation which is typically used in the calculation of such selling prices. The unit price can vary so widely that the authors are hesitant to quote typical figures. However, it is fair to say that the price per unit of circulation will be less for a weekly publication than for a daily. Also, the renewal rate on subscriptions will be a strong influencing factor. One weekly might sell for $2.00 per unit of circulation, whereas another might command $10.00. If the publication is a throw-away type, a different first step formula would be used based upon advertising volume.

VALUING THE PERSONALLY-MANAGED BUSINESS

The second step would consist of the measurement of earnings capability. In this case, an adaptation of the Excess Earnings Method described at ¶ 5.05-1 is often suitable. The amount of excess earnings so developed, however, covers all intangibles, not just goodwill. In particular, it would include the value of the subscription list, which is a very important asset of publications with paid circulations.

[¶7.05-10] AUTO WRECKING YARDS

Such businesses usually sell on the basis of their tangible net worth at market plus a bonus for goodwill. Often, this bonus can be quite substantial, constituting several months' of typical sales. The amount of goodwill bonus will usually be based on the transferability of the permit to operate in a given location and the desirability of that location. Zoning authority to operate such yards is difficult to obtain and if given on the basis of a special use permit, this permit may have a limited life or it may be confined to the individuals then operating the business. In-town locations are more valuable than those farther removed. As a rule, no goodwill bonus is paid unless it appears that the business can earn at least 20% - 25% profit before tax on its sales before deducting a salary to the owners.

[¶7.05-11] FUNERAL HOMES

At one time, funeral homes were typically priced on the basis of tangible net worth at market plus a bonus for intangibles including goodwill. The bonus was usually keyed to the number of cases handled each year. In more recent years, such formulas appear to have become obsolete, although such data might be gathered in the market and used for comparative purposes when appraising a particular home. However, the emphasis should be on localized market data and not a rule-of-thumb formula.

[¶7.06]   REAL ESTATE-RELATED BUSINESSES

There are many businesses which are so closely related to real estate that it is difficult to distinguish the value of the business from the value of the underlying assets. Hotels and motels fall in this category, as do nursing homes and mobile home parks. Nevertheless, there are formula approaches which have some validity.

[¶7.06-1] HOTELS AND MOTELS

If the valuation involves a chain of hotels or motels, the business usually is relatively large and professionally managed. As such, the valuation methods discussed in Chapter 5 would be applicable. If the assignment is to appraise a single motel or hotel, its value is normally the value of the underlying real estate. There are exceptions, however, where a particular hotel is so well known, possibly with a national reputation, that a buyer would be willing to pay a premium for use of the name.

VALUING THE PERSONALLY-MANAGED BUSINESS

A possible approach to determining the goodwill bonus applicable to such a hotel would not involve a formula but a comparison with other hotels. Thus, the income statements, room rates, and occupancy rates could be accumulated on similar hotels which do not have a similar reputation. These statements and rates can be compared to the hotel being appraised and a measure obtained as to the added income the subject hotel generates. This added income could then be valued by perhaps capitalizing the typical level of extra earnings at an appropriate rate. The value of the hotel would then be the value of the real estate plus the goodwill bonus so determined.

[¶7.06-2] NURSING HOMES

The value of the real estate should be determined for a nursing home, but a bonus might be payable over and above this value. Nursing homes often sell for amounts which are based on a unit price per bed. The price per bed would be multiplied by the number of beds in the facility. That price would include all of the assets of the business, including goodwill and real estate. If this is the case, and the per bed price is higher than the basic value of the real estate, there may in effect be a value set on goodwill and other intangibles.

[¶7.06-3] MOBILE HOME PARKS

Although the value of such parks is closely aligned with the real estate involved, a goodwill bonus may be applicable. Mobile home parks often are priced on the basis of 3 - 8 times typical monthly receipts. The usual multiplier applicable in the area where the park is located should be determined. What multiplier should be chosen for the subject firm as between the highest and the lowest market figure will depend upon the desirability of the park and its relative profitability. Once the calculation has been made, the value of the land and the depreciated value of the improvements are deducted to arrive at the value of the business itself.

[¶7.07]   SUMMARY

Personally-managed businesses present some special appraisal problems. There is the difficulty of ferreting out the facts about the business, because records are usually poor. Then, the common fallacy that these businesses sell simply by formula must be addressed. Departures from such formulas are frequent and difficult to assess. In many cases there is no discernable formula. Such businesses are highly individualistic and do not easily fit into neat patterns. Nevertheless, the appraiser should search for any formulas which exist, as they can be indicators of value, if not the final conclusion.

Regardless of the type of personal business being appraised, there are certain logical limits to their value. Generally, the business will not sell for less than its tangible net worth at market value, nor will it sell for more than five times net profit

VALUING THE PERSONALLY-MANAGED BUSINESS

before tax but after a salary allowance to the owners. The minimum value might be lower if the firm barely produces enough profit to afford a living to the owner. Seldom, however, will the maximum of five times pre-tax earnings be exceeded—and, in fact, it will be an unusual personally-managed business that will sell for that much. Businesses with a poor history of earnings should be analyzed to determine the cause for the low earnings and to see if it is correctable. Newer businesses which are not well established and one-man businesses tend to sell for their tangible net worth.

In turning to the market for data, the appraiser should realize that the marketplace is not highly organized as to valuation methods. In their negotiations, buyers and sellers often have opposite objectives, and this tends to pull negotiations away from set patterns. Also, exact selling prices and terms are often obscured.

When applicable formulas do appear, there are usually two steps involved. An example of the application of two such formulas is demonstrated in the BLM case. Method 10 is an asset-based formula which also considers profits. Method 11 is sales based, with a ceiling set by profits. Neither method is perfect, but taken together, reasonable values can be developed.

Formulas should be approached with flexibility, with the market data shaped to fit the circumstances of the business being appraised. Guidelines for sales multipliers and net profit multipliers are discussed. It is recommended that tangible assets be appraised regardless of formulas and that special care be exercised to see that owners' salaries have been considered.

When no formula is evident from the market study, the appraiser may wish to create one. Or he may develop information and methods for businesses similar to but not identical with the one being appraised. Or he may compare a non-franchise business with similar firms which are franchised to determine a possible measure for going concern value.

A number of examples are given of businesses which typically sell with some reference to a formula. The list is not all-inclusive but is intended to be illustrative of a wide variety of operations, ranging from auto repair garages to funeral homes.

Some businesses such as hotels, nursing homes, and mobile home parks are closely related to the value of their underlying real estate. Nevertheless, formulas do come into play in such real estate-oriented businesses, and these are discussed.

CHAPTER 8

WHAT IS GOODWILL?

*Each is given a bag of tools, a shapeless
mass and a book of rules;
And each must make, ere life is flown,
a stumblingblock or a steppingstone.*
                    R.L. SHARPE - 1890

TOPICS DISCUSSED IN THIS CHAPTER

[¶8.01] — The "Big Pot" Theory of Goodwill

[¶8.02] — Elements of Goodwill and Other Intangible Assets
  Group 1 - Intangible Assets Non-Severable from the Business
  Group 2 - Intangible Assets Non-Severable from the Person
  Group 3 - Intangible Assets Generally Severable from the Business

[¶8.03] — How to Distinguish Goodwill from Other Intangibles

[¶8.03-1] — General Definition of Goodwill

[¶8.03-2] — Definition of Other Intangible Assets

[¶8.03-3] — Can Goodwill and Other Intangibles Be Commingled?

[¶8.03-4] — Going Concern Value

[¶8.03-5] — Court Definitions of Goodwill

[¶8.03-6] — The Internal Revenue Service View of Intangibles

[¶8.04] — How to Determine the Existence of Goodwill

[¶8.04-1] — Earnings Test

[¶8.04-2] — Market Test

[¶8.04-3] — Question and Answer Test

[¶8.05] — Summary

CHAPTER 8

WHAT IS GOODWILL?

[¶8.01] THE "BIG POT" THEORY OF GOODWILL

Ask the typical businessman, "What is goodwill?" After a short pause, he probably will reply, "Goodwill is the going concern value of a business - its ability to produce effectively and to attract customers." Pressed a little further, he might describe it as the price a buyer would pay for a business over and above the economic value of its tangible assets.

The foregoing could be described as the "big pot" theory of goodwill. All tangible assets are identified and valued. Whatever is left over in the way of value is then metaphorically thrown into one big pot, blended, and named *goodwill*. This is a common theory, and it is even subscribed to by some appraisers.

One reason the "big pot" theory is prevalent is because the sale of intangibles is approached on a very unsophisticated basis by many buyers and sellers of businesses. This is especially true of small concerns. The buyer and seller typically will agree fairly readily on the value of the tangible assets. Then, almost as an afterthought, they bargain over the intangibles. The seller may say, "This business certainly has goodwill worth at least $30,000. Look at how the customers return year after year, and look at our steady profits." The buyer may proffer a few negatives about the business and indicate that in his opinion the goodwill is worth no more than $10,000. Finally, they compromise and agree on a value of $20,000. Neither buyer nor seller really knows what has been bought and sold, nor whether the price paid is realistic. They only know that the going business had some value over and above its tangible assets, and that $20,000 seemed to be the best price they could put on that value.

Following this approach, the buyer may suddenly wake up to the fact that the $20,000 of goodwill he has bought is a non-depreciable asset for income tax purposes. He then asks his accountant to analyze his purchase to see if part of the $20,000 could be written off. The accountant may advise him that in order for an intangible asset to be amortized, the Internal Revenue Service says it must have a measurable value and a determinable economic life. Since it appears the buyer simply acquired going concern value, it may have a measurable value, but there is no apparent way to give it a determinable economic life. As long as the business exists in its present form at its present location, this value will persist. It can't be said to decline at the rate of say $2,000 per year over ten years.

If the buyer had been more knowledgeable, he might have been aware of the problem in advance. A common solution would have been an attempt to impute a greater value, such as the entire $20,000 of goodwill, to the tangible depreciable assets. But this approach is usually detrimental to the seller's interests, because he may have depreciated these assets to very low values on his books. While the sale

WHAT IS GOODWILL?

of a depreciable asset theoretically affords him a capital gain, this is true only to the extent the gain exceeds the depreciation he has taken. Therefore, the end result is frequently a significant amount of ordinary income which the seller must recognize. This results from the so-called "depreciation recapture" provisions of the Internal Revenue Code.[31]

If both the small business buyer and seller are relatively sophisticated, the probable result is a compromise, still based on the "big pot" theory. In the foregoing situation, the tangible assets might end up overvalued by $10,000, leaving a stated value of only $10,000 for goodwill. Neither buyer nor seller arrived at a perfect solution to their tax problems. Presumably, the buyer would attempt to depreciate the extra $10,000 attributed to the tangible assets, and the seller would be faced with some depreciation recapture as a result. The seller, however, would hopefully obtain capital gain treatment on at least the $10,000 stated as goodwill, but the buyer could not write off this amount.

A different approach to this problem might have revealed a more satisfactory solution for both parties. Perhaps there was some going concern value which could not be given an economic life, but maybe this represented only $5,000 of the excess over the value of the tangible assets. Perhaps the remainder was properly attributed to the existence of a secret process and a patent. Possibly these assets were worth not $15,000, but $20,000. Thus, a closer look at the intangibles might have resulted in a value of $25,000 on all intangibles, rather than the $20,000 which resulted from the typical "broad brush" approach.

Could both buyer and seller be considered better off by such a closer analysis? The answer is probably yes, if the appraisal itself did not cost them too much. The seller would receive $25,000 for the intangibles instead of $20,000. He probably could sustain capital gain treatment on the entire $25,000. The buyer, on the other hand, is not faced with a possible Internal Revenue Service challenge to the extra $10,000 which would have been placed on tangible assets under the earlier approach, since he bought them at their sustainable market values. While he paid $5,000 more for the business, it is probable that $20,000 of the so-called goodwill value is amortizable for tax purposes. This would be true for the portion of the $20,000 attributable to the patent and probably would be true for the portion attributable to the secret process, if the process could be given a sustainable economic life.

Admittedly, a breakdown of the values contained in the "big pot" of goodwill may not be worthwhile for many small businesses. The cost of developing the values, either by hiring an appraiser or by doing the necessary research on one's own, may not be justified by the amount of goodwill involved. One could not afford to spend too much time analyzing an amount of $5,000 or $10,000 payable for goodwill.

WHAT IS GOODWILL?

On the other hand, when larger businesses change hands, the stakes are too high to allow the acceptance of intangible assets as an unidentified mass. Usually, both buyer and seller are knowledgeable in business dealings and both wish to resolve goodwill into sustainable values so that a realistic price can be placed on the business. If, for example, part of the value is in patents and secret processes, the buyer wants to know what these assets are and what they are worth. These and many other intangible assets probably do not appear on the company books because they were expensed. It therefore behooves the seller to find, identify, and value them wherever possible so that he can best represent the true worth of the business. The buyer, too, will want to be aware of any possible negative intangibles, such as an unfavorable lease or an unprofitable contract.

Both buyer and seller can have tax problems if the goodwill mass is not analyzed, preferably before the sale/purchase is consummated. For instance, the buyer may assume he has purchased only tangible assets. Then an Internal Revenue audit of the seller results in the seller sustaining a substantial value for goodwill because it was to his interest to document and prove such a value. Sensing a possible tax recovery from the buyer, the IRS then audits the buyer and disallows a substantial part of his depreciation. The unfavorable tax result under other conditions could just as well have hurt the seller instead of the buyer, or both might have been unfavorably affected in certain respects. Had goodwill been more carefully studied and valued in the first place, unfavorable or unexpected tax results could well have been avoided.

[¶8.02] ELEMENTS OF GOODWILL AND OTHER INTANGIBLE ASSETS

As a first step in overcoming the problems incident to the "big pot" theory, it is necessary to determine the individual assets which comprise goodwill. As has been intimated above, in common business usage, goodwill includes far more than the going concern value of the business. There is a tendency to group all intangible assets together and label them *goodwill*. Many, if not most, intangibles are created with time and effort and are not material in nature. The labor and overhead that go into their creation is usually absorbed as part of the general expense of the operation. Thus, the owners will recognize that they have assets which are not shown on the balance sheet, but no one has made an attempt to identify or set a value upon them.

For appraisal purposes, what one labels *goodwill*, versus other intangible assets, is not of vital importance. What is important is a definition of the intangible assets that can be found in businesses and a clear understanding of their different characteristics. With this background in mind, a careful effort can be made to identify all such assets which exist in a business. Then, having identified them, an effort can be made to assign values to each.

WHAT IS GOODWILL?

The pool of assets which may be described as *goodwill and other intangible assets* may be categorized into three basic groups: (1) intangible assets which are non-severable from the business, (2) intangible assets which are non-severable from the person, and (3) intangible assets which are usually severable from both the business and the person. Some of the more common elements within each group are summarized as follows:

Group 1 - Intangible Assets Non-Severable from the Business

The assemblage of property, plant, and equipment into a productive unit or units.
The availability of trained employees.
Systems, controls, and methods which have been developed as part of the operation.
The existence of customers.
Start-up losses which have been absorbed.
Advertising and promotion accomplishments.
Advantages of location beyond those directly attributable to the real estate itself.
The local, regional, or national reputation a business may have established by virtue of public and customer knowledge of its dependability, quality of service and product, price of service and product, and credit standing with vendors and banks.

Group 2 - Intangible Assets Non-Severable from the Person

The personal reputation of employees or owners with the general public, customers, other employees, other owners, and lenders.
The personal skills of such individuals, including their technical know-how, sales ability, financial acumen, etc.
The general skills of employees or owners in fields such as employee relations, customer relations, leadership, management, and administration.

Group 3 - Intangible Assets Generally Severable from the Business

Brand names	Secret formulas
Trademarks	Licenses
Trade names	Patents
Secret methods and processes	Franchises
Technical libraries	Drawings and patterns
Copyrights	Film rights
Newspaper morgues	Water rights

Contracts, such as covenants not to compete, employment contracts, purchase contracts, sales contracts, and advertising contracts.
Lists, such as mailing lists, customer lists, and subscription lists.

In addition to their relative degree of severability from the business, the foregoing intangible assets have these varying characteristics:
   a. **Determinable versus indeterminable life**
      Some have a reasonably determinable economic or legal life, whereas others do not.

WHAT IS GOODWILL?

b. Individual items versus group valuation
Some can be valued as individual assets; others must be valued as a group.

Group 1 assets generally have indeterminable lives and must be valued as a group. Since the life cannot be fixed, Group 1 assets cannot be amortized or depreciated. This is not to say the value so represented may not vary with the fortunes of the business, but there is no logical way to measure a steady decline in value, as would be required for an amortization schedule. An exception could be justified where the business has been organized to perform a simple contract, after which it will be liquidated.

At the other extreme, most of the assets in Group 3 can be individually valued, and most have a determinable life. For instance, a patent can be individually valued, and it has both an economic and a legal life. On the other hand, some assets in Group 3 can be individually valued, but they do not usually have determinable lives. Trade names and water rights are examples of this type. Still other Group 3 assets may sometimes have a determinable life and sometimes they may not. For instance, a license or a franchise may be granted for a specific period or for an indefinite time.

Assets in Group 2 are somewhat unique in their association with individuals. In most cases they would be viewed as having indeterminable lives. However, the special skills of an individual can be given a determinable life and a specific value if his services are placed under an employment contract.

It is important to note that even though assets in all three groupings may be present in a business, this does not mean that there is any goodwill or other intangible value in the business. Usually, the firm must be capable of generating a profit over and above that which is necessary to pay salaries to the owners before it is reasonable to assume the intangibles have an economic value. In the absence of such profits, there must be a determinable price the market is willing to pay for them. In the latter case, this generally means the assets must be separable from the business, such as a liquor license, a water right, or a favorable leasehold. Occasionally, however, as described at ¶ 8.03-4, an intangible premium may be paid for a losing business.

[¶8.03] HOW TO DISTINGUISH GOODWILL FROM OTHER INTANGIBLES

While intangible assets can be appraised without too much concern as to how they are labeled, a definition of goodwill is nevertheless desirable and helpful. This is because goodwill is referred to in court cases, business sales, tax proceedings, and generally in business. Many people purport to understand it, although few actually do. Except by coincidence, it is not the "big pot" of assets described at ¶ 8.01.

WHAT IS GOODWILL?

[¶8.03-1] GENERAL DEFINITION OF GOODWILL

For most purposes, goodwill can be defined as those elements of a business or a person which cause customers to return to that business or person and which usually enable a firm to generate profit in excess of that which is required for a reasonable return on *all* of the other assets of the business, including a return on all other intangible assets which can be identified and separately valued. Goodwill always runs with the business or individual and cannot be sold separately. Part or all of business goodwill can sometimes be sold separately from the owners and employees of the business, but it cannot be sold separately from the business. Similarly, personal goodwill can be sold in part or fully separate from a business but not separate from the individual.

To be less theoretical in definition, business goodwill usually includes the intangible assets included in Group 1 under ¶ 8.02. Personal goodwill generally includes the intangible assets included in Group 2 under ¶ 8.02. In most cases, the goodwill of an enterprise consists of business and personal goodwill. The excess profits which are earned are the result of these two elements of goodwill combined.

The excess profits which measure the value of goodwill can be evolved in a number of different ways, as discussed later in this chapter. Nevertheless, in theory, one reasons along the line of Method 3 - the Excess Earnings Method described at ¶ 5.05-1. The economic value of the tangible assets is determined, and to this is added the economic value of the intangible assets other than goodwill. These individual assets must in the aggregate show a competitive rate of return after considering the risks involved and economic depreciation and amortization where appropriate. If there is an excess of profits, goodwill is present. If no excess profits exist, there usually is no goodwill, regardless of how many elements of business and personal goodwill may be present. The principal exceptions to the latter rule are discussed at ¶ 8.03-4.

[¶8.03-2] DEFINITION OF OTHER INTANGIBLE ASSETS

Intangible assets other than goodwill are difficult to define in generalities because they have no single, all-pervasive quality. All cannot be said to be intangible in the common dictionary meaning of the term, i.e., incapable of being perceived by touch; lacking in physical substance. A technical library is an intangible asset for appraisal purposes, and yet it is quite palpable.

For appraisal purposes, intangible assets as a group are best described as being those assets of a business other than goodwill which have economic value; which consist of various kinds of rights, privileges, assemblages of data and know-how; and which can be individually identified and valued. Usually, a commercial intangible asset must either be generating an advantageous profit or it must have the likelihood of being able to do so in the near future.

WHAT IS GOODWILL?

Thus, a definition is reached by elimination. Common assets which do *not* fit the definition are: cash, accounts receivable, notes receivable, machinery, equipment, and land. In other words, most normal balance sheet assets are not intangibles for appraisal purposes. Occasionally, a patent, a copyright, or some other intangible may show up on the balance sheet with an assigned cost, but the cost is seldom the economic value. Also, from time to time, an asset may be discovered which does not appear on the balance sheet and which could be considered an intangible or merely an unrecorded tangible asset of the business. Thus, a library of books would probably be considered an unrecorded tangible asset if it were worth only the intrinsic value of the used books. If, on the other hand, the library is assembled in such a manner that it can be used to create profits, it takes on value beyond the intrinsic worth of the volumes and would then be considered an intangible asset. A favorable leasehold may not directly produce profits, but it does so indirectly because it has value only to the extent it provides a below-market rental.

Rather than belabor the definition, it is helpful to refer to the Group 3 assets listed in ¶ 8.02. These are examples of the more common intangible assets other than goodwill.

[¶8.03-3] CAN GOODWILL AND OTHER INTANGIBLES BE COMMINGLED?

To avoid the extensive commingling of various types of intangibles which is indigenous to the "big pot" theory of goodwill, an effort should always be made to separate and individually value intangible assets other than goodwill. However, as a practical matter it may be necessary on occasion to include in a single value pool goodwill and one or more of the assets described in Group 3. For instance, it may be recognized that a business has customer lists and a secret method of production, both of which have value. Nevertheless, it may appear that the cost of establishing these separate values will exceed the benefit to be realized from the result. Under such circumstances, it is appropriate to arrive at a pool of values which may be described as "goodwill and other intangible assets." The value conclusion should preferably include a notation that a secret method of production and valuable customer lists exist but were not separately valued.

[¶8.03-4] GOING CONCERN VALUE

The courts have generally agreed an intangible value sometimes attaches to the tangible assets of an assembled business. This is called going concern value. The courts have also helped distinguish going concern enhancement from its brother, goodwill.

For some valuations, particularly income tax related problems, properly demonstrating the existence and the amount, or the nonexistence, of a going concern value as distinct from goodwill may be a very important aspect of the study.

WHAT IS GOODWILL?

The term going concern value was defined by the Supreme Court in a 1933 case involving the basis for rate making for a public utility, *Los Angeles Gas & Electric Corp., 289 U.S. 287 (1933)*. This case was referred to in a more recent decision, *Northern Natural Gas 470 F.2d 1107 (CA-8, 1973)*, "This court has declared it to be self evident that there is an element of value in an assembled and established plant, doing business and earning money over one not thus advanced, and that this element of value is a property right which should be considered in determining the value of the property upon which the owner has a right to make a fair return."

Going concern is an intangible that attaches to the tangible assets of some businesses. It may exist as a value enhancement for the assemblage of a business regardless of the businesses' profitability.

For valuation purposes, going concern value may be measured separately from other assets, although it is not a property which may be sold separately. Going concern value, like goodwill, can have value only when considered as part of an operating enterprise. For income taxes both are non-amortizable.

The foggy difference between going concern value and goodwill is cleared somewhat when the valuation methods required to value each are examined. Going concern values and goodwill values are measured by different methods.

Goodwill is usually measured by some excess profit or profit advantage technique. If there is profit beyond that required to provide an economic return on tangible and identifiable intangible (patents, licenses, etc.) assets required by the business, this excess profit may indicate the existence of goodwill.

But what if there is no excess profit? If there is no expectation of excess profit, it is said there is probably no marketable goodwill. However, the taxpayer has been alerted that the tax courts and IRS take the position if there is no goodwill demonstrable by excess profit, there may be going concern value expressed and measured in a manner other than excess profit, usually by a cost to assemble or unrealized return on investment.

[¶8.03-5] COURT DEFINITIONS OF GOODWILL

Legal opinions as to what constitutes commercial goodwill have broadened over the years. The earliest known case involving a definition and value of goodwill was in England in 1620 (Broad versus Jollyfe).[32] Broad was a shopkeeper who had acquired a business from Jollyfe for the cost of the wares plus a premium for the assurance that the seller would not relocate in the area. Contrary to his agreement, the seller did so relocate and took much of the business with him. The case was tried in court, and a judgment was handed down in favor of the plaintiff. A breach of contract was involved. The case centered around the goodwill of the business which the plaintiff claimed was lost due to transfer of the patronage from one location to another. In effect, the seller had taken his location with him. It was concluded that the location constituted the goodwill.

Two centuries later, in 1810, location was still considered the basis of goodwill. In Austen versus Bois,[33] the case revolved around local goodwill (location) as

WHAT IS GOODWILL?

opposed to personal goodwill. The court concluded that location was the key benefit to the business and therefore the essence of goodwill. It primarily influenced the habits of customers and employees to the benefit of the business.

In a case one year later, the definition of goodwill was considerably broadened to a point where it more closely approximates the view expressed in many contemporary court cases. This case (Churton versus Douglas) is considered a leading case, with the definition of goodwill contained therein having been followed by many subsequent cases. In broadening the definition, reference was made to Cruttwell versus Lye[34] wherein Lord Eldon had said, "The 'good will' which has been the subject of sale is nothing more than the probability that the old customers will resort to the old place." In Churton versus Douglas, Vice Chancellor Wood said, "It would be taking too narrow a view of what was laid down by Lord Eldon to say that good will is confined to that. Good will, I apprehend, must mean every positive advantage, if I may so express it, as contrasted with the negative advantage of the late partner, not carrying on the business himself, that has been acquired by the old firm in carrying on its business, whether connected with the premises on which the business was previously carried on, or with the name of the late firm, or with any other matter carrying with it the benefit of the business."[35]

In more recent years, many court cases have cited the following definition: "Goodwill is the advantage or benefit which is acquired by an establishment beyond the mere value of the capital stock, funds, or property employed therein, in consequence of the general public patronage and encouragement which it receives from constant or habitual customers on account of its local position, or from celebrity or reputation for skill, or affluence or punctuality, or from other accidental circumstances or necessities, or even from ancient partialities or prejudices."[36]

A 1941 case, Burke versus Canfield, provided some further amplification as follows: "'Good will' is characteristic of a going business and essentially is constituted in the tendency of customers to return for trade to those with whom they are accustomed to deal, and included in the elements holding out the lure to return are an established trade-name, a specific or general location, a reputation for service, personal attention, reasonable prices, etc., and for most purposes good will must be dealt with legally in connection with the particular business involved."[37]

Other cases have established the fact that goodwill is property recognized and protected by law as such.[38] Another case stated that goodwill has no existence except in connection with the going business to which it is incident.[39]

Many other legal definitions of goodwill and amplification of its finer meanings can be found in various legal publications.[40] Despite the many cases where goodwill has been cited and the many attempts to define it, no definition seems perfect. In most instances, goodwill is defined in such broad terms that it might be interpreted to include almost everything other than the tangible assets of a business. In some instances, this may be true. Nevertheless, the courts have recognized many intangi-

WHAT IS GOODWILL?

ble assets as distinctly separate from goodwill. Whether a party to a lawsuit is able to sustain intangibles as being separate from goodwill often depends on the care the party has taken to separately identify and value them. Lack of proper preparation and careless definition can lead to several intangible assets being grouped into a "big pot" which is classed as goodwill.

[¶8.03-6] THE INTERNAL REVENUE SERVICE VIEW OF INTANGIBLES

Most of the controversy which surrounds goodwill and other intangibles is involved directly or indirectly with tax considerations. Thus it becomes important to understand how the Internal Revenue Service views goodwill and other intangibles. By way of introduction, it should be pointed out that for purposes of dealing with the IRS, the distinction between goodwill and other intangibles is significant. This is true because goodwill can neither be currently deducted as an expense, nor can it be amortized or depreciated. On the other hand, many other intangible assets can be either currently deducted or amortized.

Perhaps the best starting point is to cite Internal Revenue Service Regulations with respect to intangibles. Regulations Section 1.167 (a)-3 provides as follows:

"If an intangible asset is known from experience or other factors to be of use in the business or in the production of income for only a limited period, the length of which can be estimated with reasonable accuracy, such an intangible asset may be the subject of a depreciation allowance. Examples are patents and copyrights. An intangible asset, the useful life of which is not limited, is not subject to the allowance for depreciation. No allowance will be permitted merely because, in the unsupported opinion of the taxpayer, the intangible asset has a limited useful life. No deduction for depreciation is allowable with respect to good will."

A recent tax case tried before the U.S. District Court for the Eastern District of California illustrates the generally accepted interpretation of the foregoing regulation and other related rules. In the case of Delk vs. the U.S.,[41] Delk Pest Control Co. purchased customer service contracts from two other pest control companies. Contracts from one company were purchased for $3,129 and from the other for $4,375. The Delks wrote the cost of these contracts off as a business expense in 1968. The Internal Revenue Service denied the deduction and assessed a tax and interest of $5,183.33 on the $7,504 disallowed deduction. The IRS contended that the customer service agreements purchased were the same as goodwill and therefore not depreciable, and that the contracts did not have a useful life that could be estimated with reasonable accuracy. In his instructions to the jury, the judge set forth the following:

". . . in order for the plaintiffs [i.e., the Delks] to prevail in this action, they must establish two things by a preponderance of the evidence:

"First, they must prove that the customer service agreements purchased by Delk Pest Control of Arizona have a value which is separate and distinct from goodwill and they must establish what that value is.

WHAT IS GOODWILL?

"Next, they must show that the customer service agreements purchased by Delk Pest Control of Arizona have a useful life in the business that can be estimated with reasonable accuracy and they must establish what that life is."

The judge further instructed the jury as follows:

"In proving what the useful life of the customer service agreements purchased by Delk Pest Control of Arizona may be, the plaintiffs may not rely merely on their own unsupported opinion as to what the useful life of the contracts is. That is, the plaintiffs' opinion must be corroborated by other competent testimony or evidence establishing the useful life of the customer service agreements."

Still other judicial instructions to the jury were:

"While Congress has granted the privilege of a deduction for depreciation, there are some restrictions on the kinds of property which may be depreciated, however. For instance, where the useful life of a piece of property cannot be estimated with reasonable accuracy, no depreciation deduction can be allowed, for it would be impossible to tell what amount would be allowable as a deduction in each year. For this reason, no depreciation may be taken for what is known as goodwill. Goodwill is defined as the expectancy of continued patronage for whatever reason."

The Internal Revenue Service won the Delk case, not because the jury found that service contracts per se were non-depreciable assets, but rather because the Delks did not prove to the jury's satisfaction that the lists in question could be valued separately and distinctly from goodwill. Nor did they prove that the useful life of the lists was estimated with reasonable accuracy. Had the Delks chosen not to deduct the entire cost of the lists in one year but had set them up as depreciable assets with assigned lives, their approach would have been better based. Of greater importance, however, had they more thoroughly researched and documented their case, they might have prevailed.

The *Houston Chronicle* case[42] could be viewed as a model of proper preparation and documentation. It is also illustrative of the byplay which frequently takes place between taxpayers and the Internal Revenue Service with respect to goodwill and intangibles. The *Chronicle* purchased all of the assets of a competing newspaper, the *Houston Press*, for a purchase price of $4,500,000. The firm then hired an appraiser who was an expert witness and who had broad experience in valuing intangibles. He allocated the purchase price as follows, and the allocation was used by the *Chronicle* in making up its income tax returns:

	Price	Useful Life
Real Estate & Equipment	$1,494,000	Various
Library (Morgue)	900,000	10 years
Subscription List	71,200	5 years
Non-Competition Agreement	2,034,800	10 years
Total Purchase Price	$4,500,000	

WHAT IS GOODWILL?

The Internal Revenue Service accepted the value of the tangible assets as filed (i.e., the real estate and equipment) but it reallocated the remaining intangible assets of $3,006,000 as follows: Library (Morgue) $150,000; Subscription List -0-; Non-Competition Agreement -0-; Goodwill - $2,856,000. The *Chronicle* paid the resulting very substantial added income taxes under protest and sued in the Federal Court for a refund.

The case went to jury trial in January 1972, and the appraiser testified on behalf of the taxpayer. The jury decided the values were as follows: Library (Morgue) - $350,000; Subscription List - $71,200; Non-Competion Agreement - $1,809,400; Goodwill - $775,400 - for a total value of intangibles of $3,006,000.

The Internal Revenue Service decided not to challenge the values set by the jury nor the useful life assigned to the major intangible assets. It did decide to appeal the useful life of the subscription list. It argued that the list did *not* have a "reasonably ascertainable life" and, consequently, could not be amortized for income tax purposes. The Court of Appeals found for the taxpayer and made the following comments:

> "Judicial tolerance compels us to say that many jurists and scholars could diagnose tax non-depreciability in the muscles and tendons of list transactions. We reject, however, the establishment of a per se rule and a monolithic 'mass asset' theory that would amalgamate all subscription lists with goodwill.
>
> "Our view that amortizability for tax purposes must turn on factual bases, is more in accord with the realities of modern business technology in a day when lists are bartered and sold as discrete vendible assets. Extreme exactitude in ascertaining the duration of an asset is a paradigm that the law does not demand. All that the law and regulations require is reasonable accuracy in forecasting the asset's useful life.
>
> "The burden to prove that an asset qualifies for tax amortizability is cast upon the taxpayer, and this taxpayer has manfully carried that heavy load as weighed by the jury. After studying the Code, Regulations, cases, testimony, and the jury's verdict, all in the light of the trial judge's meticulously thorough instructions, we can find no Achilles heel to the amortizability of these subscription lists."

From the foregoing cases and regulations, these facts can be deduced:

1. For an intangible asset to be depreciated, it must be identified and valued separately from goodwill.
2. Such as asset must have a determinable life.
3. Such intangible values and lives must be sustained by well-documented facts drawn from the business or other sources, such as the industry of which the business is a part.

172

WHAT IS GOODWILL?

4. Even though a given type of intangible asset may have been denied amortization or write-off by IRS in one or more instances, it is worth pursuing the deduction if the taxpayer believes he can sustain a value separate from goodwill and can prove a determinable life.

5. Goodwill itself is never amortizable for income tax purposes.

6. If a dispute with IRS goes to court, it is helpful to have an expert witness on hand to testify to the values and economic lives claimed by the taxpayer.

7. It is desirable to make the necessary allocations and do the required documentation at the time the tax returns are filed so that a consistent position can be taken. Also, a well-documented, logical tax return sometimes discourages at the outset the instituting of an audit, or, if an audit develops, it minimizes the disputes.

From other court cases and decisions, the following additional facts can be ascertained with respect to the Internal Revenue Service approach to intangible assets:

1. Contrary to its position on tangible assets, the IRS, supported by several court decisions, generally requires that intangibles be capable of complete exhaustion in order to qualify for depreciation.[43]

2. As a general rule, only the straight line method of depreciation is permissible with respect to intangible property.[44]

3. Notwithstanding the general rule that depreciation by the declining balance, sum-of-the-digits, and other common accelerated methods are usually not applicable, the straight line method is not the exclusive approach to depreciation if the taxpayer can prove another method is reasonable.[45]

4. When lists, contracts, and similar items are purchased or valued as mass assets, the IRS may maintain they are "indivisible assets" which do not have individually determinable value and hence are non-amortizable.[46] To overcome this contention, it may be desirable to value each customer or each contract individually and to individually determine their useful lives.[47]

5. If goodwill is acknowledged to exist in a business, it may be possible to exclude this value from the sale or purchase price if the goodwill can be shown to be associated with the person rather than the business."[48]

As one reviews the Internal Revenue Code, IRS regulations, and related court decisions, it becomes apparent that Congress, the Treasury, and the courts have all failed to give practical consideration to the capitalization and amortization of intangible assets. It is true that research and development expenses were considered in the 1954 revision of the Code and some clarification was afforded on trademark and trade name expenditures in 1956. Nevertheless, the tax code

WHAT IS GOODWILL?

should be thoroughly studied and revised with respect to intangible assets to give effect to current business and market practices. For example, it is economically logical to value and depreciate a mass of customer lists without resort to analyzing the value and life of individual accounts. Because such an account by account analysis has not been made should not cause these assets to be grouped with goodwill. Nor is it logical to require the complete exhaustion of an intangible asset before it can be deemed eligible for depreciation.

Inequities and lack of logic aside, the appraiser must deal with the tax laws as he finds them. Therefore, a necessary preliminary to any appraisal for tax purposes should include a careful study of applicable sections of the Internal Revenue Code and Internal Revenue Service regulations. In addition, a study should certainly be made of related court cases as well, since the courts often do not agree with the IRS interpretation. Nor should the taxpayer be dissuaded from seeking amortization simply because past decisions have indicated a particular type of intangible may not qualify for amortization. If the two basic tests of measurable value and determinable life can be met, there is a reasonable possibility that courts may allow the deduction even if the IRS does not. As an aid to the necessary research, there is included at Appendix 2 a listing of intangibles which the courts have decided are depreciable and those which have been considered not to be. It should be noted that there are instances where similar types of intangibles have been held both depreciable and nondepreciable.

[¶8.04] HOW TO DETERMINE THE EXISTENCE OF GOODWILL

As a first step in determining the existence of goodwill, it is necessary to examine every aspect of the business which is being studied to determine whether there are separately identifiable intangible assets of the type mentioned in Group 3 of ¶8.02. If so, each such asset should be separately valued. Then, the tests described below should be applied.

[¶8.04-1] EARNINGS TEST

Since one part of the general definition of goodwill is the ability of a firm to generate profit in excess of that which is required for a reasonable return on all of the assets of the business other than goodwill (See ¶8.03-1), it is logical to first test to see whether such excess earnings exist. Often, this will entail the application of a test similar to the Excess Profits Method described at ¶5.05-1.

This test is subject to certain reservations which have been covered elsewhere, namely: (1) A company may not show goodwill under the earnings test, and yet goodwill may be present in the form of going concern value, or (2) Earnings may be good, but the business has no goodwill because it has a limited life due to being tied to a single contract, or (3) It may have no goodwill, despite its earnings, because there are only one or two customers who can withdraw their support, or (4) Past earnings may not be indicative of the future when a key man has passed on, or (5)

WHAT IS GOODWILL?

The business may be faced with potentially expensive litigation which may destroy excess earnings in the future. Finally, in some businesses, particularly of the smaller, personally-managed type, excess profit methods simply do not apply. A market-derived formula may be found to be more useful in determining goodwill in such cases.

[¶8.04-2] MARKET TEST

The use of market formulas has been discussed in detail in Chapter 7. Where such formulas exist and can be relied upon as being representative, they should be applied to see if their application indicates the existence of goodwill. If it does, the results should be accepted subject to all of the caveats about formulas suggested in Chapter 7. Important among these caveats is the caution that simply because a market formula has shown goodwill exists in a business similar to the one being appraised, there is no assurance it exists in the subject business. Each company's circumstances must be evaluated and a reasonable determination made as to what potential buyers and sellers would normally do in developing a value for that business.

[¶8.04-3] QUESTION AND ANSWER TEST

The third test concept requires one to set aside both the earnings test and the market test and ask the rhetorical question, "Does goodwill exist in this business?" By asking and answering the question, after having considered excess earnings and market formulas, the appraiser can demonstrate the thoroughness of his investigation and consideration. Quite often, neither the excess earnings nor the market formula tests will indicate the presence of goodwill. It is appropriate to then ask, "Why?"

It may be that the type of business being analyzed does not sell for a premium. For example, many businesses are easily started. In such cases, investors may be more inclined to gamble on a fresh start rather than pay an extra consideration for an existing business and perhaps acquire negative as well as positive factors. In other instances, a buyer may investigate the market just as the appraiser does. In the process, he may discover that while a business might justify a premium for goodwill based on going concern value and profits, similar concerns do not command this bonus. Therefore, logically or not, the buyer refuses to pay a premium.

On the other hand, the question test may reveal that a consideration for goodwill may be justified even though it does not show up in excess earnings or by market formula. Under these circumstances, how can the elements of goodwill be valued? The answer is to translate the time that it would take to create the positive elements seen by the appraiser into dollars. Regardless of the element of goodwill being considered, it is usually found that, as with old wine, time creates value. An individual may have special skills, but he may not be able to translate these into value over and above the normal wage for his occupation without first establishing

WHAT IS GOODWILL?

a reputation. This takes time. The same is true of businesses. If the appraiser can arrive at the amount of time required to develop the goodwill element, he can translate this time into dollars. He may estimate labor involved in developing a workable production control system, for example. He would price out the labor over the period of time involved to develop the system. If it extended over two or three years, he might apply present worth tables to reduce the expenditure to a present value.

Another method might be used if it were necessary to develop the value of a business reputation. The advertising and other promotional costs which would be necessary to build a comparable reputation could be estimated. Again, if this expenditure would extend over several years, the present value might be calculated.

Thus, the existence of goodwill can be tested. If it is found, and no other methods seem applicable to value it, the appraiser can still arrive at a plausible worth for goodwill. He needs only to think the problem through and utilize a little ingenuity using general appraisal techniques which might not at first have appeared applicable.

[¶8.05] SUMMARY

The common concept of goodwill is one which resembles a big pot. After all tangible assets of a business have been valued and some extra value is found to exist, whatever is left over is metaphorically thrown into one big pot, blended, and named "goodwill."

The trouble with the "big pot" theory is that it often results in assets being classed as goodwill which are not. Many such assets could be separately identified, valued, and depreciated to the tax advantage of the business owner. In addition, the nebulous nature of goodwill as a leftover conglomeration of assets often results in an excessive value placed on goodwill and an inability to identify the true intangible assets of the business.

There are actually three groupings of intangible assets generally found in business. The first group, which can be most aptly described as elements of business goodwill, are intangible assets which are non-severable from the business. The second group, which could be referred to as personal goodwill elements, are non-severable from the person. The final grouping of intangible assets are usually severable from the business and include such items as brand names, copyrights, various types of contracts, and licenses. Some of these assets have determinable economic lives, some do not. Some can be valued as individual assets; others must be valued as a group.

For most purposes, goodwill can be defined as those elements of a business or a person which cause customers to return to that business or person and which

WHAT IS GOODWILL?

usually enable a firm to generate profits in excess of that which is required for a reasonable return on all of the other assets of the business, including a return on all other intangible assets that can be identified and separately valued. Other intangible assets are those assets of a business other than goodwill that have economic value; which consist of various kinds of rights, privileges, assemblages of data and know-how and that can be individually identified and valued. Usually, such an asset must be related to producing a profit. Sometimes it is not economically feasible to separate other intangible assets from goodwill, and if this has not been done, the resultant pool of intangibles should be labeled to indicate it contains assets other than goodwill.

The Internal Revenue Service, as supported by the courts, has indicated there is going concern value. This value arises as a result of a business being assembled and having the potential of being profitable. However, there may be going concern value in instances when the business is not actually demonstrating a profit. A premium might be paid on the basis the business is there, it fills a void for the buyer or time is not required to establish the business. It should be noted a going concern premium in lieu of goodwill is not automatic just because the business exists.

Starting with a court case in 1620, the judicial concept of goodwill has broadened from a concept confined to location to a definition that is closer to the broad definition noted above. The contemporary judicial definition of goodwill, drawn from several court cases, is cited in this chapter.

This chapter also describes the Internal Revenue Service view of intangibles, because the valuation of goodwill and other intangibles is most often required for tax purposes. Applicable IRS definitions and court interpretations of the Internal Revenue Code are included. It is most important to distinguish other intangible assets from goodwill for tax purposes, since goodwill cannot be deducted as an expense; whereas many other intangibles can be written off, usually in the form of depreciation. The two most important IRS requirements for depreciation of intangibles are that their value be established as separate and distinct from goodwill and their useful life can be estimated with reasonable accuracy.

Tests for determining the existence of goodwill are discussed, including the excess earnings, market and question and answer tests.

CHAPTER 9

HOW TO VALUE GOODWILL AND OTHER INTANGIBLES

The greatest gains and values are farthest from being appreciated.

HENRY DAVID THOREAU - 1817-1862

TOPICS DISCUSSED IN THIS CHAPTER

[¶9.01]	—	**Goodwill Valuation and the IRS**
[¶9.01-1]	—	**Method 12 - The IRS Goodwill Formula** Basic Concept - Limitations - Advantages Procedure - Example
[¶9.02]	—	**Intangible Valuation Methods**
[¶9.02-1]	—	**Method 13 - Profit Advantage** The Concept - Example
[¶9.02-2]	—	**Method 14 - Relief from Royalty** The Concept - Example
[¶9.02-3]	—	**Variations on Profit Contribution Methods**
[¶9.02-4]	—	**Method 15 - Cost Savings** The Concept - Example
[¶9.02-5]	—	**Method 16 - Cost to Create** The Concept - Example
[¶9.02-6]	—	**Method 17 - Cost to Purchase**
[¶9.02-7]	—	**Method 18 - The Accountants' Method** The Concept - Example
[¶9.03]	—	**How to Value Specific Intangible Assets**
[¶9.03-1]	—	**Brand Names and Registered Trademarks**
[¶9.03-2]	—	**Copyrights**
[¶9.03-3]	—	**Contracts** Employment Contracts - Covenants Not to Compete - Affiliation Agreements
[¶9.03-4]	—	**Patents**
[¶9.03-5]	—	**Franchises**
[¶9.03-6]	—	**Licenses**
[¶9.03-7]	—	**Secret Processes, Methods, and Formulas**
[¶9.03-8]	—	**Lists** Specialized Mailing Lists - Customer Lists - Subscription Lists
[¶9.03-9]	—	**Leasehold Interests**
[¶9.03-10]	—	**Technical Libraries and Newspaper Morgues**
[¶9.03-11]	—	**Drawings**
[¶9.03-12]	—	**Water Rights**
[¶9.03-13]	—	**Film Rights**
[¶9.03-14]	—	**Tax Credits for Past Losses**
[¶9.04]	—	**Summary**

CHAPTER 9

HOW TO VALUE GOODWILL AND OTHER INTANGIBLES

[¶9.01]   GOODWILL VALUATION AND THE IRS

The Excess Earnings Method, described as Method 3, (¶ 5.05-1) and the various market methods discussed in Chapter 7 are generally accepted methods of arriving at the value of goodwill. In most instances, this intangible asset which has been defined as "goodwill" in Chapter 8 can be quantified and so valued.

Still another approach should be considered, however; namely, the formula method which has been developed by the Internal Revenue Service. This formula was set forth in 1920 by the Treasury Department for the purpose of providing a method for valuing intangible assets lost by breweries and other businesses connected with the distilling industry as a result of the passage of the Eighteenth Amendment to the Constitution of the United States. The formula was set forth in a Committee on Appeals and Review memorandum and is commonly referred to as ARM-34. It was later supplemented by another memorandum designated *ARM-68*. This formula was often referred to in estate and other tax cases subsequent to its use in settling with the liquor industry.

In more recent years, the Internal Revenue Service has increasingly shied away from use of the formula. The current policy can best be summarized by quoting from Revenue Ruling 68-609:

". . . the 'formula' approach may be used for determining the firm market value of intangible assets of a business only if there is no better basis available."

Notice, however, that the formula approach has not been abandoned. In fact, this same ruling goes to some length to completely restate it. Because tax considerations are so important in the appraisal of goodwill and other intangibles, a full understanding of the position of the IRS is essential. For this reason, the complete text of applicable rulings has been reproduced in Appendix 3. Here will be found the leading ruling on intangible valuation, namely, Number 68-609, as well as rulings 59-60 and 65-193, which deal with the valuation of closely-held businesses.

[¶9.01-1] METHOD 12 - THE IRS GOODWILL FORMULA

Basic Concept

A percentage return is computed on the average annual market value of the tangible assets less liabilities. The amount of this percentage return is deducted from the average annual after-tax earnings of the business. The remainder, if any, is considered to be the amount of the average annual earnings from the intangible assets of the business. This remainder is capitalized and the result is an indication of the business' goodwill value.

HOW TO VALUE GOODWILL AND OTHER INTANGIBLES

Limitations

The resulting mass of intangible assets is similar to the "big pot" of goodwill described in Chapter 8. The entire mass is essentially non-amortizable and amorphous. A different approach might well reveal intangible assets other than goodwill that could be separately valued and depreciated.

Advantages

If there are no intangible assets other than goodwill, the intangible value has some validity. When records are deficient and the amount of goodwill is small, it affords an economical approach to the valuation.

Procedure

Step 1. Determine the average after-tax earnings for a representative period. The IRS suggests no less than 5 years. However, if on study, the future business trend indicates a difference from the average 5 years, the most representative time period is used. Delete unusual years. Prosepctive earnings may be used in some instances where future events appear to be entirely different from any past year or several year average. If the business is organized as a proprietorship, partnership or Subchapter S corporation for income tax reporting purposes, deductions must be made for salary for owner labor, other normal expenses and regular corporate income taxes.

Step 2. Determine the average net tangible assets for the same period used in Step 1. The tangible assets are to be based on fair market values. If a several-year period is used for developing an average earnings base, the fair market values of the assets for the same years should be estimated and the average used.

A detailed valuation of all tangible assets for each year to correspond with the earnings period used can be difficult. A somewhat simplified procedure is suggested. The fair market values of the assets for the latest year might be used as a base with adjustments made for prior years using backtrending factors for the fixed assets. The current asset values can usually be ascertained for past years by reviewing accounting records. For BLM, book values have been used.

HOW TO VALUE GOODWILL AND OTHER INTANGIBLES

Step 3. Deduct a return on average net tangible asset investment. It is preferable to use an industry rate, if available. There are numerous studies summarizing financial ratios by industry, but these ratios are usually based on depreciated book cost of tangible assets, not fair market values. Furthermore, these ratio studies usually do not distinguish between return on tangibles and intangibles. These two asset categories usually require different rates of return. Although industry rate of return data may not be based on market values, it should be considered.

The IRS Formula assumes adequate provision for future depreciation of wasting assets has been made as an expense in computing average earnings and suggests 8% to 10%. But many companies operate with assets that have a very low or no depreciation base. Also, differing depreciation methods are allowed for tax purposes. If the depreciation expense is not adequate, the return on net tangible asset rate used in the Formula should be adjusted accordingly to make adequate provision for return of investment (depreciation) as well as return on investment.

Step 4. If there are excess earnings, this excess is capitalized at an IRS suggested rate of 15% to 20% depending upon relative hazards.

Example

1. **Calculation of Profits**

Fiscal Year	After-Tax Earnings	Adjustments	Adjusted Earnings	
3-31-72	142,949	—	142,949	
3-31-73	115,232	11,385	126,617	
3-31-74	133,079	1,485	134,564	
3-31-75	145,840	21,582	167,422	
3-31-76	117,439	18,810	136,249	
Five Year Total			707,801	
Five Year Average ($707,801 ÷ 5)			141,560	
Average Earnings				$141,560

2. **Calculation of Tangible Assets**

Fiscal Year	Total Assets	Less Intangibles	Less All Liabilities	Formula Assets	
3-31-72	955,738	75,025	149,894	730,819	
3-31-73	994,517	90,331	173,441	730,745	
3-31-74	1,026,941	105,423	172,786	748,732	
3-31-75	1,281,188	122,723	381,193	777,272	
3-31-76	1,330,304	159,211	415,120	755,973	
Five Year Total				3,743,541	
Five Year Average ($3,743,541 ÷ 5)				748,708	
Return on Formula Assets at 10%					74,871

3. **Excess Earnings** — $ 66,689
4. **Value of Intangible Assets** ($66,689 ÷ .20) — $333,445

HOW TO VALUE GOODWILL AND OTHER INTANGIBLES

In the foregoing calculation, total assets, intangibles and current liabilities were taken from Exhibit 1 and earnings from Exhibit 2. Adjustments were derived from items A through E of Exhibit 5 on an after-tax basis (i.e.: 1973 adjustment before tax was $11,500; effective tax rate was about 1%; 1.00 − .01 = .99; .99 x $11,500 = $11,385). All liabilities were deducted from total assets instead of deducting only "accounts and bills payable" as would be done if Revenue Ruling 68-609 were strictly interpreted. The authors believe all liabilities is the proper interpretation of the IRS meaning.

The value of BLM intangible assets by the IRS Formula Method compares with the following values calculated by the more sophisticated methods outlined in Chapter 6: Belmur Process - $75,000; Lamp Patent - $15,000 and Goodwill - $180,000, for a total of $270,000. Thus, the intangible asset total of approximately $333,000 obtained with the IRS Formula would result in the total BLM company being valued $63,000 higher than by other methods. In addition, instead of having $90,000 of depreciable intangible assets, none would be depreciable because all would be considered the equivalent of goodwill.

[¶9.02]   INTANGIBLE VALUATION METHODS

There are several accepted methods which are useful in valuing intangible assets other than goodwill. Which method is applicable to a particular asset in a particular business varies with the circumstances. In some cases, more than one method may be used for an asset so that there is a cross-check on the resulting values. In other instances, only one method seems appropriate. In still other cases, the appraiser may have to develop techniques of his own, using elements from one or more of the usual methods. As an aid to the reader in quickly identifying all of the standard methods of appraisal described in this book, the intangible methods have been numbered sequentially following those suggested for general business and goodwill.

[¶9.02-1]   METHOD 13 - PROFIT ADVANTAGE

The Concept

This method is useful when it is possible to estimate with reasonable accuracy the profit advantage an intangible asset generates. In concept, it is similar to the excess earnings method (Method 3 at ¶5.05-1) used in valuing an entire enterprise, except that for this method, the extra earnings are applied to a specific intangible. This method can often be used as a second valuation technique used to test the reasonableness of conclusions reached by Method 15 - Cost Savings (¶9.02-4).

HOW TO VALUE GOODWILL AND OTHER INTANGIBLES

The profit advantage referred to is the extra net profit before tax which the intangible asset being appraised affords a particular product or service over similar products or services which are not benefited by such an intangible. The advantage may be based on historical or anticipated profits. An example might be the exceptional profit generated by a patented item over similar non-patented items as a result of the legal monopoly - i.e., a patented razor blade compared to a similar non-patented blade. Another example might be the higher profit generated by a brand name product compared with a similar unbranded product, such as brand name aspirin compared to the generic drug.

Example

To more specifically demonstrate this method, it has been used to value the secret process owned by BLM Electronics known as the Belmur Process. By reference to ¶ 3.02-8 of Chapter 3, it is learned that the process is unpatented but that there is a consensus that it will afford BLM a profit advantage for about eight years. A further assumption is that the process has just come on stream and has not yet affected past earnings. It is projected that this process, which is applicable to the manufacture of one of the company's most popular diagnostic lamps, will permit the sale of 10,000 units per year for the eight year period at $1.50 per unit more than competitors can realize on similar lamps. The calculation, using the Profit Advantage Method, would be as follows:

Average Number of Units Sold Annually	10,000
Price Advantage	1.50
Total Annual Profit Advantage	15,000
Present Worth Factor (12% Rate for 8 years)	4.968
Total Value of Profit Advantage	$74,520
Value of Belmur Process (rounded)	$75,000

For a discussion of the use of Present Worth Tables, see the "Procedure" section of Method 5 - Discounted Cash Flow (¶ 5.05-4).

[¶9.02-2] METHOD 14 - RELIEF FROM ROYALTY

The Concept

The Relief-from-Royalty Method is commonly used in the valuation of patents and licensing agreements. Often, the owner of a patent will license others to use this asset for a royalty, which is usually a percentage applied to the total dollar volume generated from sales of the patented item. Such royalties will normally be in the range of 3% - 7%, with 5% being common. Frequently, the royalty percentage will vary relative to the volume of the licensee. If the owner has already licensed others, the proper royalty percentage is simple to determine. If not, the appraiser will have to assume the position of a third party and, through market analysis or cost studies, make a determination of a supportable royalty percentage.

HOW TO VALUE GOODWILL AND OTHER INTANGIBLES

A projection must then be made of sales to which the royalty will apply. If the patent is new and its market is untested, a market analysis must be made to determine the potential. Often such a study will already have been made. Nevertheless, the reasonableness of its conclusions should be verified to whatever extent deemed necessary to adequately support the value conclusions. Inherent in the sales projection, too, is a determination of the economic life of the patent or license. The legal life is known, but the economic life may well be different. There must be a realistic forecast of how long the royalty payments can be expected and at what level. If the products are new, it may be necessary and desirable to forecast estimated sales volume year by year.

The next step is a mathematical computation of the anticipated royalty receipts by applying the royalty percentage to the projected sales. If sales have been forecast on a year by year basis, the applicable calculation must be made for each year. If a typical annual sales volume and royalty percentage have been determined over the life of the patent or license, then only one calculation is involved.

Any expenses which would be incurred in maintaining the patent or license are then accounted for and deducted from the royalty income. Such expenses could include management, legal, administrative, marketing, and similar costs. Although these expenses may be relatively minor, they still should be calculated and deducted if they relate in any way to the ability of the owner to maintain the level of royalty income forecast.

The final step is to capitalize the net royalty income stream into value. This is usually a value before income taxes. As in other discussions of applicable capitalization rates (see Method 5 at ¶ 5.05-4), the rate used is relative to the risk of the income stream continuing at its projected level. As a general rule, intangible assets have a substantially higher risk than do more secure investments, such as improved real estate, mortgages, government securities, etc. It would not be uncommon to consider risk ranges for intangibles in as broad a range as 12% - 30%, with 15% - 20% being quite common. There is no fully satisfying method for determining the rate of capitalization to be applied to each intangible. It is a subjective matter, and the appraiser must be governed by the facts in each instance.

Example

For illustration, this method has been used to value the explosion-proof lamp patent owned and developed by BLM Electronics. By reference to ¶ 3.02-8 of Chapter 3, the applicable figures are obtained. The manufacturing rights have already been licensed and the rates of royalty have been set. The patent is estimated to have a ten-year economic life, at the end of which time it will be useless. The related expenses shown below were not stated in Chapter 3 but are estimated here. The calculation of value for the lamp patent by the Relief-from-Royalty Method is as follows:

HOW TO VALUE GOODWILL AND OTHER INTANGIBLES

Fiscal Year Ending:

	3-31-77	3-31-78	3-31-79	3-31-80- 3-31-86	
1. Estimated Sales	$50,000	$75,000	$100,000	$50,000 per yr.	
2. Royalty %	7%	6%	5%	7%	
3. Gross Profit	3,500	4,500	5,000	3,500	
4. Expenses	1,000	500	500	1,000	
5. Net Profit	2,500	4,000	4,500	2,500	
6. Present Worth Factor	.870	.756	.658	2.735	
7. Value of Income	2,175	3,024	2,961	6,838	
8. Total of Line 7					$14,998
9. Value of BLM Explosion-Proof Lamp Patent (rounded)					$15,000

In the above example, a present worth rate of 15% was used as representative of the level of risk associated with the lamp profits. The column headed "3-31-80 through 3-31-86" covers seven fiscal years - that is, $50,000 per year of sales and $2,500 of net profits were projected for each of these years. The present worth factor of 2.735 is calculated as follows: Present Worth Factor for ten years at 15% equals 5.019 less .870 factor for 3-31-77 less .756 factor for 3-31-78 less .658 factor for 3-31-79 equals 2.735.

[¶9.02-3] VARIATIONS ON PROFIT CONTRIBUTION METHODS

The reader will recognize that both Methods 13 and 14 are based on profits to be contributed as a result of the intangible assets discussed. However, it may not always be practical to determine a unit price advantage as was done for Method 13, nor to select a royalty as was done for Method 14. In the former case, the figure may be impractical or unavailable, and in the latter case the asset to be appraised may not be of the type which would normally be licensed to another. Yet, it is determined that the particular intangible asset does make a profit contribution to the entire enterprise which is unique and identifiable.

In such a situation, the problem becomes one of locating a starting point for the development of a valuation technique. A study might reveal, for example, that a brand name product had a higher sales volume than a similar unbranded product (or one whose brand name was not well known). An attempt would then be made to determine the profit contribution resulting from the extra sales volume.

There are a variety of ways in which such a profit contribution could be derived, depending upon the information that is available. One approach might involve a determination of the pre-tax net profit rate for the entire enterprise. This percentage would then be applied to either a typical level of extra annual sales volume or to a year-by-year forecast with appropriate adjustments in the net profit rate. Whether applied to a typical level of sales or to year by year forecasts, it may not be wise to accept the average net profit for the entire firm without some adjustments. For example, the added sales volume might actually contribute to a higher profit margin than the remaining products to which it is being indirectly compared. On the other hand, there might be some special costs which should be considered.

In some instances it may be necessary to compare the sales and profits of a product with data from the industry in general or from other selected companies. It may not be practical to compare the product in question with others manufactured by the company which owns it. Attempting to develop the unique profit contribution of an intangible based on information from outside sources can be very difficult, and many assumptions and adjustments may be required. However, if this is the only method available for determining the value, it may have to be done this way. There are many sources of industry-wide information, such as trade associations, trade publications, the Department of Commerce, the Small Business Administration, and other governmental agencies. Unfortunately, this information is rarely broken down for a single product, process, or method so that a direct comparison can be made.

In using any profit contribution or profit advantage technique, it is important to justify the results by applying suitable tests to be certain that there is an overall intangible value in the company. An intangible asset must contribute a measurable economic advantage to its owner, or it is not an asset. Usually, that measurable advantage must come in the form of excess earnings over and above those required for an economic return on all other capital invested. This would be true no matter what approach or technique has been utilized. There must be a reasonable anticipation of profits generated by the intangible being valued which is unique and in excess of the return required on all other tangibles and intangibles.

Thus, wherever possible, a test such as the Excess Earnings Method (¶ 5.05-1) should be applied to the company as a whole. If there are excess earnings available after providing for a suitable return on other assets - tangible *and intangible* - but excluding the asset being appraised, presumably this excess is generated by the intangible asset in question. If the excess earnings so computed are minimal or non-existent and the appraiser has developed an appreciable value using one of the Profit Contribution Methods, he had best go back to the drawing board and recheck his figures and his assumptions. The Profit Contribution Methods present problems because of the subjective approach required and the frequency of difficult-to-prove assumptions. The result must be realistic, believable, and defensible to be useful.

[¶9.02-4]   METHOD 15 - COST SAVINGS

The Concept

Determination of a reasonable profit contribution or advantage may be extremely difficult or impractical. On the other hand, it may be found that an intangible asset is responsible for specific cost savings which can be measured. By creat-

HOW TO VALUE GOODWILL AND OTHER INTANGIBLES

ing this saving, the intangibles, in effect, make a profit contribution. Thus a cost advantage might be created by a contract which allows the advantageous purchase of raw materials, such as oil supply contracts negotiated by some of the utilities before the Arab oil boycott. Or a labor saving process or method or a secret formula may create a cost savings. Cost savings may relate to the time required to assemble or create something. An employment contract with a valuable employee could be viewed as a form of cost saving if, because of his ability and skill, the business was able to perform certain functions more economically than were it to acquire and train a new employee to accomplish the same tasks with equal skill.

The method usually involves a determination of a specific amount of cost savings over a specific period of time. This savings is then capitalized using a present worth factor.

Example

A company has developed a streamlined, secret method for assembling a manufactured item. It has been determined that competing products cost $4.50 per unit to manufacture, of which 50% of the cost is represented by labor. The client company sells 250,000 units per year. As a result of its secret method of assemblage, the company can save 25¢ per unit on material and it can save 35% on competing labor costs. It expects this advantage to continue for six years. The value of the process using the cost savings method is as follows:

1. **Material Savings:**
    250,000 units x $.25 = $ 62,500

2. **Labor Savings:**
    Competitor's Cost for Like Product:
        250,000 units x $4.50 = $1,125,000
        Labor Content at 50%   562,500

    Labor Saving:
        35% x $562,500 =   196,875

3. **Total Saving** $259,375

4. **Life of Advantageous Cost Savings:**   Six Years

5. **Value Computation:**
    Present Worth Factor (6 years at 15%)   3.784
    Value: $259,375 x 3.784 = $981,475

6. **Value of Secret Process (rounded)** $980,000

[¶9.02-5] METHOD 16 - COST TO CREATE

The Concept

Bearing in mind that intangible assets tend to be fully or partially expensed by most businesses, the appraiser may be called upon to develop the cost to create an

HOW TO VALUE GOODWILL AND OTHER INTANGIBLES

asset such as a patent or a secret process or a mailing list. Although the cost of an intangible asset is seldom its value, this is not always true. There are times when the Cost-to-Create Method is the only feasible approach to valuation. This could be particularly true with respect to items for which a market had not yet been developed nor could one be practically estimated, and still there was sufficient evidence that a market could be generated. A new invention or a research and development project might fall into this category. A specialized, but improved, mailing list might be another example.

The costs which are part of the cost to create can be quite diverse, depending upon the situation. Typically, costs for an experimental item, such as the research leading to a patent, would include at least the labor and material to create prototypes, engineering drawings and plans, and legal fees.

The cost to create may be the final value estimate itself, or it may be only a portion of the total value of an asset which includes a buildup of other costs or values to make up the total. The Cost-to-Create Method also may be used as a means of checking the value conclusion reached by another method.

This method should be used cautiously and sparingly. As has been noted, cost is not generally indicative of value, especially of an intangible. Normally, if an intangible contributed no more to the income stream of a business than the cost to create it, there would be no advantage. Generally, an intangible asset must provide a specific and unique advantage of some sort. However, when no other method seems practical, it might be reasonable to conclude, for example, that the research and development cost of a certain item might result in some special advantages in the future. A buyer could be expected to pay a price for it, since the work had already been done. Very possibly, this price would be no more than the cost to create.

Example

Assume an appraiser was asked to develop the cost to create a research and development project. After careful study, he came up with the following costs:

Materials	$10,000
Labor (1,000 hours at $10 per hour)	10,000
Outside Research Assistance	5,000
Legal Research	5,000
Market Research	10,000
Subtotal	40,000
Return on Investment:	
Average Investment $20,000 x 10% = $2,000	
x 2 years	4,000
TOTAL COST TO CREATE	$44,000

HOW TO VALUE GOODWILL AND OTHER INTANGIBLES

One purpose for including this example is to point out the types of costs which typically must be developed - often from several sources and frequently with little help from the company's records. The second purpose is to remind the reader that return on investment should be considered as one of the expenses.

[¶9.02-6] METHOD 17 - COST TO PURCHASE

Occasionally, an intangible asset can be acquired in the market at a price judged to be equivalent to its economic value. Attempts should always be made to test the purchase price of such an asset to be certain it is not an aberration. As appropriate, test methods could include cost savings, cost to create in-house, excess profits, profit contribution, and profit advantage. The cost to purchase may be useful as a value test for franchises and licenses appraised by other means.

Many intangibles are bought and sold in the open market, and sufficient data can be obtained to develop a market value for such assets. For example, franchises to operate certain types of business can be acquired from a franchisor at established prices. In some cases, the franchise may be resold with very limited control by the franchisor, thus establishing a secondary market. Liquor licenses are another example of a salable intangible. Often these licenses sell for a price many times the original cost to the last licensee.

[¶9.02-7] METHOD 18 - THE ACCOUNTANTS' METHOD

The Concept

The accounting profession is often concerned with the allocation of the purchase price of a business among the various assets acquired. In 1970, the Accounting Principles Board of the American Institute of Certified Public Accountants issued its Opinion No. 17 regarding the proper recording of intangible assets in a business acquisition. This opinion has since been incorporated into Volume 3 of the AICPA's Professional Standards. The entire opinion contained some thirty-five paragraphs; therefore, rather than reproduce it, the key facts are summarized as follows:

Identifiable intangible assets should be recorded at the cost of purchase and included as separately identifiable assets along with the various classifications of tangible assets. The remaining portion of the purchase price is considered to be an unidentifiable asset called *goodwill*. In effect, the goodwill as a residual figure is the difference between the purchase price and the total cost of all other assets acquired less the liabilities assumed.

The specifically identifiable assets relate closely to the assets described in Group 3 at ¶8.02 of Chapter 8 - i.e., patents, licenses, franchises, contracts, etc.. When the assets are acquired as part of a total purchase price without values assigned to the individual intangible assets, the fair values of the individual assets are used as a basis for allocating the total price. Notice, however, the assignment of values approximating fair market value tends to arise only in specialized situations, such as a purchase price allocation. Usually, the accountants condone the normal business practice of writing off as expenses the costs of most intangible assets, whether or not specifically identifiable. For this reason, they do not generally appear on company books except where the assets have been purchased.

Example

A company is purchased for $500,000 cash. The acquisition consists of $500,000 in tangible assets and $100,000 of identifiable intangible assets, such as patents, copyrights, and licenses. Accounts payable and other debt of $200,000 is assumed. Based on these facts, the Accountants' Method would make the following allocation of the purchase price:

Assets		Liabilities & Capital	
Tangible Assets	$500,000	Liabilities Assumed	$200,000
Identified Intangible Assets	100,000		
Goodwill	100,000	Capital	500,000
Total Assets	$700,000	Total Liabilities & Capital	$700,000

Note that the goodwill residual is the difference between the purchase price and the total cost of identifiable assets less the liabilities assumed. That is, from the purchase price of $500,000 is subtracted $400,000 ($600,000 of identifiable tangible and intangible assets less $200,000 of liabilities assumed) leaving $100,000, which is the value assigned to goodwill.

[¶9.03] HOW TO VALUE SPECIFIC INTANGIBLE ASSETS

In the foregoing section, several standard methods have been described which are useful in valuing individual intangible assets. As noted, more than one method may be used for a given asset. The appraiser may correlate the results of two or more methods, or he may use an additional method or methods as a check on values which he has derived from a single technique he feels is most applicable. In the following paragraphs of this section, the adaptation of the foregoing methods to specific types of assets is discussed.

[¶9.03-1] BRAND NAMES AND REGISTERED TRADEMARKS

Brand names and trademarks can have immense value. Some, such as *Kleenex* and *Frigidaire* have become almost generic terms. It is rare to hear someone ask for a soft tissue. Usually, the request will be for Kleenex. Lesser-known brand names or trademarks will not approach the values of Kleenex or Frigidaire, but if there is a sales or profit advantage afforded by the trademark or name, a profit contribution method can be used to value it. A further variation on the methods discussed at ¶9.02-1 through ¶9.02-3 could involve a determination that a particular well-known label sells at a 20% higher profit margin than relatively unknown competing products. This added margin could be applied to the annual sales of the brand being valued to obtain a net income advantage which can be capitalized.

A critical problem in the valuation of brand names and trademarks is determination of the capitalization method. If a remaining economic life cannot reasonably be established, the appraiser is left with but two choices, to select an arbitrary life or to capitalize the asset in perpetuity.[49] This is a difficult choice and demonstrates the reason these assets are often grouped with goodwill into one pool of intangibles. However, it is not illogical to capitalize the brand names or trademarks in perpetuity, because any excess income considered to be goodwill would be so capitalized. Thus, if a portion of the excess profits can be isolated to a brand name, a reasonable separation of value from the balance of goodwill is achieved.

If the appraisal is for tax purposes, an indeterminate life would not be accepted for depreciation purposes. (See ¶ 8.03-6.) However, the capitalization in perpetuity would provide a separate value for balance sheet purposes. This means that if the asset is sold or otherwise disposed of at a later date, there is an established basis for taxable gain or loss.

At times, a comparative sales technique might be utilized as a primary or test method. A market check may reveal similar brand names or trademarks have been sold which afford suitable comparisons.

The Relief-from-Royalty Method (¶ 9.02-2) could be used by hypothesizing that the brand name or trademark could be licensed to a third party. Royalty income based on competitive market conditions could be calculated. This income could then be capitalized by an appropriate method.

The Cost-to-Create Method (¶ 9.02-5) might also be reasonable if it appears the asset has future value, but it is difficult to determine a definite market or profit advantage. The cost to develop a brand name can be substantial. Often included are costs of extensive art work, market studies, surveys, tests of use, promotions, and advertising. Certain oil companies have spent literally millions of dollars in developing a new brand name or a company or product identification.

[¶9.03-2] COPYRIGHTS

Appraisal methods and considerations for copyrights are similar to those for brand names and trademarks, with relatively minor exceptions. The principal difference lies in the fact that it is somewhat easier to arrive at a useful life for copyrights. This is not so much because they have a fixed legal life, but rather because copyrighted products are apt to have a limited economic life.[50] Another difference is that the Relief-from-Royalty approach would appear to have a limited applicability to copyrights.

HOW TO VALUE GOODWILL AND OTHER INTANGIBLES

[¶9.03-3] CONTRACTS

A wide variety of contracts could have value as intangible assets. Some of the more representative types are advertising contracts, employment contracts, covenants not to compete, sales contracts, purchase contracts, and affiliation contracts.

As a general rule, and particularly in tax cases, it is advisable to value each contract individually rather than attempting to assign a value to a group of assets. The tax considerations are outlined at ¶ 8.03-6, but it could be added that the greater the degree of sophistication used in appraising contracts, the more acceptable to the court the conclusions seem to be.

The valuation of contracts which provide an income can usually be valued using one of the profit contribution methods described at ¶ 9.02-1 through ¶ 9.02-3. That is, the net profit from the contract would be projected on either a year-by-year basis or at a typical figure. The results would then either be carried back to present value using appropriate tables, or the typical profit would be capitalized at a suitable rate. Identical rates should not be used for different contracts unless the risks are similar. The process of valuing each contract separately for the reasons suggested above entails individual risk valuations. It is also important to be sure that income attributed to a particular contract is exclusively for that contract and has not been mixed with other sources of income. This segregation of income can pose a major problem.

When contracts do not actually generate income per se, but rather involve specific and significant savings, these savings can be translated into profit contributions. As was noted earlier, contracts for future purposes at advantageous prices, such as oil products contracted before the Arab boycott, are prime examples.

Employment Contracts

Employment contracts afford another widespread example of contracts which can result in specific, measurable savings. For example, when one company buys another, the president of the selling company, who is a key figure in the business, contracts to remain with the company for a specified period. This is often done to help transfer customers to the new owner. The value of such a contract could be based upon the cost to replace the individual with another person who would take a period of time to become as effective. In some instances, a key man may perform the functions of two or three important posts, such as chief administrator, sales manager, and production manager. An acceptable cost to replace all of these key people could be developed through a number of sources, such as employment consulting firms and published compensation manuals.

Example

Assume a five year contract has been signed with a key person in a selling company who spends 25% of his time as chief executive officer and the remainder

HOW TO VALUE GOODWILL AND OTHER INTANGIBLES

as sales manager. Without this key man, it can be assumed the business might decline rapidly or cease altogether. Therefore, the contract is an essential ingredient for the continued success of the operation. As such, it has substantial value. A study made of comparable salaries in the industry results in findings that a full-time chief executive officer would be paid $50,000 a year and a full-time sales manager $40,000 per annum.

In a valuation of this type, it should be assumed that if one or two new people were brought in to take the place of the key man, they would, over a period of time, gradually learn the business and become equally effective. This is a theoretical but necessary consideration, because it is necessary to quantify the unique contribution the key man would make during each year of the contract. This would be related to the time required for new people to learn the key man's jobs before they became as effective. It might be calculated that during the first year, 100% of the key man's salary would be saved over using new people; during the second year, it might be estimated that 60% would be saved (the new people are assumed to be only 40% as effective); during the third year, 50%; during the fourth year, 30%; and 10% in the final year. The total savings for each year would then be brought back to a present worth basis by using present worth factors. Assuming the competing salaries cited, the base upon which the savings would be calculated is $42,500 per annum (25% of the key man's time as chief executive at $50,000 per year plus 75% of his time as sales manager at $40,000).

Year	Cost to Replace	Percent Saved	Amount Saved	15% Factor	Present Worth
1	$42,500	100%	$42,500	.870	$36,975
2	42,500	50%	21,250	.756	16,065
3	42,500	40%	17,000	.658	11,186
4	42,500	30%	12,750	.572	7,293
5	42,500	10%	4,250	.497	2,112
Total					$73,631
Value of the Contract (rounded)					$74,000

Before accepting this value of $74,000, it should be compared to the total amount of the contract. If the contract called for a salary of more than $42,500 per year, the value conclusion seems reasonable. If, however, it called for something less, such as $30,000 per year, the conclusion on value seems questionable, and a change should be made in the calculation.

Covenants Not to Compete

Covenants not to compete are often included in buy-sell agreements of businesses. Occasionally, they are included in key person employment contracts. Many court battles have been fought over the valuation of covenants not to compete and over the establishment of finite lives for them. A study of the court decisions leads to the conclusion that if at the time of sale the value of the covenant was agreed upon and a specific dollar amount was placed upon it and if this amount was reasonable, the valuation stands a good chance of being accepted by the court. Most of these cases involve tax matters.

Such covenants can be valued using a cost saving method. One approach would be to develop the cost and time required to build a business to the present level of the firm being sold. Another approach would be to make an estimate of the sales which would be lost if the previous owner were privileged to open a competing business in the same territory. The sales loss could then be translated into lost profits, and these could be valued.

Covenants not to compete are normally for a specific period of time. Consideration should be given to the fact that the new owner presumably would gradually build up his own goodwill, so that the importance of the covenant would tend to diminish. If this is the case, the diminishing value should be considered on a year by year forecasted basis. The value of the savings, or the value of the reduced loss, would then be totaled for each year. The value of these annual amounts would be compiled, probably using present worth factors, and this calculation would result in the value of the covenant not to compete.

Affiliation Agreements

Affiliation agreements, such as those entered into by a local broadcasting company with a major network, can be valuable. The advantage can be measured by the advertising rates and quantity of advertising that such a radio or television station enjoys compared with its competitors. Since advertising rates are published and these rates are related to the quantity of the station's audience, ample data is available to make such a comparison. If studies indicate that a substantial portion of the subject station's advantage over competition is due to the network affiliation, this advantage can be valued without too much complexity. The value is usually related to the capitalized value of the extra earnings created by the affiliation. Care needs to be taken to eliminate the effects of any advantages the station may possess other than the network affiliation.

There are innumerable types of contracts which are capable of being valued, and all cannot be discussed here. It should be evident from the foregoing discussion, however, that the usual method of valuing contracts is first to isolate the specific advantage the contract provides. This advantage is converted into net profit for a specific period of time, and this profit is then capitalized by a suitable method. This should be done on a contract by contract basis.

[¶9.03-4] PATENTS

The most common method for valuing a patent is the Relief-from-Royalty Method described as Method 14 at ¶9.02-2. In effect, this method assumes the patent is owned by a third party and therefore the true owner must pay a royalty for

HOW TO VALUE GOODWILL AND OTHER INTANGIBLES

the privilege of using the patented item. Since the true owner does in fact have title to the patent, he is relieved from having to pay the royalty; hence, the name "relief from royalty."

Another approach to patent valuation would be to use a Profit Contribution Method. (See ¶ 9.02-1 and ¶ 9.02-3.) Under this method, a net profit would be calculated which is directly attributable to the patented technique, formula, method or product. This income stream would then be capitalized over the economic life of the patent to arrive at its value.

The Cost-to-Create Method could also be used, but as was pointed out at ¶ 9.02-5 in the discussion of this method, it would generally be used where no definite market had yet been established. For this reason, Cost to Create is most widely used to value applications for patents and research and development work done for a potential patent.

In determining the life of a patent, it is advisable to bear in mind that the legal life, which ranges from 3½ to 17 years, may not be the same as the economic life. A market study may be required to determine the reasonable length of time over which the patent can provide sufficient protection to generate the advantageous income which has been calculated. In fact, not only may a market study be required, but also a study of potential competitive technology may be needed.

Problems are often encountered in valuing American inventions which are patented in foreign countries. Such countries do not always provide the same protections to patent holders as are afforded in the United States. Consideration needs to be given to these differences.

[¶9.03-5] FRANCHISES

A franchise is, in effect, a license granted by a manufacturer, large retailer, wholesaler, or service company granting permission to a retailer or service specialist to sell his particular product or service. There are franchises in existence in many different lines of business, and fees paid for franchises can range from $1,000 to over $100,000. The fee varies according to the strength and reputation of the franchisor, the support which the franchisor gives in the form of advertising, training, advantageous purchasing, and the basic profitability of most of the franchises.

Transferability of the franchise will be of concern. If there are limitations upon this, the degree and type of restriction must be considered for its effect on value. At times there will be a specific buy-back amount set forth in the agreement. This would naturally restrict the value, because the franchisee would not be free to sell the asset to outsiders. He would have to sell it back to the franchisor, or at least give him the right of first refusal. If a franchise is particularly successful, the franchisor will usually wish to protect it in every way possible. One way to do this is to include stringent and specific conditions in the agreement as to who can hold the privilege.

HOW TO VALUE GOODWILL AND OTHER INTANGIBLES

Establishing a determinable economic life for the franchise can present a challenge. Franchises usually run with the franchisee's business, and they are automatically renewed as long as there is no breach of contract. The potential life of the agreement has an effect on the type of capitalization rate used. If there is no determinable life, it may be necessary to capitalize into perpetuity.[51] On the other hand, if it can be found that the advantage offered by the franchise is limited to the early years, as might be true for a start-up business, and a substantial pattern can be established to prove this, a limited life can be calculated for the franchise. Any advantage can then be valued on a projected year by year basis using present worth factors.

There are several ways in which a franchise can be valued, following some of the methods suggested in ¶9.02. If there is a profit advantage over similar businesses by virtue of the franchise, a Profit Contribution or Profit Advantage Method can be used. If the franchise results primarily in cost savings, a Cost Savings Method would be appropriate. As was noted earlier, Method 17 - Cost to Purchase (¶9.02-6) should always be checked on franchises. If by chance the franchise is shown on the books, the origin of the figure should be checked (i.e., was it, for instance, the cost to purchase?), but the chances are minimal that the book figure will coincide with value.

[¶9.03-6] LICENSES

Since licenses are similar to franchises, the methods applicable to their valuation are generally parallel. However, in the case of certain licenses, such as those for the sale or dispensation of alcoholic beverages and those issued by the Federal Communications Commission, there is an added complication of weighing the effect of government policies on transferability.

[¶9.03-7] SECRET PROCESSES, METHODS AND FORMULAS

If these assets are protected by a patent, then the methods discussed for valuing patents should be used. (See ¶9.03-4.) Often, however, no patent protection exists, but a profit advantage or cost saving is afforded for some period into the future. If so, a study of the historical general business and accounting records should provide necessary information on the extent and character of the advantages provided. Allocations made from these records may involve a considerable amount of judgment on the part of the appraiser, but usually supportable figures can be derived.

A major difficulty in this type of appraisal lies in developing determinable lives for the assets. Such intangibles are often subject to a high degree of risk, particularly when there is no patent protection. The greatest risk lies with an employee taking the trade secrets with him, either before or after he leaves the company. There may be legal recourse, but that approach also involves high risks.

HOW TO VALUE GOODWILL AND OTHER INTANGIBLES

Method 13, (discussed at ¶ 9.02-1) includes an illustration of one approach to valuing a secret process - the Profit Advantage Method. The Cost Savings Method described at ¶ 9.02-4 is another frequently used approach.

[¶9.03-8] LISTS

There are many different types of lists that are bought, sold, valued, and/or compiled. No one method is applicable to all types of lists because their content and use can vary widely. To illustrate the principles, however, three types of lists are discussed below: specialized mailing lists, customer lists, and subscription lists.

Specialized Mailing Lists

While many lists are bought and sold, highly specialized lists can not be readily acquired on the outside. For example, one of the authors was faced with the need to compile a list of all recreational vehicle owners in a given state. There is a wide variety of such vehicles. Some are specially licensed, some are licensed as trucks, some as private automobiles, and some are not licensed at all when the body which converts a truck to a recreational vehicle is removable. There was no known source at that time for this specialized mailing list.

Assuming it were not available on the market, appraisal of an existing specialized list would entail an estimate of the cost to build up or create it on an in-company basis. This study would have to include an estimate of the period of time required to develop the list to its current level of effectiveness or completeness. One approach to determining the time required would involve a review of the company's experience with respect to the percentage of the list which would require revision each year. If 25% of the names needed annual revision, it is reasonable to conclude that it would take four years to build a comparable list.

Having determined the time period, an estimate should next be made of the cost to compile the list. The existing list may have been generated as a result of advertising in newspapers, periodicals, trade magazines, radio or television, direct mail, and by telephone and personal calls by salesmen. The cost of all or a portion of these activities could be allocated to the list development. In addition, clerical time and supplies should be considered. In effect, the list could be valued by the Cost-to-Create Method.

Customer Lists

While customer lists may be developed in somewhat the same way as mailing lists, some different concepts are usually involved. Whereas a mailing list provides a basis for advertising and solicitation, it does not contain an assurance that all those on the list will become customers. A customer list is made up of people with whom the firm has done business over a period of time. The list gains value to the extent customers become "regulars" and make repeat purchases. Another element

HOW TO VALUE GOODWILL AND OTHER INTANGIBLES

of value is created by the potential of lower cost sales. It takes less solicitation and effort to make sales to repeat customers.

Still other aspects of customer lists give them distinctive values, such as the pre-screened credit standing of the names; their availability as references for new customers; and the advertising value of the names of prominent people on the list for implied or actual product endorsement. The fact that a customer list contributes value to a company is not difficult to establish. The measure of this value can be a more complex matter.

One suggested approach would be to analyze the list to determine repeat sales originating from it. This analysis should be made for a period of several years. A percentage of repeat customers could thus be developed. The sales contribution on an annual basis by individual repeat customers could be determined, or repeat sales could be developed for the entire group. By either method, the repeat sales could be compared to the total sales of the business. If, for example, customers on the list were typically responsible for 50% of the total sales of the enterprise, the dollar sales contribution of the list could be determined. The sales so derived could then be converted to net profit. If customers on the list contributed $200,000 in sales and the typical net profit of the business before tax but after owners' salaries were 6%, the annual profit contribution of the list could be considered to be $12,000.[52] This figure could then be capitalized in perpetuity if no definite life could be put on the list, or a present worth factor could be applied if a life could be determined.

As in the case of specialized mailing lists, one approach to the determination of a life for the list would be a calculation of the turnover of names. Assume a historical review of the company records for a representative period indicates 20% of the customers were typically lost each year. The life of the list could then be established at five years.

Another approach for valuing the customer list might be use of the Cost-to-Create Method. The procedure would be similar to that suggested for appraising specialized mailing lists.

Subscription Lists

Newspapers, magazines, and private publications of all kinds have valuable subscription lists. Frequently, market data is available in sufficient detail to enable the compilation of typical market prices paid for them. For instance, entire newspaper enterprises often sell for a consideration which includes a specific figure for the subscription list. The price is based on so many dollars per subscriber. It may range from $10 to several hundred dollars, depending upon the type of newspaper, its advertising rates, the number of subscribers, and the total circulation. Such market data should always be given consideration in the valuation of subscription lists.

HOW TO VALUE GOODWILL AND OTHER INTANGIBLES

The Cost-to-Create Method might also be used in much the same way as was done with respect to mailing and customer lists. In addition, a Profit Contribution Method might seem reasonable if it is possible to develop a profit advantage from customers on the subscription list as opposed to those who were not so included.

The economic life of a subscription list would be estimated using the same approaches outlined for mailing and customer lists. As in the case of contracts, it is desirable to value the lists individually, rather than to use group averages. This is particularly true when the appraisal is being made for income tax purposes.

[¶9.03-9] LEASEHOLD INTERESTS

A leasehold interest is basically a tangible asset not an intangible. It involves basic real estate valuation procedures. The starting point is to find out whether such an interest exists. The usual approach to this determination is to compare the lease rental with the economic or going rental for comparable space. The economic rental can be determined by a market survey. In making comparisons, suitable weight should be given to variations in location, physical condition, expense responsibilities, and other factors which would distort the results. If it is found that the lease rental is advantageous because it is less than the economic rental on a net-after-expenses basis to the tenant, it can be concluded that a leasehold interest exists.

In rental comparisons, the appraiser must know what the market rentals include. Terminology can often be confusing. For example, there are distinct differences between net usable space and net rentable space. Net rentable space is that which the owner of the property is able to rent. If the owner includes common areas on a pro rata basis to each tenant, then this space is part of the net rentable area, but it is not exclusively usable by the tenant.

Leases must be carefully read to determine the existence and effect of special provisions, such as acceleration clauses. Such clauses may provide for lump sum payments at the end of an accounting period to allow for increases in operating expenses or real estate taxes. The amount of such adjustments may be difficult to estimate, but it must be given consideration, because this added rent may have the effect of negating the leasehold interest.

Once a supportable, economic rental advantage has been established, the typical annual amount of the advantage is usually capitalized over the remaining period of the lease. Often there are options to renew, and the terms of these options dictate how any rental advantage attributable to the option periods should be handled. It is apparent that a lease which has only a short time to run and has no advantageous renewal options would have a limited value even if the rent were well below market on the balance of the base term.

HOW TO VALUE GOODWILL AND OTHER INTANGIBLES

[¶9.03-10] TECHNICAL LIBRARIES AND NEWSPAPER MORGUES

The type of technical library which falls into the intangible category generally has been created over a long period of time, and the expenses of assembling it have usually been expensed.[53] Nevertheless, the library can have immense economic value - in some cases being the most important asset of an enterprise. Newspaper morgues are approached for appraisal purposes in the same manner.

The Cost-to-Create Method (see ¶ 9.02-5) is usually the most practical for such assets. In compiling the costs, all essential expenses should be considered, including the labor, material, and supplies involved in assembling the data as well as the cost of books, drawings, papers, maps, charts, records, tapes, and microfilm. In essence, all costs should be totaled with the exception of furnishings and equipment.

Because of the passage of time, many items in such a library can be virtually irreplacable. Careful analysis needs to be given to the time that would be involved in attempting to replace the library, beginning with conditions as they exist at the date of appraisal. For example, an important document in the library may have been readily available in 1935, but if it had to be recreated at a current date, original research and other expenses would be required. It would be much more costly to obtain the document today. Many similar situations often arise, each of which needs to be studied carefully and individually evaluated.

While technical libraries and newspaper morgues may have a great deal of value, there is usually some obsolescence as well. The cumulative costs to create should be reduced by obsolescence to the extent it exists.

[¶9.03-11] DRAWINGS

Drawings which relate to the productive capacity of an enterprise can have substantial economic value if they are still used. Even if not used on a regular basis, the value may be significant if they are useful at any time to help solve a problem or to create a special product for which there may be only occasional demand. Sometimes drawings which appear to be crudely done may have great utility, whereas some of the finest engineered drawings or plans may have no value whatsoever. Written specifications which accompany drawings may be important to their utility and should be considered in valuing the data, especially if a Cost-to-Create technique is used.

There are occasions when drawings can be the essence of an entire business. One of the authors was engaged to appraise such a business. The company specialized in automotive ignition parts and prided itself on being able to furnish such parts for virtually every model of automobile ever built. The key to its ability was a complete file of drawings accumulated over many years. Information with respect to older ignition parts was gleaned by searching through junkyards or any other place where old ignition systems could be located. Such systems were then acquired

HOW TO VALUE GOODWILL AND OTHER INTANGIBLES

and torn apart. Drawings of all of the integral parts were made and filed. They were crude in appearance, being recorded freehand on inexpensive cardboard. However, they had great value because comparable information could be gathered only in the way the company had done it. No such information was available for most of the older vehicles from factory records, owner's manuals, or other published data. As a result, the firm gained a reputation for being the manufacturer of specialized parts that could be obtained nowhere else. The fact that the firm could manufacture from the drawings on file was as essential ingredient in its success.

While not always as vital to the business as for the ignition parts manufacturer, valuable drawings are common among many enterprises. They tend to be overlooked because they have been expensed. The custom of expensing the cost is particularly applicable to drawings because they usually are the result of many diverse activities which are normal expense items, such as research, surveys, studies, appraisals, and photographs. Even were the time to make the drawings capitalized, this would normally be an insignificant part of the full cost.

While several valuation methods could be applied, depending upon the circumstances, two are often used. The Cost-to-Create Method (¶ 9.02-5) is obviously applicable. Factors to be considered are similar to those involving the creation of mailing lists, technical libraries, and research and development. The labor, material, and other costs incident to developing the drawings are summarized. Obsolescence of some of the drawings should be considered and quantified. The resulting cost after obsolescence would be the value, or at least one measure of it.

The second frequently used approach would be an income method (¶ 9.02-1 through ¶ 9.02-3) if a measurable advantage can be developed through having the drawings versus not having them. As in the case of the ignition manufacturer, the drawings may create a virtual monopoly, causing customers to return to the same place of business since they cannot be satisfied elsewhere. From company records, it should be possible to estimate the degree of influence the drawings have on obtaining customers. A sales or profit contribution could be derived. This contribution could then be capitalized.

It will be recognized that one of the problems associated with the valuation of drawings is the establishment of determinable life for income tax purposes. If this cannot be done on a sustainable basis, it will be necessary to group the drawings with goodwill for tax write-off purposes. However, as has been noted earlier with respect to other intangibles, it may still pay to place a value on the drawings in the event of subsequent sale or as an aid in determining the detail on all of the assets of a firm.

[¶9.03-12] WATER RIGHTS

Exclusive rights to use water from a stream, river or well can be an extremely valuable asset. Such rights can become an integral part of the value of real estate.

HOW TO VALUE GOODWILL AND OTHER INTANGIBLES

Sometimes the rights flow with the land. They are then said to be appurtenant to the land. In other cases, the rights may be separately sold, usually as shares of stock, each share carrying a specific water allowance.

Water rights are usually valued by normal real estate appraisal techniques. Land which has water rights can be valued and compared to similar land without rights. Provided there are not other factors which affect the relative values which have not been isolated, the differences between the value of the land with rights and the dry land is a measure of the worth of the rights.

Another approach, where applicable, would be to estimate the cost savings resulting from the use of the water for power generation compared with the cost to buy energy (usually in the form of electricity) from other sources. The cost savings can then be estimated and capitalized in perpetuity, unless the right has a time limit.[54] If limited, present worth factors would be used to capitalize the projected income stream.

If the rights are transferable, as by the sale of stock with water rights, a market approach should be checked. There may be sufficient sales of such stock to afford at least some test of value. The problem with this approach may be the lack of regularity of sales and the difficulty of deriving suitable facts, since such shares almost always are private transactions.

For property tax purposes, county assessors sometimes value water rights based on the going market price for water, such as the price per acre foot for agricultural uses. An estimate is made of the acre feet of water created by the right. This is then multiplied by the going price per acre foot and the result is capitalized at a rate thought appropriate. Such a formula can result in unrealistic values, however, if expenses of delivering the water are not deducted to arrive at a measure of profitability or if too low a capitalization rate is used.

[¶9.03-13] FILM RIGHTS

Film rights usually attach to so-called "film in the can." The latter term refers to a movie, commercial, or instructional film which has been completed and is ready for showing. The income created by the film can be many times the original cost to produce it, even after deduction of marketing costs and the expenses of maintaining the film in usuable condition. Income from the right is often related to a percentage of the receipts from those who pay to use the film. Frequently, there is a specified minimum fee.

In most cases, the potential gross income from the film can be estimated on a year by year basis. By deducting the appropriate expenses, it is then possible to calculate net profits. These profits can be capitalized into value by use of present worth factors. The factors used should reflect the risks inherent in the projection, as would be true for other appraisals using this approach.

HOW TO VALUE GOODWILL AND OTHER INTANGIBLES

[¶9.03-14] TAX CREDITS FOR PAST LOSSES

The Internal Revenue Code allows the carryback and carryforward of certain types of losses designated as operating losses and capital losses. For most corporations both types of losses can be carried back for three years, but the carryforward periods differ. That is, operating losses can be carried forward for seven years, whereas only five years are allowed for capital losses.[55] Thus, if a business has either kind of loss in the current year, this loss can be carried back to offset profits in the three preceeding years. If the business sustained losses in prior years, these losses can be carried forward for five or seven years (depending on the type of loss) to offset the current year's profits and profits of subsequent years. In either case, there is a tax saving.

It is apparent that such tax credits can have an appreciable economic value. This value is not normally reflected on balance sheets, except perhaps as a footnote. However, there are many restrictions on their use, particularly where control of an enterprise has changed or where there has been a major change in the type of business carried on. If the credit is to be valued for the present owners for a purpose other than sale, the task can be fairly straightforward. Basically, the anticipated tax savings can be estimated, and this savings can be capitalized into value. Choice of the capitalization rate must be carefully considered, however, as this is a high risk asset. If the company has not been profitable in past years, it is quite possible that it will not be uniformly profitable in the future, and hence will not be able to use part or all of the tax credit. If it was profitable in the past but is currently losing money, the risk of losing the credit is lessened.

In all cases, when loss carryover provisions are to be valued, there exists the risk of IRS disallowance by audit. This is an almost imponderable risk which depends a great deal upon how carefully and conservatively the company's records and tax returns have been handled. It also is influenced by the nature of the items included in the losses. For example, there can often be a considerable controversy over the question of whether a loss is an operating or a capital loss. If it is an operating loss, it is generally more broadly available than were it a capital loss. If the valuation is to be made for acquisition or sale of the business, the proposed change in control will almost surely result in an IRS challenge to use of the credits.

There are circumstances where a successor corporation can use the credits built up by a predecessor, or where new owners of a corporation can use loss credits incurred by the corporation while it was under the former owners' control. The Tax Reform Act of 1976 made substantial changes in the law governing use of such acquired losses. This means new regulations must be promulgated by the IRS, and these regulations and the law itself must be court tested. Given the complex nature of these credits and the recent change, an appraiser would be well advised to have an opinion from a competent tax attorney to back up his valuation of the risks inherent in the loss being usable or not usable and under what circumstances. The attorney's opinion would be particularly desirable when new ownership is contemplated.

HOW TO VALUE GOODWILL AND OTHER INTANGIBLES

[¶9.04]   **SUMMARY**

Goodwill can be valued by the Excess Earnings Method (¶ 5.05-1), by various market methods described in Chapter 8, and by use of the Internal Revenue Service Goodwill Formula - Method 12. The advantages and disadvantages of the IRS formula are explored. In essence, it usually results in a higher value for intangibles than other methods might provide and the end result is an amorphous, non-depreciable pool of assets. Even the IRS uses the approach sparingly and with reservations.

Six basic methods for valuing intangibles other than goodwill are discussed. The first method requires the determination of a profit advantage gained by possession of the intangible asset in question. This advantage is then capitalized to arrive at a value. The Belmur process is used as an illustration. The second method assumes a third party owned an asset such as a patent and licensed it back to the true owner for a royalty. The amount of this theoretical royalty is then capitalized to yield a value for the asset. The BLM explosion-proof lamp patent serves as an example. The third method is based on cost savings which can be attributed to the intangible. When the saving has been determined, preferably on a projected year-by-year basis, it is capitalized using present worth factors. An example is given based on valuation of a secret process. The fourth method requires determination of the cost to re-create the asset being valued. It can be used independently or in conjunction with other methods. Giving due consideration to a return on the funds invested as part of the costs, the costs to create when totaled become the value. A fifth method is useful when comparable assets are available on the market. It is called the Cost-to-Purchase Method. This method can also be used to check other value conclusions. Finally, the method used by public accountants is discussed. This method is used primarily to allocate the purchase price of a business so as to set a value on goodwill. Essentially, all tangible and identifiable intangibles are assigned values. The residual, whatever it may be, is designated as goodwill.

The balance of the chapter is devoted to a discussion of how to value specific intangible assets such as brand names, copyrights, licenses, technical libraries, drawings, and film rights. In each case, the most widely used intangible valuation methods are suggested. Appraisal problems incident to the specific asset are discussed. The chapter concludes with an explanation of possible approaches to the valuation of tax credits with particular emphasis on loss carryforwards.

CHAPTER 10

VALUING GOODWILL IN EMINENT DOMAIN CASES

The law is a sort of hocus-pocus science.

CHARLES MACKLIN - 1690 - 1797

TOPICS DISCUSSED IN THIS CHAPTER

[¶10.01] — California Innovation in Goodwill Loss Compensation

[¶10.02] — Legal History of Goodwill in Eminent Domain Actions

[¶10.03] — Uniform Eminent Domain Code Proposed

[¶10.04] — Goodwill Under the Eminent Domain Code

[¶10.04-1] — Loss of Patronage

[¶10.04-2] — Expanded Concept of Goodwill

[¶10.04-3] — Goodwill Must Be Lost

[¶10.04-4] — Compensation for Goodwill Loss Must Not Be Duplicative

[¶10.04-5] — No Betterments May be Created

[¶10.05] — Special Considerations

[¶10.05-1] — Businesses With Improving Trends

[¶10.05-2] — Owner Preferences and Physical Condition

[¶10.05-3] — Personal Goodwill Versus Business Goodwill

[¶10.05-4] — Tenancy Versus Ownership

[¶10.05-5] — History and Longevity of the Business

[¶10.05-6] — Multiple Businesses

[¶10.05-7] — Total Versus Partial Loss

[¶10.06] — Appraiser's Definition of Goodwill Loss
Part 1 - Existence of Goodwill
Part 2 - Goodwill loss

[¶10.07] — Goodwill Loss Valuation Methods

[¶10.07-1] — Goodwill as a Special Purpose Property

[¶10.07-2] — Method 19 - Capitalization of Excess Earnings Lost
Basic Concept - Limitations - Advantages - Procedure: Complete Loss of Goodwill - Procedure: Partial Loss of Goodwill
Example: Partial Loss of Goodwill

[¶10.07-3] — Method 20 - Goodwill Loss Based on Market Formulas
Basic Concept - Limitations and Advantages - Procedure - Example

[¶10.07-4] — Method 21 - Cost to Restore Goodwill Loss
Basic Concept - Limitations - Advantages - Procedure - Example

[¶10.08] — Summary

CHAPTER 10

VALUING GOODWILL IN EMINENT DOMAIN CASES

[¶10.01] CALIFORNIA INNOVATION IN GOODWILL LOSS COMPENSATION

True to its reputation as an innovator in many fields, in 1976 California became the first state to give full recognition to the desirability of compensating for the loss of goodwill in eminent domain takings. As part of an overall revision of its Eminent Domain Law, the legislature included the following provisions:

Article 6. Compensation for Loss of Goodwill

1263.510 (a) The owner of a business conducted on the property taken, or on the remainder if such property is part of a larger parcel, shall be compensated for loss of goodwill if the owner proves all of the following:

(1) The loss is caused by the taking of the property or the injury to the remainder.

(2) The loss cannot reasonably be prevented by a relocation of the business or by taking steps and adopting procedures that a reasonably prudent person would take and adopt in preserving the goodwill.

(3) Compensation for the loss will not be included in payments under Section 7262 of the Government Code.

(4) Compensation for the loss will not be duplicated in the compensation otherwise awarded to the owner.

(b) Within the meaning of this article, "goodwill" consists of the benefits that accrue to a business as a result of its location, reputation for dependability, skill or quality, and any other circumstances resulting in probable retention of old or acquisition of new patronage.[56]

The California action is of interest, and not just to those pursuing condemnation matters within the boundaries of that state. It is an innovative step that will probably be reflected in similar laws in other states. It therefore behooves all parties interested in eminent domain to understand what the California law provides and how goodwill loss can be valued.

[¶10.02] LEGAL HISTORY OF GOODWILL LOSS IN EMINENT DOMAIN ACTIONS

To understand fully the significance of the new California law, it is necessary to review briefly the legal history of goodwill loss in eminent domain proceedings. In essence, the courts have established that goodwill loss is not protected by the U.S. Constitution. Only where compensation is provided by statute can it be directly considered.

VALUING GOODWILL IN EMINENT DOMAIN CASES

Although Amendment V to the U.S. Constitution provides,"nor shall private property be taken for public use, without just compensation," goodwill has not been considered property in this sense. Typical of one view were the judge's comments in Sawyer v. Commonwealth: "There are many serious pecuniary injuries which may be inflicted without compensation. No doubt a business may be property, and property of great value. But a business is less tangible in nature and more uncertain in its vicissitudes than the rights which the constitution undertakes to protect."[57] Hence, losses of goodwill and related assets would not be compensable.

Another typical view is stated in Klein v. United States, where the judge said "It is settled law that in the absence of specific statutory mandate, compensation under the Fifth Amendment may be recovered only for property taken and not for incidental or consequential losses, the rationale being that the sovereign need only pay for what is actually taken rather than for all that the owner has lost. [Cases were then cited.] Hence the incidental spoilation of the plaintiff's inventory and equipment, *the reduction or loss of its goodwill and profits,* [Italics added] and the expenses incurred in having to readjust its manufacturing operations are non-compensable under long-established legal principles."[58] This position is further amplified in Banner Milling v. State of New York, wherein the judge said: "Here the good will may be damaged by inconvenience and removal of the business but it is not taken. The owner of the business may remove to another place, establish his business and carry his good will with him."[59] However, in another leading case, Mitchell v. United States, the court held that even though there were no alternative premises to which the displaced business could be moved, goodwill loss still could not be compensated for.[60]

The courts have not been unsympathetic to the inequities which develop from the foregoing reasoning. On occasion they have recognized the problem and stated in effect that the courts could do nothing about it. Resort must be made to legislation. In Oakland v. Pacific Coast Lumber & Milling Co., a leading California case decided in 1915 and 1916, the position is well stated. The appellant, which was the business injured by the condemnation taking, contended "that business is property, and when the taking by the state or its agencies interferes with, impairs, damages, or destroys a business, compensation may be recovered therefor." In reply, the judge said, "We are not to be understood as saying this should not be the law when we do say that it is not our law. It is quite within the power of the legislature to declare that a damage to that form of property known as business or the goodwill of a business shall be compensated for; . . ."[61]

Recognizing the inequities of the constitutional situation, some of the states have enacted laws which provide partial compensation for goodwill loss. In Florida, for example, compensation for business damage or destruction in right of way takings has been afforded by statute. However, the business must have been in existence for five years and the land taken and the business thereon must both be owned by the same party. A lessee who operates such a business is not protected.

VALUING GOODWILL IN EMINENT DOMAIN CASES

In Vermont and New York compensation is now provided by statute for damages to business *on the land taken*. Limited compensation for elements of goodwill loss has been provided by statute in Texas and Oklahoma. None of the other states has provided the comprehensive statutory right to compensation for goodwill loss that now exists in California. However, there is a strong likelihood that others will so provide in the future because of an action recently taken by leaders in the legal profession.

[¶10.03] UNIFORM EMINENT DOMAIN CODE PROPOSED

In 1974 the National Conference of Commissioners on Uniform State Laws adopted a recommended Uniform Eminent Domain Code. The Commissioners are leading attorneys, judges, and teachers of law selected from each of the fifty states plus the District of Columbia and Puerto Rico. The object of the National Conference, which meets annually, is "to promote uniformity in state laws on all subjects where uniformity is deemed desirable and practicable."[62] If the conference decides to take up a subject, it refers the subject to a special committee which prepares a draft of an act. After due consideration and necessary modification, final drafts of proposed uniform laws are then approved by the Conference and are submitted to the American Bar Association for its approval. The Conference has been successful in seeing many of its drafts enacted into law, often with relatively little modification.

It is significant, therefore, that the Conference included as part of its proposed Eminent Domain Code the following:

Section 1016. [Loss of Goodwill]

(a) In addition to fair market value determined under Section 1004, [of the Uniform Code] the owner of a business conducted on the property taken, or on the remainder if there is a partial taking, shall be compensated for loss of goodwill only if the owner proves that the loss (1) is caused by the taking of the property or the injury to the remainder, (2) cannot reasonably be prevented by a relocation of the business or by taking steps and adopting procedures that a reasonably prudent person would take and adopt in preserving the goodwill; (3) will not be included in relocation payments under Article XIV, and (4) will not be duplicated in the compensation awarded to the owner.

(b) Within the meaning of this section, "goodwill" consists of the benefits that accrue to a business as a result of its location, reputation for dependability, skill, or quality, and any other circumstances resulting in probable retention of old or acquisition of new patronage.[63]

Notice how closely the California law parallels the Uniform Eminent Domain Code. In fact, as the drafters of the California legislation state, "Section 1263.510 [of the California law] . . . is the same in substance as Section 1016 of the Eminent Domain Code . . ."[64]

VALUING GOODWILL IN EMINENT DOMAIN CASES

[¶10.04] GOODWILL UNDER THE EMINENT DOMAIN CODE

The definition of goodwill is identical under the Eminent Domain Code and under the California law. There is no evidence in the legislative history which would lead one to believe that the drafters of the Code and of the California law meant to attribute different meanings to the same language. Therefore, a discussion of the meaning of the definition to appraisers should be equally applicable to California and to other states where the same definition is adopted. At least this is a fair position to take until the definition has been tested in the courts. To date no such tests have been possible, since the California law did not become effective until July 1, 1976, and no other states are known to have adopted the goodwill definition at the date of this writing.

[¶10.04-1] LOSS OF PATRONAGE

The primary emphasis in the Uniform Code definition of goodwill appears to be upon patronage. For purposes of the Code, it is stated that "goodwill" consists of the benefits that accrue to a business [as a result of various named assets] resulting in probable retention of old or acquisition of new *patronage*."[Italics added.] While the ability to retain or expand patronage is certainly an important element in court definitions of goodwill cited at ¶ 8.03-5, it is not to the exclusion of other factors, as is the case under the Eminent Domain Code. For the latter purposes, if patronage will be lost as a result of an eminent domain taking, there is in effect a presumption that there may be a compensable loss. The presumption is rebuttable for the reasons cited at ¶ 10.04-3.

[¶10.04-2] EXPANDED CONCEPT OF GOODWILL

In Chapter 8, an attempt was made to distinguish the differences between goodwill and other intangible assets. The goodwill elements were described as basically those which tended to be non-severable from the business or the person. Those intangible assets which could be separately identified and which could generally be sold apart from the business were defined as usually not being a part of goodwill. However, an eminent domain proceeding sets up an artificial set of circumstances requiring a reanalysis of the general rules.

The Code definition of goodwill contains a very broad expression of the factors which may affect patronage, and hence goodwill. Not only are the historic goodwill factors of "location, reputation for dependability, skill, or quality" to be considered, but also "*any other circumstances* [italics added] resulting in probable retention of old or acquisition of new patronage." Failing drafters' comments, legislative history, or court decisions to the contrary, and there are none at present, it would appear that the Code definition of goodwill is meant to expand beyond the ordinary concept. Thus if the value of a franchise or license is impaired as the result of an eminent domain taking, and if this impairment results in a loss of patronage, there ap-

VALUING GOODWILL IN EMINENT DOMAIN CASES

pears to be a compensable goodwill loss (again subject to the qualifications at ¶ 10.04-3).

Assume, for example, that a restaurant property is being acquired. The owner of the business possesses a franchise which allows him to operate as part of a well-known chain. The owner paid for the franchise and it is apparent that it has substantial value and is responsible for generating patronage because of the well-known name and other advertising benefits. If, for some reason such as market area restrictions in the contract, the franchise is not transferable to another location, then the loss in value attributable to the franchise must be considered as part of compensable goodwill loss. This would be true even though the franchise might be classed as an intangible asset aside from goodwill for other purposes.

In the above example, the result would be different, however, if the franchise had a residual value, such as a refund right from the franchisor. Assume in the example that the total value of goodwill and the franchise was $50,000, $25,000 was refundable from the franchisor, the total property is taken, and the business cannot be relocated. Although the franchise might be the key factor in drawing patronage to the business, the compensable loss would not be $50,000, but rather $25,000, because of the residual value of the franchise after the taking.

Another example might involve a special use permit. Typical of such a situation might be an auto salvage yard operating under a special use permit which is not transferable to another location. The permit may be salable apart from the business to someone else who would operate a like business at that location, and it might have a value normally separate from goodwill. However, as a result of the taking, neither the affected business nor any other can use the permit at this location. So the loss of patronage is complete and the loss of the permit value is complete. This loss would be compensated for as part of the goodwill loss in a taking.

It can be seen from the foregoing that the key factors in determining which intangible losses are compensable as goodwill loss under the Uniform Code differ from the ordinary situation. Usually it is the degree of severability and susceptibility to independent valuation which determines whether an asset will be treated as a separately identified intangible or as goodwill. Under the Code definition, however, it is the degree of transferability to another location and the affect on patronage which govern. Thus, if an intangible asset is freely transferable from one location to another without diminution in value and without an adverse affect on patronage it would not result in a compensable loss. On the other hand, if an intangible asset which would usually be classed as separate from goodwill could not be transferred and if this fact affected patronage adversely, there would be a loss to be considered.

This discussion should not leave the reader with the false impression that it is not important to consider separate valuations of goodwill and other intangibles in

VALUING GOODWILL IN EMINENT DOMAIN CASES

eminent domain proceedings. On the contrary, it is vitally important to value all assets individually. In many instances, it will be found that there are intangibles which have values and markets separate from the business itself. In certain approaches to value, such as the Excess Earnings Method, failure to segregate these intangibles could lead to the erroneous conclusion that all excess earnings are attributable to goodwill. If this conclusion were used as the basis for calculating any potential damage, a significant error could arise. However, if any marketable intangible assets which would not be affected by the taking were segregated and separately valued and were an appropriate return on investment on these assets deducted from earnings, the error would be avoided.

A frequently encountered example of the above situation could involve a liquor store. Assume such a business were to be affected by the taking of the real estate which houses the operation. In California such businesses must be licensed within the county where they are located. The licenses are salable and have readily established values. Were such a store appraised entirely on the basis of its excess earnings without a proper deduction for a return on the market value of the license, the excess earnings figure would be too high. Furthermore, if the value of the business were then added to the capitalized value of these improper excess earnings, the total value of the business would be distorted.

[¶10.04-3] GOODWILL MUST BE LOST

Although the definition of goodwill may be expanded for purposes of the Eminent Domain Code, there must be a loss of the goodwill so defined in order to have a compensable goodwill loss. This may sound like double-talk, but further discussion clarifies the point. Put another way, a business may create patronage and profits. Some, or all, of this patronage and profit may be lost as a result of an eminent domain taking, but there still may be no goodwill loss. While the Code definition of goodwill is broader than that generally applicable in business, the basic concept of goodwill outlined in Chapter 8 still pertains. The business must create not just earnings, but *excess earnings*, or market checks must reveal that such businesses do sell for a goodwill premium, or there must be some other sustainable reason to believe goodwill as defined does indeed exist. A variation of the tests for the existence of goodwill described at ¶8.04 must be applied. If the business does not create profits in excess of those necessary to provide a reasonable return on the tangible assets plus those intangibles which are not affected by the taking plus an adequate salary to the owners, there probably is no goodwill. This contention could be refuted if similar businesses are shown to sell for a goodwill premium nevertheless, or other tests reveal the existence of goodwill. The point is that the Eminent Domain Code does not compensate for lost profits or lost patronage per se. Such losses must be those attributable to goodwill.

For example, a business might prove the loss of $100,000 in patronage as a result of an eminent domain taking. This may also mean a loss of $10,000 in profits.

However, if $9,000 of these profits is necessary to provide an adequate return on investment and to compensate the owner, only $1,000 of profits remains applicable to goodwill and other unidentified intangibles. Hence the profit to be considered as part of the goodwill loss cannot exceed $1,000. Similarly, if a business shows that its volume drops from $300,000 to $200,000 as a result of a taking, perhaps with a resultant drop in profits, there may be no compensable goodwill loss if a market study reveals that similar businesses never sell for a goodwill premium.

By the same token it seems that the goodwill loss portion of the Code is not intended to compensate for the mere interruption of business. Goodwill must be present in order to have a compensable goodwill loss under any circumstances. In the foregoing examples, were the businesses interrupted by the taking with a loss of $100,000 in sales and $10,000 in profits, only the $1,000 in profits attributable to goodwill would be compensable. In the second instance where a market study revealed no goodwill, none of the lost profits would be compensable. The important conclusion is that the goodwill loss must be effectively permanent.

[¶10.04-4] COMPENSATION FOR GOODWILL LOSS MUST NOT BE DUPLICATIVE

The Uniform Eminent Domain Code provides that the loss for which compensation is sought ". . . (3) will not be included in relocation payments under Article XIV, . . ." The article referred to deals with allowances made for moving and related expenses pursuant to the Federal Uniform Relocation Assistance and Real Property Acquisition Policies Act (42 USC §4601 et seq) and interlocking state statutes, such as the California Relocation Assistance Act (Gov. Code §7260 et seq). In other words, if elements of goodwill loss will be compensated for under these acts, duplicate compensation can not be claimed under §1016 of the Code.

The Code also provides that compensation for goodwill loss "(4) will not be duplicated in the compensation [otherwise] awarded to the owner." This language applies to any compensation which would duplicate that which would otherwise be described as part of the goodwill loss, but the authors probably had at least one specific problem in mind. The California Law Revision Commission makes this comment at page 1035 of its recommendations: "The Commission recommends that improvements pertaining to the realty include any facility, machinery, or equipment installed on the property to be taken or on the remainder, regardless of the method of installation, that cannot be removed without a substantial loss in value or without substantial damage to the property on which it is installed. This will assure that such property having *special in place value* [italics added] will be taken and compensated as part of the realty." This recommendation resulted in §1263.205 of

VALUING GOODWILL IN EMINENT DOMAIN CASES

the California Eminent Domain Law which provides that such substantial loss in value will be determined by considering the value of the subject machinery or equipment in place as part of the realty "compared with its value if it were removed and sold."[65]

Prior to the enactment of this section in the California law, some machinery and equipment losses resulting from a taking went uncompensated. This was particularly true of some losses associated with installation costs. Thus a piece of machinery might have a market value of $10,000, but it cost $2,000 to install it. This $2,000 could have been lost under certain circumstances in the past. By providing reimbursement for the $2,000, the Committee may have seen an overlap with that element of goodwill described under Group 1 at ¶ 8.02 of this book as "The assemblage of property, plant, and equipment into a productive unit or units." The authors, however, are therein referring principally to what can best be described as the going concern value of such equipment rather than installation costs. However, the use of the term "special in place value" by the Committee has led to some conjecture that the Committee really meant to compensate not only for installation costs but also for elements of going concern value. Either way, the Code would prevent any duplication of compensation between the realty and the goodwill provisions through item (4) of the goodwill loss provisions cited above. Also, as mentioned, the Code would prevent any other possible duplicate payments.

[¶10.04-5] NO BETTERMENTS MAY BE CREATED

It can be properly concluded that provision for the compensation of goodwill losses does not contemplate compensation which would better the position of the business. Rather, it should provide an amount which compensates for goodwill lost but not an amount which would:
    a. Create goodwill after the taking which did not exist before.
    b. Improve the financial position of the firm, as by converting an unprofitable business into a profitable one after the taking.
    c. Provide a better plant and equipment after the taking than existed before.
    d. Pay for the taking of reasonable action to prevent goodwill loss which a prudent business owner should have taken himself to prevent the loss. This latter point is specifically covered by Section 1016 (a)(2) of the Uniform Code.

As noted under the previous section, there specifically should also be no duplicate compensation which would result in a betterment.

[¶10.05]   SPECIAL CONSIDERATIONS

In addition to the general considerations cited in the preceding section, there are a number of other factors which must be evaluated. All are not applicable to

VALUING GOODWILL IN EMINENT DOMAIN CASES

every business involved in a taking, but some may be present, and if so, they must be weighed.

[¶10.05-1] BUSINESSES WITH IMPROVING TRENDS

The Eminent Domain Code does not restrict goodwill compensation to reimbursement for loss of existing patronage. It defines goodwill as the benefits which accrue to a business from circumstances "resulting in probable retention of old *or acquisition of new patronage.*" [Emphasis added.] Many businesses affected by eminent domain taking may have recent histories of improving financial conditions which would indicate a probable increase in patronage and profits. It might then be argued that the goodwill loss should not only consider reductions from current business levels but also from the higher levels which could reasonably be expected were it not for the proposed eminent domain taking.

Whether or not such added consideration should be included in the appraisal must be determined on the basis of reasonable estimates and expectations. Not all businesses continue upward trends indefinitely. Many industries and individual businesses within these industries are cyclical, with peaks and valleys in their sales and profit histories. The analyst must carefully consider whether an indicated uptrend in a business being appraised can reasonably be expected to continue for a near-term projected period. If the circumstances strongly suggest a projected uptrend could be sustained, then this fact should be reflected in the pro forma financial statements which the appraiser will prepare on a before and after taking basis. The probable result would be to increase the goodwill loss as a result of anticipated new patronage and profits. As was stated in Chapter 4, in speaking of projected statements generally, the forecast should be held to a near term, preferably no more than a year. Even the most successful and well-established businesses can be dramatically affected by unexpected changes in market demands, laws, shortages of materials, loss of key personnel, new competitors, and a host of other conditions which make long term projections neither realistic nor reasonable.

[¶10.05-2] OWNER PREFERENCES AND PHYSICAL CONDITION

In some instances, the owner of a business may choose not to relocate even though a suitable alternative location is available. He may present many arguments as to why relocation is not possible. The appraiser should be on guard not to let his conclusions be colored by contentions which really proceed from the owner's personal preferences. An impartial study should be made to determine realistically whether a business can be relocated and, if so, to what possible locations. The loss of goodwill in moving to an alternative location can then be properly determined.

[¶10.05-3] PERSONAL GOODWILL VERSUS BUSINESS GOODWILL

One of the most difficult tasks facing an appraiser is the determination of the real source of goodwill. Is it attached to the business or to an individual, or is it possibly a mixture of both? An Excess Earnings Method test may indicate that goodwill does exist in the business affected by the taking. However, this test will not reveal how the excess earnings or goodwill are generated. If most of the goodwill appears to be due to the personal skills of the owner, the chances are that most, if not all, of the goodwill is transferable to another location. Hence, it would not be compensable under goodwill loss provisions of the Code. The appraiser must carefully evaluate the owner's unique contribution to the business. Then he must make a judgment as to how much of the goodwill attaches to the business itself, continuing whether the owner were present or not. The latter will probably form the principal goodwill which will be subject to loss in the eminent domain proceeding.

A problem related to the question of personal goodwill may arise if the owner of a business is aged or infirm. He may contend that he cannot physically move the business and hence should be compensated for the entire loss of goodwill - personal and business. As justified as the owner's contention may be, the appraiser must still conclude that personal goodwill is essentially a transferable asset and non-compensable. He must also conclude that if the concern is capable of being moved to another location with no loss of business goodwill, there is no compensable goodwill loss.

[¶10.05-4] TENANCY VERSUS OWNERSHIP

An important consideration in determining whether a business has goodwill arising from its location is the security of its tenancy. If the property is owned, this question is mute. If, however, there is only a short term lease with no renewal options, or the business is on a tenant-at-will basis, the question arises whether the business could remain at its present location even without the proposed eminent domain taking. If a move seems probable anyway, this fact would often reduce the amount of goodwill loss attributable to the taking. However, care must be exercised in drawing such conclusions. In any event economic rent should be deducted as an expense to the business before computing goodwill to be certain that any leasehold interest is not mixed into the goodwill value.

[¶10.05-5] HISTORY AND LONGEVITY OF THE BUSINESS

A consideration closely related to the circumstances of tenancy can be the history and longevity of a business. If the firm has been at a single location for many years and leases have historically been renewed, this would certainly lead to a strong presumption that the business can continue at its present location for the foreseeable future. Nevertheless, a long history at a given location is not a guarantee that the business can perpetuate itself there. All circumstances must be carefully reviewed.

VALUING GOODWILL IN EMINENT DOMAIN CASES

A long history can have other possible affects on goodwill. It may be that the reputation of the business is so well established that its patrons will follow it to almost any location within reason. If this is the case, there is probably little goodwill to be lost in the taking, at least in so far as it pertains to location. On the other hand, if the business has a long history but its goodwill is heavily dependent on a particular location, the potential goodwill loss incident to the taking could be considerable, influenced, of course, by the security of the tenancy.

Aside from location, the age of the business itself can influence the amount of goodwill. A business with little or no history (less than a year old, for example) would seldom have goodwill related to the business itself. There may be goodwill related to the owners, but this is usually a transferable asset, as noted at ¶ 10.05-3. Goodwill is a high-risk asset and one which is usually built up over many years. The fact that a new business may have excess earnings does not necessarily indicate that there is valuable goodwill. The risk associated with the goodwill of a new business is normally substantially higher than that applicable to a more established enterprise.

[¶10.05-6] MULTIPLE BUSINESSES

Not infrequently, several related businesses may operate at a single location which will be affected by an eminent domain taking. The gross income, expenses, and profit of these businesses may be consolidated into a single balance sheet and a single income statement. However, each of the businesses may not be equally affected by the taking. Some of the businesses may be capable of operating almost anywhere, while others may be very dependent on the existing location. An example could be a manufacturing plant with a related retail outlet. Manufacturing facilities can often be placed in a wide variety of locations, assuming the needed industrial amenities are available. Retail businesses, on the other hand, usually require local identity and are more dependent on a specific location. It is probable such a manufacturing operation need suffer little if any goodwill loss as a result of a taking, whereas the retail store might have a significant loss. At any rate, the several operations must be segregated so that the effect of the taking can be assessed for each business.

[¶10.05-7] TOTAL VERSUS PARTIAL LOSS

If a business cannot be relocated within the same or a very similar market, any goodwill and related intangible assets affected by the taking should probably be considered totally lost. If the business can remain where it is or can be relocated close by, there may be only a partial loss of goodwill and intangibles.

For example, it may be found that a business at its present location or when moved to another location will lose but a portion of its patronage for a year and will then be back at its previous level. The compensable loss will then be confined to this single year. The same would be true if the loss were estimated to extend over two years. However, should the loss be estimated to extend over a period longer than two years, or perhaps indefinitely, all of the goodwill owned by the enterprise probably should be considered lost. This follows the previously stated position that estimates beyond a year or two are highly speculative. This statement is particularly pertinent to smaller businesses. In larger, well-established concerns, forecasting may be more reliable and a somewhat longer projection may be in order.

Another problem may arise where a business is forced to cease its operations completely as a result of the taking. Assume there is no useful market data indicating a set formula, or a given amount is typically paid for goodwill. Assume further that the excess profits test results in a zero goodwill answer. Since the business is being forced to terminate, there can be no question about the loss of patronage. Here the appraiser is forced back to the Question and Answer Test for goodwill cited at ¶ 8.04-3. If he finds goodwill does exist, he may use a cost approach to establish the amount of goodwill loss, much as was suggested at ¶ 8.04-3. He must hypothesize as to the reasonable costs involved in generating new patronage, assuming the business were to be started again in a similar market area. That portion of the costs applicable to goodwill restoration will then form the basis of his goodwill loss calculation - i.e., costs incident to mere profit restoration must not be included. (See ¶ 10.04-3.) He must be particularly careful in such circumstances to be sure that the condemning authority is not bailing out a troubled business. The failure of the excess earnings test and the market test to indicate goodwill may be an indication the business is really marginal and has no goodwill. The appraiser must be certain that his answer to the question, "Is there nevertheless goodwill present?" can be answered with conviction.

[¶10.06] APPRAISER'S DEFINITION OF GOODWILL LOSS

For appraisal purposes in cases brought under statutes which include the Eminent Domain Code definition of goodwill, the following amplified definitions will prove useful:

Part 1 - Existence of Goodwill

The existence of goodwill is manifested by (a) historical excess earnings, or (b) by the reasonable probability of excess earnings in the immediate future, or (c) by market data which clearly indicates a goodwill bonus is usually paid for similar businesses, or (d) by special circumstances which cause the appraiser to conclude goodwill is present. Included as part of goodwill for this purpose are intangible assets such as franchises and licenses which contribute to the attraction of patronage.

VALUING GOODWILL IN EMINENT DOMAIN CASES

Comment

Excess earnings are determined in the same manner as that described under the Excess Earnings Method (Method 3 at ¶ 5.05-1). In arriving at excess earnings for purposes of the Code care needs to be taken that there is an adequate amount deducted from the profit to provide an economic return on intangible assets such as certain franchises and licenses. These may or may not be considered part of goodwill under the Code. The purpose of the Excess Earnings Method is to isolate those excess earnings which pertain to goodwill. If goodwill is to be expanded by adding other assets to it, then the value of such assets should be added separately. As in the ordinary use of the Excess Earnings Method, overall company profits should first be reduced by any adjustment needed to provide a competitive salary to the owner. Category (d) special circumstances, refers to goodwill which is determined by use of the Question and Answer Test described at ¶ 8.04-3.

Part 2 - Goodwill Loss

If a business can be relocated, the potential loss of goodwill is measured by the difference in the value of goodwill before and after the taking. However, as a general rule, the loss should not exceed the lower of the cost to restore the lost goodwill or the total value of the goodwill before the taking. If the business cannot be relocated within the same market area, all of the goodwill owned by the business should be considered as lost. Also, if the goodwill loss cannot be restored within a reasonable period, the entire amount of the loss should be considered irretrievable.

[¶10.07]   GOODWILL LOSS VALUATION METHODS

Although there are a number of techniques which may be used to develop the value of goodwill partially or totally lost, these methods generally fall into three basic categories: Excess Earnings Capitalization; Market Formulas; and Cost-to-Restore (essentially lost patronage). Before discussing these techniques further, it is helpful to amplify certain characteristics of goodwill.

[¶10.07-1]   GOODWILL AS A SPECIAL PURPOSE PROPERTY

In many cases, including some involving eminent domain takings, the courts have awarded compensation based on the loss of a portion of a going business, its goodwill or other intangibles on the basis of evidence that market value has been lost. However, market value has not always been the criterion because it has sometimes been considered impractical. This is particularly true of special purpose properties, such as churches, schools, and some manufacturing or processing facilities. A special purpose property usually has value to a particular user, and any alternative use results in a sale at approximately the liquidation value of the property.

VALUING GOODWILL IN EMINENT DOMAIN CASES

Therefore, market data is of little use in developing the value of a property to a user who has possession and can effect a unique utilization of the asset. The California eminent domain law recognizes that value may not always be determinable from market transactions. It states at §1263.320(b): "The fair market value of property taken for which there is no relevant market is its value on the date of valuation that is just and equitable."

Goodwill is, in a sense, a special purpose property. It has value only when related to a specific enterprise or person. It is not customarily marketable as a separate asset. There are instances where a market analysis will reveal a specific amount paid for goodwill as part of a going concern, but only as part of a going concern. Where there is a paucity of market data and goodwill loss must be determined, there is no reasonable choice but to consider other appraisal techniques deemed "just and equitable." The Excess Earnings Method is one of the more widely accepted goodwill valuation techniques. When utilized on a before and after taking basis, it can be quite useful. Another approach could involve the use of some variation on the Cost-to-Create Method (Method 16 at ¶9.02-5). In this instance, it might involve the cost to restore goodwill through advertising and other promotional activities.

[¶10.07-2] METHOD 19 - CAPITALIZATION OF EXCESS EARNINGS LOST

Basic Concept

If it appears that all goodwill stands to be lost in the taking, the Excess Earnings Method (¶5.05-1) with minor variations may provide an effective measure of goodwill loss. If, on the other hand, a partial loss of goodwill seems likely, the Excess Earnings Method can still be used, but it will be necessary to calculate the excess earnings both before and after the taking. The difference between these before and after levels of excess earnings, in turn, can be used to measure goodwill loss.

Limitations

A business may show no excess earnings and still have goodwill.

Advantages

When goodwill loss can be developed using this approach, there is a logical explanation for the result which is relatively easy to substantiate in court.

Procedure - Complete Loss of Goodwill

If it is anticipated all goodwill can be expected to be lost, historical earnings are developed before capital charges and before income taxes but after owner's salary, as was done for the Excess Earnings Method described at ¶5.05-1. This latter method is used to develop the value of goodwill with the following changes:

VALUING GOODWILL IN EMINENT DOMAIN CASES

1. If the business owns the real estate to be taken, substitute a fair rental value for the depreciation and return on investment which would otherwise be calculated on this asset.
2. Exclude from depreciation and return on investment any intangible assets which are to be considered as part of goodwill for eminent domain purposes because they contribute to patronage.

The excess earnings can then be capitalized at an appropriate rate, such as 15% to 20%, and the resulting figure is the value of goodwill lost.

Comment

The rental value of owned real estate is substituted for economic depreciation and return on investment with respect to this asset to avoid possible contentions of duplication with other eminent domain awards. While theoretically the same results could be obtained by leaving the real estate in the calculation, a fair return on investment in the land and buildings and depreciation on the latter may be subject to more challenge than would be true of the rental value. If the return on investment or depreciation were debated as being too high or too low, it would cast doubt on the residual excess profits and lead to the contention that the value of the goodwill was too high or too low. If goodwill were established as including profits actually applicable to the real estate, there would be some duplication in payment, since the real estate will be paid for in the taking. At any rate, the simplest approach to describe is often best for court testimony purposes.

Intangible assets to be included as part of goodwill for eminent domain purposes must be excluded from depreciation and return on investment so that the residual excess profits will include a return on all of the goodwill, including these intangibles.

Procedure - Partial Loss of Goodwill

The same procedure described above may be followed with respect to the Excess Earnings Method to determine goodwill before the taking, except that the final step of capitalizing the excess earnings so derived may not be necessary. Having computed the excess earnings before the taking, the same procedure can be followed for the period after the taking by preparing new pro forma sales and earnings giving effect to the changed conditions. From this it is then possible to obtain the difference between the pre-taking excess earnings and those after the taking. This result can then be capitalized into the value of goodwill lost.

Example - Partial Loss of Goodwill

Assume a business whose property is to be taken has earnings after owner's salary of $50,000 per year before the taking. As a result of the taking, it is anticipated there will be a loss of patronage for two years thereafter that can be expected to reduce profits during this two-year period. Marketable intangibles with a value of $50,000 have no appreciable effect on patronage and are not to be included as

VALUING GOODWILL IN EMINENT DOMAIN CASES

part of goodwill. A calculation of goodwill loss given these presumptions and others inherent in the figures noted hereafter could be as follows:

GOODWILL LOSS VALUE

Using Excess Earnings Before and After a Taking

	Before		After First Year	After Second Year
1. After-tax Earnings	$50,000			
2. Plus Depreciation Expense (after tax)	5,000			
3. Plus Interest Expense (after tax)	5,000			
4. Earnings Before Capital Charges	60,000	$60,000	$47,500	$52,500
5. Deduct Economic Depreciation:				
Office Furniture & Fixtures (8 yr. life) (5,000 x .125)	(625)			
Machinery and Equipment (6 yr. life) (50,000 x .167)	(8,350)			
Trucks (4 yr. life) (20,000 x .25)	(5,000)			
Marketable Intangibles (15 yr. life) (50,000 x .067)	(3,350)	(17,325)	(17,325)	(17,325)
6. Deduct Economic Return on Investment:				
Working Capital (100,000 x .12)	(12,000)			
Fixed Assets (120,000 x .12)	(14,400)			
Marketable Intangibles (50,000 x .14)	(7,000)	(33,400)	(33,500)	(33,500)
7. Excess Earnings		$9,275	-0-	$ 1,675

SUMMARY OF GOODWILL LOSS

First Year:		
Excess Earnings Lost		$9,275
Second Year:		
Excess Earnings Lost (9,275 - 1,675)	7,600	
Present Worth of Loss (15% for 1 yr., deferred 1 yr.)	.7561	5,746
GOODWILL LOSS		$15,021*

*This figure would probably be rounded to $15,000.

VALUING GOODWILL IN EMINENT DOMAIN CASES

[¶10.07-3] METHOD 20 - GOODWILL LOSS BASED ON MARKET FORMULAS

Basic Concept

Using market derived formulas, goodwill is valued before and after the taking. That is, a market formula or approach is used to determine the value of the business and its goodwill before the taking, and the same approach is then used to derive the same values after assuming conditions incident to the taking.

Limitations and Advantages

This approach is no better than the formulas upon which it is based. For a discussion of the limitations and advantages of these, see ¶7.04.

Procedure

Except for the imposition of presumed conditions after the taking, the procedure would be as described under ¶7.04-1 and ¶7.04-2.

Example

To avoid the necessity of added assumptions and figures, assume the land and buildings for the BLM Fast Burger operation were to be taken. The pre-taking results are then identical to those developed pursuant to Methods 10 and 11 at ¶7.04-1 and ¶7.04-2. These facts are summarized in the first column which follows under "Before." In computing the "After" column, it is assumed as a result of the taking sales are reduced by $100,000 and profits by $5,000. Assume further that the franchise is freely transferable to another location.

See Example on next page:

VALUING GOODWILL IN EMINENT DOMAIN CASES

GOODWILL LOSS VALUE

Based on Market Formulas Before and After a Taking

	Before	After
Method 10 - Asset-Based Formula		
Total Tangible Assets	$ 75,000	$ 75,000
Less: Liabilities	(15,000)	(15,000)
Plus: Value of Franchise	20,000	20,000
Tangible Net Worth at Market	80,000	80,000
Plus: One Year Net Profit (for Goodwill)	28,300	20,000
Total Value of the Business	$108,300	$100,000
Method 11 - Sales-Based Formula		
Typical Annual Sales	$500,000	$400,000
Market Multiplier	.25	.25
Indicated Value of the Business	$125,000	$100,000
Typical Annual Profits	28,300	20,000
Market Multiplier	4	4
Indicated Value of the Business	$113,200	$ 80,000
Correlation		
Method 10	$108,300	$100,000
Method 11		
Step 1	125,000	100,000
Step 2	113,200	80,000
Conclusion as to Value	$108,000	$ 90,000
Allocation of Values		
Net Tangible Assets	60,000	60,000
License	20,000	20,000
Total	80,000	80,000
Residual to Goodwill	28,000	10,000
Indicated Goodwill Loss	$18,000	

VALUING GOODWILL IN EMINENT DOMAIN CASES

[¶10.07-4] METHOD 21 - COST TO RESTORE GOODWILL LOSS

Basic Concept

If the Excess Earnings Method and the Market Formula Methods result in either excessive or too low figures for goodwill loss, or if only to check these results, the appraiser may wish to estimate the costs of restoring lost goodwill. If these costs are realistic and do not add up to an amount which exceeds the total value of goodwill before the taking, the method can have validity.

Limitations

If the loss cannot be restored within a reasonable period of time, the estimated costs become highly speculative. One may be forced to conclude in such a case that any goodwill present has been entirely lost.

Advantages

Specific, provable items of expense to restore patronage and other aspects of goodwill lend credibility to the value set on goodwill loss.

Procedure

The procedure to be followed for this method is best explained by the following example. It is important to realize, however, that cumulative costs should be sufficient only to restore goodwill and not all profits and patronage which might be lost. (See ¶ 10.04-3.)

Example

Assume various tests indicate the business in question definitely has goodwill. After the taking and as a direct result of it, patronage will be decreased by 100,000 in the year following and by $50,000 in the second year. The firm earns 5% profit after provision for the owner's salary, so these patronage losses translate into profit losses of $5,000 and $2,500 respectively. These profits are directly applicable to goodwill and are not just a reduction in business profits. (See ¶ 10.04-3.) To help restore volume, it will be necessary to spend $3,000 per year on advertising and promotion for the two year period. There is also a possibility that other expenses will be required which must be passed along to patrons and hence may have the effect of reducing patronage. In the example shown below, there is an assumed increase in rent over and above the economic rent applicable to the former location. At a new location the business will be required to pay $16,000 per annum rent, which is $2,000 more than the economic rent of $14,000 at the former site. Assume the increased rent of $2,000 must be paid over a three year period. The present worth of this $2,000 per year for three years is therefore added to the cost to restore goodwill loss.

VALUING GOODWILL IN EMINENT DOMAIN CASES

COST TO RESTORE GOODWILL LOSS

Loss of Sales First Year	$100,000	
Normal Net Profit	5%	
First Year Profit Loss	5,000	
Present Worth of this Loss at 12% Rate	.8929	$ 4,465
Loss of Sales Second Year	50,000	
Normal Net Profit	5%	
Second Year Profit Loss	2,500	
Present Worth of this Loss at 12% Rate	.7972	1,993
Increase Cost of Promotion over Two Years	$ 3,000 per year	
Present Worth at 12% Rate	1.6901	5,070
Increase Rental Expense over Three Years	$ 2,000 per year	
Present Worth at 12% Rate	2.4018	4,801
Cost to Hire and Train Two New Employees		2,500
Total Cost to Restore Goodwill Loss		$18,829*

*This figure would probably be rounded to either $18,000 or $19,000.

[¶10.08] SUMMARY

California has become the first state to give full recognition to the desirability of compensating for the loss of goodwill in eminent domain takings. This action is important for two reasons. First, in California it overcomes a basic injustice in the common law which gives no Federal or state Constitutional protection against goodwill losses when governments acquire property by eminent domain. Second, because it follows the basic language used by the prestigious National Conference of Commissioners on Uniform State Laws in their Uniform Eminent Domain Code, the California action may well reflect the shape of things to come in the other 49 states.

Key emphasis in the Code is placed on continuing patronage as a vital factor in goodwill. Through a broad definition of possible matters which may affect patronage, the Code appears to expand the usual definition of goodwill to include other intangibles. However, loss of patronage and profits incident thereto does not necessarily mean there is compensable goodwill loss. There must be goodwill in the business before the taking, and only that portion of the patronage loss which is traceable to goodwill is compensable. Also, the compensation for goodwill must not duplicate payments for the same elements under other governmental programs or under other sections of the Eminent Domain Code. Nor, as a result of the goodwill loss compensation, can the business be any better off after the taking than it was before.

VALUING GOODWILL IN EMINENT DOMAIN CASES

In analyzing potential goodwill loss, thought must be given to a number of special considerations. If a business is steadily adding to its goodwill prior to the taking, goodwill loss may be greater than historical precedent would indicate. The fact an owner may be unable or unwilling to relocate does not affect the basic transferability of the business for eminent domain purposes. Personal goodwill is generally non-compensable. If a business is on short tenancy, a determination must be made as to whether it has much compensable goodwill incident to its location. Where a displaced business actually consists of several businesses or operations, the effect of the taking on the goodwill of each segment must be considered. Whether the goodwill of a business is determined to be partially or fully taken may hinge on the length of time it would take to restore it to its former position. A lengthy period to restore probably indicates a total loss of goodwill.

The concept of goodwill as a special purpose property is discussed, and three methods are suggested for valuing goodwill loss.

CHAPTER 11

VALUING FRACTIONAL INTERESTS IN CLOSELY-HELD BUSINESSES

A foolish consistency is the hobgoblin of little minds.
RALPH WALDO EMERSON 1803-1882

TOPICS DISCUSSED IN THIS CHAPTER

[¶11.01] — The History of Minority-Interest Discounts

[¶11.02] — Minority-Interest Valuation Methods

[¶11.02-1] — Method 22 - Cost to Market

[¶11.02-2] — Method 23 - Comparable Letter Stock

[¶11.02-3] — Method 24 - Dividend Yield

[¶11.03] — Valuing Majority Interests

[¶11.04] — Blockage

[¶11.05] — Stocks Held in Trust

[¶11.06] — Restrictive Agreements

[¶11.07] — Valuing Different Classes of Stock

[¶11.08] — Summary

CHAPTER 11

VALUING FRACTIONAL INTERESTS IN CLOSELY-HELD BUSINESSES

[¶11.01] THE HISTORY OF MINORITY-INTEREST DISCOUNTS

The owner of a minority interest in a closely-held business is generally in a rather undesirable position. His investment is virtually locked in. There may be no market at all for his shares, or to the extent they can be sold, the only buyers are often his fellow owners or the corporation itself. At the same time, the business may pay out little or no dividends or partnership distributions. As a minority holder he is virtually powerless to change this situation.

Such a minority interest often results from a special set of circumstances which lacks the impartiality characteristic of minority interests in public companies which trade on one of the exchanges or in the over-the-counter market. In a closely-held firm, the minority interest frequently comes about because of a personal relationship with other owners or because of a special relationship with the company. An employee may receive stock as part of a bonus or profit-sharing plan. The minority interest so acquired may be uniquely valuable to its owner, but it can have considerably less value to an impartial third party. To such a buyer who is seeking an economically justifiable investment, any interest in a closely-held business which is less than a majority will be worth substantially less. In fact, the value per share to him will often be less than the average value per share of all of the outstanding stock in the enterprise. Therefore, resale of minority interests in closely-held firms tends to be at substantial discounts.

This situation has not always been as true as it is today. Prior to the 1930's, such minority interests could be freely marketed to anyone who would be interested in owning the stock. There was no Securities and Exchange Commission and there were few state agencies effectively regulating stock issuance and sale. No registration statements were needed and no prior notice of sale was required. Shares could be sold as expedient to do so. There were fewer and less complex laws in general. Income taxes were not significant. Most incorporated closely-held firms tended to issue only one class of unrestricted, voting, common stock. If a partnership, the ownership could be expanded or contracted with virtually no governmental interference. As a result, minority interests tended to be valued more nearly in direct ratio to their share of the total value of the concern. Thus a 25% interest was worth $250,000 if the entire operation was valued at $1 million.

The courts reflect the trends in the marketplace, albeit on a somewhat delayed basis. In consequence, between 1920 and 1929, all major court cases involving the valuation of minority interests in closely-held firms resulted in no discount being applied. In the 1930's, about 20% of such cases involved discounts. By the 1970's, about two-thirds of the cases recognized minority interest discounts, and whereas during the earlier period the maximum discount was 33%, in the 1970's it reached 55%.[66] Thus the courts have given recognition to the ever increasing restrictions on minority interests and the resulting lack of marketability. It seems probable that even greater discounts will be allowed by the courts in the future, since even greater discounts prevail in the marketplace. One knowledgeable writer suggests that discounts of up to 90% may now be in order.[67]

This is not to say that all minority interests will or should carry a discount. If, for example, a minority interest in the equity of a business carried voting control, such a minority could well be worth a premium. Likewise, if a minority block would enable another minority holder to achieve a majority with control or if the minority were needed to reach the percentage of ownership needed to merge or file consolidated statements, the stock would have added value. The appraiser must be aware of all special values and restrictions which apply to the minority interest being valued.

[¶11.02] MINORITY-INTEREST VALUATION METHODS

The starting point for arriving at the discounted value of a minority interest is a determination of the value of all of the shares of the business considered as a block. For purposes of the ensuing discussion, this result will be referred to as the *basic share value*. The usual approach is to start with the total equity value of the company as a whole determined by the methods described in the preceding chapters of this book. This total equity value is then divided by the total number of shares issued and outstanding, and the result is the basic share value. Another approach used particularly by the courts is to divide either the book value or adjusted book value of the equity in the entire enterprise by the issued and outstanding shares. Such an approach is most appropriate when the business is essentially a holding company the assets of which have readily determinable market values such as real estate or listed securities. Once the basic share value has been selected, this is the base to which an appropriate minority interest discount is applied.

Selection of the appropriate discount method is then necessary. This is not always a simple problem because the appraiser is usually dealing with a hypothetical situation in which no actual impartial buy-and-sell situation has been encountered. If there have been any sales of minority interests in the firm, they have probably been made between related parties or others who could not deal from the same arm's length approach found in the securities market. Particularly with respect to such situations, it is appropriate to cite an often quoted section of Internal Revenue Ruling 59-60: "A sound valuation will be based upon all the relevant facts, but the elements of common sense, informed judgment and reasonableness must enter into the process of weighing those facts and determining their aggregate significance."[68] Despite the importance of the judgment factor, selected appraisal methods should rely as much as possible on provable facts.

VALUING FRACTIONAL INTERESTS IN CLOSELY-HELD BUSINESSES

[¶11.02-1]   METHOD 22 - COST TO MARKET

In determining the basic share value, the appraiser has in effect assumed that there is an established market for 100% of the company's stock. Therefore, one appropriate method for determining the discount applicable to a minority holding would entail an estimate of the cost of creating a market for that holding. Considerable information with respect to such costs can be obtained from underwriters and from Securities and Exchange Commission filings. When all such potential expenses have been cumulated, the total should be divided by the number of shares in the minority block, and this becomes the per share discount. This in turn is subtracted from the basic share value to arrive at the value of the minority holding.

Despite the logic of this method, it has many practical limitations. One is the frequently encountered situation where the total value of the entire enterprise is not sufficient to warrant the creation of a public market, let alone a market for a minority interest. This is partially because there are many costs to such a marketing effort, including legal fees, registration expenses, advertising, and underwriter's fees. In total, these charges may be even more than the total value of the block of stock being appraised. Another practical limitation may be the minimums set by underwriters. In many instances, it will be impossible to find an underwriter who would attempt to create a market for the small number of shares involved. This is particularly true in periods such as the present when so-called "best efforts" underwritings are exceedingly scarce.

[¶11.02-2]   METHOD 23 - COMPARABLE LETTER STOCK

Since minority interest discounts are primarily the result of limited marketability, it is appropriate to consider a method which relies on a similar discount for restricted marketability. Specifically, there can be a reasonable degree of comparability between the discount applicable to the so-called *letter stock*[69] of publicly traded firms and that which is applicable to the minority shares of closely-held firms. In both cases, the basic discount is for lack of marketability. Both are typically minority interests. In both instances, regulatory clearance with attendant expenses is probably required before sale. Comparability may break down somewhat because the shares of an already publicly-owned firm may be easier and less expensive to market than those of a closely-held business. Also, the letter stocks tend to involve larger blocks than the typical closely-held minority interest. However, with some adjustment for any such differences, a discount based on those applied to letter stock has reasonable validity.

The primary problem is one of cumulating the necessary data to form an acceptable data base. Letter stock transactions probably occur daily, but the needed information can be extremely difficult to obtain unless it happens to be published in the annual report of the companies involved. Even so, it may be necessary to review many such reports to unearth the needed data in sufficient quantity and detail to support appraisal conclusions.

VALUING FRACTIONAL INTERESTS IN CLOSELY-HELD BUSINESSES

Fortunately, some of the type of information needed is readily available. In 1969, the Securities and Exchange Commission began requiring investment companies registered under the Investment Company Act of 1940 to disclose pertinent details regarding their acquisition of restricted securities. Among other things, it is incumbent upon the investment company to state how the securities have been valued. The appropriate regulations can be found in SEC Accounting Series Releases 113 and 118 of October 21, 1969 and December 23, 1970 respectively. This information reveals the price paid for letter stock and other restricted securities, and these prices can in turn be compared with the annual revaluations of these same securities by the boards of directors of the investment companies. A comparison can also be made with the price at which registered shares of the same portfolio companies are selling in the market. Thus, some supportable data can be derived on the discount for non-marketability.

It is pertinent to note that a few Small Business Investment Companies are registered under the Investment Company Act of 1940, and these portfolio securities must be valued by the above procedures. Also, some of these companies invest in firms which have an already established market for their shares, so that comparisons can be made between their letter stock and that which is unrestricted. The significance of this source is that such portfolio companies are more apt to be directly comparable to the closely-held firms discussed here than are the companies whose stock is held by the larger investment companies. Care must be exercised, however, to be certain that the SBIC portfolio securities have the same rights and privileges as the related publicly-traded shares - i.e., do not compare preferred with common, warrants with stock, etc.

Assuming that the SBIC data is either too incomplete or lacks real comparability, the general investment company data outlined certainly affords an excellent general means of determining discounts for non-marketability. It is interesting to note information gleaned from some of these reports by the investment banking firm of Moroney, Beissner & Co. of Houston, Texas published in *Taxes* magazine for March 1973. The portfolios of ten investment companies were analyzed involving purchase of 146 blocks of "restricted equity securities." Discounts ranged from 3% to 90%, but very few purchases were made at the low end of the spectrum. Most seemed to fall in the range of 30% to 50%. This study was made several years ago and market conditions vary sufficiently to call for use of the latest statistics in any valuation. However, it is indicative of the substantial discounts some very sophisticated buyers feel are appropriate for the cash purchase of restricted securities.

Procedurally, when the appropriate discount has been determined, it would be applied to the basic share value of the company being appraised to arrive at the value of the minority interest. This procedure is similar to that for Methods 22 and 24.

[¶11.02-3]   METHOD 24 - DIVIDEND YIELD

A minority shareholder has little or no say in management decisions, company

VALUING FRACTIONAL INTERESTS IN CLOSELY-HELD BUSINESSES

policy, salaries, benefits, and so on. Therefore, from an economic point of view, the investor's only chance to realize an economic return on his investment is through dividends received. If the company is sufficiently well established and has a history of paying dividends, these payments may form one of the best methods available for computing a discount applicable to minority holdings in that firm.

In applying this method, the appraiser compares the actual dividend payment history of the subject company with what the probable payment would have been had the company's stock been publicly traded. The most recent several years (usually the last five) should be used. The logic of this appraoch is as follows: If the shareholder were free to sell his stock and make an alternative investment having at least equal economic benefits, then the value of the minority interest should not exceed the value indicated by the dividend yield.

For example, assume a company earned an average of approximately $100,000 per year and during the selected period of the study typically paid out 15%, or $15,000, in annual dividends. A market survey indicates that a yield on investments with comparable risks and restrictions was 6%. Therefore, the capitalized value of the $15 annual dividend is $250 ($15 ÷ .06 = $250). This, then, is the indicated value of each minority share using this method. To arrive at the percentage of discount, compare this amount to the basic share value of the entire company. If the latter is assumed to be $500 per share, then the minority interest worth $250 per share is the subject of a 50% discount. Such a discount can be attributed not only to lack of marketability but also to all other factors which restrict or limit the economic value of a minority interest in a closely-held business.

[¶11.03] VALUING MAJORITY INTERESTS

As a general rule, the value of a majority interest in a closely-held firm is assumed to be a prorate of the value of the entire operating enterprise. In other words, if the equity value of the whole business is $100,000 and there are 100 outstanding shares, the value of each share is $1,000. This is identical to the basic share value described at ¶ 11.02. Whereas minority interests would normally carry a discount from this basic share value, majority interests are usually assumed to have a value on a par with it. In the foregoing situation, therefore, a 55% interest, or 55 shares, would be worth $55,000.

Nevertheless, it is reasonable to inquire whether the value of a majority interest may not be greater than the basic share value. If a minority interest usually must be discounted, why shouldn't a majority interest carry a premium? In some cases this may be true, but much depends on the assumptions which were used in valuing the entire enterprise in the first place.

While the value of a closely-held business is usually based on many considerations, substantial reliance is typically based upon market data such as price earn-

VALUING FRACTIONAL INTERESTS IN CLOSELY-HELD BUSINESSES

ings ratios, dividend payouts, and dividend yields. In valuing the closely-held business using market data, adjustments have presumably been made for various risk factors inherent in the private firm, but typically no adjustment has been made for the relative lack of marketability. It usually is assumed that lack of marketability is offset by the fact that an entire enterprise is being valued. Such a total enterprise, or at least majority interest control of it usually is quite marketable. Therefore, the liquidity advantage of the publicly-held stock is presumed offset by the obvious advantages of having control of a privately-held business. This being the case, no additional premium should be added to the majority interest.

There are exceptions to this conclusion. For example, if there were no majority interest in a firm, but one would be desirable, and if it were presumed that one of the stockholders sought such a majority, he might be willing to pay a premium for one or more minority holdings to achieve it. If there were substantial evidence to indicate this would be true, then the average per share value of the majority interest might be more than the basic share value of the entire enterprise. However, to arrive at this premium means that the basic tendency of minority interests to be discounted must be overcome and that, in fact, these minority interests acquired to achieve control will bear a premium.

If a premium is applicable to the control block, a further question arises as to what percentage of the stock should be subject to the premium. In theory, an interest of 51% represents the maximum utility, and any investment beyond that declines in value. In other words, 51% provides control, and beyond that any acquisition should be at a discounted level applicable to most minority holdings. Often this will be the case, but not always. If, for instance, sufficient control is sought to authorize a merger without the consent of the remaining shareholders, 66⅔% or more may be required. Similarly, if it seems desirable to file a consolidated income tax return, 80% is needed.

[¶11.04] BLOCKAGE

Blockage is a term applied to the circumstance in which a relatively large block of registered stock in a publicly-held company is sold at a discount below the quoted market price of the stock. Such large blocks are often sold in private transactions to avoid the negative impact on the public market were such a large amount offered for public sale at one time. Because large blocks are more difficult, time-consuming, and perhaps more expensive to sell than smaller holdings, a discounted price is not infrequently paid.

It is sometimes argued that, in certain circumstances, blockage has application in valuing the shares of closely-held companies. It seems this might be true if the block to be acquired comprised a majority interest in excess of that needed for effective control. As such, it might be considered as an offset against any potential premium for acquisition of control. In rare occasions it might apply to a large min-

VALUING FRACTIONAL INTERESTS IN CLOSELY-HELD BUSINESSES

ority interest. For instance, the minority interest might be so large and involve so much money that the potential market would be considerably narrowed. However, the appraiser must be very cautious not to duplicate discounts. That is, if a discount has already been applied for lack of marketability of the minority interest, the blockage discount must not duplicate the same lack of marketability consideration.

[¶11.05] STOCKS HELD IN TRUST

Stocks held in trust may lack marketability regardless of the size of the block in the trust. This is true because trusts typically provide special restrictions on sale. Therefore, even though the trust may represent a majority holding and control, there may be very limited, if any, marketability. Under such circumstances, even a majority interest might require a significant discount for lack of marketability. If the trust holding were a minority, a discount might be required in consideration of the special restrictions of the trust as well as a discount for normal non-marketability of the minority interest.

[¶11.06] RESTRICTIVE AGREEMENTS

The effect of stock restrictions must be considered in valuing either majority or minority interests. Such restrictions may generally be defined as contracts or agreements between two or more persons or entities which have the effect of controlling the sale or transfer of the business interests represented by the subject stock. They normally fall into three categories as follows:

1. **Buy-Sell Agreements**

Under such agreements, the owner of a business interest is obliged to sell and a buyer (usually another stockholder or the corporation itself) must purchase at a predetermined price. Due to the lack of market prices for closely-held stock, the price will usually be set by a formula described in the agreement, although it may be keyed to fair market value as set by an appraiser. The transaction is generally contingent upon certain events, such as the death, retirement, or impairment of one of the parties.

2. **Option Agreements**

The owner of an option has the right to purchase a specified amount of stock at a predetermined price or at a price set by a formula described in the agreement. The purchase usually must be made within a specific period of time.

3. **Right of First Refusal**

This is an agreement whereby the owner of an interest must first offer it to the company, other owners, or specifically named parties before it can be offered to the public or other private parties.

VALUING FRACTIONAL INTERESTS IN CLOSELY-HELD BUSINESSES

For estate, gift, and income tax purposes, the courts have frequently taken the position that if a price is specified in such a restrictive agreement, that price may serve to peg the value if certain other conditions are met. These conditions usually are: (1) there must be a clear written restriction that the owner cannot sell his interest during his lifetime without first offering it to the parties named in the agreement at the predetermined price; (2) the owner must not be able to easily remove the restrictions; and (3) the agreement must give evidence of being a bona fide, arm's length transaction. The probability of Internal Revenue Service and court acceptance of the price is improved if there have been actual sales made according to the agreement.

If sales of shares presumably restricted by such agreements have been made at prices which do not conform, these agreements probably will have a minimal effect for tax purposes. Likewise, the appraiser will give them little weight in his valuation. However, he may tend to look through such agreements for other reasons as well. For example, if the financial condition of the company is substantially poorer than it was when the agreement was executed and when the prices were established, the appraiser may conclude that it is impractical to suppose the company or other named buyers will in fact make purchases at the specified prices even if presumably required to do so. On the other hand, if a formula or price setting method specified in the agreement seems to make reasonable allowance for variations in financial condition, the effect of the agreement should be given serious consideration.

[¶11.07]   VALUING DIFFERENT CLASSES OF STOCK

As tax laws, financing arrangements, and business operations in general have become more complex, the structure of the equity interests in closely-held firms have likewise become more complex. It is not uncommon to find two or more classes of stock which may include one or more classes of preferred and perhaps voting and non-voting common. Different classes may have different dividend privileges, conversion rights, etc. Loans may be made to the firm with conversion privileges or options to acquire stock.

Given the personal nature of the closely-held business, some very unusual arrangements may be found, particularly when the holdings are within a single family. Thus a founder may gradually give away or sell stock to his sons, other members of the family, key employees, or to a personally controlled charitable foundation. At the same time, however, he takes care to retain control even as he lowers his equity. Often this is done through issuance of non-voting stock to those he intends to benefit. He may have effective control with as little as one share of voting stock, whereas his actual equity is minimal. In such a situation, and in less drastic variations of it, the appraiser is faced basically with valuation of the right to control.

VALUING FRACTIONAL INTERESTS IN CLOSELY-HELD BUSINESSES

So extensive and complex are the possible arrangements, it is not practical to hypothesize as to all and set forth suggested valuation methods. The best advice which can be offered when complex capital structures are encountered is to be certain to isolate all of the rights and privileges having a bearing upon the equity. Having done so, each such right or privilege must be separately valued. It is usually possible to find some market or public information which will be helpful in this process. For example, there is substantial market information available from publicly-held and traded stock transactions which will help to quantify the value of voting rights, such as the market difference between voting and non-voting common. Since financing agreements are matters of public record with state corporation commissioners and with the SEC, these can be helpful in valuing conversion rights. In general, public sources should be carefully explored for comparable data. Some of the appraisal principles discussed earlier in this book can then be adapted to fit the need.

[¶11.08] SUMMARY

The quotation on the title page of this chapter, while intended to be jocular, nevertheless states a caution worthy of notice. In valuing minority, majority, and large block interests in closely-held businesses, the appraiser cannot consistently apply the overall share value determined by dividing the value set for the whole firm by the issued and outstanding shares. This value, referred to in this chapter as the basic share value, is usually discounted when a minority interest is being valued. It is usually the appropriate value when a majority interest is appraised.

Over the years as the tax laws, financing agreements, and business in general have become more complex, minority interests in closely-held firms have tended to become relatively illiquid and hard to market. For this reason, the courts, the IRS, and the market generally have recognized that higher and higher discounts should be applied. Three methods for valuing minority interests are suggested in this chapter. Considerations are also discussed in valuing majority interests, including those which provide control. The effect of blockage on the value of closely-held business interests is covered. Also reviewed for their effect on value are trust holdings and restrictive agreements. A final section describes some of the considerations involved when the firm being valued has different classes of stock and other securities outstanding.

CHAPTER 12

QUESTIONS AND ANSWERS

And when the queen of Sheba heard of the fame of Solomon . . . she came to prove him with hard questions.

THE BIBLE - I KINGS 10:1

TOPICS DISCUSSED IN THIS CHAPTER

Question Number	Topic
1.	Estate Tax - Decease of Key Owner
2.	Divorce - Valuation of Professional Business
3.	Intangible Valuation - Choice of Method
4.	Intangible Valuation - Multiple Assets
5.	Intangible Valuation - Choice of Remaining Life
6.	Intangible Valuation - Loss in Value of Assets
7.	Definition - IRS "Fair Market Value"
8.	Definition - IRS "Closely-Held Corporation"
9.	Definitions - Market Value, Value in Exchange, Value in Use, Value in Place, User-in-Possession Value, Going Concern Value
10.	Definition - Working Capital for Appraisal Purposes
11.	Special Purpose Properties - Choice of Appraisal Method
12.	Stock Valuation - Employee Stock Ownership Trusts (ESOTS)
13.	Stock Valuation - Majority Interest in Trust
14.	Stock Valuation - Minority Interest Transfers Within Family
15.	Stock Valuation - Appraisal of Tangible Assets
16.	Stock Valuation - Preferred Stock
17.	Appraisal Methods - Capitalization Rate Versus Multiplier
18.	Comparability - Use of Similar Businesses
19.	Comparability - Importance of Location
20.	Excess Earnings Method - Handling Interest Expense
21.	Goodwill in Tax Cases - Inclusion of Other Intangibles
22.	Goodwill in Eminent Domain - Inclusion of Tangible Assets
23.	Real Estate - Separation of Business Values
24.	Debt Consideration - Real Estate Versus Business Operations
25.	Business Sales - Large Versus Small Businesses
26.	Market Data - Reliability
27.	Multiple Entities - Approach to Segregation
28.	Appraisers - Used as Consultants
29.	Appraisers - Procedure in Hiring
30.	Appraisers - Trial Preparation
31.	Appraisers - As Witnesses
32.	Appraisers - Tips for Trial Attorneys

CHAPTER 12

QUESTIONS AND ANSWERS

1. ESTATE TAX - DECEASE OF KEY OWNER

Question

What factors should be considered in valuing the stock of a closely-held company for estate tax purposes under the following assumptions: (a) the majority owner has been active in the business, and (b) prior to his decease, the company enjoyed a substantial amount of goodwill?

Answer

If much of the goodwill was due to the special efforts of the deceased, it may not be transferable to the estate or to potential purchasers. The valuation of any business is based largely upon the future and not the past. Therefore, even though past financial statements may indicate substantial goodwill, this asset may have largely or completely disappeared, and this fact must be reflected in the estate tax valuation. For that matter, if the decease caused diminution in the value of any asset, be it tangible or intangible, the appraisal must reflect this. For instance, the owner may have been personally building technical equipment from details contained only in his mind. Had he lived, the capitalized costs would have great value, but upon his decease there may be no one else capable of completing the work, and the costs may have to be written off.

As a matter of appraisal principle, when faced with determining fair market value, a disinterested third party must be assumed to be the potential buyer. If prudent, he would not pay for assets which could not be utilized or which may no longer exist.

2. DIVORCE - VALUATION OF PROFESSIONAL BUSINESS

Question

What considerations are involved in valuing a business under these circumstances: (1) the purpose of the appraisal is to form a basis for division of property in a divorce action; (2) one of the assets is a closely-held professional business; (3) this business depends upon the technical skill of one of the marriage partners; and (4) historical earnings indicate the existence of a substantial amount of goodwill or other valuable intangibles?

Answer

The value of the goodwill may well become a major matter of contest. This means a cautious, well-thought-out approach to the problem is doubly important. Assume a prosperous medical practice is involved where the husband's earnings

QUESTIONS AND ANSWERS

are very high because of a special skill which he possesses. The valuation of his earnings will be crucial to the overall appraisal of the business.

As a starting point, consideration should be given to the salary he could command if he were to work for someone else. If there are excess earnings over and above such a potential salary, this excess is probably attributable in large part to intangibles—assuming, as is usually the case, that the practice includes little in the way of tangible assets. Nevertheless, these excess earnings are not necessarily goodwill per se. They can best be described as the result of technical skill. If these earnings are to be capitalized into a value, what capitalization rate should be used? The answer depends upon the remaining life of the husband's skill. As is true of most professional fields, there are constant changes in medicine. Unless he keeps up with these changes, his skill can become nearly obsolete in a relatively short period of time. However, to keep up requires additional investment of time, capital, and effort. With respect to the latter, even the husband's age and physical condition can affect his ability to show extra earnings. Another consideration was mentioned at ¶ 7.05-5, namely, do ethical considerations permit the sale of goodwill-type assets in a medical practice?

3. INTANGIBLE VALUATION - CHOICE OF METHOD

Question

This book describes several methods for valuing intangible assets, such as Cost to Create, Relief from Royalty, and Profit Advantage. How does one determine which method is preferable?

Answer

The choice will be dictated to a considerable degree by three factors: (1) the type of data available; (2) the character of the asset, and (3) the purpose of the appraisal. As a general rule, at least two techniques should be used in developing the value of an intangible. Wherever possible, one of these should be the Cost-to-Create Method. (See ¶ 9.02-5.) This is not necessarily because it is the best measure of value, but it does provide a realistic frame of reference in correlation with one or more other methods. However, there may not be enough reliable data to permit its use. If the asset originated from research, development, and testing, the labor costs of this may be completely obscured in the payroll records and no competitive data may be available. If this is the case, the Cost-to-Create Method cannot be used. The same could hold true with regard to one or more alternative methods. If the asset is of a type that can be expected to produce earnings, a method or methods based on potential income, such as the Profit Advantage Method, should be used. (See ¶ 9.02-1.) If the purpose of the appraisal is to arrive at a selling price for the asset, a careful analysis should be made to see if like assets are traded in the marketplace.

QUESTIONS AND ANSWERS

4. INTANGIBLE VALUATION - MULTIPLE ASSETS

Question

How does one segregate the value of a particular intangible which is part of a total business enterprise having many kinds of assets which contribute to sales and profits?

Answer

Make a careful, systematic study of the particular advantages of the asset being appraised together with other profit-contributing assets within the same company. For example, if there is a particular secret process used to manufacture an item, what are the measurable advantages of that process compared with other manufacturing methods currently or previously used by the same company for a similar product? Going to the outside and comparing general industry data with the asset being appraised is desirable, but often industry data tends to be available only in broad averages. Specifics are hard to come by.

Apropos of the above discussion, one of the authors was once treasurer of a firm that manufactured molded rubber parts known as "O" rings, as well as a multitude of other rubber products. A new secret process for manufacturing "O" rings was developed which enabled these parts to be cured in one minute, whereas the method previously used by the company required 20 minutes. Cost studies were available within the company records which showed quite clearly the impact this saving had on profits. To value this process would have been quite simple using intra-company data adapted to the appraiser's needs.

5. INTANGIBLE VALUATION - CHOICE OF REMAINING LIFE

Question

What is the best approach to estimate the remaining useful life of an intangible asset?

Answer

There is no simple answer. Historical records of the company and the industry of which it is a part should be studied to determine the period of time in which similar assets were capable of generating a profit. Product obsolescence records should be studied to determine how rapidly new products of similar character came along to replace older ones. Were one to evaluate a secret process for making calculators, for example, considerable evidence would be available as to the rapidity with which technology is rendered obsolete. In the case of mailing and subscription lists, studies can be conducted to determine how often names on the list turn over. Thus a turnover rate of 20% per year would indicate the list in question had a life of five years.

QUESTIONS AND ANSWERS

It is important to stress the desirability of developing statistical data to back up conclusions on economic life. The remaining life may be heavily weighted by the appraiser's judgment, but court cases require backup evidence as well. Factual support is demanded for most appraisal purposes.

6. INTANGIBLE VALUATION - LOSS IN VALUE OF ASSETS

Question

In Chapter 10, there is considerable discussion regarding the valuation of lost goodwill. How might one appraise the decline in value of other intangibles, such as could occur as the result of a copyright infringement?

Answer

Appraising the loss in value of any intangible asset can be handled much as one would handle goodwill losses. Damages may be measured by reduction in value caused by loss in sales, reputation, original investment, momentum which may have been created, and by required increases in expenses. This same approach can be taken for losses in value of patents, contracts, and franchises. A basic necessity is to determine the value of the asset before it was taken, infringed upon, or terminated. Using available data, the asset can be valued just prior to the loss and a suitable technique for appraising the loss can be developed. Whether the loss is total or partial depends on the circumstances.

7. DEFINITION - IRS "FAIR MARKET VALUE"

Question

How does the Internal Revenue Service define "fair market value" for purposes of estate, gift, and income taxes?

Answer

Internal Revenue Service Regulations §20.2031-1(b) defines "fair market value" as: "the price at which the property would change hands between a willing buyer and a willing seller, neither being under any compulsion to buy or to sell and both having reasonable knowledge of relevant facts." It also generally assumed that the buyer has adequate financial resources to make the purchase.

The heart of the above definition did not originate with the Internal Revenue Service but with the courts. See, for example, a leading case, Commissioner of Internal Revenue vs. Marshman CA-6, 279 F 2d 27, Cert.denied, 364 US 918.

While the definition is not as all-inclusive as might be desired, it does mean that fair market value *cannot* result from a forced sale or one resulting from an un-

QUESTIONS AND ANSWERS

usual or rigged market. Nor can it be the result of purely subjective factors such as sentimental value or the special use value to a particular owner.

8. DEFINITION - IRS "CLOSELY-HELD CORPORATION"

Question

How does the Internal Revenue Service define a "closely-held corporation"?

Answer

As defined in pertinent Revenue Rulings, "Closely held corporations are those corporations the shares of which are owned by a relatively limited number of stockholders. Often the entire stock issue is held by one family. The result of this situation is that little, if any, trading in the shares takes place. There is, therefore, no established market for the stock, and such sales as occur at irregular intervals seldom reflect all of the elements of a representative transaction as defined by the term "fair market value."' See §2.03 of Revenue Ruling 59-60 at Appendix 3.

9. DEFINITIONS - APPRAISAL TERMINOLOGY FOR VALUE

As in most professions, appraisers have developed a jargon of their own. The terminology is a sort of shorthand that appraisers understand, but which can leave the uninitiated more befuddled than enlightened. This is particularly true of various terms for value. The following questions are aimed at explaining in non-technical language the meaning of some of the more common concepts of value.

Question

What is meant by "market value"?

Answer

The basic concept of this term can best be summarized as the most probable price a property would bring in a competitive market, assuming: (1) a buyer and seller who know allo of the relevant facts about the property and the market; (2) that both are intelligent and economically motivated - not, for example, sentimental about the property; and (3) the buyer is in a position to pay cash. It is comparable in concept to the term "fair market value" discussed in question 7 above. The courts and various taxing bodies have given many definitions to "market value" and "fair market value." Due to differences in emphasis on some of the market factors, when litigation is contemplated, it is advisable to check the definition in vogue in the legal jurisdiction involved.

QUESTIONS AND ANSWERS

Question

What is meant by "value in exchange"?

Answer

It generally refers to a market value determined by comparing the subject property with other comparable properties. The subject property and the comparables are usually what can best be described as "general purpose properties" as opposed to single use or "special purpose properties."

Land is commonly valued by this method. It is usually assumed to be vacant and ready for development. It fits this approach under the theory that it will sell for its highest, best, and most profitable use at a price which is in close proximity to the selling prices set by the general market for similar land.

General purpose buildings, too, are often appraised by this method. Available competitive buildings which may serve the same purposes and which are in all other respects reasonably comparable provide the prospective purchaser with a choice. The amount the purchaser is willing to pay is dictated to some extent by the price which has been paid recently for similar properties.

The foregoing concept works well for land, land improvements, and buildings for which there can be more than one buyer or user. However, often the appraisal will involve a special purpose property which does not fit this concept. See *value-in-use* discussed below.

Question

What is meant by "value in use"?

Answer

The term usually refers to the market value of a special purpose property which has only a single use and therefore has a very limited market other than to the present user. Examples of special purpose improvements include such facilities as churches, athletic stadiums, dry docks, oil refineries, steel mills and newspaper printing plants. Generally, these properties have value when used for the purpose for which they were designed but have a very limited value for alternative purposes. Therefore, the "value in use" concept becomes the basis for developing the market value of such properties.

The comparable sales method used to arrive at "value in exchange" generally does not fit these properties. If sales of comparable properties are found, they often represent distress sales or sales for some alternative uses. A sale for an alternative use involves a built-in discount for reduced utility, and the price would reflect the costs the new owner would incur in converting the property to his requirements. For

QUESTIONS AND ANSWERS

these reasons, the cost approach and on occasion some form of income method are the most commonly used techniques for valuing special purpose properties.

Properly conceived and developed, the "value in use" of an asset should be no greater than the value if there were a comparable market.

Question

What is meant by "value in place"?

Answer

"Value in place" is most often used in connection with the appraisal of machinery and equipment. It essentially represents the market value of machinery and/or equipment installed in a factory or in whatever similar place it will be used. Hence the term "value in place."

To fully understand the concept, it is helpful to start with the machinery on the dealer's showroom floor where it has a market value to him. This value is based upon his costs plus provision for overhead and profit, the latter additions normally being dictated by competition. This is the first level of market value.

Next, the machinery is moved to the factory and installed. The value in place includes the first level of market value plus applicable sales taxes, freight, and all costs of installation, including special foundations, power services, engineering, leveling, and testing. Properly applied, this cumulation of costs should represent market value. This assumes that the equipment in place can be utilized to generate an economic income which would provide not only a proper return on the investment in the equipment, including all labor and other expenses, but also a profit to the enterprise. However, the profit to the business beyond the return on investment in the equipment should *not* be included as part of the equipment value. To do so would include an intangible value which may be part of goodwill or some other identifiable intangible asset.

Question

What is meant by "user-in-possession value"?

Answer

Such a value requires additional consideration beyond the level of the "value in place" concept discussed above. Basic to this value is the theory that there may be a special use value to the user in possession which is greater than that to any other user not having the advantage of occupying the property. This concept may be appropriate when appraising a portion of a facility, such as the value of a steel plate

QUESTIONS AND ANSWERS

rolling mill which is only a part of a much larger steel mill operation. It is commonly used in appraisals made for the General Services Administration of the U.S. Government when disposing of special facilities owned by one of the armed forces. These facilities usually have been built for a specific weapons program and for convenience were constructed near or even among the privately-owned facilities of the contractor.

One method for arriving at the required addition to "value in place" is to develop the present worth of the loss of return on investment which would be experienced by the user in possession were the facilities not already assembled. For example, if facilities would take a year to develop and become operational and the business regularly developed a 20% return on its tangible net worth, the present worth of 20% return on the facility for one year might be a feasible measure of the special use value to be added to "value in place."

There can be several ways to develop "user-in-possession value", but most methods tend to result in some element of intangible value being included. This is the primary distinction between "value in use" and "user-in-possession value." However, the two terms may be synonymous if no intangible values are involved.

Question

What is "going concern value"?

Answer

The term "going concern value" was defined by the Supreme Court in a 1933 case involving the basis for rate making for a public utility, *Los Angeles Gas & Electric Corp., 289 U.S. 287 (1933).* This case was referred to in a more recent decision, *Northern Natural Gas, 470 F.2d 1107 (CA-8, 1973).*

"This court has declared it to be self evident that there is an element of value in an assembled and established plant, doing business and earning money over one not thus advanced, and that this element of value is a property right which should be considered in determining the value of the property upon which the owner has a right to make a fair return."

10. DEFINITION - WORKING CAPITAL FOR APPRAISAL PURPOSES

Question

Is *working capital* for appraisal purposes synonymous with the same term for accounting purposes?

Answer

No. From an accounting standpoint, working capital is the difference between current assets and current liabilities as shown on the balance sheet. For appraisal purposes, this may or may not be considered the proper level of working capital to be utilized. For example, what occurs when a business has more current liabilities

QUESTIONS AND ANSWERS

than current assets and as a result shows negative working capital according to accounting definitions? From a practical standpoint, working capital is required if the business is to be maintained. Therefore, in valuing such a business, the proper level of working capital must be developed regardless of what the balance sheet indicates. For many businesses, the proper working capital level is related to several months of cash operating expenses (often two to four months).

The importance of using a realistic working capital level is apparent when one considers the Excess Earnings Method (¶ 5.05-1). Were working capital used at a level which was too low to maintain the business, little or no return would be required on that portion of the business investment. As a result, less is deducted from profits, and the final result is an inappropriately high level of excess earnings. Were the proper level of working capital substituted, lower and more realistic excess earnings would result.

An excess of working capital can also distort the appraisal. Assume a business had just received a large sum of cash from the sale of assets no longer required in the business. It may be temporarily overcapitalized and such excess capital should be deducted. The business can then be appraised based upon competitive and reasonable asset levels. If appropriate, the excess cash can then be added to the value of the business at the conclusion of the appraisal. This same approach is used in real estate appraisals when there is excess land.

11. SPECIAL PURPOSE PROPERTIES - CHOICE OF APPRAISAL METHOD

Question

Is it ever appropriate to use the "value in exchange" concept to value a special purpose property?

Answer

Yes. While the definition of "value in use" contained at Question 9 above would indicate this is not usually true, it can become appropriate if the special purpose property has become obsolete. This might come about due to changes in technology or in market demand for the product, for instance. Under such circumstances it is appropriate to consider sales of comparable properties and "value in exchange." The buyer of such an obsolete facility would normally not be willing to pay more for it than he would for alternative units which had similar obsolescence.

12. STOCK VALUATION - EMPLOYEE STOCK OWNERSHIP TRUSTS (ESOTS)

Question

How should stock in a closely-held business be valued for purposes of a proposed ESOT?

QUESTIONS AND ANSWERS

Answer

As a general rule, the stock given to individual employees through these plans involve fractional interests. In many cases, all of the stock set aside for the trust is a minority interest. As part of the original plan which must be approved by the Department of Labor and by the Treasury Department, the stock must be appraised at a fair market value. In view of the minority interest generally involved, the normal considerations given to the valuation of such interests must apply; that is, limited marketability, limited voice in management, and lack of control over dividends. For more details on valuing minority interests, see Chapter 11. As in all appraisals, the circumstances surrounding the particular stock issue must be considered.

A unique valuation problem which many ESOT plans include is a guarantee to buy the stock back at a future date. This would imply that no discount is needed for lack of marketability. However, careful consideration must be given to the inherent risk that the company may not fulfill its obligation. For example, how probable is it that the company might experience financial difficulties and not be able to raise the cash necessary to make the buy-back?

13. STOCK VALUATION - MAJORITY INTEREST IN TRUST

Question

If the controlling interest in a closely-held company is held in trust, would this interest be subject to a discount?

Answer

Yes, it could be desirable to apply a discount, depending upon the ownership of the trust and the restrictions applied. The control of the trust may actually have the effect of making a majority interest into several minority holdings. If so, this would reduce the effective control which might normally be exercised by one individual owning the majority on an unrestricted basis. Furthermore, a minority interest held in trust for a specific individual may actually be subject to an additional discount over that which would normally apply to a minority holding by the individual.

14. STOCK VALUATION - MINORITY INTEREST TRANSFERS WITHIN FAMILY

Question

In a situation where transfer of a minority interest of stock (whether by gift or sale) is contemplated to a member of a family where other members of the family already have a majority interest, would the minority interest be subject to a discount?

QUESTIONS AND ANSWERS

Answer

There is no general answer. Each situation must be examined individually for circumstances which may affect value. However, such appraisals usually require the determination of the fair market value of the minority holding. This means consideration should be given to those conditions which would be weighed by a disinterested third-party buyer. If the stock were transfered by an outright purchase, the price paid could be influential in setting value, although some weight might be given to the fact that the transaction could be less than arm's length.

A minority interest is a minority interest, regardless of who holds it - a member of the family or an outsider. (This assumes the minority is a normal voting interest with no special restrictions.) While it is true that blood runs thicker than water and perhaps the minority interest added to the family majority enables effective control of dividends, etc., this cannot be taken for granted. Many families do not get along. To do the job properly, the appraiser should usually consider the value of the stock to a third party in an open market transaction.

15. STOCK VALUATION - APPRAISAL OF TANGIBLE ASSETS

Question

In valuing all of the stock of a closely-held company, is it always necessary to appraise for fair market value all of the tangible assets, including real estate, machinery and equipment, et cetera?

Answer

Not necessarily, although a total appraisal is ideal. If the appraiser concludes that the earnings of the enterprise are the most meaningful indicator of value, the fair market value of the fixed assets may be of little consequence. However, if the purpose of the appraisal includes a requirement to allocate values to individual assets, the full appraisal may be required. Also, if the business is a fixed asset intensive operation where machinery, equipment, and real estate represent significant portions of the total value, it may be desirable to have these assets appraised. In some such cases it may be absolutely essential even when valuing the enterprise by its earning power.

16. STOCK VALUATION - PREFERRED STOCK

Question

If there are several classes of stock involved in an appraisal, including preferred and common, how should the preferred be valued?

QUESTIONS AND ANSWERS

Answer

While several techniques may be utilized, the normal procedure is to first value the entire enterprise. Then the preferred stock would be valued, giving consideration to such factors as voting and non-voting rights, redemption privileges, etc. The residual value would then apply to the higher-risk common shares.

In following the above procedure, it is pertinent to note that the preferred stock often has some restrictions on its value, such as being redeemable at a certain level, often at par. These restrictions must be considered in ascribing value. On occasion, the result may be a value attributed to the preferred which is greater than the value of the entire enterprise. In such a situation, the value of the preferred must be lowered so as not to exceed the value of the business. This may indicate, however, that the common is valueless, which is not likely. Therefore, the rights of all classes of stock must be analyzed. It might develop that the common shares had voting rights and the preferred had none. Consideration could then be given to the fact that the common owners could recapitalize or otherwise reorganize the company so as to give these shares value. The resulting allocation of value between classes of shares must be realistic based on the rights and privileges of each class.

17. APPRAISAL METHODS - CAPITALIZATION RATE VERSUS MULTIPLIER

Question

In valuing excess earnings, cash flow, net profit, and so forth, is it preferable to use a capitalization rate or a multiplier?

Answer

It depends upon the circumstances and how the appraiser has approached the entire valuation problem, not merely one step in the process. However, multipliers are usually more easily explained to others. Therefore, when a jury trial or other extensive public explanation is anticipated, use of a multiplier should be considered if it fits the valuation approach.

18. COMPARABILITY - USE OF SIMILAR BUSINESSES

Question

When there is very little data available on businesses comparable to the one being appraised, is it reasonable to use information gathered on other businesses which are not necessarily the same?

QUESTIONS AND ANSWERS

Answer

Yes, it is reasonable on some occasions. For example, if the appraisal problem involves a retail business which is unique and for which no comparable sales can be found, it may be feasible to cumulate sales on other types of retail businesses that have similar financial characteristics. These similarities might include comparable levels of sales and profits, similar inventory requirements, etc. After all, investment opportunities are competitive. Unless a business constitutes a monopoly or is a very difficult business to enter, it cannot remain extraordinary and exclusive for very long. Under these circumstances, the valuation of investment characteristics becomes extremely important, and the particular product or service may be of only secondary importance.

19. COMPARABILITY - IMPORTANCE OF LOCATION

Question

In developing market data to be used for comparison with a business being appraised, is there any particular geographic limitation on the area from which comparables should be drawn?

Answer

It is helpful if like businesses can be found within a reasonable radius of the company being appraised, but it is not usually essential. Close geographic proximity is almost requisite only if the business is heavily real estate oriented so that the sale of comparable land or buildings would influence the result significantly. Otherwise, when no similar businesses can be found within the immediate community, it is acceptable to survey a much broader area. In some cases, sales of like businesses may be considered on a nationwide basis. When reliance is placed upon price-earnings ratios taken from the stocks of publicly-traded companies, in effect comparisons are being made with firms which are national or even international. Such comparisons are reasonable and common practice, so long as any particular effect of local circumstances is also taken into consideration.

20. EXCESS EARNINGS METHOD - HANDLING INTEREST EXPENSE

Question

In applying the Excess Earnings Method (Method 3 at ¶ 5.05-1) how should interest on debt be handled?

Answer

Since there was no outstanding debt in the BLM case, this question was not fully

QUESTIONS AND ANSWERS

covered. One phase of the question was dealt with in the case, namely, the situation where long term debt is not in existence but is deemed necessary. It was assumed that $50,000 would be needed on a long term basis and that it would cost 12% in interest to obtain the funds. This amount of $6,000 per annum was deducted as part of the required economic return on investment.

However, to more fully answer the question posed, assume a situation with the following facts:

Current Assets	
Cash	$ 75,000
Accounts Receivable	300,000
Inventory	500,000
Total Current Assets	$875,000
Current Liabilities	
Accounts Payable	$100,000
Note Payable (at 9% interest)	300,000
Mortgage (current portion, 9.5% interest)	10,000
Total Current Liabilities	$410,000
Working Capital ($875,000 – $410,000)	$465,000
Long Term Debt (mortgage, 9.5% interest)	$200,000

Computation of Excess Earnings

Pro Forma Income before Capital Charges		$300,000
1. Deduct Economic Depreciation on Tangible Assets		(150,000)
2. Deduct Return on Investment in Land & Buildings		(55,000)
3. Deduct Return on Working Capital as follows:		
Interest on $300,000 note payable at 9%	27,000	
Interest on $10,000 current portion of mortgage at 9.5%	950	
Return on balance of working capital ($155,000 at 10%)	15,500	(43,450)
4. Deduct Interest on $200,000 long term portion of mortgage at 9.5%		(19,000)
5. Excess Earnings		$ 32,550

21. GOODWILL IN TAX CASES - INCLUSION OF OTHER INTANGIBLES

Question

It seems to be generally accepted by many taxpayers that certain intangibles such as advertising contracts and licenses with automatic renewal clauses must be considered part of the goodwill pot. As a result, these assets are not depreciable. Is this proper?

QUESTIONS AND ANSWERS

Answer

In many instances it may be, but this approach should not be considered a general rule. If there is adequate evidence that such assets have a determinable life and a value which can be defined, every effort should be made to support these conclusions. Developing a proper data base may be a difficult problem, but if the potential tax savings are significant, the extra effort can be quite rewarding. Probably the most common reason taxpayers lose their cases in court is lack of adequate preparation and documentation. When the taxpayer goes in well prepared, he is often successful even in the face of generally adverse court rulings on similar cases. The taxpayer and his appraiser should never be lured into the conclusion that success is impossible because similar cases have gone against the taxpayer.

22. GOODWILL IN EMINENT DOMAIN - INCLUSION OF TANGIBLE ASSETS

Question

In eminent domain cases when potential goodwill loss is valued by the Excess Earnings Method using values before and after the taking, how is the possible change in tangible assets to be handled?

Answer

As explained at ¶ 10.07-2, any real estate can be eliminated as an asset for purposes of the Excess Earnings Method by substituting its market rental value. Non-real estate fixed assets should be considered at the same level both before and after the taking, even though some of these assets may be taken. This is because in using the Excess Earnings Method, the potential goodwill loss is measured by the earnings which remain after provision for an economic return on fixed assets, among other things. If it is assumed a business required $100,000 of non-real estate fixed assets to produce the patronage and sales which existed before the taking, it can be presumed to require the same level after the taking. It is not appropriate to reduce the fixed assets to $40,000 in the Excess Earnings Method formula because the eminent domain proceeding would take $60,000 in such assets. To do so would eliminate the return required on $60,000 of investment, resulting in an overstatement of excess earnings after the taking. Since this would have the effect of reducing the difference between the before and after levels of goodwill, it would result in goodwill loss being understated. Furthermore, if the $40,000 of remaining assets were used, it is unlikely the business could regain the same patronage and sales level it enjoyed when $100,000 of assets were available.

QUESTIONS AND ANSWERS

23. REAL ESTATE - SEPARATION OF BUSINESS VALUES

Question

When a business is closely related to real estate, is it possible to arrive at a value for the business which is distinct from the real property? Examples of such businesses would include hotels, nursing homes, marinas, and ski resorts.

Answer

If the business has a value separate from the real estate and other tangible property, this value can be determined. Note the word "if." Not all hotels or motels, for example, have such a distinct business value. In many instances, however, this separate value does exist and the market often recognizes it even though it may not be separately allocated.

One of the major problems in valuing such businesses is the difficulty in segregating income generated by the business from that resulting from the real estate. When faced with such a problem, it is desirable to first value the real property using a depreciated cost approach or comparable sales. Using the value of the real estate so determined, its fair rental value can be evolved. By deducting this rental value from the total sales or income of the enterprise, and if income still remains, the business itself probably is generating receipts. From this a value can be developed for the business. The brevity of this answer should not lead the reader to believe the problem is simple. It is not.

24. DEBT CONSIDERATION - REAL ESTATE VERSUS BUSINESS OPERATIONS

Question

In appraising real estate versus going business enterprises, what is the basic difference in the manner in which debt is handled?

Answer

Real estate is usually appraised as though it were free and clear of debt. That is, the entire property is appraised as though unencumbered, even though the ability to obtain a mortgage with certain terms may influence its value in several ways. On the other hand, in the valuation of a going enterprise, it is usually only the equity which is ultimately appraised. In arriving at the market value of the equity, the fixed assets and certain other assets owned by the business may be appraised on a free and clear basis, but the ultimate value of the business is generally considered to be the owner's equity (all of the assets less all of the liabilities). This is true whether the business is being valued using the book value or some earnings method.

QUESTIONS AND ANSWERS

For example, in the case of real estate, if the total value of the land and buildings is $500,000, that is usually the figure that will be stated in an appraisal. Although it is a simple matter to deduct a mortgage liability in order to determine the owner's equity, this is generally a separate step. The market value would be quoted as $500,000, not $500,000 less the mortgage.

Were the appraisal to involve a business enterprise, the total value of the assets could also be $500,000, but this would not normally be the quoted market value of the business. Assuming liabilities of $300,000, these would first be deducted with resulting equity of $200,000. This figure of $200,000 would be shown as the market value of the enterprise.

25. BUSINESS SALES - LARGE VERSUS SMALL BUSINESSES

Question

What is the basic difference in the manner in which a small business usually sells versus sale of a larger firm?

Answer

The smaller business generally sells selected assets, such as inventory, shelving, equipment, and perhaps selected accounts receivable and even selected liabilities. Larger businesses more often sell as operating enterprises. If the larger firm is incorporated, this will include all assets and all liabilities - whatever makes up the business.

The method used in valuing a business is often influenced by the manner in which similar firms sell. It is for this reason that formula techniques most often apply to smaller businesses. The formulas usually relate to specific assets or multipliers of net sales or net profit. When multipliers are used, certain selected assets are frequently considered to be included in the resultant value. However, very often all of tha assets owned by the business are not included. This is particularly true of cash, accounts receivable, and debt items. If additional assets or liabilities are to be included which are not normally included in the value resulting from the multiplier, these items will be added to or subtracted from the multiplier value as appropriate. Many very small businesses sell strictly for the market value of selected assets with little or no regard for multipliers of sales or profits.

The larger the enterprise, the more likely it will be organized as a corporation, and the valuation techniques are influenced accordingly. The net worth of the business and various means of weighing earnings are usually given considerable weight. Formulas tend to become less relevant.

QUESTIONS AND ANSWERS

26. MARKET DATA - RELIABILITY

Question

How reliable is the information regarding prices paid for goodwill and other specific assets when obtained from buyers or sellers of smaller businesses?

Answer

Often the information provided is somewhat suspect and should not be accepted without thorough questioning. Remember that buyer and seller usually have opposing objectives when it comes to allocation of the purchase price. The seller wishes as much of the price as possible to represent goodwill, since for tax purposes this represents a capital gain to him. By the same token, the more value put on depreciable assets, the more likely he is to face ordinary income on recaptured depreciation. The buyer, on the other hand, wishes as little goodwill as possible, since this is not a depreciable asset. In addition, he wishes the maximum value in depreciable tangible assets because of the added tax deductions he will obtain.

Because of these opposing objectives, the prices quoted for various assets, especially goodwill, may be arbitrary and not factual. By asking enough questions, the appraiser may be able to determine the weight placed upon tax considerations and evaluate the answers accordingly.

27. MULTIPLE ENTITIES - APPROACH TO SEGREGATION

Question

In valuing a closely-held company, it often is discovered that there are actually several companies involved. How does one handle such a problem?

Answer

It depends upon the circumstances. Usually there will be extensive adjustments required in the income statements and balance sheets. This is particularly true when there have been inter-company transfers, sales, arbitrary allocations of expenses to various functions, etc. The appraiser should obtain adequately documented support for any adjustments to be made to the statements. If it is necessary to determine a separate value for each of the enterprises, this can be handled in two ways: first, by separating the enterprises and valuing each independently, or second, by valuing the total enterprise and making reasonable allocations to each business. The choice between the methods depends a great deal upon the relationship between the businesses. If, for example, the several operations are actually more like divisions of a single firm and are very closely related, it may be most practical to value the enterprise as a single unit. Then an allocation can be made as a final step.

QUESTIONS AND ANSWERS

28. APPRAISERS - USED AS CONSULTANTS

Question

Is it ever advisable to use a qualified appraiser as a consultant?

Answer

Yes. This can be very helpful when a deal is being made. Often the principals in a proposed business sale, for example, will work out all aspects of a transaction and then call in the experts to give them the best position for taxes, valuation, and legal support. Before the position of opposing parties becomes "hardened" a settlement is more easily negotiated. Too frequently an appraiser will be asked to value a company and provide a segregation of asset values after the deal has been set. Had he been consulted earlier, he might well have advised on the best way to arrange the transaction so as to minimize goodwill, for instance. After all is done, it cannot be restructured to accomplish such an end.

Do not, however, expect a professional appraiser to be a negotiator, and especially do not expect him to negotiate his own opinion of value. Appraisers can act as advisors in negotiations, settlement conferences, depositions, and may be helpful in deciding strategy. However, negotiations should be carried on by the property owner himself or by his legal representative.

29. APPRAISERS - PROCEDURE IN HIRING

Question

How should one go about hiring an appraiser?

Answer

If the problem is particularly complex or a given value level is extremely important, ask the appraiser for a preliminary opinion. Hire him on a per diem basis to do only the work necessary to arrive at such an opinion. In his preliminary review, he may discover information previously unknown. This is also a good way to control costs and avoid a large billing for a thoroughly documented appraisal which may be of no value.

Tell the appraiser everything you know and think pertinent to the appraisal except your value opinion. Let him know the purpose and function of the appraisal and expose all of the skeletons in the closet. He will probably find out anyway, and it is better to avoid surprises.

Do not understate the problem in your initial contact with the appraiser. Answer his questions fairly in order that he may accurately estimate time, expertise, and fee requirements.

QUESTIONS AND ANSWERS

Appraisers' charges are based upon per diem rates, range estimates, and flat fees. Make it absolutely clear who the appraiser is working for and who is paying the bill.

30. APPRAISERS - TRIAL PREPARATION

Question

How can an appraiser assist an attorney in preparation for a trial?

Answer

No one should be in a better position to know the weaknesses of his own appraisal or the potential weaknesses of the opposing appraisal than your appraiser. Therefore, have him write out questions and answers which he thinks he should be asked and which might be helpful in cross-examination. This not only helps the attorney in planning the trial, but it also forces the appraiser to view his work product in a critical manner. It is probably the best way for him to prepare.

31. APPRAISERS - AS WITNESSES

Question

Do you have any suggestions for attorneys as to how an appraiser may be used most effectively as a witness?

Answer

We have found the following suggestions to be helpful:

Remember that an appraiser is basically a technician and not a salesman. However, the basic function is to *sell* his value to the jury or the judge. A conflict is therefore set up which must be resolved with thoughtful pre-trial preparation and conferences.

  a. Keep statements simple and avoid complex formulas, math, and explanations which no one will understand.
  b. Have the appraiser make an introductory statement explaining how he went about making his appraisal and arriving at his opinion of value. This statement should not be interrupted by questions. When completed, this statement (which should be a brief but adequate presentation of the total work done by the appraiser) may be followed by the attorney's questioning to fill in voids, amplify, and emphasize. This technique is better than the constant question-and-answer exchanges which often leave the court confused as to what

QUESTIONS AND ANSWERS

      the appraiser really did and how the elements fit together.

   c. Thoroughly qualify the witness, particularly with regard to ethics, designations, and professionalism. Have a complete presentation of the appraisal profession, specifically as a quick offense/defense against such questions as "How long have you been in this neighborhood?" "Have you ever actually sold a liquor store?", etc.

32. APPRAISERS - TIPS FOR TRIAL ATTORNEYS

Question

Do you have any other tips for attorneys which will help them keep their appraisers from being tripped up in a trial and in cross-examination?

Answer

Yes, indeed. While many more could be added, there are five suggestions we feel are worth citing.

1. Watch mathematics. Don't assume that appraisers are always good at math, particularly under pressure on the stand. Attorneys are not always expert mathematicians either, and nothing can be more disastrous than computational errors over math.
2. Blackboards can be dangerous to use, except for simple drawings or plans. Avoid the use of blackboards for math, formulas, and so forth at almost all costs. They are an excellent tool for attorneys during cross-examination. Appraisal practice involves many basic assumptions and matters of judgment. It is easy to confuse the opposition by asking hypothetical questions such as, "If you used a 12% cap rate instead of a 10% rate, what would have happened, and would you please put the answer on the blackboard?"
3. Definitions can be dynamite. Be sure that all basic definitions and concepts are written out before the trial and that the appraiser has memorized them in advance.
4. Elaborate use of exhibits can backfire. Although a few well-done exhibits may help sell a value, very often the jury may see things in the exhibits that the attorney does not. For example, photos have a tendency to make things look much better or much worse than they actually are.
5. Get to know everything you can about the opposing expert witness; for example, articles he has written, how he is viewed by his peers, his position in the community, et cetera.

You won't have to face the queen of Sheba, but you, like Solomon, will be proved with hard questions when you have your day in court.

APPENDIX

LIST OF APPENDIXES

APPENDIX 1 - *Ratio Analysis for Small Business*—Excerpts
Business Ratios and How They Work
Standard or Typical Ratios
Sources of Ratio Studies
For Further Study

Editorial Note: Some of the material in both *Sources of Ratio Studies* and *For Further Study* is outdated but it, nevertheless, provides a useful lead as to where this material can be found and as to its scope.

APPENDIX 2 - Court Decisions Regarding Depreciation of Intangibles
Air space - Agreements Not to Compete - Broadcasting Licenses - Business Expansion Costs - Business Licenses and Franchises - Contracts - Copyrights and Patents - Customer Lists - Drawings - Easements, Pipeline - Exchange Memberships - Going Concern Value - Goodwill - Hospital Staff Privileges - Insurance Expiration Lists - Patient Charts - Personal Service Contracts: Baseball Players - Secret Processes - Various Intangibles

APPENDIX 3 - Revenue Rulings Respecting Valuation
Revenue Ruling 59-60 - Valuation of Stocks and Bonds
Revenue Ruling 65-193 - Valuation of Stocks and Bonds
  Modifies Revenue Ruling 59-60
Revenue Ruling 68-609 - Valuation of Stocks and Bonds
  Updates and restates applicable portions of ARM 34 and ARM 68 (issued in 1920) and OD 937 (issued in 1921). It also supersedes these old rulings completely.

APPENDIX 1

RATIO ANALYSIS FOR SMALL BUSINESS - EXCERPTS*

BUSINESS RATIOS AND HOW THEY WORK

A BALANCE SHEET tells how a business stands at one given moment in the business year. A profit-and-loss statement sums up the results of operations over a period of time.

Of themselves, these two types of financial documents are a collection of inanimate figures. But when the assorted financial symbols are interpreted and evaluated, they begin to talk.

A single balance sheet is like the opening chapters of a book—it gives the initial setting. Thus, one balance sheet will show how the capital is distributed, how much is in the various accounts, and how much surplus of assets over liabilities exists. A lone profit-and-loss statement indicates the sales volume for a given period, the amount of costs incurred, and the amount earned after allowing for all costs.

When a series of balance sheets for regularly related intervals, such as fiscal or calendar yearends, is arranged in vertical columns so that related items may be compared, the changes in these items begin to disclose trends. The comparative balance sheets then no longer remain snapshots, but are converted into X-rays, penetrating outward tissue and outlining skeletal structure of all basic management actions and decisions.

Thus, decisions to increase basic inventories because of upward price changes may be revealed in large quantities of merchandise on hand from one period to the next. If credits are relaxed and collections slow up when sales remain constant, there may be a successive increase in receivables. If expansion is undertaken, debts may run higher; and if losses are sustained, net worth declines.

Similarly, comparative profit-and-loss statements reveal significant changes in what took place. Were prices cut to meet competition? Then look for a lower gross profit—unless purchasing costs were reduced proportionately. Did sales go up? If so, what about expenses? Did they remain proportionate? Was more money spent on office help? Where did the money come from? How about fixed overhead? Was it controlled? It is only by comparing operating income and cost account items from one period to another that revealing answers are found.

---

*For the full reference and Superintendent of Documents order number, see Footnote 9.

APPENDIX 1

STATEMENTS REVEAL IMPORTANT RELATIONSHIPS

In order to make comparisons meaningful, it is helpful to use relationships. If inventories are increased $50,000, for instance, the significance is difficult to evaluate unless the item is compared with sales and working capital. In other words, could the business really afford that much addition to stock? Did the merchandise turn over as fast as formerly? Or was the result an accumulation of unsalable goods? Thus you need to relate asset and liability items to something else to make their significance easy to grasp.

Similarly, when you analyze costs in relation to sales, you can translate the cost figures into percentages of the sales. Then, by comparing the percentages from one period to another, you can see whether or not aggregate dollar totals of individual items meant progress or setbacks. Hence, profit-and-loss statements prepared by accountants show not only dollar totals, but usually also the percentages of sales represented by each item. Percentages, of course, are expressions of arithmetical proportions. Proportions are ratios.

THREE KINDS OF RATIOS

Broadly speaking, there are three kinds of ratios. The first are balance sheet ratios which refer to relationships between various balance sheet items. The second are the operating ratios which show the relationships of expense accounts to income. The third group is made up of ratios which show the relationship between an item in the profit-and-loss statement and one on the balance sheet.

TEN KEY RATIOS

How many different ratios are significant? As might be expected, there is among the experts considerable difference of opinion on this question. An early authority, Alexander Wall, while Secretary and Treasurer of Robert Morris Associates, listed 10 ratios in his book, *Basic Financial Statement Analysis*. Roy A. Foulke, another pioneer, lists 14 important ratios.[1] A study by American Trade Association Executives[2] found 34 separate types of financial ratios being compiled by 26 trade associations a number of years ago.

That study suggested, however, that "It should be understood that the range of possible ratios is limited by the number and classification of accounts that are used in various types of business enterprises. Ratio study needs simplification more than to multiply examples. Ratios may lose their significance and accuracy when they become excessively detailed and therefore unduly attenuated."

---

[1] *Practical Financial Statement Analysis.* McGraw-Hill Book Co., Inc. 6th edition. 1968.
[2] The official name of this organization is now American Society of Association Executives.

APPENDIX 1

Along this line, a primary objective in this booklet was to narrow down the field of ratios to a working minimum for small business use. Because of this objective, a certain selection and rejection of material has obviously been necessary. The following ratios, for instance, reflect chiefly balance sheet relationships. A few combine balance sheet and profit and loss items, while one, net profit on net sales, is based exclusive (sic) on data from the profit and loss statement. The procedures for preparing an all-balance-sheet study follow the same pattern as those outlined in connection with combined balance-sheet and income-statement analyses.

Against this background, then, the following 10 ratios are suggested as key ones for small business purposes:
1. Current assets to current liabilities.
2. Current liabilities to tangible net worth.
3. Turnover of tangible net worth.
4. Turnover of working capital.
5. Net profits to tangible net worth.
6. Average collection period of receivables.
7. Net sales to inventory.
8. Net fixed assets to tangible net worth.
9. Total debt to tangible net worth.
10. Net profit on net sales.

Brief definitions of these ratios appear below, followed by specific examples using data taken from the balance sheet and profit-and-loss statement on pages 13 and 14. Explanation of the terms of the financial statements, used in calculating the ratio, is also included in the discussion of each ratio.

1. Current Assets To Current Liabilities.

Widely known as the "current ratio," this is one test of solvency, measuring the liquid assets available to meet all debts falling due within a year's time.

$$\text{Example:} \frac{\text{Current assets}}{\text{current liabilities}} = \frac{\$37,867}{\$19,242} = 1.97 \text{ times.}$$

Current assets are those normally expected to flow into cash in the course of a merchandising cycle. Ordinarily these include cash, notes and accounts receivable, and inventory, and at times, in addition, short term and marketable securities listed on leading exchanges at current realizable values. While some concerns may consider current items such as cash-surrender value of life insurance as current, the tendency is to post the latter as noncurrent.

Current liabilities are short term obligations for the payment of cash due on demand or within a year. Such liabilities ordinarily include notes and accounts payable for merchandise, open loans payable, short term bank loans, taxes, and accruals. Other sundry short term obligations, such as maturing equipment obliga-

APPENDIX 1

tions and the like, also fall within the category of current liabilities.

2. Current Liabilities To Tangible Net Worth.

Like the "current ratio," this is another means of evaluating financial condition by comparing what is owed to what is owned. If this ratio exceeds 80 percent, this is considered a danger sign.

$$\text{Example: } \frac{\text{Current liabilities}}{\text{tangible net worth}} = \frac{\$19{,}242}{\$33{,}970} = 56.6 \text{ percent.}$$

Tangible net worth is the worth of a business, minus any intangible items in the assets such as goodwill, trademarks, patents, copyrights, leaseholds, treasury stock, organization expenses, or underwriting discounts and expenses. In a corporation, the tangible net worth would consist of the sum of all outstanding capital stock—preferred and common—and surplus, minus intangibles. In a partnership or proprietorship, it could comprise the capital account, or accounts, less the intangibles.

A word about "intangibles." In a going buisness, these items frequently have a great but undeterminable realizable value. Until these intangibles are actually liquidated by sale, it is difficult for an analyst to evaluate what they might bring. In some cases, they have no commercial value except to those who hold them: for instance, an item of goodwill. To a profitable business up for sale, the goodwill conceivably could represent the potential earning power over a period of years, and actually bring more than the assets themselves. On the other hand, another business might find itself unable to realize anything at all on goodwill.

3. Turnover Of Tangible Net Worth.

Sometimes called "net sales to tangible net worth," this ratio shows how actively invested capital is being put to work by indicating its turnover during a period. It helps measure the profitability of the investment. Both overwork and underwork of tangible net worth are considered unhealthy.

$$\text{Example: } \frac{\text{Net sales}}{\text{tangible net worth}} = \frac{\$189{,}754}{\$33{,}970} = 5.6 \text{ times.}$$

Turnover of tangible net worth is determined by dividing the average tangible net worth into net sales for the same periods. The rato is expressed as the number of times the turnover is obtained within the given period.

4. Turnover Of Working Capital.

Known, as well, as the ratio of "net sales to net working capital," this ratio also measures how actively the working cash in a business is being put to work in terms of sales. Working capital or cash is assets that can readily be converted into operat-

APPENDIX 1

ing funds within a year. It does not include invested capital. A low ratio shows unprofitable use of working capital; a high one, vulnerability to creditors.

Example: $\dfrac{\text{Net sales}}{\text{working capital}} = \dfrac{\text{net sales}}{\text{current assets - current liabilities}}$

$= \dfrac{\$189,754}{\$37,867 - \$19,242} = 10.1$ times.

Deduct the sum of the current liabilities from the total current assets to get working capital, the business assets which can readily be converted into operating funds. A business with $100,000 in cash, receivables, and inventories and no unpaid obligations would have $100,000 in working capital. A business with $200,000 in current assets and $100,000 in current liabilities also would have $100,000 working capital. Obviously, however, items like receivables and inventories cannot usually be liquidated overnight. Hence, most businesses require a margin of current assets over and above current liabilities to provide for stock and work-in-process inventory, and also to carry ensuing receivables after the goods are sold until the receivables are collected.

5. Net Profits To Tangible Net Worth.

As the measure of return on investment, this is increasingly considered one of the best criteria of profitability, often the key measure of management efficiency. Profits "after taxes" are widely looked upon as the final source of payment on investment plus a source of funds available for future growth. If this "return on capital" is too low, the capital involved could be better used elsewhere.

Example: $\dfrac{\text{Net profits (after taxes)}}{\text{tangible net worth}} = \dfrac{\$5,942}{\$33,970} = 17.5$ percent.

This ratio relates profits actually earned in a given length of time to the average net worth during that time. Profit here means the revenue left over from sales income and allowing for payment of all costs. These include costs of goods sold, writedowns and chargeoffs, Federal and other taxes accruing over the period covered, and whatever miscellaneous adjustments may be necessary to reduce assets to current, going values. The ratio is determined by dividing tangible net worth at a given period into net profits for a given period. The ratio is expressed as a percentage.

6. Average Collection Period Of Receivables.

This ratio, known also as the "collection period" ratio, shows how long the money in a business is tied up in credit sales. In comparing this figure with net maturity in selling terms, many consider a collection period excessive if it is more than 10 to 15 days longer than those stated in selling terms. To get the collection period

APPENDIX 1

figure, get average daily credit sales, then divide into the sum of notes and accounts receivable.

Example: $\dfrac{\text{Net (credit) sales for year}}{365 \text{ days a year}}$ = daily (credit) sales ($519).

$$\text{Average collection period} = \dfrac{\text{notes and accounts receivable}}{\text{daily (credit) sales}}$$

$$= \dfrac{\$26{,}765}{\$519} = 51.5.$$

This figure represents the number of days' sales tied up in trade accounts and notes receivable or the average collection received. The receivables discounted or assigned with recourse are included because they must be collected either directly by borrower, or by lender; if uncollected, they must be replaced by cash or substitute collateral. A pledge with recourse makes the borrower just as responsible for collection as though the receivables had not been assigned or discounted. Aside from this, the likely collectibility of all receivables must be analyzed, regardless of whether or not they are discounted. Hence all receivables are included in determining the average collection period.

7. Net Sales To Inventory.

Known also as a "stock-to-sales" ratio, this hypothetical "average" inventory turnover figure is valued for purposes of comparing one company's performance with another, or with the industry's.

$$\text{Example: } \dfrac{\text{Net sales}}{\text{inventory}} = \dfrac{\$189{,}754}{\$10{,}385} = 18.3 \text{ times.}$$

A manufacturers' inventory is the sum of finished merchandise on hand, raw material, and material in process. It does not include supplies unless they are for sale. For retailers and wholesalers, it is simply the stock of salable goods on hand. It is expected that inventory will be valued conservatively on the basis of standard accounting methods of valuation, such as its cost or its market value, whichever is the lower.

Divide the average inventory into the net sales over a given period. This shows the number of times the inventory turned over in the period selected. It is compiled purely and only for purposes of making comparisons in this ratio from one period to another, or for other comparative purposes. This ratio is not an indicator of physical turnover. The only accurate way to obtain a physical turnover figure is to count each type of item in stock and compare it with the actual physical sales of that particular item.

Some people compute turnover by dividing the average inventory value at cost into the cost of goods sold for a particular period. However, this method still gives

APPENDIX 1

only an average. A hardware store stocking some 10,000 items might divide its dollar inventory total into cost of goods sold and come up with a physical average; this however, would hardly define the actual turnover of each item from paints to electrical supplies.

8. Afixed Assets To Tangible Net Worth.

This ratio, which shows the relationship between investment in plant and equipment and the owners' capital, indicates how liquid is net worth. The higher this ratio, the less the owner's capital is available for use as working capital, or to meet debts.

$$\text{Example: } \frac{\text{Fixed assets}}{\text{tangible net worth}} = \frac{\$15,345}{\$33,970} = 45.2 \text{ percent.}$$

Fixed assets means the sum of assets such as land, buildings, leasehold improvements, fixtures, furniture, machinery, tools, and equipment, less depreciation. The ratio is obtained by dividing the depreciated fixed assets by the tangible net worth.

9. Total Debt To Tangible Net Worth.

This ratio also measures "what is owed to what is owned." As this figure approaches 100, the creditors' interest in the business assets approaches the owner's.

$$\text{Example: } \frac{\text{Total debt}}{\text{tangible net worth}} = \frac{\text{current debt} + \text{fixed debt}}{\text{tangible net worth}}$$

$$= \frac{\$19,242}{\$33,970} = 56.6 \text{ percent.}$$

Total debt is the sum of all obligations owed by the company such as accounts and notes payable, bonds outstanding, and mortgages payable. The ratio is obtained by dividing the total of these debts by tangible net worth.

10. Net Profit On Net Sales.

This ratio measures the rate of return on net sales. The resultant percentage indicates the number of cents of each sales dollar remaining, after considering all income statement items and excluding income taxes.

A slight variation of the above occurs when net operating profit is divided by net sales. This ratio reveals the profitableness of sales—i.e., the profitableness of the regular buying, manufacturing, and selling operations of a business.

To many, a high rate of return on net sales is necessary for successful operation. This view is not always sound. To evaluate properly the significance of the ratio, consideration should be given to such factors as (1) the value of sales (2) the

APPENDIX 1

total capital employed and (3) the turnover of inventories and receivables. A low rate of return compared with rapid turnover and large sales volume, for example, may result in satisfactory earnings.

$$\text{Example: } \frac{\text{Net profits}}{\text{net sales}} = \frac{\$5,942}{\$189,754} = 3.1 \text{ percent.}$$

ANALYZING THE PROFIT-AND-LOSS (INCOME) STATEMENT

Based solely on data taken from the profit-and-loss (P & L) statement, operating ratios show the precentage relationships of each item to a common base of net sales. These percentages may be compared with those of previous periods to measure a firm's performance. They also may be compared to the typical percentages of businesses in similar trades or industries when they are available. Such comparisons will indicate the competitive strengths and weaknesses of a business.

The items included in profit and loss statements vary from business to business. For example, some businesses break down their sales expense to show the costs of salesmen's salaries and commissions, advertising, delivery costs, supplies, and so forth; some do not. In the following explanation of the P & L items, only major items are included.

The following explanations briefly discuss each item in the accompanying condensed profit-and-loss statement (see page 14):

Net Sales.

This figure represents gross dollar sales minus merchandise returns and allowances. Some accountants also deduct cash discounts granted to customers on the theory that these are actually a reduction of the net selling price; others credit the discounts to "other" expense. "Trade" and "quantity" discounts are, of course, concessions off price, and should be deducted from the gross sales. In setting up the profit-and-loss statements in percentages, the net sales are shown as 100 percent.

APPENDIX 1

FIGURE 1

ANY SMALL BUSINESS, INC.

Balance Sheet

December 31, 19—

Assets

Current Assets:			
Cash on hand and in banks			$ 4,320
Notes receivable		$ 4,820	
Less notes discounted		3,000	1,820
Accounts receivable		$21,945	
Less reserve for bad debts		1,875	20,070
Inventories			10,385
Prepayment of expenses			1,272
Total current assets			$37,867
Plant and equipment:			
Land and building		$14,495	
Equipment, fixtures, and furniture		4,800	
Less allowances for depreciation		3,950	15,345
Intangibles:			
Goodwill		$ 500	
Patents, franchises, etc.		500	1,000
Total assets			$54,212

Liabilities

Current liabilities:	
Notes payable)to banks)	$ 4,000
Accounts payable (trade)	10,322
Taxes payable	3,600
Other payables (including accruals)	1,320
Total current liabilities	$19,242
Fixed liabilities	0
Total liabilities	$19,242

Capital

Capital stock (preferred)	$ 5,000	
Capital stock (common)	20,000	
Surplus	9,970	
Total		$34,970
Total liabilities and capital		$54,212

APPENDIX 1

FIGURE 2

ANY SMALL BUSINESS, INC.
Profit and Loss Statement
For year ending December 31, 19—

Item	Amount		Percent
Gross sales		$193,472	
Less returns and allowances		3,718	
Net Sales		$189,754	100.00
Cost of goods sold		147,348	77.65
Gross profit on sales		$ 42,406	22.35
Selling expenses	$ 10,479		5.52
General and administrative expenses	19,510		10.28
Financial expenses	1,312		.69
Total expenses		31,301	16.49
Operating profit		$ 11,105	5.86
Extraordinary expenses		300	.16
Net profit before taxes		$ 10,805	5.70
Federal, State, and local taxes		4,863	2.56
Net profit after taxes		$ 5,942	3.14

Cost of goods sold. For retailers and wholesalers, this figure is the inventory at the beginning, plus purchases, plus "Freight in," and less inventory at the end of the period. "Freight out" is generally shown as delivery expense, either under separate or other sections of the statement.

For manufactures, there are various additional items to be considered. They include supervision, power, supplies, the direct costs of manufacturing labor (including social security and unemployment taxes on factory employees), that portion of depreciation which enters into cost of production, and many others.

Gross profit on sales. This figure is obtained by deducting cost-of-goods sold from net sales.

Selling expenses. These expenses include such items as salaries of salesmen and sales executives, wages of other sales employees, commissions, travel expense, entertainment expense, and advertising.

Operating profit. This is the difference between the gross profit on sales and the sum of the selling expenses.

APPENDIX 1

General and administrative expenses. These expenses include officers' salaries, office overhead, light, heat, communication, salaries of general office and clerical help, cost of legal and accounting services, "fringe" taxes payable on administrative personnel, sundry types of franchise and similar taxes, and other expenses.

Financial expenses. This item would include interest, doubtful accounts, and discounts granted if not already deducted from sales.

Other operating expenses and income. Here might be included various unusual expense items not elsewhere classified, such as moving expenses, against which might be credited income from investments and miscellaneous credits and debits.

Extraordinary charges (if any). Such expenses do not occur very often, but occasionally unusual costs such as losses on sale of unused fixtures and equipment do arise.

Net profit before taxes. This figure is the profit after deducting the regular and extraordinary business charges mentioned above.

Taxes. This item includes the Federal, State, and local taxes paid by the company out of its earnings.

Net profit after taxes. This figure is the final figure showing earnings available for distribution or retention.

Figure 2 illustrates how a condensed profit-and-loss statement would be expressed, first in terms of dollars, then in terms of percentages of net sales.

STANDARD OR TYPICAL RATIOS

How much rent should I pay? How much am I entitled to charge against income for my salary? What should it cost me for making deliveries? What's the average cost of doing business in my line? How much should I pay my salesmen?

Hardly academic questions these. They are asked by businessmen every day, as they talk among themselves, or as they discuss business problems with association executives, bankers, and credit men.

NEED FOR MEASUREMENTS

On occasion, financing problems arise which give impetus to further questions. One of the most common is this one: "How much should my business earn on invest-

APPENDIX 1

ed capital?" Others are: "I want to buy some machinery. Can I swing the purchase on my present capital, or should I invest more money in the business?" "My competitor's business is for sale; if I buy him out, will my operating capital be enough to finance both businesses?" "How fast should my inventory turn over?" "What size reserve should I carry for bad debts?"

The availability of information by which a small business owner may measure his performance is important. Indeed, yardsticks and standards in the form of typical or standard ratios for different lines of business have caused many a small entrepreneur to make a worthwhile reappraisal of his business thinking.

Some time ago, for instance, a trade association representing a phase of the contracting business held a symposium of members to discuss problems in bid pricing. A problem in bidding was placed on the table. Participants were given a set of specifications and material prices on a mythical job. The problem was to analyze the costs and bid on the job at a price which would return a reasonable margin of profit.

Bids ran a gamut ranging from 13 to 31 percent above material costs. Meanwhile, a trained cost accountant had already predetermined that the bid margin should be 26 percent. Discussing the wide variation in the results of this exercise in bid pricing, an officer of the association said:

"Our people just don't have an adequate understanding of their costs. They can figure the obvious items which they handle every day, but they don't allow enough for their fixed and indirect overhead costs, which aren't recognized fully until they come to check up at the end of the year. Frankly, our membership has too little understanding of all the factors that go into making up a price. As a result, very few of them are earning a fair return. But today's study of these factors in an actual case was an eye opener to these men."

At the other end of the scale, a rapidly growing number of businessmen have come to look to ratios for their trade and industry as management tools in pinpointing situations and conditions in their business which merit attention.

GROWTH OF STANDARD RATIO STUDIES

Ratio analysis is not an entirely new development. As early as 1913, the Bureau of Business Research of Harvard University conducted a study of the expenses of shoestores. Since then, the conducting of ratio studies has been accelerated by the efforts of various trade associations, Government agencies, mercantile agencies, banks, research departments of industrial and accounting firms, and schools and universities. Recognition of the importance of good operating ratios will do more than any other present influence to standardize the best procedures and results now being attained and to make for constant improvement in management.

APPENDIX 1

TECHNIQUES OF COMPILATION

The first step taken by the compiling organizations in developing comparative operating ratios is to obtain detailed profit-and-loss statements of concerns in the line of business under study. It is hardly to be expected that every concern in a given line would furnish figures. Some decline to cooperate, and withhold the information. Some don't have sufficiently detailed records. Some don't keep records on a comparable basis—a highly important point.

But suppose every concern in the line did furnish comparable figures. The job of assembling, evaluating, and digesting such a mass of information would be so vast and so time-consuming that it would be difficult to complete the study. It would be impossible to complete it quickly and cheaply enough to give the results any practical significance.

The answer to this problem is "sampling." "Sampling" means the technique by which statisticians obtain information from a small random number of concerns located in dispersed areas. The concerns thus selected are known to be reasonably typical of all the concerns in the area under study. As a result, what is true of the sample will also be generally true of all the concerns.

An illustration of the technique of sampling would be to check the quality of bread baked in a commercial bakery by testing, say, one loaf out of every thousand. Better still, you might sample that one loaf by trying a single slice. If the entire output of that particular bakery were produced under uniform conditions, it is quite likely that a few slices of the bread, selected at random from the large number being baked, would be indicative of the bakery's entire output.

When a large-enough sample is obtained from units of reasonable similarity at random intervals, the characteristics of the sampling are quite closely indicative of the characteristics which exist in all units in that area. Thus, when adequately made, a sample of the operating results of a small group of business concerns in a line and region, tends to reflect the overall situation for that line and area.

The proper scope of the sampling is usually determined by a number of tests based on mathematical formulae, which are too technical to warrant exploration here. Actually, the size of the sample may be influenced by the number of cooperating concerns and the area to be covered—as well as by the aggregate number of concerns in the line against which the sample is to be drawn.

To illustrate this point, consider several recent examples. One nationwide survey of ratios made by Dun & Bradstreet was based on a sample of 104 wholesalers of drugs and druggists' sundries. Another was based on material gathered from 239 department stores. By contrast, one individual company's survey of drugstores was based on a review of figures from over 2,000 drugstores in a nationwide segment.

APPENDIX 1

OBTAINING THE FIGURES

Once a method has been worked out for sampling the line, the next step is to select names of concerns in given random areas. These are obtained from lists either furnished by an association, or drawn from mailing lists, lists of customers, reference books, or whatever other sources are available.

The next step is to send out requests for detailed profit-and-loss statements as of a given date to concerns whose cooperation is to be elicited. Sometimes, the surveying organization will request that the figures be returned on its own specially prepared forms so as to insure uniformity and comparability.

ASSEMBLING THE RESULTS

As soon as the information begins to flow back to the statisticians, the job of assembling and compiling begins. There are several methods of doing this, all of which yield some kind of middle-ground figures which try to reflect as nearly typical a result as possible. Once these middle ground figures have been determined, they are often arranged in an overall summary reflecting in percentages the composite situation for all concerns covered. In other cases, figures may be reported in terms of dollar averages so as to show, for example, typical dollar sales.

Often, the figures are also regrouped in terms of size categories, such as stores with sales volume of $20,000–$50,000, stores doing $50,000 to $100,000 annual volume, and so on. Or, the figures may be regrouped to show differences according to area, or city versus country, or credit versus cash sales.

Finally, the studies usually pinpoint relationships of certain key items, such as dollar amount of owner's salary, or salary per sales person, or sales per square foot, average stock turnover, and so forth.

One overall summary of a cost-of-doing-business study is illustrated in Figure 3.

OPERATING RATIOS VS. FINANCIAL RATIOS

The number of sources which compile comparative balance sheet ratios is relatively small, as compared with those which conduct studies of operating ratios. Much of the information which is available relative to comparative balance sheet ratios is on larger businesses.

Branches of the Federal Government, such as the Federal Trade Commission and the Securities and Exchange Commission, have compiled various balance-sheet ratios on large corporations, and similar studies have been made by a limited number of schools and universities. A few trade associations have supplemented their studies on operating ratios in their lines with ratios on selected balance-sheet items. Banks make private ratio studies based on their own files, and use the excellent studies prepared for them by Robert Morris Associates. The compiling of comparative financial statement ratios has also been done for many years by Dun & Bradstreet, Inc.

APPENDIX 1

FIGURE 3

SUMMARY OF OPERATING RATIOS

OF 379 "PROFITMAKING" RETAIL HARDWARE STORES

		Percent of Sales
Net sales		100.00
Cost of goods sold		66.05
Margin		33.95
Salary Expense:		
Owners and managers	7.15	
Salespeople, office, and other	9.60	
Total Salaries		16.75
Other Expense:		
Office supplies and postage	0.40	
Advertising	1.55	
Donations	0.05	
Telephone and telegraph	0.30	
Losses on notes and accounts receivable	0.15	
Delivery expense (exclusive of wages)	0.50	
Depreciation of delivery equipment	0.25	
Depreciation of furniture, fixtures, and tools	0.35	
Rent	2.70	
Repairs to building	0.10	
Heat, light, water, and power	0.80	
Insurance	0.80	
Taxes (not including Federal income tax)	1.10	
Interest on borrowed money	0.05	
Unclassified (including store supplies)	1.20	
Total Expense (not including interest on investment)		27.05
Net Profit		6.90

Source: The National Retail Hardware Association.

SOURCES OF RATIO STUDIES

Ratio sources may be classified into two groups; those agencies which compile data for a number of individual industries; and, those which confine their work to a particular industry or a group of related industries. The best known of the former are Dun & Bradstreet, Inc., Robert Morris Associates, and The Accounting Corporation of America. The latter group is composed of trade associations, publishers of trade magazines, specialized accounting firms, industrial companies (e.g. National

APPENDIX 1

Cash Register Co.), and colleges and universities. In addition to these two groups, Federal Government agencies provide a wealth of data covering somewhat broader industry classifications in most cases than the private sources.

DUN & BRADSTREET, INC.

Dun & Bradstreet, Inc, has been publishing its "Key Business Ratios" annually since 1932 in *Dun's Review and Modern Industry*, a monthly magazine. They also appear in separate pamphlet form. The data are essentially a byproduct of Dun & Bradstreet's very extensive financial and reporting services. The report covers 125 lines of business activity consisting of 71 manufacturing and construction industries, 32 wholesaling industries, and 22 lines of retailing.

In addition to the annual reports, Dun & Bradstreet, Inc. publishes *Cost of Doing Business* studies covering a number of retail industries. The National Credit Office, an affiliate of Dun & Bradstreet, Inc., also publishes a number of intermittent reports on the industries in which it specializes. Following are lists of the types of businesses covered in the ratio study and in the cost-of-doing business study:

KEY BUSINESS RATIOS

RETAILING

Children's and infants' wear stores
Clothing and furnishings, men's and boys'
Department stores
Discount stores
Discount stores, leased departments
Family clothing stores
Farm equipment dealers
Farm and garden supply stores
Furniture stores
Gasoline service stations
Grocery stores
Hardware stores
Household appliance stores
Jewelry stores
Lumber and other building materials dealers
Miscellaneous general merchandise stores
Motor vehicle dealers
Paint, glass and wallpaper stores
Shoe stores
Tire, battery and accessory stores
Variety stores
Women's ready-to-wear stores

WHOLESALING

Air conditioning and refrigeration equipment and supplies
Automotive equipment
Beer, wine and alcoholic beverages
Chemicals and allied products
Clothing and accessories, women's and children's
Clothing and furnishings, men's and boys'
Commercial machines and equipment
Confectionery
Dairy products
Drugs and druggists' sundries
Electrical appliances, TV and radio sets
Electrical apparatus and equipment
Electronic parts and equipment
Farm machinery and equipment
Footwear
Fresh fruits and vegetables
Furniture and home furnishings
Groceries, general line
Hardware
Industrial machinery and equipment
Lumber and construction materials
Meats and meat products
Metals and minerals
Paints and varnishes
Paper and its products
Petroleum and petroleum products
Piece goods
Plumbing and heating equipment and supplies

APPENDIX 1

Poultry and poultry products
Scrap and waste materials
Tires and tubes
Tobacco and its products

MANUFACTURING AND CONSTRUCTION

Agricultural chemicals
Airplane parts and accessories
Bakery products
Blast furnaces, steel works and rolling mills
Blouses and waists, women's and misses'
Books; publishing and printing
Broad woven fabrics, cotton
Canned and preserved fruits, vegetables and sea foods
Commercial printing except lithographic
Communication equipment
Concrete, gypsum and plaster products
Confectionery and related products
Construction, mining and handling machinery and equipment
Converted paper and paperboard products
Cutlery, hand tools and general hardware
Dairy products
Dresses: women's, misses' and junior's
Drugs
Electric lighting and wiring equipment
Electric transmission and distribution equipment
Electrical industrial apparatus
Electrical work
Electronic components and accessories
Engineering, laboratory and scientific instruments
Fabricated structural metal products
Farm machinery and equipment
Footwear
Fur goods
General building contractors
General industrial machinery and equipment
Grain mill products
Heating apparatus and plumbing fixtures

Heavy construction, except highway and street
Hosiery
Household appliances
Industrial chemicals
Instruments, measuring and controlling
Iron and steel foundries
Knit outerwear mills
Malt liquors
Mattresses and bedsprings
Meat packing plants
Metal stampings
Metalworking machinery and equipment
Millwork
Miscellaneous machinery, except electrical
Motor vehicle parts and accessories
Nonferrous foundries
Office and store fixtures
Outerwear, children's and infants'
Paints, varnishes, lacquers and enamels
Paper mills, except building paper
Paperboard containers and boxes
Passenger car, truck and bus bodies
Petroleum refining
Plastics, materials and synthetics
Plumbing, heating and air conditioning
Sawmills and planing mills
Screw machine products
Shirts, underwear and nightwear, men's and boys'
Soap, detergents, perfumes and cosmetics
Soft drinks, bottled and canned
Special industry machinery
Suits and coats, women's and misses'
Suits, coats and overcoats, men's and boys'
Surgical, medical and dental instruments
Toys, amusement and sporting goods
Trousers, men's and boys'
Underwear and nightwear, women's and children's
Wood household furniture and upholstered
Work clothing, men's and boys'

COST OF DOING BUSINESS

RETAILING

Apparel and accessories
Automotive dealers
Building materials
Drug and proprietary stores
Eating and drinking places
Farm equipment dealers

Furniture and home furnishings
Gasoline service stations
General merchandise
Grocery stores, meat, fish, fruit and vegetable markets
Hardware stores
Liquor stores
Tire, battery and accessory dealers

APPENDIX 1

WHOLESALING

Farm products—raw materials
Groceries and related products
Other wholesale trades

MANUFACTURING

Apparel and other finished products
Food and kindred products
Lumber and wood products, except furniture
Machinery, except electrical
Printing, publishing and allied industries

CONSTRUCTION

General trade contractors
Special trade contractors

SERVICES

Accounting, auditing and bookkeeping
Automotive
    Automobile repair shops
Business
Educational
Engineering and architectural
Legal
Lodging services
Medical services
    Dentists and dental surgeons
    Physicians and surgeons
Personal services
    Beauty and barber shops
    Laundries, cleaning and dyeing plants
Recreational
Repair, except automotive

TRANSPORTATION, COMMUNICATION AND SANITARY SERVICES

Motor freight transportation and warehousing

FINANCE, INSURANCE AND REAL ESTATE

Insurance agents and brokers
Real estate operators (except developers) and lessors
Security and commodity brokers and dealers

MINING

AGRICULTURE, FORESTRY AND FISHERIES

ACCOUNTING CORPORATION OF AMERICA

The Accounting Corporation of America publishes semiannually the *(Mail-Me-Monday) Barometer of Small Business*. Its data are derived as a by-product of the Accounting Corporation's accounting services to clients throughout the Nation.

The *(Mail-Me-Monday) Barometer* classifies its operating ratios for the various industry groups on the basis of gross volume. The classifications vary with the industry group but seldom do they exceed $300,000. The emphasis on small business units is apparent from the fact that, among the 50 basic types of business reported in mid-year 1969, the average annual gross volume for the combined firms in each line of business equals $300,000 in only one line (new car dealers); nine other lines ranged between $100,000 and $200,000; the balance was under $100,000. Following is a list of types of business for which there are ratios:

Apparel, children's and infants
Apparel, men's specialty
Apparel, men's and women's
Apparel, women's specialty
Appliance stores
Auto parts and accessories
Bakeries
Beauty shops
Cocktail lounges

Confectionery stores
Contractors—building
Contractors—specialty
Dairies
Dentists
Doctors of medicine
Dry cleaning shops
Drug stores
Feed and seed stores
Florists

APPENDIX 1

Food stores—combination	Nursery and garden supplies
Food stores—specialty	Paint, glass and wallpaper
Furniture stores	Photographic supply stores
Garages	Plumbing and heating equipment
Gift and novelty stores	Printing shops
Hardware stores	Professional—others
Jewelry stores	Repair services
Laundromats and hand laundries	Restaurants
Laundries, plant	Service stations
Liquor stores	Shoe stores
Lumber and building material	Sporting goods stores
Machine shops	Taverns
Meat markets	TV radio sales and service
Motels	Transportation
Music stores	Used car dealers
New car dealers	Variety stores

SPECIALIZED INDUSTRY SOURCES

The most important specialized industry sources for ratio data are trade associations. In addition, however, accounting firms, trade magazines, universities, and some large companies publish ratio studies.

TRADE ASSOCIATIONS.

National associations which have published ratio studies in the past include the following:

Air-Conditioning & Refrigeration Wholesalers, 22371 Newman Avenue, Dearborn, Mich. 48124
Air Transport Association of America, 1000 Connecticut Avenue NW., Washington, D.C. 20036
American Bankers Association, 90 Park Avenue, New York, N.Y. 10016
American Book Publishers Council, One Park Avenue, New York, N.Y. 10016
American Booksellers Association, 175 Fifth Avenue, New York, N.Y. 10010
American Carpet Institute, 350 Fifth Avenue, New York, N.Y. 10001
American Institute of Laundering, Doris and Chicago Avenues, Joliet, Ill. 60433
American Institute of Supply Associations, 1505 22d Street NW., Washington, D.C. 20037
American Meat Institute, 59 East Van Buren Street, Chicago, Ill. 60605
American Paper Institute, 260 Madison Avenue, New York, N.Y. 10016
American Society of Association Executives, 2000 K Street, NW., Washington, D.C. 20006
American Electric Association, 16223 Meyers Street, Detroit, Mich. 48235
American Supply Association, 221 North LaSalle Street, Chicago, Ill. 60601
Automotive Service Industry Association, 230 North Michigan Avenue, Chicago, Ill. 60601
Bowling Proprietors' Association of America, Inc., West Higgins Road, Hoffman Estates, Ill. 60172
Florists' Telegraph Delivery Association, 900 West Lafayette Boulevard, Detroit, Mich. 48226
Food Service Equipment Industry, Inc., 332 South Michigan Avenue, Chicago, Ill. 60604
Laundry and Cleaners Allied Trades Association, 1180 Raymond Boulevard, Newark, N.J. 07102
Material Handling Equipment Distributors Association, 20 North Wacker Drive, Chicago, Ill. 60616

APPENDIX 1

Mechanical Contractors Association of America, 666 Third Avenue, Suite 1464, New York, N.Y. 10017
Menswear Retailers of America, 390 National Press Building, Washington, D.C. 20004
Motor and Equipment Manufacturers Association, 250 West 57th Street, New York, N.Y. 10019
National-American Wholesale Lumber Association, 180 Madison Avenue, New York, N.Y. 10016
National Appliance and Radio-TV Dealers Association, 1319 Merchandise Mart, Chicago, Ill. 60654
National Association of Accountants, 525 Park Avenue, New York, N.Y. 10022
National Association of Building Owners and Managers, 134 South LaSalle Street, Chicago, Ill. 60603
National Association of Electrical Distributors, 600 Madison Avenue, New York, N.Y. 10022
National Association of Food Chains, 1725 Eye Street, N.W., Washington, D.C. 20006
National Association of Furniture Manufacturers, 666 North Lake Shore Drive, Chicago, Ill. 60611
National Association of Insurance Agents, 96 Fulton Street, New York, N.Y. 10038
National Association of Music Merchants, Inc., 222 West Adams Street, Chicago, Ill. 60606
National Association of Plastic Distributors, 2217 Tribune Tower, Chicago, Ill. 60611
National Association of Retail Grocers of the United States, 360 North Michigan Avenue, Chicago, Ill. 60601
National Association of Textile and Apparel Wholesalers, 350 Fifth Avenue, New York, N.Y. 10001
National Association of Tobacco Distributors, 360 Lexington Avenue, New York, N.Y. 10017
National Automatic Merchandising Association, Seven South Dearborn Street, Chicago, Ill. 60603
National Beer Wholesalers' Association of America, 6310 North Cicero Avenue, Chicago, Ill. 60646
National Builders' Hardware Association, 1290 Avenue of the Americas, New York, N.Y. 10019
National Electrical Contractors Association, 1200 18th Street, NW., Washington, D.C. 20036
National Electrical Manufacturers Association, 155 East 44th Street, New York, N.Y. 10017
National Farm and Power Equipment Dealers Association, 2340 Hampton Avenue, St. Louis, Mo. 63130
National Home Furnishings Association, 1150 Merchandise Mart, Chicago, Ill. 60654
National Kitchen Cabinet Association, 918 Commonwealth Building, 674 South 4th Street, Louisville, Ky. 40204
National Lumber and Building Material Dealers Association, Ring Building, Washington, D.C. 20036
National Office Products Association, Investment Building, 1511 K Street, NW., Washington, D.C. 20015
National Machine Tool Builders Association, 2071 East 102d Street, Cleveland, Ohio 44106
National Oil Jobbers Council, 1001 Connecticut Avenue, NW., Washington, D.C. 20036
National Paper Box Manufacturers Association, 121 North Bread Street, Suite 910, Philadelphia, Pa. 19107
National Paper Trade Association, 220 East 42nd Street, New York, N.Y. 10017
National Parking Association, 1101 17th Street, NW., Washington, D.C. 20036
National Restaurant Association, 1530 North Lake Shore Drive, Chicago, Ill. 60610
National Retail Furniture Association, 1150 Merchandise Mart Plaza, Chicago, Ill. 60654
National Retail Hardware Association, 964 North Pennsylvania Avenue, Indianapolis, Ind. 46204
National Retail Merchants Association, 100 West 31st Street, New York, N.Y. 10001
National Shoe Retailers Association, 200 Madison Avenue, New York, N.Y. 10016
National Sporting Goods Association, 23 East Jackson Boulevard, Chicago, Ill. 60604
National Stationery and Office Equipment Association, Investment Building, 1511 K Street, NW., Washington, D.C. 20005
National Tire Dealers and Retreaders Association, 1343 L Street, NW., Washington, D.C. 20005

APPENDIX 1

National Wholesale Druggists' Association, 220 East 42d Street, New York, N.Y. 10017
National Wholesale Jewelers Association, 1900 Arch Street, Philadelphia, Pa. 19103
National Wholesale Hardware Association, 1900 Arch Street, Philadelphia, Pa. 19103
Northamerican Heating & Airconditioning Wholesalers Association, 1200 West 5th Avenue, Columbus, Ohio 43212
Optical Wholesalers Association, 222 West Adams Street, Chicago, Ill. 60606
Paint and Wallpaper Association of America, 7935 Clayton Road, St. Louis, Mo. 63117
Petroleum Equipment Institute, 525 Dowell Building, Tulsa, Okla. 74114
Printing Industries of America, 711 14th Street, NW., Washington, D.C. 20005
Robert Morris Associates, Philadelphia National Bank Building, Philadelphia, Pa. 19107
Scientific Apparatus Makers Associates, 20 North Wacker Drive, Chicago, Ill. 60606
Shoe Service Institute of America, 222 West Adams Street, Chicago, Ill. 60606
Super Market Institute, Inc., 200 East Ontario Street, Chicago, Ill. 60611
United Fresh Fruit and Vegetable Association, 777 14th Street, NW., Washington, D.C. 20005
United States Wholesale Grocers' Association, 1511 K Street, NW., Washington, D.C. 20005
Urban Land Institute, 1200 18th Street, NW., Washington, D.C. 20036
Wine and Spirits Wholesalers of America, 319 North Fourth Street, St. Louis, Mo. 63102

NATIONAL CASH REGISTER COMPANY

The National Cash Register Company publishes an annual "Expenses in Retailing." This booklet examines the cost of operation in over 50 lines of business. The ratios are obtained from primary sources, most of which are trade associations. For some lines of business, the expense percentages are broken down into "controllable expense" and "fixed expense." Following is a list of businesses covered in a recent NCR study:

Appliance and radio-TV dealers
Automobile dealers
Auto parts dealers
Bakeries
Bars
Beauty shops
Book stores
Building material dealers
Candy stores
Children's and infant's wear
Cocktail lounges
Confectionery stores
Delicatessens
Department stores
Dentists
Doctors
Drug stores (retail pharmacies)
Dry cleaners
Electrical appliance stores
Family shoe stores
Florists
Food stores
Furniture stores
Garages
Gift, novelty and souvenir stores
Hardware stores
Hotels
Jewelry stores
Laundries
Liquor stores
Lumber and building materials dealers
Meat markets
Men's wear stores
Motels
Music stores
Novelty stores
Nursery and garden supply stores
Office supply and equipment dealers
Paint and wallpaper dealers
Photographic studio and supply stores
Professional services
Radio-TV dealers

APPENDIX 1

Restaurants
Service stations
Shoe stores (family)
Souvenir stores
Specialty foods (delicatessen, etc.)
Specialty stores
Sporting goods stores
Stationery stores
Super markets
Taverns
Tourist courts
Transportation and service
Used car dealers
Variety stores
Wholesaling
Women's apparel and specialty stores

ROBERT MORRIS ASSOCIATES

Long noted among the banking fraternity for extensive work in the field of ratio compilation and analysis is Robert Morris Associates, the National Association of Bank Loan and Credit Officers (sic). Founded in 1914, this organization's size is indicated by the fact that its membership comprises more than 1,200 commercial banks. Its activities include maintenance and advancement of standards of correct credit practice.

Robert Morris Associates has developed ratio studies for over 225 lines of business as indicated below. Owners and managers of small concerns wishing further information on the availability of this material may address inquiries to the Executive Manager, Robert Morris Associates, Philadelphia National Bank Building, Philadelphia, Pennsylvania 19107. Following is a list of lines of business for which Robert Morris Associates provides ratios:

MANUFACTURING

Advertising displays and devices
Apparel and other finished fabric products:
  Canvas products
  Children's clothing
  Curtains and draperies
  Furs
  Hats
  Men's and boys' sport clothing
  Men's work clothing
  Men's, youths' and boys' separate trousers
  Men's, youths' and boys' shirts, collars and nightwear
  Men's, youths' and boys' suits, coats and overcoats
  Women's dresses
  Women's suits, skirts, sportswear and coats
  Women's undergarments and sleepwear
Beverages:
  Flavoring extracts and syrups
  Malt liquors
  Wines, distilled liquor and liqueurs
Caskets and burial supplies
Chemicals and allied products:
  Drugs and medicines
  Fertilizers
  Industrial chemicals
  Paint, varnish and lacquer
  Perfumes, cosmetics and other toilet preparations
  Plastic materials and synthetic resins
  Soap, detergents and cleaning preparations
Food and Kindred products:
  Bread and other bakery products
  Candy and confectionery supplies
  Canned and dried fruits and vegetables
  Dairy products
  Flour and other grain mill products
  Frozen fruits, fruit juices, vegetables, and specialties
  Meat packing
  Prepared feeds for animals and poultry
  Vegetable oils

APPENDIX 1

Furniture and fixtures:
   Mattresses and bedsprings
   Metal household furniture
   Store, office, bar and restaurant fixtures
   Wood furniture—except upholstered
   Wood furniture—upholstered

Jewelry, precious metals

Leather and leather products:
   Footwear
   Luggage and special leather products
   Tanning, currying, and finishing

Lumber and wood products:
   Millwork
   Prefabricated wooden buildings and structural members
   Sawmills and planing mills
   Veneer and plywood
   Wooden boxes and containers

Machinery, equipment and supplies—electrical:
   Electronic components and accessories
   Equipment for public utilities and industrial use
   Household electrical appliances
   Lighting fixtures
   Radios, TV and phonographs
   Radio and TV transmitting, signaling and detection equipment

Machinery, except electrical equipment:
   Ball and roller bearings
   Construction and mining machinery and equipment
   Farm machinery and equipment
   General industrial machinery and equipment
   Industrial and commercial refrigeration equipment and complete air conditioning units
   Machine shops—jobbing and repair
   Machine tools and metal working equipment
   Oil field machinery and equipment
   Special dies and tools, die sets, jigs and fixtures
   Special industry machinery

Metal industries—primary:
   Iron and steel forgings
   Iron and steel foundries
   Non-ferrous foundries

Metal products—fabricated (except ordnance, machinery, and transportation equipment):
   Coating, engraving, and allied services
   Cutlery, hand tools and general hardware
   Enameled iron, metal sanitary ware and plumbing supplies
   Fabricated structural steel
   Heating equipment, except electric
   Metal cans
   Metal doors, sash, frames, molding and trim
   Metal stampings
   Miscellaneous fabricated wire products
   Miscellaneous non-ferrous fabricated products
   Screw machine products, bolts, nuts, screws, rivets and washers
   Sheet metal work
   Valves and pipe fittings, except plumbers' brass goods

Paper and allied products:
   Envelopes, stationery and paper bags
   Paperboard containers and boxes
   Pulp, paper and paperboard

Printing, publishing and allied industries:
   Book printing
   Bookbinding, and miscellaneous related work
   Books: publishing, and printing
   Commercial printing, except lithographic
   Commercial printing, lithographic
   Newspapers: publishing and printing
   Typesetting

Professional, scientific, and controlling instruments:
   Engineering, laboratory and scientific and research instruments
   Photographic equipment and supplies
   Surgical, medical and dental equipment and supplies

Rubber and miscellaneous plastics products:
   Miscellaneous plastics products

APPENDIX 1

  Rubber footwear and fabricated rubber products
Stone, clay and glass products:
  Brick and structural clay tile
  Concrete brick, block and other products
  Minerals and earths, ground or otherwise treated
  Pressed and blown glass and glassware
  Ready-mixed concrete
Textile mill products:
  Broad woven fabric—cotton, silk and synthetic
  Broad woven fabric—woolens and worsteds
  Dyeing and finishing
  Hosiery—anklets—children's, men's and boys'
  Hosiery—women's—full fashioned and seamless
  Knitting—Cloth, outerwear and underwear
  Narrow fabrics and other smallwares
  Yarn—cotton, silk, and synthetic
Toys, amusement, sporting and athletic goods:
  Games and toys, except dolls and children's vehicles
  Sporting and athletic goods
Transportation equipment:
  Aircraft parts (except electric)
  Motor vehicle parts and accessories
  Motor vehicles
  Ship and boat building and repairing

WHOLESALING

Automotive equipment and supplies:
  Automobiles and other motor vehicles
  Automotive equipment
  Tires and tubes
Beauty and barber supplies and equipment:
Drugs, drug proprietaries and druggists' sundries
Electrical equipment:
  Electrical supplies and apparatus
  Radios, refrigerators and electrical appliances
Flowers and florists' supplies

Food, beverages and tobacco:
  Coffee, tea and spice
  Confectionery
  Dairy products and poultry
  Fish and sea foods
  Frozen foods
  Fruits and vegetables
  General groceries
  Grain
  Meats and meat products
  Tobacco and tobacco products
  Tobacco leaf
  Wine, liquor and beer
Furniture and home furnishings:
  Floor coverings
  Furniture
General merchandise
Industrial chemicals
Iron, steel, hardware and related products:
  Air conditioning and refrigeration equipment and supplies
  Hardware and paints
  Metal products
  Metal scrap
  Plumbing and heating equipment and supplies
  Steel warehousing
Lumber, building materials and coal:
  Building materials
  Coal and coke
  Lumber and millwork
Machinery and equipment:
  Agricultural equipment
  Heavy commercial and industrial machinery and equipment
  Laundry and dry cleaning equipment and supplies
  Mill supply house
  Professional equipment and supplies
  Restaurant and hotel supplies, fixtues and equipment
  Transportation equipment and supplies, except motor vehicles

APPENDIX 1

Paper and paper products:
   Printing and writing paper
   Wrapping or coarse paper and products

Petroleum products:
   Fuel oil
   Petroleum products

Scrap and waste materials:
   Textile waste

Sporting goods and toys:

Textile products and apparel:
   Dry goods
   Footwear
   Furs
   Men's and boys' clothing
   Women's and children's clothing
   Wool

RETAILING

Aircraft:
   Aircraft—new and used

Apparel and accessories:
   Family clothing stores
   Furs
   Infants' clothing
   Men's and boys' clothing
   Shoes
   Women's ready-to-wear

Books and office supplies:
   Books and stationery
   Office supplies and equipment

Building materials and hardware:
   Building materials
   Hardware stores
   Heating and plumbing equipment dealers
   Lumber
   Paint, glass and wallpaper stores

Cameras and photographic supplies

Department stores and general merchandise:
   Department stores
   Dry goods and general merchandise

Drugs

Farm and garden equipment and supplies:
   Farm equipment
   Feed and seed—farm and garden supply

Flowers

Food and beverages:
   Dairy products and milk dealers
   Groceries and meats
   Restaurants

Fuel and ice dealers:
   Fuel, except fuel oil
   Fuel oil dealers

Furniture, home furnishings and equipment:
   Floor coverings
   Furniture
   Household appliances
   Radio, television and record players

Jewelry

Liquor

Luggage and gifts

Marine hardware, boat and supply

Motor vehicle dealers:
   Autos—new and used
   House trailers
   Tire, battery, and accessories
   Trucks—new and used

Musical instruments and supplies

Road machinery equipment

Sporting goods

Vending machine operators, merchandise

SERVICES

Advertising agencies
Auto repair shops
Auto and truck rental and leasing
Bowling alleys
Business and management consulting
Commercial research and development laboratories
Engineering and architectural services
Equipment rental and leasing
Funeral directors

APPENDIX 1

Insurance agents and brokers
Intercity bus lines
Laundries and dry cleaners
Linen supply
Local trucking and storage—including household goods
Local trucking—without storage
Long distance trucking
Motels, hotels and tourist courts
Nursing homes, sanatoria, convalescent and rest homes
Real estate holding companies

Refrigerated warehousing, except food lockers

CONTRACTORS

Oil well servicing contractors
Oil and gas well drilling

NOT ELSEWHERE CLASSIFIED

Bottler—soft drinks
Commercial feed lots
Poultry, except broiler chickens
Radio and/or TV stations
Seed companies (vegetable and garden)

GOVERNMENT SOURCES

Federal Government publications provide a wealth of data covering somewhat broader industry classifications in most cases than the private sources.

The most current and completely developed ratio data are published jointly by the Federal Trade Commission and the Securities & Exchange Commission in the form of the Quarterly Financial Report for Manufacturing Corporations. These are available, however, only for broadly defined industry groups. The data cover all manufacturing corporations, except newspapers and related sub-groups.

The Internal Revenue Service of the U.S. Treasury Department publishes annually, with an approximate three year lag at present, the Statistics of Income, Corporation Income Tax Returns and Statistics of Income, Business Income Tax Returns. The reports represent selected income statement, balance sheet, and tax items obtained from Federal Income Tax returns. It is possible to utilize the basic dollar data presented to derive valuable ratio information.

The Census of Business, published by the Bureau of the Census, is conducted at 5-year intervals and provides limited ratio and dollar financial data, mostly in the wholesale trade area. The advantages of the Census data lie primarily in the detailed industry and size breakouts of data, and in certain other detailed classifications of data not elsewhere available.

OTHER SOURCES

A number of accounting and management consultant firms have done or are doing ratio studies under contract with trade associations and other industry groups. In the past, ratios have been published by these sources for the restaurant, hotel, home furnishing, laundry and dry cleaning businesses. Various trade publishers also publish ratio data from time to time. Two of the better-known companies that publish ratios for their dealers are the Eli Lilly & Company (drugs) and the Eastman Kodak Company (photography).

APPENDIX 1

The Credit Research Foundation, affiliated with the National Association of Credit management, publishes quarterly data on the average collection period for accounts receivable and an aging of receivables in a number of manufacturing and distribution industries.

FOR FURTHER STUDY

The following publications are listed for those who may wish to explore further the many and varied aspects of ratio analysis. The list is necessarily selective in keeping with the objectives of this book. No discourtesy is intended toward authors whose works are not cited.

Barometer of Small Business. Midyear Edition. $6 a copy. Year Book, $10 a copy. Annual subscription, including 2 issues, $12.50. Accounting Corporation of America, 1929 First Avenue, San Diego, Calif. 92101. For a number of basic types of small businesses, this study gives sales volumes and trends, as well as operating ratios. For higher volume groups, it shows typical financial statements.

Expenses in Retail Businesses. Published periodically. Available on request. The National Cash Register Co., Marketing Services Department, Dayton, Ohio 45409. Operating ratios give typical experiences for various lines of retail business. For many lines, there is a breakdown by size class, as well. Average ratios, according to the compiler, "should be used by the businessman according to his own experience with his specific business and its peculiar characteristics."

Key Business Ratios in 125 Lines. Annual. Single copies free on request. Dun & Bradstreet, Inc., Business Information Systems, 99 Church Street, New York, N.Y. 10007. The 14 ratios, shown in terms of medians, cover approximately 125 lines of retail, wholesale, manufacturing, and construction business.

Cost of Doing Business: Partnerships, Proprietorships. Available on request. Dun & Bradstreet, Inc., Business Information Systems, 99 Church Street, New York, N.Y. 10007. For a number of lines of retail and wholesale trade, manufacturing, construction, services, and the like, this states operating ratios (as a percent of sales) derived from representative samples of Federal income tax returns.

Manual of Performance Ratios for Business Analysis and Profit Evaluation, by Leo Troy. 1966. $45. Prentice-Hall, Inc., 70 Fifth Avenue, New York, N.Y. 10011. This reference-type work uses Internal Revenue Service data to give operating factors, selected financial ratios, and selected financial factors, for about 70 nonmanufacturing industries and 20 manufacturing industries.

Operating Costs and Ratios—Retail. Revision in preparation. Free. Small Business Bibliography No. 8. Small Business Administration, Washington, D.C. 20416 (or the nearest SBA office). Bibliography of books, pamphlet material, periodicals and other sources to be used either in calculating operating ratios or in studying existing ratios by line of retail business.

APPENDIX 1

Operating Costs and Ratios—Wholesale. Revision in preparation. Free. Small Business Bibliography No. 11. Small Business Administration, Washington, D.C. 20416 (or the nearest SBA office). Bibliography of books, pamphlet material, periodicals and other sources, to be used either in calculating operating ratios or in studying existing ratios by line of wholesale business.

Practical Financial Statement Analysis, by Roy A. Foulke, 6th ed. 1968. $11.50. McGraw-Hill Book Company, Inc., 330 West 42d Street, New York, N.Y. 10036. This book describes the background, evolution, and techniques for analyzing financial statements. By tables, it shows an interquartile range of ratios for 72 lines of business activity.

Quarterly Financial Report for Manufacturing Corporations, by Federal Trade Commission-Securities and Exchange Commission. $2 a year. Superintendent of Documents, U.S. Government Printing Office, Washington, D.C. 20402. This continuing series of quarterly reports, based on corporation income tax returns, shows the financial characteristics and operating results for all U.S. manufacturing corporations. Reader can use data to make his own ratio analysis.

Sources of Composite Financial Data: A Bibliography, 2d ed. 1967. Members 50¢; nonmembers $1.00. The Robert Morris Associates, Research Department, Philadelphia National Bank Building, Philadelphia, Pa. 19107. Lists and annotates 90 sources for further information on "cost of doing business," operating results, and the like, for over 200 industries, including manufacturing, wholesaling, retailing, and service firms.

Statement Studies. Annual. $10 a year. The Robert Morris Associates, Research Department, Philadelphia National Bank Building, Philadelphia, Pa. 19107. Eleven key business ratios are presented, in terms of medians, for approximately 225 different lines of business, including manufacturers, wholesalers, retailers, and services. Businesses are broken down by size class.

APPENDIX 2

COURT DECISIONS REGARDING DEPRECIATION OF INTANGIBLES

The following list is by no means all-inclusive but rather indicates the broad range of assets which may be subject to depreciation or amortization and conditions where the deductions may or may not be allowed.

AIR SPACE

Excavations purchased by a refuse operation were held depreciable when it was shown usefulness of the pits would be exhausted as they were filled.
Sexton 42 TC 1094. (IRS acquiesced in results only.)

AGREEMENTS NOT TO COMPETE

No depreciation allowed when definite life could not be proved.
B.T. Babbitt, Inc., 32 BTA 693.

Amortization allowed even though agreement was oral.
Standard Lumber & Hardware Co., TC Memo 1959-159.

Depreciation allowed when broken out from goodwill in purchase agreement.
Silberman, 22 TC 1240 (A); Herndon, TC Memo 1962-184; J.S.L. Restaurants, Inc., TC Memo Docket No. 23382 - 2/28/51; Danksch v. Busey, 125 F Supp 130.

Depreciation not allowed when agreement could not be separated from goodwill.
Walker, TC Memo 1954-71; Asch, TC Memo 1954-244; Burke, 18 TC 77.

Agreement can be separately valued although the contract does not do so.
Wilson Athletic Goods Mfg. Co., Inc. v. Com., 222 F (2d) 355.

BROADCASTING LICENSES

FCC radio and TV licenses have usually been held nondepreciable on the basis that the agency until recently always renewed them and hence they did not have a determinable life.
KWTX Broadcasting Co., Inc., 31 TC 952, aff'd 272 F (2d) 406; Times World Corp. v. US, 251 F Supp 43.

One district court allowed amortization over a three year period when evidence was submitted that there was some question about automatic renewal. However, neither the Treasury nor the Tax Court followed this reasoning.
WDEF Broadcasting Co. v. US, 215 F Supp 818.

BUSINESS EXPANSION COSTS

Capitalized costs of business expansion held nondepreciable.
Mid State Products Co., 21 TC 696.

APPENDIX 2

BUSINESS LICENSES AND FRANCHISES

When such licenses are indefinitely renewable, no depreciation is allowed.
    Nachman, 12 TC 1204 (A); Blackett, TC Memo Docket No. 25689 9/28/51.

When not indefinitely renewable, depreciation is allowed.
    D.J. Campbell Co., Inc. v. US, 370 F (2d) 336.

CONTRACTS

Amortization is permitted if a time period can be proven over which the rights of the contract will be exhausted.
    Atlantic Carton Corp., 2 BTA 380.

No depreciation or amortization is allowed if there is not a limited life.
    Western Valve Bag Co., 13 BTA 749.

COPYRIGHTS AND PATENTS

A license to use a patent is amortizable over the useful life of the patent.
    Service Recorder Co., 2 BTA 96 (A) rev'd on other ground 24 F (2d) 875.

Supplementary patents may be written off over the life of the patent which they supplement.
    Hyatt Roller Bearing Co. v. US, 43 F (2d) 1008.

Pending applications are not amortizable since they have no definite life.
    Borg & Beck Co., 24 BTA 995 (A); Hershey Mfg. Co., 14 BTA 867 (NA) affirmed 43 F (2d) 298; Sarkes Tarzian, Inc. v. US, 140 F Supp 863 Rev'd and rem'd on other issue 240 F (2d) 467, or remand 159 F Supp 253.

Small loan manual held depreciable over the life of the copyright even though frequently revised.
    Domestic Management Bureau, Inc., 38 BTA 640 (A).

CUSTOMER LISTS

Depreciation allowed when purchaser of retail fuel accounts proved customer losses of 9% per year.
    Holden Fuel Oil Co., TC Memo 1972-45.

Depreciation allowed where 20% of laundry customer accounts were shown to be lost each year.
    Manhattan Co. of Va., Inc., 50 TC 78.

APPENDIX 2

DRAWINGS

Deduction was allowed for drawings, blueprints, etc., where a useful life was established.
    Wallis Tractor Co., 3 BTA 981 (A).

EASEMENTS, PIPELINE

When an easement for a pipeline loses its value when the particular pipeline itself is fully depreciated, amortization or depreciation has been allowed.
    Panhandle Eastern Pipe Line Co. v. US 408 F (2d) 690; Commonwealth Natural Gas Corp. v. US, DC VA 12/22/66 195 F (2d) 493; Badge Pipe Line Co. v. US 401 F (2d) 799; Shell Pipe Line Corp. v. US 267 F Supp 1014.

EXCHANGE MEMBERSHIPS

Commodity exchange seat found nondepreciable.
    Cummins, 19 TC 246.

GOING CONCERN VALUE

Found nondepreciable.
    US v. Cornish, 348 (2d) 175.

GOODWILL

Cannot be exhausted and hence nondepreciable.
    Red Wing Malting Co. v. Willcuts, 15 F (2d) 626; X-Pando Corp., 7 TC 48, app. dism'd (CCA-2) 2/7/48.

HOSPITAL STAFF PRIVILEGES

A doctor was allowed to depreciate his payment for hospital staff privileges over the four year remaining life of the hospital since a new hospital was being built.
    Wells-Lee v. Com, 360 F (2d) 665 rev'g, aff'g and rem'g, TC Memo 1964-315.

INSURANCE EXPIRATION LISTS

Held to be depreciable.
    Savings Assurance Agency, Inc., TC Memo 1963-52.

Nondepreciable as mass assets with an indefinite life.
    S.S. Ballin Agency, Inc. v. Com, 446 F (2d) 554 aff'g TC Memo 1969-203; Morris, TC Memo 1968-295; Salome, Tr. v. US, 395 F (2d) 990, aff'g DC Texas, 7/18/67; Squires v. US, 289 F Supp 597; Blaine, Sr. v. US, 441 F (2d) 917, rev'g and rem'g DC Texas 11/15/69, cert den 11/9/71.

APPENDIX 2

PATIENT CHARTS

An obstetrician-gynecologist was permitted to amortize the cost of patient charts (or medical histories) purchased from another doctor over six years. Due to fast population turnover and the history of childbirth in the area, the charts were held useless after six years. However, 10% of the purchase price of the charts was held to be nondepreciable as goodwill.

    Johnson, Jr. v. US, DC Texas 2/24/61.

PERSONAL SERVICE CONTRACTS: BASEBALL PLAYERS

The IRS states that the effect of the "reserve clause" in major league baseball player contracts is to bind the player to his club for his useful life in baseball. Hence these contracts must be capitalized and depreciated over this life. Prior to the 1967 ruling by IRS, both the IRS and courts allowed the contracts to be deducted currently because they were considered to have a basic one year life.

    Rev Ruling 67-379, CB 1967-2, 127; Com v. Pittsburgh Athletic Co., 72 F (2d) 883; Com v. Chicago National League Ball Club, 74 F (2d) 1010.

SECRET PROCESSES

Held nondepreciable under the facts of the case.

    Kaltenbach v. US, 66 Ct Cl 581.

VARIOUS INTANGIBLES

Trade names, trademarks, brand names, newspaper subscription lists, formulas and royalty rights on copyrighted books were all held nondepreciable when their useful lives were found indeterminate.

    Meredith Publishing Co. v. Com. 64 F (2d) 890, cert den 290 US 676; Norwich Pharmacal Co., 30 BTA 326; National Weeklies Inc. v. Com, 137 F (2d) 39; Pohlen v. Com, 165 F (2d) 258.

APPENDIX 3

REVENUE RULINGS RESPECTING VALUATION

REVENUE RULING 59-60 - VALUATION OF STOCKS AND BONDS

In valuing the stock of closely held corporations, or the stock of corporations where market quotations are not available, all other available financial data, as well as all relevant factors affecting the fair market value must be considered for estate tax and gift tax purposes. No general formula may be given that is applicable to the many different valuation situations arising in the valuation of such stock. However, the general approach, methods, and factors which must be considered in valuing such securities are outlined.

Sec. 1. Purpose.

The purpose of this Revenue Ruling is to outline and review in general the approach, methods, and factors to be considered in valuing shares of the capital stock of closely held corporations for estate tax and gift tax purposes. The methods discussed herein will apply likewise to the valuation of corporate stocks on which market quotations are either unavailable or are of such scarcity that they do not reflect the fair market value.

Sec. 2. Background and Definitions.

.01 All valuations must be made in accordance with the applicable provisions of the Internal Revenue Code of 1954 and the Federal Estate Tax and Gift Tax Regulations. Sections 2031(a), 2032 and 2512(a) of the 1954 Code (sections 811 and 1005 of the 1939 Code) require that the property to be included in the gross estate, or made the subject of a gift, shall be taxed on the basis of the value of the property at the time of death of the decedent, the alternate date if so elected, or the date of gift.

.02 Section 20.2031-1(b) of the Estate Tax Regulations (section 81.10 of the Estate Tax Regulations 105) and section 25.2512–1 of the Gift Tax Regulations (section 86.19 of Gift Tax Regulations 108) define fair market value, in effect, as the price at which the property would change hands between a willing buyer and a willing seller when the former is not under any compulsion to buy and the latter is not under any compulsion to sell, both parties having reasonable knowledge of relevant facts. Court decisions frequently state in addition that the hypothetical buyer and seller are assumed to be able, as well as willing, to trade and to be well informed about the property and concerning the market for such property.

.03 Closely held corporations are those corporations the shares of which are owned by a relatively limited number of stockholders. Often the entire stock issue is held by one family. The result of this situation is that little, if any, trading in the

APPENDIX 3

shares takes place. There is, therfore, no established market for the stock and such sales as occur at irregular intervals seldom reflect all of the elements of a representative transaction as defined by the term "fair market value."

Sec. 3. Approach to Valuation.

.01 A determination of fair market value, being a question of fact, will depend upon the circumstances in each case. No formula can be devised that will be generally applicable to the multitude of different valuation issues arising in estate and gift tax cases. Often, an appraiser will find wide differences of opinion as to the fair market value of a particular stock. In resolving such differences, he should maintain a reasonable attitude in recognition of the fact that valuation is not an exact science. A sound valuation will be based upon all the relevant facts, but the elements of common sense, informed judgment and reasonableness must enter into the process of weighing those facts and determining their aggregate significance.

.02 The fair market value of specific shares of stock will vary as general economic conditions change from "normal" to "boom" or "depression," that is, according to the degree of optimism or pessimism with which the investing public regards the future at the required date of appraisal. Uncertainty as to the stability or continuity of the future income from a property decreases its value by increasing the risk of loss of earnings and value in the future. The value of shares of stock of a company with very uncertain future prospects is highly speculative. The appraiser must exercise his judgment as to the degree of risk attaching to the business of the corporation which issued the stock, but that judgment must be related to all of the other factors affecting value.

.03 Valuation of securities is, in essence, a prophesy as to the future and must be based on facts available at the required date of appraisal. As a generalization, the prices of stocks which are traded in volume in a free and active market by informed persons best reflect the consensus of the investing public as to what the future holds for the corporations and industries represented. When a stock is closely held, is traded infrequently, or is traded in an erratic market, some other measure of value must be used. In many instances, the next best measure may be found in the prices at which the stocks of companies engaged in the same or a similar line of business are selling in a free and open market.

Sec. 4 Factors To Consider.

.01 It is advisable to emphasize that in the valuation of the stock of closely held corporations or the stock of corporations where market quotations are either lacking or too scarce to be recognized, all available financial data, as well as all relevant factors affecting the fair market value, should be considered. The follow-

APPENDIX 3

ing factors, although not all-inclusive are fundamental and require careful analysis in each case:

(a) The nature of the business and the history of the enterprise from its inception.
(b) The economic outlook in general and the condition and outlook of the specific industry in particular.
(c) The book value of the stock and the financial condition of the business.
(d) The earning capacity of the company.
(e) The dividend-paying capacity.
(f) Whether or not the enterprise has goodwill or other intangible value.
(g) Sales of the stock and size of the block of stock to be valued.
(h) The market price of stocks of corporations engaged in the same or a similar line of business having their stocks actively traded in a free and open market, either on an exchange or over-the-counter.

.02 The following is a brief discussion of each of the foregoing factors:

(a) The history of a corporate enterprise will show its past stability or instability, its growth or lack of growth, the diversity or lack of diversity of its operations, and other facts needed to form an opinion of the degree of risk involved in the business. For an enterprise which changed its form of organization but carried on the same or closely similar operations of its predecessor, the history of the former enterprise should be considered. The detail to be considered should increase with approach to the required date of appraisal, since recent events are of greatest help in predicting the future; but a study of gross and net income, and of dividends covering a long prior period, is highly desirable. The history to be studied should include, but need not be limited to, the nature of the business, its products or services, its operating and investment assets, capital structure, plant facilities, sales records and management, all of which should be considered as of the date of the appraisal, with due regard for recent significant changes. Events of the past that are unlikely to recur in the future should be discounted, since value has a close relation to future expectancy.

(b) A sound appraisal of a closely held stock must consider current and prospective economic conditions as of the date of appraisal, both in the national economy and in the industry or industries with which the corporation is allied. It is important to know that the company is more or less successful than its competitors in the same industry, or that it is maintaining a stable position with respect to competitors. Equal or even greater significance may attach to the ability of the industry with which the company is allied to compete with other industries. Prospective competition which has not been a factor in prior years should be given careful attention. For example, high profits due to the novelty of its product and the lack of competition often lead to increasing competition. The public's appraisal of the future prospects of competitive industries or of competitors within an industry may be indicated by price trends in the markets for commodities and for securities. The loss of the manager of a so-called "one-man" business may have a depressing effect upon the

APPENDIX 3

value of the stock of such business, particularly if there is a lack of trained personnel capable of succeeding to the management of the enterprise. In valuing the stock of this type of business, therefore, the effect of the loss of the manager on the future expectancy of the business, and the absence of management-succession potentialities are pertinent factors to be taken into consideration. On the other hand, there may be factors which offset, in whole or in part, the loss of the manager's services. For instance, the nature of the business and of its assets may be such that they will not be impaired by the loss of the manager. Furthermore, the loss may be adequately covered by life insurance, or competent management might be employed on the basis of the consideration paid for the former manager's services. These, or other offsetting factors, if found to exist, should be carefully weighed against the loss of the manager's services in valuing the stock of the enterprise.

(c) Balance sheets should be obtained, preferably in the form of comparative annual statements for two or more years immediately preceding the date of appraisal, together with a balance sheet at the end of the month preceding that date, if corporate accounting will permit. Any balance sheet descriptions that are not self-explanatory, and balance sheet items comprehending diverse assets or liabilities, should be clarified in essential detail by supporting supplemental schedules. These statements usually will disclose to the appraiser (1) liquid position (ratio of current assets to current liabilities); (2) gross and net book value of principal classes of fixed assets; (3) working capital; (4) long-term indebtedness; (5) capital structure; and (6) net worth. Consideration also should be given to any assets not essential to the operation of the business, such as investments in securities, real estate, etc. In general, such nonoperating assets will command a lower rate of return than do the operating assets, although in exceptional cases the reverse may be true. In computing the book value per share of stock, assets of the investment type should be revalued on the basis of their market price and the book value adjusted accordingly. Comparison of the company's balance sheets over several years may reveal, among other facts, such developments as the acquisition of additional production facilities or subsidiary companies, improvement in financial position, and details as to recapitalizations and other changes in the capital structure of the corporation. If the corporation has more than one class of stock outstanding, the charter or certificate of incorporation should be examined to ascertain the explicit rights and privileges of the various stock issues including: (1) voting powers, (2) preference as to dividends, and (3) preference as to assets in the event of liquidation.

(d) Detailed profit-and-loss statements should be obtained and considered for a representative period immediately prior to the required date of appraisal, preferably five or more years. Such statements should show (1) gross income by principal items; (2) principal deductions from gross income including major prior items of operating expenses, interest and other expense on each item of long-term debt, depreciation and depletion if such deductions are made, officers' salaries, in total if they appear to be reasonable or in detail if they seem to be excessive, contributions (whether or not deductible for tax purposes) that the nature of its business and its

APPENDIX 3

community position require the corporation to make, and taxes by principal items, including income and excess profits taxes; (3) net income available for dividends; (4) rates and amounts of dividends paid on each class of stock; (5) remaining amount carried to surplus; and (6) adjustments to, and reconciliation with, surplus as stated on the balance sheet. With profit and loss statements of this character available, the appraiser should be able to separate recurrent from nonrecurrent items of income and expense, to distinguish between operating income and investment income, and to ascertain whether or not any line of business in which the company is engaged is operated consistently at a loss and might be abandoned with benefit to the company. The percentage of earnings retained for business expansion should be noted when dividend-paying capacity is considered. Potential future income is a major factor in many valuations of closely-held stocks, and all information concerning past income which will be helpful in predicting the future should be secured. Prior earnings records usually are the most reliable guide as to the future expectancy, but resort to arbitrary five-or-ten-year averages without regard to current trends or future prospects will not produce a realistic valuation. If, for instance, a record of progressively increasing or decreasing net income is found, then greater weight may be accorded the most recent years' profits in estimating earnings power. It will be helpful, in judging risk and the extent to which a business is a marginal operator, to consider deductions from income and net income in terms of percentage of sales. Major categories of cost and expense to be so analyzed include the consumption of raw materials and supplies in the case of manufacturers, processors and fabricators; the cost of purchased merchandise in the case of merchants; utility services; insurance; taxes; depletion or depreciation; and interest.

(e) Primary consideration should be given to the dividend-paying capacity of the company rather than to dividends actually paid in the past. Recognition must be given to the necessity of retaining a reasonable portion of profits in a company to meet competition. Dividend-paying capacity is a factor that must be considered in an appraisal, but dividends actually paid in the past may not have any relation to dividend-paying capacity. Specifically, the dividends paid by a closely held family company may be measured by the income needs of the stockholders or by their desire to avoid taxes on dividend receipts, instead of by the ability of the company to pay dividends. Where an actual or effective controlling interest in a corporation is to be valued, the dividend factor is not a material element, since the payment of such dividends is discretionary with the controlling stockholders. The individual or group in control can substitute salaries and bonuses for dividends, thus reducing net income and understating the dividend-paying capacity of the company. It follows, therefore, that dividends are less reliable criteria of fair market value than other applicable factors.

(f) In the final analysis, goodwill is based upon earning capacity. The presence of goodwill and its value, therefore, rests upon the excess of net earnings over and above a fair return on the net tangible assets. While the element of goodwill may be based primarily on earnings, such factors as the prestige and re-

APPENDIX 3

nown of the business, the ownership of a trade or brand name, and a record of successful operation over a prolonged period in a particular locality, also may furnish support for the inclusion of intangible value. In some instances it may not be possible to make a separate appraisal of the tangible and intangible assets of the business. The enterprise has a value as an entity. Whatever intangible value there is, which is supportable by the facts, may be measured by the amount by which the appraised value of the tangible assets exceeds the net book value of such assets.

(g) Sales of stock of a closely held corporation should be carefully investigated to determine whether they represent transactions at arm's length. Forced or distress sales do not ordinarily reflect fair market value nor do isolated sales in small amounts necessarily control as the measure of value. This is especially true in the valuation of a controlling interest in a corporation. Since, in the case of closely held stocks, no prevailing market prices are available, there is no basis for making an adjustment for blockage. It follows, therefore, that such stocks should be valued upon a consideration of all the evidence affecting the fair market value. The size of the block of stock itself is a relevant factor to be considered. Although it is true that a minority interest in an unlisted corporation's stock is more difficult to sell than a similar block of listed stock, it is equally true that control of a corporation, either actual or in effect, representing as it does an added element of value, may justify a higher value for a specific block of stock.

(h) Section 2031(b) of the Code states, in effect, that in valuing unlisted securities the value of stock or securities of corporations engaged in the same or a similar line of business which are listed on an exchange should be taken into consideration along with all other factors. An important consideration is that the corporations to be used for comparisons have capital stocks which are actively traded by the public. In accordance with section 2031(b) of the Code, stocks listed on an exchange are to be considered first. However, if sufficient comparable companies whose stocks are listed on an exchange cannot be found, other comparable companies which have stocks actively traded in on the over-the-counter market also may be used. The essential factor is that whether the stocks are sold on an exchange or over-the-counter there is evidence of an active, free public market for the stock as of the valuation date. In selecting corporations for comparative purposes, care should be taken to use only comparable companies. Although the only restrictive requirement as to comparable corporations specified in the statute is that their lines of business be the same or similar, yet it is obvious that consideration must be given to other relevant factors in order that the most valid comparison possible will be obtained. For illustration, a corporation having one or more issues of preferred stock, bonds or debentures in addition to its common stock should not be considered to be directly comparable to one having only common stock outstanding. In like manner, a company with a declining business and decreasing markets is not comparable to one with a record of current progress and market expansion.

APPENDIX 3

Sec. 5 Weight To Be Accorded Various Factors.

The valuation of closely held corporate stock entails the consideration of all relevant factors as stated in section 4. Depending upon the circumstances in each case, certain factors may carry more weight than others because of the nature of the company's business. To illustrate:

(a) Earnings may be the most important criterion of value in some cases whereas asset value will receive primary consideration in others. In general, the appraiser will accord primary consideration to earnings when valuing stocks of companies which sell products or services to the public; conversely, in the investment or holding type of company, the appraiser may accord the greatest weight to the assets underlying the security to be valued.

(b) The value of the stock of a closely held investment or real estate holding company, whether or not family owned, is closely related to the value of the assets underlying the stock. For companies of this type the appraiser should determine the fair market values of the assets of the company. Operating expenses of such a company and the cost of liquidating it, if any, merit consideration when appraising the relative values of the stock and the underlying assets. The market values of the underlying assets give due weight to potential earnings and dividends of the particular items of property underlying the stock, capitalized at rates deemed proper by the investing public at the date of appraisal. A current appraisal by the investing public should be superior to the retrospective opinion of an individual. For these reasons, adjusted net worth should be accorded greater weight in valuing the stock of a closely held investment or real estate holding company, whether or not family owned, than any of the other customary yardsticks of appraisal, such as earnings and dividend paying capacity.

Sec. 6. Capitalization Rates.

In the application of certain fundamental valuation factors, such as earnings and dividends, it is necessary to capitalize the average or current results at some appropriate rate. A determination of the proper capitalization rate presents one of the most difficult problems in valuation. That there is no ready or simple solution will become apparent by a cursory check of the rates of return and dividend yields in terms of the selling prices of corporate shares listed on the major exchanges of the country. Wide variations will be found even for companies in the same industry. Moreover, the ratio will fluctuate from year to year depending upon economic conditions. Thus, no standard tables of capitalization rates applicable to closely held corporations can be formulated. Among the more important factors to be taken into consideration in deciding upon a capitalization rate in a particular case are: (1) the nature of the business; (2) the risk involved; and (3) the stability or irregularity of earnings.

APPENDIX 3

Sec. 7. Average of Factors.

Because valuations cannot be made on the basis of a prescribed formula, there is no means whereby the various applicable factors in a particular case can be assigned mathematical weights in deriving the fair market value. For this reason, no useful purpose is served by taking an average of several factors (for example, book value, capitalized earnings and capitalized dividends) and basing the valuation on the result. Such a process excludes active consideration of other pertinent factors, and the end result cannot be supported by a realistic application of the significant facts in the case except by mere chance.

Sec. 8. Restrictive Agreements.

Frequently, in the valuation of closely held stock for estate and gift tax purposes, it will be found that the stock is subject to an agreement restricting its sale or transfer. Where shares of stock were acquired by a decedent subject to an option reserved by the issuing corporation to repurchase at a certain price, the option price is usually accepted as the fair market value for estate tax purposes. See Rev. Rul. 54-76, C.B. 1954-1, 194. However, in such case the option price is not determinative of fair market value for gift tax purposes. Where the option, or buy and sell agreement, is the result of voluntary action by the stockholders and is binding during the life as well as at the death of the stockholders, such agreement may or may not, depending upon the circumstances of each case, fix the value for estate tax purposes. However, such agreement is a factor to be considered, with other relevant factors, in determining fair market value. Where the stockholder is free to dispose of his shares during life and the option is to become effective only upon his death, the fair market value is not limited to the option price. It is always necessary to consider the relationship of the parties, the relative number of shares held by the decedent, and other material facts, to determine whether the agreement represents a bonafide business arrangement or is a device to pass the decedent's shares to the natural objects of his bounty for less than an adequate and full consideration in money or money's worth. In this connection see Rev. Rul. 157 C.B. 1953-2, 255, and Rev. Rul. 189, C.B. 1953-2, 294.

Sec. 9. Effect on Other Documents.

Revenue Ruling 54-77, C.B. 1954–1, 187, is hereby superseded.

REVENUE RULING 65-193 - VALUATION OF STOCKS AND BONDS

Revenue Ruling 59-60, C.B. 1959–1, 237, is hereby modified to delete the statements, contained therein at section 4.02 (f), that "In some instances it may not be possible to make a separate appraisal of the tangible and intangible assets of the business. The enterprise has a value as an entity. Whatever intangible value there is, which is supportable by the facts, may be measured by the amount by which the

APPENDIX 3

appraised value of the tangible assets exceeds the net book value of such assets."

The instances where it is not possible to make a separate appraisal of the tangible and intangible assets of a business are rare and each case varies from the other. No rule can be devised which will be generally applicable to such cases.

Other than this modification, Revenue Ruling 59-60 continues in full force and effect. See Rev. Rul. 65-192.

REVENUE RULING 68-609 - VALUATION OF STOCKS AND BONDS

The purpose of this Revenue Ruling is to update and restate, under the current statute and regulations, the currently outstanding portions of A.R.M. 34, C. B. 2, 31 (1920), A.R.M. 68, C.B. 3, 43 (1920), and O.D. 937, C.B. 4, 43 (1921).

The question presented is whether the "formula" approach, the capitalization of earnings in excess of a fair rate of return on net tangible assets, may be used to determine the fair market value of the intangible assets of a business.

The "formula" approach may be stated as follows:

A percentage return on the average annual value of the tangible assets used in a business is determined, using a period of years (preferably not less than five) immediately prior to the valuation date. The amount of the percentage return on tangible assets, thus determined, is deducted from the average earnings of the business for such period and the remainder, if any, is considered to be the amount of the average annual earnings from the intangible assets of the business for the period. This amount (considered as the average annual earnings from intangibles), capitalized at a percentage of say, 15 to 20 percent, is the value of the intangible assets of the business determined under the "formula" approach.

The percentage of return on the average annual value of the tangible assets used should be the percentage prevailing in the industry involved at the date of valuation, or (when the industry percentage is not available) a percentage of 8 to 10 percent may be used.

The 8 percent rate of return and the 15 percent rate of capitalization are applied to tangibles and intangibles, respectively, of businesses with a small risk factor and stable and regular earnings; the 10 percent rate of return and 20 percent rate of capitalization are applied to businesses in which the hazards of business are relatively high.

The above rates are used as examples and are not appropriate in all cases. In applying the "formula" approach, the average earnings period and the capitalization rates are dependent upon the facts pertinent thereto in each case.

The past earnings to which the formula is applied should fairly reflect the prob-

APPENDIX 3

able future earnings. Ordinarily, the period should not be less than five years, and abnormal years, whether above or below the average, should be eliminated. If the business is a sole proprietorship or partnership there should be deducted from the earnings of the business a reasonable amount for services performed by the owner or partners engaged in the business. See *Lloyd B. Sanderson Estate V. Commissioner* [1930 CCH ¶ 9386], 42 F. 2d 160 (1930). Further, only the tangible assets entering into net worth, including accounts and bills receivable in excess of accounts and bills payable, are used for determining earnings on the tangible assets. Factors that influence the capitalization rate include (1) the nature of the business, (2) the risk involved, and (3) the stability or irregularity of earnings.

The "formula" approach should not be used if there is better evidence available from which the value of intangibles can be determined. If the assets of a going business are sold upon the basis of a rate of capitalization that can be substantiated as being realistic, though it is not within the range of figures indicated here as the ones ordinarily to be adopted, the same rate of capitalization should be used in determining the value of intangibles.

Accordingly, the "formula" approach may be used for determining the fair market value of intangible assets of a business only if there is no better basis therefor available.

See also Revenue Ruling 59-60, C.B. 1959–1, 237, as modified by Revenue Ruling 65-193, C.B. 1965–2, 370, which sets forth the proper approach to use in the valuation of closely held corporate stocks for estate and gift tax purposes. The general approach, methods, and factors, outlined in Revenue Ruling 59-60, as modified, are equally applicable to valuations of corporate stocks for income and other tax purposes as well as for estate and gift tax purposes. They apply also to problems involving the determination of the fair market value of business interests of any type, including partnerships and proprietorships, and of intangible assets for all tax purposes. A.R.M. 34, A.R.M. 68, and O.D. 937 are superseded, since the positions set forth therein are restated to the extent applicable under current law in this Revenue Ruling. Revenue Ruling 65-192, C.B. 1965–2, 259, which contained restatements of A.R.M. 34 and A.R.M. 68, is also superseded.

FOOTNOTE REFERENCES

1. *Standard Industrial Classification Manual,* Superintendent of Documents, U.S. Government Printing Office, Washington, D.C. 20402.
2. *California Code of Civil Procedure,* Part 3, Chapter 9, Article 6, §1263.510(a).
3. *Montgomery's Auditing,* Defliese, Johnson & Macleod, p.706, Ronald Press Co., New York, N.Y.
4. *Accounting Terminology Bulletin No. 1,* ¶ 56, American Institute of Certified Public Accountants, New York, N.Y.
5. Computations of depreciation in the example are as follows:
   a. *Straight Line:* $6,000 cost − $500 salvage value = $5,500 ÷ 5 years = $1,100 depreciation applicable to 1976.
   b. *Sum of the digits:* $6,000 cost x 5/15 = $2,000 depreciation applicable to 1976.
   c. *Double Declining Balance:* $6,000 cost x 40% (twice the straight line rate of 20%) = $2,400 depreciation applicable to 1976.
6. *Montgomery's Auditing,* See footnote 3 above; *Handbook of Modern Accounting,* edited by Davidson, McGraw-Hill Book Co., New York, N.Y.; *Accountants' Handbook,* Wixon, Kell & Bedford, Ronald Press Co., New York, N.Y.
7. *Unaccountable Accounting* and *More Debits Than Credits,* Abraham J. Briloff, Harper & Row, New York, N.Y.
8. *Business Finance Handbook,* Prentice-Hall, Inc., New York, N.Y.; *Understanding Corporate Reports: a Guide to Financial Statement Analysis,* Leopold A. Bernstein, Dow Jones-Irwin, Inc., Homewood, Ill.
9. Key portions of this booklet are reproduced at Appendix 1. The complete booklet can be purchased from Superintendent of Documents, U.S. Government Printing Office, Washington, D.C. 20402 under the title *Ratio Analysis for Small Business,* Small Business Management Series No. 20, Stock No. 045,000,00098-2/Catalog No. SBA 1.12:20/3.
10. See footnote 1.
11. *Annual Statement Studies,* 1975 edition, Robert Morris Associates, Credit Division, Philadelphis National Bank Bldg., Philadelphia, Pa. 19107.
12. The prodecure described assumes all inventories are finished goods. If other inventories are involved, values would normally be set as follows: raw material inventories - appraise at current replacement cost; work-in-process inventories - appraise at estimated selling price of the finished goods less (a) cost to complete, (b) normal cost to sell, and (c) normal profit margin.
13. In arriving at pro forma earnings it is assumed any necessary adjustment was made to reflect competitive salaries to owner-managers. Thus no further adjustment for salaries is required in this computation.
14. The intangibles included at this step may embrace some which were not amortized under Step 5. For instance, a trademark may not always be subject to amortization because of difficulty in establishing a definitive life. Nevertheless, an economic return should be calculated on its value.

FOOTNOTE REFERENCES

15. In the BLM case, the working capital reflected on the Economic Balance Sheet at March 31, 1976 (see Exhibit 4) was $407,899 ($649,091 of current assets less $241,192 of current liabilities). Since, however, there was only $18,935 of cash, the appraiser judged this to be inadequate. Therefore, he added $50,000 in long term debt, which has the effect of boosting working capital. For a discussion of the difference between working capital for accounting purposes and for appraisal purposes, see Question 10 in Chapter 12.

16. *Real Estate Appraisal Terminology*, edited by Byrl N. Boyce, Ballinger Publishing Co., Cambridge, MA.

17. The actual multiplier derived from dividing 100 by 20 is 5.0 to infinity. Multiplying $42,285 by the rounded figure of 5.0 does produce $211,425.

18. Present worth and compound interest tables are available from a number of sources. One compilation which is widely used by appraisers is the *Ellwood Tables* compiled by L.W. Ellwood, MAI, for the American Institute of Real Estate Appraisers. The Institute also publishes the tables. Its address is 155 East Superior St., Chicago, IL. 60611.

19. In security analysis, earnings are usually synonymous with net profit after tax. These terms are used interchangeably in this book.

20. In current commercial usage, the term *pro forma earnings* generally refers to projected earnings, and that is the way in which the term is used in this book. Some accounting textbooks, however, prefer to describe pro forma earnings more in line with what this book designates as *adjusted historical earnings*.

21. The typical dividend yield rate would usually be based on the average yields for the comparable companies. To find the average dividend yield for a given firm, one would select an average price paid for the stock during the year being evaluated and divide this into the dividend paid during the same year. The average stock price could be a simple average, a median price, or a weighted average. For example, assume the selected average price for a given year was $16 and a dividend of $1 was paid during the year. The average dividend yield would then be 6.25% ($1.00 divided by $16). This yield would differ from that which might be calculated based on the price of the stock on a given day.

22. Adjusted historical cash flow might also be used and capitalized by a dividend rate similarly derived from market data.

23. Adjusted historical profits are the same as would be the case for Method 6.

24. See *Internal Revenue Rulings* reproduced at Appendix 3.

25. Applicable cases can be found in one of the standard Federal Tax reporters, such as *Commerce Clearing House*, *Prentice-Hall*, or *Research Institute of America* under captions such as "Valuation of Corporate Stocks."

26. Notice that this profit is *not* the same as the figure developed for Method 4, Capitalization of Net Profit (¶ 5.05-3). Method 4 was based on pro forma or projected earnings, whereas this method is based on adjusted historical earnings. Since the dividend yield rate computed for comparable companies is historical

FOOTNOTE REFERENCES

in nature, it is logical to use historical earnings for the company being appraised when this Method 7 is utilized.

27. In the example only five comparative companies have been used. A much larger sampling would be preferable for the development of this ratio. Also, the asset mix of the comparative companies should be studied carefully to be sure that there is at least some resemblance of comparability to the subject.
28. See *Internal Revenue Code* Sections 1245 and 1250.
29. These figures can be reconciled with BLM share of earnings shown in the previous paragraph as follows:

Fiscal Yr. Ending	Total Earnings	BLM %	BLM Share
1972	$ 9,400	53%	$ 5,000
1973	18,900	53%	10,000
1974	28,300	53%	15,000
1975	28,300	53%	15,000
1976	28,300	53%	15,000

30. A distinction is drawn between licenses and franchises. It would not be appropriate to compare a restaurant with a liquor license, for instance, with one which did not have one. However, a franchised fast food operation might be compared with a similar non-franchised operation for purposes of evaluating going concern values in the non-franchised operation. The latter process is described in the text following this footnote.
31. See *Internal Revenue Code* Sections 1245 and 1250.
32. Broad versus Jollyfe, Cro Jac 596.
33. Austen versus Bois, 27 LJ, Chap. 714-718.
34. Cruttwell versus Lye, 17 Vesey 335.
35. Churton versus Douglas, 5 Jur, N.S. 887, 890.
36. In some cases the word "affluence" has been replaced by the word "influence." For a detailed listing of cases which have followed this definition, see *Words & Phrases*, West Publishing Co, St. Paul, MN, page 217 of the volume which includes Good Will.
37. Burke versus Canfield, 121 F. 2d 877, 74 App. DC 6.
38. Mann versus Fisher, 51 F Supp 550, DC MO 1943; Rees versus U.S., 187 F Supp. 924 affirmed, 295 F 2d 817, DC OR 1960.
39. Grace Bros. versus C.I.R., 173 F 2d 170, CA 9, 1949.
40. A good source for such material is *Words & Phrases*, West Publishing Co., St. Paul, MN, page 210 et seq of the volume which includes Good Will.
41. Charles C. Delk and Mary Arlee Delk, husband and wife, Plaintiffs, versus the U.S., Defendant, US District Court, Eastern District of CA, No. F-869 Civil 9/18/74.
42. Houston Chronicle Publishing Co. versus the U.S., 481 F 2d, 1240, cert den 414 US 1129.
43. Elmore Milling Co. versus Helvering, 70 F 2d, 736; Cement Gun Co., Inc., versus CIR, 36 F 2d, 107; Thatcher, 24 BTA 1130.

FOOTNOTE REFERENCES

44. Johnson versus CIR, 302 F 2d, 86, cert den 371 US 904; IRC §167 (c); also Revenue Ruling 57-352, CB 1957-2, 150 as to 150% D.B.
45. KIRO, Inc., 51 TC 155; Panhandle Eastern Pipe Line Co. versus U.S.., 408 F 2d, 690.
46. Daniel J. Klein, TC Memo 1965 - 207, affirmed, 372 F 2d, 261.
47. Seaboard Finance Co., 367 F 2d, 646 (9th Circuit, 1966), affirming TCM 1964 - 253.
48. Frank E. Zorniger, 62 TC 435, Acquiesced in results, IRB 1975-11, 5.
49. *Capitalize in perpetuity.* Technically, one would not capitalize an asset in perpetuity but would capitalize some form of income in perpetuity to arrive at the value of an asset. For example, if one concluded that a brand name created a fairly typical annual profit advantage of $8,000 per year, and if he concluded that investments of like risk typically were yielding 15% per annum, he could capitalize this annual profit advantage in perpetuity. He would divide $8,000 by 15%, which would yield a capitalized value of $53,333.33. This value is the calculated value of an asset that can be expected to create $8,000 per year of profit advantage for the foreseeable future, or in perpetuity.
50. Starting in 1978, the copyright laws as revised through 1976 give protection for 50 years beyond the creator's lifetime. For valuation purposes, this is virtually the same as a perpetual grant. Therefore, the law does not in itself really set a determinable life. Rather, it is necessary to determine the economic life of the copyright and use that as a basis for valuation.
51. As in the instance of the brand name discussion at Footnote 49, it is the typical income advantage of the franchise which would be capitalized in perpetuity.
52. Whether or not such an overall profit rate is justified is subject to the same considerations discussed at ¶ 9.02-3. For instance, do customers on the list necessarily purchase products with an average profit, or as a class do they tend to buy wider or lower margin items? It is also important to consider any expenses of maintaining lists when considering their profit contribution.
53. See ¶ 8.03-2 for the distinction between tangible and intangible libraries.
54. A cost saving can be capitalized in perpetuity in the same manner as a receipt of income or a profit advantage. See Footnote 49 for a further discussion of the term "capitalize in perpetuity."
55. See *Internal Revenue Code* §1212(a) for corporate capital losses, and see IRC §172(b) as amended by the Tax Reform Act of 1976 for operating losses.
56. The Eminent Domain Law of California which includes this quotation at §1263.510 was approved by the Governor on October 1, 1975 and filed with the Secretary of State on October 1, 1975. The goodwill loss provisions were effective July 1, 1976.
57. Sawyer versus Commonwealth, 182 Mass. 245, 65 NE 52.
58. Klein versus U.S., 375 F 2d, 825.

    Banner Milling Co. versus State of New York, 240 NY 533, 148 NE 668 (1925), cert den 269 US 582, 46 S Ct 107 (1925).

FOOTNOTE REFERENCES

60. Mitchell versus U.S., 267 US 341, 69 L Ed 644, 45 S Ct 293.
61. City of Oakland versus Pacific Coast Lumber & Mill Co. (1915), 171 Cal 392, 398, 153 P 705, 707.
62. Constitution of the National Conference of Commissioners on Uniform Laws cited at page iv of *Uniform Laws Annotated*, Master Edition, Vol. 13, West Publishing Co., St. Paul, MN.
63. *Uniform Laws Annotated*, Master Edition, Vol. 13, West Publishing Co., St. Paul, MN, page 859.
64. *California Legal Revision Commission Reports*, Vol. 12, 1974, page 1839.
65. California Eminent Domain Law, §1263. 205(b).
66. See article entitled: "Courts Increasing Amount of Discount for a Minority Interest in a Business" by Thomas W. Dant, Jr. in *The Journal of Taxation*, August 1975.
67. See article entitled: "Most Courts Overvalue Closely-Held Stocks" by Robert E. Moroney, an investment banker, in the magazine *Taxes*, March 1973.
68. For the full text of this and related revenue rulings, see Appendix 3.
69. *Letter Stock* is stock issued pursuant to an agreement letter that it will not be sold to the general public unless registered with the Securities and Exchange Commission. Such stock is usually issued to institutions or to a limited number of individuals who are assumed to be sufficiently knowledgeable and sophisticated to receive the stock without the formal disclosures usually required by the SEC.

INDEX

Accounting Methods | Page
- cash vs. accrual (¶ 2.03)............... 25
- deficiencies for appraisal purposes (¶ 2.03)....................... 24
- depreciation methods vary (¶ 2.03)..... 26
- inventory costing methods differ (¶ 2.03) 25
- research & development accounting (¶ 2.03)........................ 27

Accounting Practices (¶ 7.05-4) 152

Accounting Principles
- deficiencies for appraisal purposes (¶ 2.03)........................ 24

Advertising Agencies (¶ 7.05-6) 153

Appraisal Methods
- affiliation agreements (¶ 9.03-3)....... 196
- balance sheet methods (¶ 5.04)........ 93
- basic limits of value (¶ 7.02) 140
- blockage (¶ 11.04).................. 238
- capitalization of net profit - Method 4 (¶ 5.05-3) 103
- capitalization rate vs. multiplier (Question 17) 256
- choice of method affected by business sale customs (Question 25).......... 261
- correlation of results - formulas (¶ 7.04-3)....................... 148
- correlation of results, professionally managed business (Chap. 6)......... 131
- discounted cash flow - Method 5 (¶ 5.05-4)....................... 107
- dividend capitalization - Method 7 (¶ 5.05-6)....................... 119
- earnings & cash flow methods (¶ 5.05) .. 96
- excess earnings
  - Method 3 (¶ 5.05-1) 97
  - expense (Question 20) 257
- excess earnings method - tangible assets taken in eminent domain (Question 22) 259
- formula
  - asset-based - Method 10 (¶ 7.04-1) ... 144
  - IRS goodwill - Method 12 (¶ 9.01-1) ... 181
  - sales-based - Method 11 (¶ 7.04-2) ... 146
  - searches (¶ 7.03) 142
- formulas
  - flexibility (¶ 7.04-4) 148
  - guidelines (¶ 7.04-5) 148
  - when none can be found (¶ 7.04-6) ... 149
- goodwill (¶ 9.01) 181
  - accountants' - Method 18 (¶ 9.02-7)... 191
  - in professional business (Question 2).. 245
- goodwill loss (¶ 10.07)................ 221
  - capitalization of excess earnings lost - Method 19 (¶ 10.07-2) 222
  - cost to restore - Method 21 (¶ 10.07-4) 227
  - market formula - Method 20 (¶ 10.07-3) 225
  - tangible assets related to excess earnings (Question 22) 259
- intangible asset methods (¶ 9.02) 184

intangibles | Page
- accountants' approach - Method 18 (¶ 9.02-7) 191
- appraising loss of value (Question 6) .. 248
- choice of method (Question 3) 246
- choice of remaining life (Question 5) .. 247
- cost savings - Method 15 (¶ 9.02-4) ... 188
- cost to create - Method 16 (¶ 9.02-5).. 189
- cost to purchase - Method 17 (¶ 9.02-6) 191
- profit advantage - Method 13 (¶ 9.02-1) 184
- relief from royalty - Method 14 (¶ 9.02-2) 185
- segregation from multiple assets (Question 4) 247
- variations on profit contribution methods (¶ 9.02-3) 187

majority interests (¶ 11.03)............ 237
majority interest held in trust
Market Data Comparison Methods (¶ 5.06)..111
methods as framework for judgment (¶ 5.02)........................ 91
minority interests: comparable letter stock - Method 23 (¶ 11.02-2) 235
minority interests: cost to market - Method 22 (¶ 11.02-1) 235
minority interests: dividend yield - Method 24 (¶ 11.02-3) 236
minority interests: transfers within family (Question 14) 254
multiplier vs. capitalization rate (Question 17) 256
net worth per books - Method 1 (¶ 5.04-1)....................... 93
note valuation - Method 9 (¶ 6.03-1) 132
price earnings ratio - Method 6 (¶ 5.06-1)....................... 111
professionally-managed businesses (Chapter 5) 91
ratio of market price to book equity - Method 8 (¶ 5.06-3) 123
real estate-related businesses (¶ 7.06)........................ 155
stock: differing classes (¶ 11.07)....... 240
stock: differing classes, including preferred (Question 16) 255
stock: ESOTS (Question 12) 253
tangible net worth - Method 2 (¶ 5.04-2). 95
trust ownership of stock (¶ 11.05) 239
typical formula approach (¶ 7.04) 144

Appraisal Methods: Numerical
- method 1 - net worth per books (¶ 5.04-1)....................... 93
- method 2 - tangible net worth at market (¶ 5.04-2) 95
- method 3 - excess earnings (or excess... 97
  profit) (¶ 5.05-1)
  expense (Question 20) 257
- method 3 - excess earnings - tangible assets taken in eminent domain (Question 22) 259

317

INDEX

	Page
capitalization of net profit - Method 4 (¶ 5.05-3)	103
method 5 - discounted cash flow (¶ 5.05-4)	107
method 6 - price earnings ratio (¶ 5.06-1)	111
method 7 - dividend capitalization (¶ 5.05-6)	119
method 8 - ratio of market price to book equity (¶ 5.06-3)	123
method 9 - note valuation (¶ 6.03-1)	132
method 10 - asset-based formula (¶ 7.04-1)	144
method 11 - sales based formula (¶ 7.04-2)	146
method 12 - IRS goodwill formula (¶ 9.01-1)	181
method 13 - profit advantage (¶ 9.02-1)	184
method 14 - relief from royalty (¶ 9.02-2)	185
method 15 - cost savings (¶ 9.02-4)	188
method 16 - cost to create (¶ 9.02-5)	189
method 17 - cost to purchase (¶ 9.02-6)	191
method 18 - accountants method (¶ 9.02-7)	191
method 19 - capitalization of excess earnings lost (¶ 10.07-2)	222
method 20 - goodwill loss - market formula basis (¶ 10.07-3)	225
method 21 - goodwill loss - cost to restore (¶ 10.07-4)	227
method 22 - minority interests: cost to market (¶ 11.02-1)	235
method 23 - minority interests: comparable letter stock (¶ 11.02-2)	235
method 24 - minority interests: dividend yield (¶ 11.02-3)	236
Appraisal Purposes	
allocation of purchase price (¶ 1.05-2)	12
buy-and-sell agreements (¶ 1.05-13)	14
condemnation (¶ 1.05-11)	14
dissident owners (¶ 1.05-9)	14
divorce (¶ 1.05-3)	12
effect of purpose on value (¶ 1.02)	3
employee benefit plans (¶ 1.05-12)	14
estate and inheritance taxes (¶ 1.05-5)	13
financing (¶ 1.05-14)	15
gift tax (¶ 1.05-6)	13
liquidation of a business (¶ 1.05-10)	14
miscellaneous (¶ 1.05-16)	15
property taxes (¶ 1.05-15)	15
return on investment determination (¶ 1.05-8)	13
sale of business assets (¶ 1.05-4)	12
sale or purchase of business (¶ 1.05-1)	12
spinoff of part of a business (¶ 1.05-7)	13
Appraisers	
how to hire (Question 29)	263
tips for trial attorneys (Question 32)	265
trial preparation (Question 30)	264
use as consultants (Question 28)	263

	Page
when is professional appraiser needed (¶ 1.06)	15
witnesses (Question 31)	264
Auto Repair Garages (¶ 7.05-1)	151
Auto Wrecking Yards (¶ 7.05-10)	155
Bars and Cocktail Lounges (¶ 7.05-8)	154
Blockage, Valuation Considerations (¶ 11.04)	238
Brand Names and Trademarks (¶ 9.03-1)	192
Business Appraisals	
accounting practices (¶ 7.05-4)	152
advertising agencies (¶ 7.05-6)	153
auto repair garages (¶ 7.05-1)	151
auto wrecking yards (¶ 7.05-10)	155
bars and cocktail lounges (¶ 7.05-8)	154
funeral homes (¶ 7.05-11)	155
groceries, convenience (¶ 7.05-7)	154
hotels and motels (¶ 7.06-1)	155
insurance agencies (¶ 7.05-3)	152
legal practices (¶ 7.05-5)	153
liquor stores (¶ 7.05-2)	151
mobile home parks (¶ 7.06-3)	156
newspaper morgues (¶ 9.03-10)	202
newspapers and periodicals (¶ 7.05-9)	154
nursing homes (¶ 7.06-2)	156
Business Classifications	
businesses difficult to classify (¶ 1.04-3)	7
class of trade (¶ 1.04-5)	11
closely-held businesses (¶ 1.04)	5
legal entities (¶ 1.04-4)	7
personal businesses (¶ 1.04)	5
personal businesses (¶ 1.04-2)	6
Business Sales	
effect of customary sales procedures on appraisal method (Question 25)	261
Buy-Sell Agreements (¶ 11.06)	239
Case Study: BLM	
appraisal methods used	
book value - Method 1 (¶ 5.04-1)	93
capitalization of net profit - Method 4 (¶ 5.05-3)	103
correlation of methods (Chapter 6)	131
discounted cash flow - Method 5 (¶ 5.05-4)	107
dividend capitalization - Method 7 (¶ 5.05-6)	119
excess earnings (or excess profit) - Method 3 (¶ 5.05-1)	97
(¶ 7.04-1)	144
Fastburger operation with Method 11 (¶ 7.04-2)	146
goodwill by IRS - Method 12 (¶ 9.01-1)	181
note valuation - Method 9 (¶ 6.03-1)	132
patented lamp by Method 14 (¶ 9.02-2)	185
price earnings ratio - Method 6 (¶ 5.06-1)	111
ratio of market price to book equity - Method 8 (¶ 5.06-3)	123

INDEX

secret process by Method 13
  (¶ 9.02-1) 184
tangible net worth - Method 2
  (¶ 5.04-2) 95
balance sheet, adjusted historical &
  economic (Exhibit 4) 81
balance sheets, comparative historical
  (Exhibit 1) 43
basic facts (¶ 3.02) 51
income statements
  adjusted historical (Exhibit 5) 83
  comparative historical (Exhibits 2 & 3) . 45
  pro forma (Exhibit 6) 85
industry data compared (Exhibit 7) 87
multiple entities (¶ 2.07) 39
ratios (¶ 2.06-2) 29
reasons for use (¶ 2.05) 28
statement analysis (¶ 2.06-3) 36
Class of Trade
  selecting proper class (¶ 1.04-5) 11
Comparables
  choice of comparable businesses
    (Question 18) 256
  importance of location in choosing
    (Question 18) 256
Contracts (¶ 9.03-3) 194
Copyrights (¶ 9.03-2) 193
Copyright Infringement (Question 6) 248
Court Decisions Regarding Intangible
  Depreciation (Appendix 2) 297
Court Definitions of Goodwill (¶ 8.03-5) 168
Covenants Not to Compete (¶ 9.03-3) 195
Customer Lists (¶ 9.03-8) 199
Debt Consideration, real estate vs. business
  (Question 24) 260
Definitions
  capitalize in perpetuity (Footnote 49) ... 314
  capitalization rate (¶ 5.05-2) 102
  closely-held business (¶ 1.04) 5
  closely-held corporations (IRS)
    (Question 8) 249
  earnings (Footnote 19) 312
  fair market value (IRS) (Question 7) 248
  going concern value (Question 9) 252
  goodwill (¶ 8.03-1) 166
  goodwill, court definitions (¶ 8.03-5) 168
  goodwill loss, appraisers' definition
    (¶ 10.06) 220
  intangibles other than goodwill
    (¶ 8.03-2) 166
  letter stock (Footnote 69) 315
  market value (Question 9) 249
  multiplier (¶ 5.05-2) 102
  personal businesses (¶ 1.04-1) 5
  professional business appraisal
    (¶ 1.03) 5
  professionally-managed businesses
    (¶ 1.04-2) 6
  pro forma earnings (Footnote 20) 312
  user in possession (Question 9) 251

value in exchange (Question 9) 250
value in place (Question 9) 251
value in use (Question 9) 250
working capital for appraisal purposes
  (Question 10) 252
Depreciation: Court Decisions (Appendix 2) .. 297
Divorce
  valuation of professional business
    (Question 2) 245
Drawings (¶ 9.03-11) 202
Eminent Domain - see Goodwill..........
Employment Contracts (¶ 9.03-3) 194
ESOTS, Stock Valuation (Question 12) 253
Estate Tax, Decease of Key Owner
  (Question 1) 245
Exhibits
  balance sheets (BLM), 5 years
    (Exhibit 1) 43
  balance sheets (BLM), adjusted historical
    (Exhibit 4) 81
  balance sheets (BLM), economic
    (Exhibit 4) 81
  income statement detail (BLM), 5 years
    (Exhibit 3) 47
  income statements (BLM), 5 years
    (Exhibit 2) 45
  income statements (BLM), adjusted
    historical (Exhibit 5) 83
  income statements (BLM), pro forma
    (Exhibit 6) 85
  industry comparison with BLM (Exhibit 7) 87
Exhibits, Numerical
  exhibit 1, balance sheets (BLM), 5 years . 43
  exhibit 2, income statements (BLM),
    5 years 45
  exhibit 3, income statement detail (BLM),
    5 years 47
  exhibit 4, balance sheets (BLM), adjusted
    historical & economic 81
  exhibit 5, income statements (BLM),
    adjusted historical 83
  exhibit 6, income statements (BLM),
    pro forma 85
  exhibit 7, industry comparison w/BLM ... 87
Film Rights (¶ 9.03-13) 204
Financial Statements
  adjustment principles (¶ 4.06) 77
  appraisers' view (¶ 2.04) 27
  balance sheet adjustments required
    (¶ 4.02) 66
  balance sheet, key percentages
    (¶ 4.02-2) 68
  balance sheet, preparing adjusted
    historical (¶ 4.02-1) 66
  balance sheet, preparing economic
    (¶ 4.02-3) 68
  BLM adjusted statements (Exhibits 4-6) . 81
  BLM historical statements (Exhibits 1-3) . 43
  comparative arrangement for analysis
    (¶ 2.06-1) 28

319

INDEX

	Page
consolidated statement problems (¶ 2.07)	39
deficiencies in accounting for appraisal use (¶ 2.03)	24
generally accepted accounting principles (GAAP) (¶ 2.02)	23
historical nature (¶ 2.01)	23
income statement adjustment required (¶ 4.03)	70
income statements, preparing pro forma (¶ 4.04)	74
industry comparisons (¶ 4.05)	75
industry comparisons (BLM case) (Exhibit 7)	87
ratio analysis (¶ 2.06-2)	29
required for valuation purposes (¶ 4.01)	65
steps in statement analysis (¶ 2.06)	28
unusual items (¶ 2.06-3)	36

Formulas:

asset-based - Method 10 (¶ 7.04-1)	144
basic limits of value (¶ 7.02)	140
businesses sold by formula (¶ 7.05)	151
goodwill: IRS - Method 12 (¶ 9.01-1)	181
guidelines (¶ 7.04-5)	148
how to appraise secret formulas (¶ 9.03-7)	198
sales-based - Method 11 (¶ 7.04-2)	146
search for formulas (¶ 7.03)	142
when none can be found (¶ 7.04-6)	149

Franchises (¶ 9.03-5) 197
Funeral Homes (¶ 7.05-11) 155
Going Concern Value (¶ 8.03-4) 167

Goodwill

big pot theory (¶ 8.01)	161
commingling with other intangibles (¶ 8.03-3)	167
definition (¶ 8.03-1)	166
definition of intangibles other than goodwill (¶ 8.03-2)	166
definitions by courts (¶ 8.03-5)	168
elements of goodwill & other intangibles (¶ 8.02)	163
eminent domain (Chapter 10)	209
business age & history (¶ 10.05-5)	218
California innovation (¶ 10.01)	209
goodwill loss (¶ 10.03)	211
handling tangible assets taken (Question 22)	259
legal history of goodwill loss (¶ 10.02)	209
multiple businesses (¶ 10.05-6)	219
owner preferences & condition (¶ 10.05-2)	217
personal vs. business goodwill (¶ 10.05-3)	217
tenancy vs. ownership (¶ 10.05-4)	218
total vs. partial loss (¶ 10.05-7)	219
uniform code (¶ 10.03 & 10.04)	211
eminent domain code	
businesses with improving trends (¶ 10.05-1)	217

	Page
expanded concept of goodwill (¶ 10.04-2)	212
goodwill must be lost (¶ 10.04-3)	214
loss of patronage (¶ 10.04-1)	212
no betterments allowed (¶ 10.04-5)	216
non-duplicative compensation for loss (¶ 10.04-4)	215

goodwill loss

appraisers' definition (¶ 10.06)	220
appraisal methods (¶ 10.07)	221
how to determine its existence (¶ 8.04)	174
how to distinguish from other intangibles (¶ 8.03)	165
Internal Revenue Service view (¶ 8.03-6)	170
professional business, goodwill valuation (Question 2)	245
special purpose property (¶ 10.07-1)	221
tax cases, inclusion of other intangibles (Question 21)	258

tests

earnings (¶ 8.04-1)	174
market (¶ 8.04-2)	175
question and answer (¶ 8.04-3)	175
valuation (Chapter 9)	181
accountants' approach - Method 18 (¶ 9.02-7)	191
excess earnings Method 3 (¶ 5.05-1)	97
goodwill loss - Method 19 (¶ 10.07-2)	222
goodwill loss - Method 20 (¶ 10.07-3)	225
goodwill loss - Method 21 (¶ 10.07-4)	227
IRS approach (¶ 9.01)	181
IRS goodwill - Method 12 (¶ 9.01-1)	181
what is goodwill? (Chapter 8)	161

Groceries, Convenience (¶ 7.05-7) 154
Hotels and Motels (¶ 7.06-1) 155

Industry Comparisons

BLM statement comparisons (Exhibit 7)	87
financial statement comparisons (¶ 4.05)	75

Insurance Agencies (¶ 7.05-3) 152

Intangible Assets

appraising loss of value (Question 6)	248
choice of valuation method (Question 3)	246
commingling with goodwill (¶ 8.03-3)	167
commingling with goodwill in tax cases (Question 21)	258
definition: goodwill (¶ 8.03-1)	166
definition: other than goodwill (¶ 8.03-2)	166
depreciation: court decisions (Appendix 2)	297
elements of goodwill & other intangibles (¶ 8.02)	163
remaining life, choice of (Question 5)	247
segregation among multiple assets (Question 4)	247
valuation (Chapter 9)	181
valuation: methods (¶ 9.02)	184

INDEX

Intangible Valuation
    accountants' approach - Method 18
        (¶ 9.02-7) 191
    brand names and trademarks (¶ 9.03-1) . 192
    contracts (¶ 9.03-3) 194
    copyrights (¶ 9.03-2) 193
    cost savings - Method 15 (¶ 9.02-4) 188
    cost to create - Method 16 (¶ 9.02-5) 189
    cost to purchase - Method 17 (¶ 9.02-6) .. 191
    customer lists (¶ 9.03-8) 199
    drawings (¶ 9.03-11) 202
    film rights (¶ 9.03-13) 204
    franchises (¶ 9.03-5) 197
    leasehold interests (¶ 9.03-9) 201
    licenses (¶ 9.03-6) 198
    lists (¶ 9.03-8) 199
    mailing lists, specialized (¶ 9.03-8) 199
    newspaper morgues (¶ 9.03-10) 202
    patents (¶ 9.03-4) 196
    profit advantage - Method 13 (¶ 9.02-1) . 184
    profit contribution method, variations
        (¶ 9.02-3) 187
    relief from royalty (¶ 9.02-2) 185
    secret processes, methods, formulas
        (¶ 9.03-7) 198
    subscription lists (¶ 9.03-8) 199
    tax credits (¶ 9.03-14) 205
    technical libraries (¶ 9.03-10) 202
    water rights (¶ 9.03-12) 203

Internal Revenue Service
    estate tax, decease of key owner
        (Question 1) 245
    goodwill in tax cases (Question 21) 258
    IRS goodwill formula - Method 12
        (¶ 9.01-1) 181
    revenue rulings respecting valuation
        (Appendix 3) 301
    view of intangibles (¶ 8.03-6) 170

Interviews, format (Chapter 3) 51
Interviews, who should be contacted
    (¶ 3.01) 51
Inventories, raw material & work in process
    (Footnote 12) 311
Leasehold Interests (¶ 9.03-9) 201

Legal Entities
    corporations, ordinary (¶ 1.04-4) 9
    corporations, pseudo or subchapter S
        (¶ 1.04-4) 9
    multi-form businesses (¶ 1.04-4) 10
    partnerships (¶ 1.04-4) 8
    proprietorships (¶ 1.04-4) 7
    trusts (¶ 1.04-4) 10

Legal Practices (¶ 7.05-5) 153
Licenses (¶ 9.03-6) 198
Liquor Stores (¶ 7.05-2) 151
Lists (¶ 9.03-8) 199
Mailing Lists (¶ 9.03-8) 199

Majority Interests
    held in trust (Question 13) 254
    valuation (¶ 11.03) 237

Market Data Reliability (Question 26) 262
Market Price Premiums (¶ 5.06-4) 126

Minority Interests
    appraisal method 22: cost to market
        (¶ 11.02-1) 235
    appraisal method 23: comparable letter
        stock (¶ 11.02-2) 235
    appraisal method 24: dividend yield
        (¶ 11.02-3) 236
    discount history (¶ 11.01) 233
    transfers within family (Question 14) ... 254

Mobile Home Parks (¶ 7.06-3) 156
Multiple Businesses, Segregating Value
    (Question 27) 262
Newspaper Morgues (¶ 9.03-10) 202
Newspapers and Periodicals (¶ 7.05-9) 154
Nursing Homes (¶ 7.06-2) 156
Option Agreements (¶ 11.06) 239
Owner's Decease, Key Man - Estate Tax
    (Question 1) 245
Patents (¶ 9.03-4) 196

Ratios
    collection period, accounts receivable
        (¶ 2.06-2) 31
    current (¶ 2.06-2) 29
    debt to worth (¶ 2.06-2) 32
    fixed assets to worth (¶ 2.06-2) 35
    inventory turnover (¶ 2.06-2) 31
    net profit on net worth (¶ 2.06-2) 33
    net profit on sales (¶ 2.06-2) 34
    net worth turnover (¶ 2.06-2) 33
    purchases to trade payables (¶ 2.06-2) .. 35
    quick (¶ 2.06-2) 30
    ratio analysis (¶ 2.06-2) 29
    ratio analysis for small business
        (Appendix 1) 269

Real Estate-Related Businesses
    separation of business values
        (Question 23) 260
    valuation methods (¶ 7.06) 155

Restrictive Agreements
    buy-sell agreements (¶ 11.06) 239
    option agreements (¶ 11.06) 239
    right of first refusal (¶ 11.06) 239

Right of First Refusal (¶ 11.06) 239
Secret Processes, Methods, Formulas
    (¶ 9.03-7) 198
Special Purpose Properties, choice of method
    (Question 11) 253
Stock Classes: Differing Values (¶ 11.07) 240
Subscription Lists (¶ 9.03-8) 200
Tangible Assets, necessity for appraisal
    (Question 15) 255
Tax Credits (¶ 9.03-14) 205
Technical Libraries (¶ 9.03-10) 202
Trademarks and Brand Names (¶ 9.03-1) 192

Trials
    appraisers as witnesses (Question 31)... 264
    tips for trial attorneys on appraiser
        testimony (Question 32) 265
    trial preparation for appraisers
        (Question 30) 264

INDEX

Trust Ownership
    effect on stock value (¶11.05)........ 239
    majority interest held in trust
      (Question 13) 254

Valuation Procedure
    checking market formulas (¶5.03) 92
    comparability - location as a factor
      (Question 19) 257
    comparability - use of similar businesses
      (Question 18) 256
    correlation of methods, formulas
      (¶7.04-3) 148
    correlation of methods, professionally-
      managed business (Chapter 6) 131
    debt handling, real estate vs. business
      (Question 24) 260
    market data reliability (Question 26).... 262
    personally-managed businesses
      (Chapter 7) 139
    professionally-managed businesses
      (Chapter 5) 91
    search for formulas (¶7.03) 142
    segregating value of multiple entities
      (Question 27) 262
    tangible asset appraisal as part of
      business appraisal (Question 15) 255
    ten step process (¶1.07) 16
    when no formulas can be found
      (¶7.04-6) 149

Value: Business
    basic limits of value (¶7.02) 140
    business value in general (¶1.02)...... 3
    effect of appraisal purpose on value
      (¶1.02)......................... 3
    special problems with personally-
      managed businesses (¶7.01)........ 139
    statement of debt (Question 24) 260
    subjective nature (¶5.01) 91

Water Rights (¶9.03-12) 203